Unequal Worlds

Unequal Worlds

Discrimination and Social Inequality in Modern India

edited by
Vidhu Verma

OXFORD
UNIVERSITY PRESS

OXFORD
UNIVERSITY PRESS

Oxford University Press is a department of the University of Oxford.
It furthers the University's objective of excellence in research, scholarship,
and education by publishing worldwide. Oxford is a registered trademark of
Oxford University Press in the UK and in certain other countries

Published in India by
Oxford University Press
YMCA Library Building, 1 Jai Singh Road, New Delhi 110 001, India

© Oxford University Press 2015

The moral rights of the authors have been asserted

First Edition published in 2015

ISBN-13: 978-0-19-945328-3
ISBN-10: 0-19-945328-4

Typeset in Adobe Garamond Pro 11/13
by Tranistics Data Technologies, New Delhi 110 019
Printed in India by Rakmo Press, New Delhi 110 020

Contents

PART III STRUCTURAL DISCRIMINATION

PART IV LEGISLATION AND NEWER FORMS OF DISCRIMINATION

Acknowledgements

I would like to thank all those who enabled me to deepen my understanding of various themes in this volume. Many colleagues and students in my centre have given me a clear sense of the direction in which I could explore more effective responses to the multidimensional knots of injustice in our societies. In putting together this collection, I wish to thank the contributors for their cooperation and support during the submission process. Though I have wrestled with ideas on equality and justice for a long time, it was in the friendly atmosphere of the Centre for the Study of Discrimination and Exclusion in Jawaharlal Nehru University (JNU), which I chaired during 2013–2014, that many of my theoretical perspectives got clarified. I got fresh insights into the institutionalized patterns of discrimination that have an impact on everyday lives. Some of the papers are drawn from the interactions, seminars, and discussions we had during that period. The Indian Council of Social Science Research (ICSSR) project on Legal Justice also helped me in developing the subsequent research papers on law and discrimination which are now part of this volume.

I am deeply appreciative of the editorial team at Oxford University Press for encouraging me to go ahead with this project. I am pleased to record my gratitude to the team for being very kind with its advice and understanding of the subject during the period of assembling this manuscript. Thanks are due to my research assistant Leeda Phillips for her patience and alertness to many editing errors. However, none of the persons mentioned are to be held responsible for the views articulated in this book.

The author and publishers gratefully acknowledge the permission to reproduce the following essay: Meena Radhakrishna's article, 'Colonial Construction of a "Criminal" Tribe: Yerukulas of Madras Presidency', *Economic and Political Weekly*, 8–15 July, 2000, pp. 2553–63.

Vidhu Verma
Centre for Political Studies
Jawaharlal Nehru University

Introduction

Vidhu Verma

The question of discrimination and the concerns with equality, justice, and fairness have been around for a long time. It is an old but still current question that has to be answered anew. Discrimination undermines the idea of equality, which is considered as one of the major characteristics of modernity and also the core notion underlying the status of citizenship within the context of nation-states. The problem of addressing discrimination within our societies is that it represents a diverse spectrum of human relations and refers to a complex set of rules embedded in public institutions that disadvantage individuals due to their membership in some social group. Cornel West, in addressing this question, asserts that the consequences of an 'enlightenment conception of reason and science continue to haunt the modern West: on the non-discursive level, in ghetto streets, and on the discursive level, in methodological assumptions in the disciplines of the humanities' (West 1982). Prior studies have reduced this question to harmful effects and prejudices but these are mostly accounts drawn from psychological resources that conjoin behavioural and attitudinal elements on states of disgust or hatred towards some groups. In statistical models discrimination is measured when all other variables are controlled but these cannot effectively account for factors or unmeasured causes relevant to unequal outcomes. Discourse analysis increasingly focuses on how meanings are constituted and negotiated through verbal, linguistic, and visual discrimination but the connections between conceptualization of power and processes of the social structure are ambiguous. There is also a theoretical challenge in distinguishing discrimination from harmful social arrangements that sustain exploitation, domination, and oppression and which compel the working class organizations to overthrow capitalism. Since class is the legitimate axis of social stratification in the Marxist tradition only those features of caste discrimination are relevant that sustain class identities.

The essays collected in this present volume are an attempt to examine this question in the light of new dimensions of social inequality in the neo-liberal era. Disparities between the rich and poor continue along with various forms of discrimination that continue to shape our societies and worlds in fundamental ways. Dalits who make up a large proportion of the population, live below the poverty level and are much more vulnerable to such changes. It is not surprising that recent analyses reformulate class to understand labour markets as constituting a microcosm of capitalist society where problems of social reproduction and discrimination are manifest in contradictory forms. Parallel to this work is an examination of the caste system as not only a type of social hierarchy based on graded inequality but also what Ambedkar once called, 'the division of labourers (Ambedkar 1989a: 47). Such an examination not only breaks with earlier inquiries, by acknowledging various forms of group domination in labour markets and production processes but it also alters the terms of the debate so that the class-caste nexus can be seen as resulting from interlocking forms of private and public social structures. Societal discrimination is found to have a disproportionately exclusionary impact on marginalized groups applying for employment. In the last two decades, most studies emphasize the institutional and structural reasons for the exclusion of lower castes in addition to prejudiced discrimination.

Areas of distributive inequality, broadly called vertical inequalities are related to distribution of income and assets that rely on opportunities for work, access to knowledge, well-being, and political participation. In this volume we focus more on horizontal inequalities arising out of differences due to membership of social groups reflecting attributes of sex, caste, and the religious or ethnic origin of citizens. Since a study of these issues raised requires a multidisciplinary approach, this collection of essays range across political theory, cultural anthropology, economics, sociology, and legal histories. Most of their attention is on how caste continues to be a significant force in Indian politics taking on new forms even as older pervasive hierarchies enter into our present worlds. The remedies that leading theorists have historically looked to are articulated within the framework of individual rights in the Indian constitution that are poorly suited to address the multiple discriminations that groups suffer from. The essays argue against tendencies to assume an unquestioned similarity of discriminations that fail to address the processes through which inequalities are promoted. In addressing the way discriminatory practices have been linked to conceptualization of power in political institutions, we hope to question existing frameworks for thinking about these normative issues and to stimulate discussions for further research. In this introduction, the editor follows the struggles against caste discrimination in a historical perspective and describes the political context out of which policies of non-discrimination emerged in India.

The Evolving Discourse on Equality in the Context of India

The hope of ordering social structures through constitutional and legal reforms stretches back to the colonial period when attempts at overthrowing discriminatory caste practices emerged. There is no doubt that the idea of discrimination served medieval and early modern rulers in India in prejudices about themselves and others. But with the advent of modernity and colonial rule, hereditary occupational specialization through castes was seen as central to a cultural understanding of Hindu society. It is also not difficult to encounter governmentality at work in the dynamics of colonial recognition of castes and their subsequent classification. None-the-less, non-discrimination and the battle against untouchability was at the heart of a constructed national identity in the process of being formulated during the freedom movement. Indians in the political

process were keen to identify their country as democratic and distinguish it from a growing numbers of fascist regimes around the
world. One attempt at conceptualizing the constituents of this identity is to point out the ways Indians thought of themselves as having
inherited a range of values, rights, and institutions from the West,
which they then tried to understand given their own historical experiences rooted in modernity.[1] The personal identity of Jawaharlal
Nehru, the first prime minister of independent India, was inextricably linked to the search for a national identity. Representing the
aspirations of several Indians, Nehru wrote in *The Discovery of India*
that 'the spirit of the age is in favour of equality though practice
denies it everywhere'. He goes on to add that 'the spirit of the age
will triumph' (1961, 561). The second way is to see the manner in
which non-discrimination was transfigured as democratic equality
and also seen as a crucial part of the story on the evolution of the
Indian polity. The term 'discrimination' gravitated into the language
of the constituent assembly as a threat to fair equality of opportunity, which was pointed out by B.R. Ambedkar. He warned in his
explanatory notes that 'discrimination is a menace which must be
guarded against if the fundamental rights are to be real rights. In a
country like India where it is possible for discrimination to be practiced on a vast scale and in a relentless manner fundamental rights
can have no meaning' (cited in Rao 2006b: 98–9). He argued that
along with deliberate intervention by the state in combating social
structures of inequality it was necessary to ensure that the norm
of equal inclusion of every citizen was reflected through an equal
participation of disadvantaged sections in the political processes.
The Objective resolution moved by Nehru on 13 December 1946
addressed some of the threats posed by Ambedkar as it pledged
to provide in the constitution adequate safeguards for minorities,
backward and tribal areas, and depressed and other backward classes
(See Rao 2006b: 128–9). After much bitter struggle, and not a few
setbacks, the constitution subsequently outlawed untouchability
and expressed equality towards all cultural and religious groups.
The heavy emphasis on the historical past of caste discrimination,
which was to be rectified, played an important role in the justification of social justice and public policies of reservations following
independence.

The constitution, by its abolition of untouchability and by its mandate to the state to provide for social welfare and reform, had some forward-looking arguments too. A common argument in support of equal treatment in income, status, or opportunity was that it might promote social cohesion or greater efficiency as opposed to caste hierarchies and divisions. Further, the benefit of equality in a sense of social solidarity would bring about greater equality of circumstances, representation in institutions, and manner of life.[2] It is this shared standard of non-discrimination that provides the moral terms of a social revolution which for some scholars 'meant to get (India) out of the medievalism based on birth, religion, custom and community' in order to 'reconstruct the social structure on modern foundations of law, individual merit and secular education' (Austin 2000: 26).

With this in mind, we can point to some distinctive features of India's legal framework, that provides acts to prevent forms of caste discrimination such as The Bonded Labour System (Abolition) Act (1976), The SCs and STs (Prevention of Atrocities) Act, 1989, and the SCs and STs (Prevention of Atrocities) Amendment Ordinance 2014.[3] Many theorists view the constitution of India as providing a very interesting example of how a commitment to equality as respect for persons can be translated into a constitutional scheme that is 'freestanding' in Rawls' sense, that is, grounded in no divisive religious or metaphysical doctrine but only in a practical commitment to individual rights.

This legal framework is still in place but it has not been able to undermine a regime of discrimination and stereotyping, ideologies of natural inferiority, and economic domination. Neither has the institutional design of caste-based affirmative action been effective at the policy level. The government has set up several bodies and commissions to monitor progress, and some of these measures have enabled Dalits to lead better lives. Yet untouchability, bonded labour, poverty, manual scavenging, segregation, landlessness, and violence are the everyday reality whatever the laws and special measures prescribe.

This raises the question about whether constitutional protections and legislative enactments have failed to address the current problem of caste discrimination. For these reasons, I think it is important to examine how current practices relate to some of the limitations of the liberal democratic project of our polity. Methodological questions arise as discrimination becomes extremely equivocal, as a consequence of its increasingly multiple uses, in the form of denunciations and critiques of doctrines and policies without investigation of the conditions in which caste discrimination merges with other formations. Some scholars claim that caste acquired certain attributes under British rule or that it was typical for a certain era in modern history, which has tended to recede or become superseded by other forms of collective discrimination and violence (Dirks 2001). Many think it to be too much of an oversimplification to describe persistence of hierarchical values associated with caste, as a factor, in the way in which government works in modern India (Harriss 2012). Rather, it should focus on the way that caste is negligible as an ideology to legitimate power and wealth, while continuing to be significant as a source of cultural capital that reproduces class differences. There is little doubt older forms of dominance through caste were invented a millennia ago but on our reading new mechanisms chiefly through 'opportunity hoarding' or blocking access, operate when 'members of a categorically bounded network acquire access to a resource that is valuable, renewable and subject to monopoly' (Tilly 1999: 10).

A second mechanism which blocks access, unlike earlier caste hierarchies, but deprives groups especially in the informal sector of their productive contribution, is exploitation. All these raise a new set of questions to consider in studying caste in contemporary India. Monopolistic controls over land, labour, and credit by big business groups have historically constituted a basis of exploitation while landowners have imposed debt peonage and slavery: Are caste and class important in their own right or are they merely epiphenomenal to other patterns that effect outcomes, for example, globalization? Indeed, a deeper understanding of the role of caste in modern India in terms of differentiation, exclusion, and stigmatization may help us understand this transition of caste in modern India. The inequalities arising out of membership of oppressed groups that experience aversion, misrecognition, or stereotyping undermine their sense of being in an equal world. One can proceed further and argue that caste has not receded at all but proliferated in new forms and new sites, targeting new groups, speaking a new language. The second question then is: how do initially symmetric or uniform structures of caste relations give rise to highly complex functional structures when they encountered modern processes of production where caste becomes something else? Through these questions, there is a need to arrive at a more specific understanding of caste discrimination and the reason for its astonishing resistance. For this we need to be sure that we are indeed theorizing about caste, and not about other very general phenomena like culture, society, or economy, of which it is a symptom and whose conflicts it reveals.

A third question is about how the anti-discrimination principle, as one binding the state alone, imposes higher obligations on state institutions, when compared to private ones, so that we can see problems in housing, membership of organizations, temple entry, and matrimonial alliances still as very valid. Fourth, at its inception, the anti-discrimination principle was very limited to face-to-face interactions but over the years most international documents now recognize its purview to be indirect discrimination, prejudices, and violation of human rights. How and in what context are forms of discrimination likely to be salient in Indian society in the coming decade? There is a need to map the forces that keep people out of structures but also identify those that continue to place and locate people within unjust hierarchical social relations.

As we shall see in this volume, there is a growing recognition among social activists, academia, and policy-makers that Indian democracy has not addressed the question of discrimination adequately. Lacking support from the state, disadvantaged groups including displaced persons, denotified tribes, backward classes, and religious minorities have raised demands for recognition of newer kinds of discrimination and competing interpretations of social justice. Subtle discrimination that is built of 'micro-inequities' or little acts of disrespect, apparently small events that are often unintentional and unrecognized as yet, are mechanisms of evidence against people who are different but need to be studied as historical actors.[4] Drawing upon diverse theories, the current focus is on examining the power relations that intersect with each other and where for example, gender, caste, and class are structural categories that lead to unequal allocation of resources and misrecognition. These events affect us all in day-to-day life in housing, education, and health care, in families, neighbourhoods, and governance in general.

Rise of Democratic Equality

Discrimination is usually a response to particular manifestations of inequality which are embedded in the historical, cultural, and political context of a given society. India's transformation into a nation was accompanied by two major forces: democratic equality that integrates principles of distribution with expressive demands of equal respect (Turner 1986: 1); social movements in which egalitarianism was a key value and through which a new social justice imagination emerged through interventions of Dalits, working classes, and women movements (Omvedt 1993). Feudal claims to property, bondage of labour, or restricted mobility in occupations to particular caste groups were undermined with the rise of democratic politics. Other distinct ways of understanding economic equality, related to distribution of resources, land, wealth, income, education, and power, became increasingly linked to emancipatory projects that propagated the revolutionary overthrow of class rule. The tremendous role of these forces can be seen in questioning structural and ideological formations, which were clearly overlapping in the singular histories of that time. This volume will attempt to distinguish these to examine the claims that have been central in theorizations and perceptions of various kinds of discrimination in modern India.

The philosophical premises in this debate have been addressed by scholars who argue that strengthening of the idea of equality, was first of all, closely related to the affirmation of individualism as well as to the making of nation-states. Sumit Sarkar views the anti-colonial, national movements and debates of the constituent assembly as crucial to the making of a democratic polity. Before being implemented, these principles and convictions were contested in the constituent assembly and became part of the 'historical inheritance' of Indian democracy (Sarkar 2002: 23–46). Myron Weiner claims that 'the principle of equality implied a revolutionary transformation in India' (2002: 193–225). Scholars like Sudipta Kaviraj have relied on Alex Tocqueville's argument to propose a distinction between democratic government in the narrow sense, and the workings of the democratic principle on the whole of social life—its low but irreversible transformative impact on fundamental institutions and the imaginative apparatus of modern societies (Kaviraj 2012:

20–49).Grounded in the principle of equality, democracy challenges inherited hierarchies and predisposes people to think in egalitarian ways (Kaviraj 2001: 226).

Javeed Alam notes the positive developments that subsequently took place in 'ritual status inequalities', but he is critical of 'the democratic process' that subsequently, 'detached itself from the institutional infirmities surrounding it', and, 'acquired an autonomy of its own' (Alam 2004: 36). There is thus a widespread acceptance of democracy even when the 'working of capitalism' with which it is closely tied, fails to provide solutions to the basic necessities of the common people (Alam 2004: 40). Economic inequality generated by the expansion of capitalist production has faded from the centre of equality debates: 'Social inequality of the traditional type has been seriously undermined by the power of democratic politics; but the logic of democracy has not seriously opposed the logic of capitalist development and inequalities associated with that process' (Kaviraj 2001: 115).

Second, most of the members of the constituent assembly relied upon the tradition–modernity paradigm in their analysis of non-discrimination in which certain values were seen as obstructing rights of modern citizenship. Implicit is the assumption of a simple correlation between development and progress and replacement of traditional structures like caste by new ones. Various processes of modernity, it was argued, would corrode the social inequalities inherent in traditional social stratification recognized as obstacles to development. Following this was the assumption of 'a radical plasticity of the social' so that social structures along with political institutions would be eventually transformed in this process (Kaviraj 2001: 98).

Finally, they shared the assumption that a clear statement of rational ideals and principles in the constitution could be transformatory. Upendra Baxi points out that 'no previous constitutional model envisaged such an explicit and comprehensive transformation of a traditional society and installed a description of a constitutionally desired social order and good life and ways of deep contention regarding these' (Baxi 2002: 31–63). The assumptions behind these actions initiated an era of legislative enactments and state intervention in matters affecting social conduct that eventually culminated in the questioning of the category of modernity itself.[5]

Antinomies of Equality

Equality emerges as a modern notion closely related to the development of democratic societies in the West struggling against political absolutism and despotism and the collapse of feudalism. Anne Phillips has been univocal in asserting that democracy implies a rough equality between people in their influence on political affairs and 'this expression rests on and reinforces profound notions about social equality' (2004: 2). Expansion of citizenship has been bound up with social movements to establish equality in modern society whether instituted through socialist, social democratic, or authoritarian regimes (Turner 1986: 19). But this has also forced rethinking of fundamental categories of political discourse like equality, entirely flattened out and distorted as it is more about reason and its correct representations. If we look closely we find that the modern subject is constituted only through a series of exclusions and differentiations and autonomy of the individual is after all but a mere illusion. Unlike Western political theory that excluded women, slaves, religious minorities, and unpropertied classes as lacking rationality, the newly ascendant concept of democratic equality coexisted in the Indian context with relations of domination in caste hierarchies, bonded labour, denial of property to women, and atrocities against Dalits. Secondly, differentiation of groups rights with policies of reservation for SCs and STs although poorly implemented, were developed much earlier than civil and political rights for people. Both these rights have an enhanced hypervisibility compared to social rights for citizens in the current context following the implementation of neo-liberal policies. As the market is viewed as the primary site for economic transactions, civil and legal rights, then questions of discrimination emerge in an energized way. Equal political and civil rights present an emancipatory potential as there is a need to overcome exclusions and stigmatization associated with citizens dependent on the state welfare machinery.

Thirdly, Indian debates primarily address the concept of proportional equality to redefine the policies of group difference as effects of historical discrimination. These debates culminate in three interpretations over how to address group injustice within liberal institutions in India: (a) equality of outcomes in the form of affirmative action;

(b) non-discrimination and inter-group equality; (c) contextual analysis of difference or disadvantage of groups.

Which of these concerns has in practice been uppermost in fuelling the call for redefining equality for opportunity where the unit of analysis is the individual, is hard to say. But there is no doubting that there are contestations and these are likely to issue therefore in different ideas about how to make that concept operationalize. These can be called the 'antinomies of equality' or the marks of inequality that lie in the contradictions, oppositions, and tensions inherent in the social ideal of equality in which individuals move between the polarities of rights and duties or membership and exclusion of the political community. Significantly I shall argue that the particular staging of equality of opportunity runs parallel to the formation of a democratic arrangement that underpins many radical notions of equality. Advancing radical notions of equality implies two intertwined and historically constituted conditions of democracy—free and equal participation of the people and democracy's self-grounding and self-constitution. Indeed the second implies the impossibility of finally ever revealing democracy's true form. But in India these resulted in an array of interpretations and conceptualization of what equality means in democracy which I will briefly examine now.

Equality of Opportunity

In the constituent assembly, a general consensus prevailed on the liberal concept of equality as a distinctive modern value that belonged to the enlightenment discourse. Equality provided a framework for ideas of rationality, scientific spirit, and freedom, and moved in opposition to religion, arbitrary political power, and metaphysics. Yet the idea of equality of opportunity as employed within this unique context was subjected to critique. Although very valuable as creating parity of conditions or a level playing field, in such a way that individuals achieve their objectives through effort or choice, independent of circumstances, it was critically interrogated.

In these debates it was acknowledged that different circumstances, related to social discrimination, more than effort and choice, faced by individuals, were bound to give rise to different outcomes.[6] For these reasons in the Indian constitution, social justice was seen as a corrective remedy for caste discrimination. Reservations policies were justified when a group suffered from historical discrimination and its present disadvantaged status or backwardness was substantially attributable to that discrimination. It is not surprising to find the text speaks in two different languages: it has several formal-legal aspects of political institutions that capture the spirit of non-discrimination in its Preamble and clauses related to fundamental rights developed from Articles 14 to 18, to protect individuals from arbitrary discrimination by government officials.

The dual impulse is evident when debates step outside this paradigm of juridical equality as a neutral provision by acknowledging social practices based on caste discrimination and plead to outlaw untouchability as one of the great hindrances to developing an equal and just society. The debates implicitly accept principles of equality and non-discrimination which guarantee inclusiveness to all those who are located in equal circumstances; however, these can marginalize those who are subject to burdens of historically disadvantaged group membership; they can also sustain a deep insensitivity to entrenched social inequalities and demonize affirmative action policies. Govind Ballabh Pant pointed out that we have to 'atone for our omissions'; K.T. Shah argued that they have been 'neglected in the past' and their rights and claims to enjoy as equal citizens 'happens to be denied to them because of their backwardness.[7]

For these reasons the Articles intended to cover actions taken by state officials—which were clearly subject to norms of non-discrimination—but later it went to also to include actions in civil society. This difference was made with the understanding that since individuals should be allowed a fair chance of developing their lives, they must have fair access to employment and public space. Subsequently, the equality clauses in the Indian constitution does not require identical treatment in all circumstances as provisions were made for social groups like the scheduled castes and scheduled tribes who have been discriminated in the past.[8] Article 15 confined the prohibition against discrimination only to state action and Article 16 to state employment, while Article 29 restricted it to educational institutions. These principles form part of a 'specific conception of justice' but they seek to provide systematic guidance in overcoming social discrimination viewed as a major impediment to enjoyment of political liberties.[9]

In these discussions, however, discrimination and social inequality are viewed as 'structure neutral' or the approach is to claim that reduction of caste inequalities can be achieved through a framework of industrialization and capitalist economy without curbing the legal inequalities related to rights of property or exchanges of commercial society (Kaviraj 2001: 89–119). Exploitation as an aspect of social relations between dominant and subordinate groups, through controls over land, labour, or credit is mentioned but not subverted in any fundamental way.

Since the drafting of the constitution, the Indian government and judiciary have been involved through constitutional provisions and legal judgments to abolish social discrimination. Despite efforts by the government, equality of opportunity remains an elusive ideal and several basis of discrimination continue to undercut or subvert a concern with formal and substantive equality. Democratic equality has been modifying and restructuring many processes but the failure in the implementation of constitutional provisions on untouchability is apparent in the light of documented evidence issued by the National Commission for Scheduled Castes and Scheduled Tribes (GoI 2002; Jan Sahas and UNICEF 2009). Their reports support the claim that 'untouchability'—the imposition of social disabilities on persons by birth in certain castes—is still practised in many forms throughout the country. Apart from reports of atrocities on Dalits, it is found that they are under-represented in the labour market and that they are significant unemployment gaps for people at a 'disadvantage', such as persons with disabilities, other backward castes, religious minorities, women, and tribals.

Ambedkar on Graded Inequality

B.R. Ambedkar was possibly one of the greatest influences on subaltern groups even while being recognized as the architect of the Indian constitution. He had great faith in the capacity of political institutions to slowly undermine the basic principles of the caste system. We need to draw upon Ambedkar's notion of general equality that could serve as a basis for a state or any form of government.[10] In one of his earliest articles, he explained that democracy is not merely a form of government but primarily 'a mode of associated living, of conjoint communicated experience' in which fraternity which is another name of democracy, exists (Ambedkar 1989a: 57).

In a preface to the book, *The Untouchables*, Ambedkar argued that untouchability was a 'diabolical contrivance to suppress and enslave humanity' (Ambedkar 1990b). Throughout his life starting with the submissions in the Southborough committee in 1919, he emphasized social conditions characterized by untouchability and social ostracism that not only arrest the 'growth of personality' but also come in the way of citizenship rights and 'material well-being' (Ambedkar 1989b: 256). In this situation, equal rights could not be secured unless we attack the systemic historical subjugation of a set of people due to the caste system that had religious sanction.

Despite his explanation of the caste system as having a religious sanction, Ambedkar's initial programs attempt to integrate the Dalits into society and politics through modern political institutions and not through religion. He put his faith in the constitution and the legislative process, as well as the representative bodies to correct social and economic injustices. Equality must be accepted as the 'governing principle' so for Ambedkar it was an intrinsic good that possessed an independent value (Ambedkar 1989a: 58). While Ambedkar saw the prescriptive uses of the concept of equality in moral and political arguments as quite useful, he was conscious of the inequality of treatment based on caste and tradition. To bring about a more substantial equality must involve treating people differently, which is contrary to the formal principle. For such reasons, he advocated a separatist policy for the Dalits, which might create caste distinctions at an initial stage but eventually make these identities unimportant.

Once he was appointed the chairman of the drafting committee of the assembly on 23 December 1947, he drafted a memorandum on political safeguards to the assembly that suggested remedies against social discrimination and economic exploitation. The problem of 'deprivation' related to the lack of access to income-earning capital assets like agricultural land and capital, services necessary for business, employment, and educational skills; all these must be understood as an outcome of denials of equal rights for Dalits due to their historical exclusion from these domains for a long time. The anti-discriminatory measures are important but Ambedkar realized their limitation in overcoming the deprivation caused by the historical denial of economic and social rights over a period of time. Thus he argued that freedom from discrimination is a necessary but far from sufficient means of achieving equality. Indeed Ambedkar cautions us that:

> On the 26th of January 1950, we are going to enter into a life of contradictions. In politics we will have equality and in social and economic life we will have inequality. In politics we will be recognizing the principle of one man one vote and one vote one value. In our social and economic life, we shall, by reason of our social and economic structure, continue to deny the principle of one man one value (CAD 1949: 979).

This powerful articulation of equality accepts an insuperable opposition between liberal individualism and the democratic ideal. In retrospect, it is evident that for Ambedkar the phrase 'equality of all individuals' rests upon the exclusion of all those social differences that are perceived to be the sources of discrimination in society. Implicit in this passage is the view that democratic equality would be a pure abstract; equality can exist only through its specific meanings in particular spheres as political equality, economic equality and so forth. What matters for him is the possibility of tracing the line of demarcation between those who belonged to the demos and exercised equal rights and those who cannot have same rights because they are not part of the demos.

Ambedkar also presents a second, more inclusive, rephrasing of his conception of equality in many of his works that extends the boundaries of politics by using the rights of civil society and associations. Now he says that unlike inequality, 'graded inequality' that relies upon differentiation of grades is more dangerous as it does not create general discontent. He explains that the 'possibility of a general common attack by the aggrieved parties is non-existent' as they are not on a common level (Ambedkar 1989c: 101–2; 1990a: 10). In a chapter on the problem of discrimination, he claims that it is 'merely another name for absence of freedom' There is no freedom in the market, he argues 'divorced from the realities of a specific time and place' and it involves 'the power of choice between alternatives—a choice which is real, not merely nominal, between alternatives' (Ambedkar 1989c: 110). In privileging the brahminical priests and proposing a division of labourers, sanctioned by religion, 'the caste system does not make the sufferers combine against a common foe as it makes each group unequal both in terms of the benefits and burdens they receive in that social status.... Based on an ascending scale of reverence and descending scale of contempt it divided untouchables from the low caste Hindus and rendered collective social revolt unrealistic' (Ambedkar 1987: 46–47).

Finally, in Ambedkar's writings we find a creative interpretation of democratic liberalism to craft a new kind of group politics in India for Dalits. Through state guarantees for reservations and through the individual's conversion to Buddhism he was able to posit the ideas of imagining Dalits as equal even though outside the fold of Hinduism. Furthermore, caste social hierarchies and unequal resources undergirded two different kinds of exclusions that got entangled and produced different patterns of exclusion and unjust distributions. Hence Ambedkar saw conversion as a context within which individuals can actualize freedom as a mode of thought in action and gain a sense of self-respect and dignity.

Socialist Ideas on Equality and Distributive Justice

Although communist parties were not part of the constituent assembly, many influential ideas on economic equality and justice came from diverse socialist traditions to the Congress party heading the national movement. In 1931, the Karachi resolution stated that political freedom must be accompanied by economic rights and redistribution but when the constitution was adopted, it relegated economic freedoms to the directive principles of state policy. The traditional left did not comprehend the autonomy of caste discrimination as central to the Indian democratic project. They were united on focusing more on the category of class in trade union movements than caste in understanding social formations. Despite these conflicting ideological orientations, Myron Weiner claims that many Congress leaders were inspired by socialist ideas. They believed that a socialist welfare state based on planning would accelerate investment and growth that would benefit all classes

(Weiner 2002). A broad agreement across Gandhians, socialists, and Congress workers was that economic policy should aim for the progressive removal of poverty, inequalities in Indian society and result in the complete disappearance of arbitrary distinctions.[11] To a large extent they concurred on the need to limit sharply the existing scope of an acquisitive instinct in Indian economic life and to create a new set of cooperative motives. As far as possible institutional changes should be introduced to substitute cooperative principles of economic organization for the prevailing system based on private enterprise.

But it was the strategy of economic development based on the P.C. Mahalanobis model that finally won as its guiding spirit was pressed by a buoyant Nehru. Here the reference to overcoming backwardness was a special component for indicating economic progress. This model laid emphasis on the development of heavy industry in various five-year plans and assumed that development would trickle down from top to bottom.[12] Explaining the doctrine of 'mixed economy' B.R. Nanda explains that Nehru advocated nationalization of key industries while leaving a wide field 'for private enterprise' (Nanda 2004: 190; see Bagchi 2002). Nehru was aware of the limitations of both capitalism and communism and the welfare state was seen as a mixed brew of both these systems. He emphasized on a more purposeful vision for reorganization of the social and economic structures. Here his stress was on a socialist society with an active and expanding public sector.

The idea of equality thus was no ordinary principle propounded by legal and constitutional experts but had far wider implications in our political discourse, state policy, and public opinion. The state building project relied on the way citizenship was located on grounds of homogeneity and authenticity, to distance it from primordial notions of culture, religion, and ethnicity. A developmental ideology 'was a constituent part of the self-definition of the post-colonial state' when the state was positioned as a provider and protector. Poverty was thus defined as a broad-based set of absences or missing capabilities that were produced by oppressive social forces that could quickly be removed (Corbridge and Harriss 2005: 56). However, contestations within the nation challenged such abstract legal notions of citizenship because although the state had succeeded in establishing itself as responsible for people's welfare, it also sustained many identities. Planning in India during these decades was mainly concerned with economic growth till the social welfare field began to grapple with complex issues of class and caste. These notions sustained a terrain of dissent that engaged with the rhetoric of rights and distributive justice in the interests of specific groups. Thus constructed in conditions of economic inequality that were institutionalized by the growing power of the state and bureaucracy, radical formulations of equality and justice that focused on cultural oppression became more apparent when the marginalized and powerless groups insisted on being substantially included in the polity.

The emphasis on political domination invokes the importance of political voice or the question of who participates in the debate on democracy. Centrally, it emphasizes democratic inclusion of social groups that would eventually unsettle institutionally accepted norms of formal equality.

Changing Terms of the Discourse on Equality: Who is Equal and Why?

Although in 1946 there were more than a dozen women members in the Indian constituent assembly they did not argue for quotas or affirmative action programmes for women as it was believed that the recognition of women as equal citizens by the constitution and the fundamental rights would lead to equality in political and economic life. This belief stemmed from the assumption that the woman's question was primarily a welfare or social question, which had little to do with the structural aspects of society within which they are situated. In these debates on the constitution they supported a non-discrimination approach in Articles 14 and 15 or a gender-blind approach, that is, they viewed gender as irrelevant in enjoyment of fundamental rights and citizenship rights. The normative task of a non-discrimination perspective aimed at 'inclusion', which implies that gender ought to be non-pertinent in considerations for equality of treatment. At the same time, protections for women were upheld on the ground that according to 15(3) the state is empowered to make special provisions for women (Galanter 1984: 426).

The legislative debates during the late 1950s underscored the wholesale nature of the gender neutrality mandate. Significantly, this was the period leading up to the Kalelkar Commission where much of the discussion centred on the issue of preferential treatment in the case of Other Backward Classes (henceforth OBCs). Kaka Kalelkar, who chaired the commission, expressed his dissatisfaction on women's participation in the Indian polity: 'The position of women in India is peculiar. We have always felt that they have lived under great social handicaps and must therefore, as a class be regarded as backward but since they do not form a separate community it has not been possible for us to list them among the backward classes.' (GoI 1955: 31) Though the commission estimated backward groups to be about 32 per cent of the population it did not include women as a separate group (Galanter 1984: 169).

However, by the early 1970s, a perception had set in that women were 'backward'. International organizations such as the UN held several conferences highlighting the status of women in the third world. In response to such developments the government of India prepared a report on women's status for which a national-level committee was constituted that drew attention to rising gender disparities in all the sectors (UN 1979). The authors, in the report *Towards Equality* asserted that economic development 'has sometimes contributed to reduction of social inequalities, but has also aggravated them' (CWDS 2012: 254). In future, any policy or movement for the emancipation and development for women has to form a part of a total movement for removal of inequalities and oppressive social institutions. The committee also stated that the centuries of 'neglect, discrimination and exploitation had acquired a dimension of geometric progression' and thus 'positive discrimination was the only way to turn women's rights into a potential from de jure to de facto' (CWDS 2012: xxviii). Although the committee first considered the option of quotas, Lotika Sarkar and Vina Majumdar noted in their dissent that they had never supported special representation for women. They reiterated that the 'application of the theoretical principle of equality in the context of unequal situations only intensifies inequalities because inequality in such situations merely means privileges for those who have them already and not for those who need them' (CWDS 2012: xxviii).

Towards the end of Chapter 7 of this report, the framework within which the debate on equality had been conducted was questioned. The authors argued that women's participation has shown a steady increase but their ability to impact the political process has been negligible because of 'the inadequate attention paid to their political education and mobilization by both political parties and women's organizations'. They accused these organizations of seeing women voters and citizens as 'appendages of the males and have depended on heads of families to provide block votes and support for their parties and candidates' (CWDS 2012: 221). They caution that 'though women do not numerically constitute a minority, they are beginning to acquire the features of a minority community' (CWDS 2012: 214). Since the right to political equality has not enabled women to play their roles as partners and constituents in the political process it says that these rights only 'helped to build an illusion of equality and power which is frequently used as an argument to resist protective and acceleratory measures to enable women to achieve their just and equal position in society'. It is therefore argued that time has now come 'to move out of this token provision for women's representation to a more meaningful association of women in the structure of local administration' (CWDS 2012: 223). These formulations changed the terms of the discourse by actually questioning the formal idea of equality that was limited to equal treatment of individuals and that ignored structural inequalities like discrimination in employment and remuneration for women. It framed the question for the coming years: who is equal and why?

The committee's recommendation for entry of women in the political process and engaging them in development was not implemented but it led to an impetus for further changes. The Report of CSWI recommended that women panchayats be formed in every village as an integral part of the structure of local government. However, it was only in the 1990s that this became possible through an important milestone, the National Perspective Plan for Women (NPPW 1988–2000), a document prepared under the Rajiv Gandhi government that recommended a reservation of at least 33 per cent of total seats for women from village councils to district councils (MWCD and MHRD 1988). Some of these were adopted by the 73rd and 74th amendment acts to the Indian constitution (Ghosh and Pramanik 1999: 220–1).

Mandal Commission: Equality of Outcome

The political mobilization and assertion of the backward castes and Dalits, against the government's policy to delay implementing the recommendations of the Mandal Commission gave a new impetus to debates on equality. An entirely different position is developed by the Mandal Commission report that revisits the idea of an unequivocal declaration of equality in the present and explains that it is equality of results which is the real acid test of effective equality.[13] Arguing against open positions and the claim that they attract superior talent or encourage superior performance, the report came out in favour of social programs of positive discrimination in favour of disadvantaged groups (Other backward castes, scheduled castes and scheduled tribes). These programmes are meant to compensate for significant inequalities of condition in order to overcome obstacles to fair access to opportunities. Reflecting a socialist and Ambedkarite approach to reservations, the objective was to give OBCs access to power through public employment and institutions of higher education (BCC 1990: 57).[14] Relying upon Ram Manohar Lohia, who viewed 'economic inequality and caste inequality as twin demons which have both to be killed' proponents of the Mandal report claim to reposition and intensify the debates on caste discrimination. However by reducing caste to the question of reservation it rules out any abolition of this system in the near future (Jaffrelot 2003: 361).

The report points out the inadequacies of the equality of opportunity principle since 'when we allow weak and strong to compete on an equal footing, we are loading the dice in favour of the strong and holding only a mock competition in which the weaker partner is destined to failure right from the start' (BCC 1990: 26). Equality of opportunity is viewed as a libertarian principle since it assumes all individuals begin on similar terms on the basis of fairness in the competition for advantage. Promoting the idea of equality of condition is about promoting opportunities in the strong sense—about enabling and empowering people to exercise what might be called real choices among real options. People who started their lives at a disadvantage can never catch up due to the 'invisible and cumulative hindrances' which they face. The commission thus pleaded for 'equality of results' as 'the real acid test of effective equality' in implementing the mandates of Articles 15(4) and 16(4); But 'which may require unequal opportunity or treatment for the initially disadvantaged so that they eventually wind up equal in resources or rights' (BCC 1990: 27). Equalities of result are possible through legislation and public policies since groups with different circumstances or forms of life should be able to participate in public institutions without suffering disadvantages because of them.

Significantly, the Mandal report argued that the caste system was the cause of structural inequality and therefore notions of merit could not apply in the same way as they did in an individualistic society. It claimed that 'caste is also a class of citizens and if the caste as a whole is socially and educationally backward, reservation can be made in favour of such a caste on the ground that is a socially and education-ally backward class of citizens within the meaning of article 15(4)' (BCC 1990: 67). Yet the commission did not regard caste as the sole criterion for the definition of the OBCs. In fact, it evolved an index based on eleven indicators subdivided into three categories—social, educational, and economic.

Hollowing-out of Citizenship[15]

The Mandal Commission in principle accepted the occurrence of caste discrimination among non-Hindu groups, Muslims, Sikhs, and Christians as well. Drawing data from the census of 1931, it identified 82 different social groups among Muslims as OBCs. This new approach posed a major challenge to the constitution in hol-lowing out a universal notion of citizenship by recognizing multiple social and religious identities. Despite an awareness of the category of 'backwardness' amongst Muslims through reports and surveys, till the seventh five-year plan, religious minorities continued to get development benefits along with OBCs. It was only in 2006, that a separate Ministry of Minority Affairs (MMA) was created, and a committee set up under Justice Rajinder Sachar, to prepare a report on the status of the Muslim community (GoI 2006). The socio-economic profile that the government-appointed Sachar Committee estimates draw of Muslim Indians is disheartening. In what is a well-publicized report, the Sachar Committee Report (SCR) corroborated earlier findings, that the Muslim community has endured economic, social, and cultural discrimination and suffered impediments in access to material and non-material resources. As a community, they experienced increasing hostility in the form of intentional and unintentional discrimination from the police, public officials, and in biased educational curricula and cultural reproductions. In all major socio-economic indicators, Muslims as a community are on average worse off than members of the majority community.

These demands for substantive equality for religious minorities are complex and challenging for public policies as they sometimes fail to distinguish sufficiently the backwardness faced by a minority group from caste discrimination. As twin models of justice, both are bounded by explicit abhorrence to status hierarchy but proponents ignore the difference and underestimate the alienation and unfreedom that lie beneath these two domains.

The era of liberalization since the 1990s has opened up sectors of the industrial economy but it was also a moment at which the advancement of identity interests had intensified. Proponents of Dalit capitalism now discuss possibilities for confronting the illegitimate dominance of the Hindu caste order, through the creation of an educated middle class and employment. The booming small-scale industry presents a unique opportunity for the Dalit middle class to grow into an economic force. However, problems remain as Dalit entrepreneurs still lack social networks that other dominant business caste groups have access to. These claims of celebrating a Dalit capitalism present a caste-neutral approach towards building ownership and development of business. Thus formal segregation and stigmatization reproducing upper-caste supremacy continue and a range of newer kinds of discrimination occur (Teltumbde 2011: 10–11). Reservation or the protective discrimination policy has improved access to education and employment for the marginalized social groups but the state has not been able to implement major policies to remove their disadvantaged and insecure positions. Some scholars go so far as to argue that claims of caste have grown stronger in important areas of Indian politics and the state remains as resilient as ever. It is argued that state regulation and the decades of planned development has strengthened rather than weakened caste linkages because caste has endured as the prime network for contacts, for subcontracting and for labour recruitment in the informal economy.

Thus the globalization process has a variable impact on different sectors of the economy, leading to uneven and imbalanced growth under which the process of social exclusion of groups has been intensified. Indeed, the most important aspects of the development discourse of the state lie in its uneven consequences for marginalized groups not defined in class terms—scheduled castes, tribes, women, displaced people, and migrants.

Discrimination, Social Exclusion, and Intersectionality

In the 1990s, with the advent of new economic policies, financial institutions shifted the focus of the agenda away from redistribution to economic growth and marketization of the public sector. Scholars focused on how liberalization had an impact on different sectors of the economy leading to uneven and imbalanced growth and social exclusion of groups that were not always reducible to class. Visions of development were viewed as a discursive legitimization for the acquisition of land that further encouraged displacement and accumulation by dispossession amongst the urban poor, farmers, and tribals. They pointed to the low levels of welfare, education, health, or employment status of groups as, the effect of the neoliberal policies was to strengthen market forces while ignoring social protection policies. In light of the foregoing analysis, it is important that the current debate around equality confront the problem of multiple discriminations and move toward a compelling alternative. The concept of social exclusion emerged as a contested, discursive terrain during this period in response to the demand for such an alternative. Questions have been raised about the conceptual clarity of social exclusion, its theoretical underpinnings, or its relevance to the debates on social justice. While the notion of inclusion is quite distinct from equality, many see the social exclusion discourse as part of a broader concern to explore alternatives to mainstream development, anti-poverty approaches and their conceptualization of social disadvantage. For us the question is to what extent does this concept contribute to our understanding of discrimination and inequalities of various groups in countries like India?

Like equality of opportunity, social inclusion seeks to put disadvantaged people in a position in which they are able to participate in the economy and other aspects of social life. Like egalitarian notions of distributive justice, social inclusion is concerned about outcomes or justice in distributive patterns. But instead of seeking the same equivalent outcome for every citizen, it addresses the disadvantage of particular groups in society. The objective is to secure a minimum welfare for every citizen who is a member of groups who suffer discrimination. It tries to combine some of the objectives of liberal and radical egalitarianism by ensuring an equal distribution of resources or opportunities along with a 'type of welfarism in the sense that the outcome sought is to improve the welfare of disadvantaged groups' (Collins 2003: 16–43) A perfectionist element in the idea of social inclusion is that there is a conception of the essential elements of well-being that include material goods such as food and shelter, along with opportunities to participate in meaningful ways in social life. Non-material goods include a fulfilling level of education, participation in politics, cultural activities, and paid work.

Although many aspects of social exclusion are discussed in the Indian context, one broad area of agreement is that institutions embody different patterns of rules, norms, and asset distributions, which together help to spell out people's membership of different kinds of social groups, shape their identities, and define their interests (Kabeer 2008: 28). Similarly 'disadvantage' results in social exclusion 'when the various institutional mechanism through which resources are allocated and value assigned operate in such a way as to systematically deny particular groups of people the resources and recognition which would allow them to participate fully in the life of that society' (Kabeer 2008: 24).

Access and exclusion in one institutional domain can be offset or exacerbated by access and exclusion in another; for instance, the disadvantages associated with caste or gender within the household or community may be offset by the ability to access resources in the marketplace or the legal system. The second theme common in most writings is that social exclusion is the product of actual social practices through which group behaviour generates these patterns. The first is described as mobilization of 'institutional bias', which can operate to exclude those who might threaten the status quo without conscious decisions being taken by those who represent that status quo or any awareness on their part (Lukes 2005). A second form of exclusionary mechanism is social closure through which 'social collectivities seek to maximize rewards by restricting access to resources and opportunities to a limited circle of eligible' (Parkin 1979). Parkin uses the example of 'credentialism' to illustrate the widely used means of social closure to deny groups in society to access resources and other economic opportunities. A third category of mechanisms, according to Nancy Fraser, through which exclusion occurs is that of 'unruly practices' (Fraser 1989). These refer to the gap between rules and their implementation, which occur in all institutional domains. Examples are distribution of public goods by public service providers in social sectors like health and education that take the form of unruly practices.

India has grappled with the question of social closure, credentialism and unruly practices right from the moment it started drafting its constitution. But with emerging identity politics, there is a growing recognition that many people suffer from discrimination on a number of grounds at the same time. Newer claimants have emerged as the nature and dynamics of discrimination faced by groups such as sexual minorities, backward Muslims, denotified tribes, and displaced persons is complex, because the multiple positions occupied by them are shaped by numerous social attributes. This has triggered the search for a more effective basis for combating 'multiple discriminations' covering different grounds.

The theoretical conundrum is that people have multilayered identities yet those who have faced discrimination may choose to emphasize precisely those disparaged identities in order to subvert more invidious distinctions through group-based organizations and policies. Thus different kinds of 'group disadvantage' need to be also addressed while the concept of group based on fixed and exclusive attributes is critically accepted. Group membership is no longer a sufficient criterion to establish and identify disadvantage of an individual. The rise of sub-groups within a group that are disadvantaged in comparison to members of their own group means that multiple axes of disadvantage need to be addressed.

Outline of the Volume

All the essays in this collection refer to contestations and debates on equality surveyed in the previous sections. They raise critical questions about the contrasting approaches to study discrimination in social sciences. They identify societal complexity and interdependence as creating a paradoxical relationship between democratic equality and discrimination. With increasing complexity, differentiation, and interdependence, individuals have greater choice and opportunity. At the same time they have a reduced ability to participate in the decisions that shape one's life. What is distinctive about the papers of this volume is that they argue that wrongfulness of discrimination is tied to the fact that the act is directed against members of a salient social group. Discrimination is linked to inequalities, lack of recognition, institutional mindsets, denial of self-respect to fellow-beings, and the denial of liberty. However, discrimination cannot only be explained as a function of the attributes and actions of individuals. It refers to the vulnerabilities to domination and deprivation that some groups experience due to social-structural processes.

The volume is divided into four parts. The first part has three chapters that introduce key concepts like exclusion, discrimination, and non-discrimination. In the opening essay, Sukhadeo Thorat and Nidhi Sadana Sabharwal suggest a new theoretical logic in linking poverty and caste structures with patterns of exclusion in public policies. Across most development indicators, the excluded groups belonging to lower castes are significantly worse than that of others. This paper relies on a welfarist analytical framework to understand the link between poverty of low castes in India and policies to address their social exclusion. The second chapter on the promise and challenge of non-discrimination by Vidhu Verma examines the liberal concern for non-discrimination and the way it contrives to evade the implications of that neutral ideal in a restricted notion of egalitarianism. In explicating the approach propounded by liberal egalitarians and its critique by difference theorists who emphasize the idea of group justice, this chapter invites us to reconsider their approaches to two policies—non-discrimination laws and affirmative action. Finally, it argues for looking at institutional processes and social relations that are crucial to the remedial effectiveness of an inclusive equality analysis and also what this conceptualization means in terms of violations of harm principle, dignity, and denials of misrecognition more generally. The third chapter by Anand Teltumbde specifically looks at the political economy of discrimination and examines the way class, caste, and market are interacting and producing newer kinds of discrimination. The main argument is that caste discrimination remains as powerful as ever in the post-independent period as it was under colonialism. Even after more than sixty years of implementing laws prohibiting caste discrimination, Dalits are relatively disadvantaged in housing, employment, and education. This chapter concludes that caste discrimination is increasingly contested and challenged but nothing short of a major radical change in political economy can annihilate the caste system.

The chapters in the second part of the book are on comparative perspectives on anti-discrimination laws and affirmative action policies. Tarunabh Khaitan's chapter provides an overview of the architecture of discrimination law as one binding the state alone, and its gradual extension through judicial law-making and then through legislation to private persons. Although all the jurisdictions concerned impose anti-discrimination obligations on public as well as private bodies, most of them seem to impose higher obligations on public bodies when compared to private ones. The chapter presents the substantive doctrinal aspects of the practice of discrimination law in the chosen jurisdictions but the author claims that despite jurisdictional differences, a common, if relatively thin, structure can be discerned. Daniel Sabbagh offers a historical review on affirmative action policies that benefit groups whose existence remains independent from the will of their individual members and whose status determines their social experience and subjective identity to a large extent. This chapter identifies common trends that obtain despite major differences in national models of citizenship among countries that have set up affirmative action programmes. It also emphasizes the importance of numbers as a factor accounting for the divergences that persist.

The chapters in the third part of the volume on structural discrimination discuss in some empirical detail inequalities in intellectual-cultural capital, notions of stigma and discrimination, and the link to reproduction of social difference, their conceptual inadequacy, and their usefulness in designing effective interventions.

The chapter by Narender Kumar claims that despite the abolition of physical untouchability, it persists in various forms in rural and less in urban India. Interestingly, untouchability is reflecting in newer and nuanced forms in the modern institutions, With narratives from individuals' writings and memoirs, it looks into how the universities/colleges as modern institutions are encircled in the traditional mindset that dictates such institutions to either not allow the former untouchables to enter and if somehow they enter then to disgrace and humiliate during their engagements in the processes inside. The second chapter in this section on gender discrimination by Vidhu Verma dissects sexual harassment laws in India and their limits in providing gender justice in contemporary India. Work constitutes one of the important domains for distribution of goods and also provides a foundation for citizenship, community, and self-respect. While workplace harassment cases are playing a more prominent role in employment, different women from oppressed groups face exclusion from higher paying positions and face collective violence in different forms.

Badri Narayan's chapter critically examines the project of empowering communities through state resources as their implementation produces the sense of marginalization among various sections of society. He explores how state-led categories lead to the misdistribution of the resources. Through an empirical study of the Musahars, who belong to the scheduled castes and are one of the most marginalized Dalit castes, he develops a narrative of their experiences of democracy. Much of the paper by Aseem Prakash argues against the claim that disjunction between political equality and the vast economic inequality between the upper and lower castes can potentially be bridged by free market policies. It attempts to analyse the outcome of the political and economic desire on the part of Dalits to enter the market as owners of capital, and trade in various goods and services. Based on the exploration of some questions with the help of recorded business histories, the paper points out that the Dalits experience an unfavourable inclusion in the markets that is structured through upper-caste inspired and controlled social networks.

The final part of this volume refers to new intersections in discrimination and the newer kinds of discrimination related to disability, sexual minorities and denotified tribes; doctrinal and legal ambiguities due to newer kinds of discrimination and questions raised in recent Supreme Court judgments and challenges of intersectionality. They highlight the manner in which stigma feeds upon, strengthens, and reproduces existing inequalities of caste, religion, tribe, gender, and sexuality and limits access to certain new groups in the public, market, and private domains.

The chapter by Meena Radhakrishna examines how nomadic communities have been a target of the fears and suspicions of sedentary communities. The Yerukulas of Madras Presidency were criminalized in the twentieth century and the British started the process of reforming them. The attitude of the law-makers as well as the police towards these communities has not changed since independence. Indiscriminate detention, arrest without warrant, taking photographs and fingerprints of people belonging to DNTs, and custodial torture of the people continue in different parts of the country. The chapter by Renu Addlakha examines the approach of the Indian government towards the landmark United Nations Convention on the Rights of Persons with Disabilities in 2006. Thereafter, a number of legislative and executive steps have been initiated in a bid to comply with the Convention. The chapter specifically deconstructs the above mentioned draft laws to highlight new concepts and paradigms impacting the process with a particular focus on how gender and disability intersect along with other important variables.

Poonam Kakoti Borah studies discrimination towards sexual minorities in India, from the perspective of existing laws. While sexual minorities have remained at the peripheries of our political imagination for a long time, today identities forged on grounds of sexual orientation have assumed the middle-ground protesting against the legal and social discrimination that they face. This chapter argues that a reassessment of ideas of privacy and tolerance become imperative in order to fight discriminations that emanates from our binary thinking. The last chapter by Aftab Alam analyses the demands of various groups such as Dalit Muslims and explores the issues related to the silence imposed historically, socio-economically, and politically on the Dalit Muslims. It brings to the fore their voices and visions, issues and struggles, shares their achievements, and critically highlights weaknesses and limitations. There is an attempt to address the issues of discrimination and exclusion of Dalit Muslims, their identity and their ambiguous relationship with other Dalits in the assertion of their rights and dignity.

It will be clear to the reader that this collection does not express a unified theory. As is often the case in periods of transformation such as the one we are living through, many assumptions are challenged while others are defended in good faith. These essays cannot fully capture the rich debates on equality and discrimination. In some ways, it is my hope that the intensity of debates presented here will inspire others to do more research in these areas.

Notes

1. For modernity as an aspiration and ideology in colonial India, see Sanjay Joshi (2005).
2. For the assertion that untouchability is an inescapable part of caste, see debates on discrimination, CAD III, pp. 413–14, 29 April 1947.
3. The Amendment Ordinance 2014 was signed by the President on 4 March 2014 and came into force immediately. (Since it is an ordinance, it will need to be ratified by [the next] parliament within six [6] months or it will lapse).
4. The micropolitics of caste can intrude into the electoral arena. See, M. Vijaybaskar and A. Wyatt (2013).
5. Lloyd and Susanne Rudolph question the claim that the presence of caste as a relic of pre-modernity is antithetical to ideas on equality and justice. (See Rudolph and Rudolph 1967).
6. See B. Shiva Rao, Advisory Committee Proceedings (2006a: 221), vol. I, 21–2 April 1947, in which Alladi Krishnaswami Ayyar is led to ask: Is this a chapter on fundamental rights or is it a chapter of discriminatory provisions?
7. See G.B. Pant's speech moving the Objective Resolution, in Rao (2006b, 63). Vol. II. Also K.T. Shah's comment on Article 9 of the draft constitution, see CAD, vol vii, 29 November 1948, 655.
8. Several safeguards amongst others include Article 335 mandating claims of SCs/STs to services and posts in the Union of India and the States. Articles 330–333 provide for reservations for seats for SC and ST (except the STs of autonomous districts of Assam) in the Lok Sabha and in the state legislative assemblies.
9. Both Articles 15 and 16 extend the equality guarantees of Article 14, by providing for rights against discrimination. Article 15 : (1) The state shall not discriminate against any citizen on grounds only of religion, race, caste, sex, place of birth or any of them; (2) No citizen shall on grounds only of religion, race, caste, sex, place of birth or any of them be subject to any disability, liability restriction or condition with regard to:

a) access to shops, public restaurants, hotels and places of public entertainment or

b) the use of wells, tanks, bathing ghats, roads and places of public resort maintained wholly or partly out of state funds or dedicated to the use of general public.

3. Nothing in this article shall prevent the state from making any special provisions for women and children.

10. For Ambedkar's response, see CAD, Vol. VII, pp. 700–1, 30 November 1948.

11. See the debate on Article 18 on the need to abolish titles and on Conferment of Decorations on Persons (Abolition) Bill, 1969 in the Lok Sabha by Acharya J.B. Kripalani. It was alleged that the spirit and purpose of this new injunction was lost when the government sought to bring back the same old inequities by conferring titles and decorations by an executive order.

12. See CWC meeting at Wardha, Haripura, formation of NPC. (Chatterjee 1997).

13. V.P. Singh, prime minister of a coalition of parties, called Janata Dal, announced plans for a greatly expanded OBC reservations under the Mandal Commission (BCC 1990: 22).

14. The Mandal Commission introduced quotas for backward castes for recruitment to the central and state governments, to private undertakings receiving financial assistance from the government, and to all government universities and affiliated colleges. Supplementing reservations already existing for SCs and STs set as 22.5% the commission resigned itself to maximum quotas of 27% in order to remain within the limits of the law laid down in a number of Supreme Court judgements.

15. I borrow this title from David Marquand who has written for a different context (Marquand 2004).

References

Alam, J. 2004. *Who Wants Democracy?* New Delhi: Orient Longman.

Ambedkar, B.R. 1987. 'The Triumph of Brahmanism: Regicide or the Birth of Counter-Revolution', in V. Moon (ed.), *Dr. Babasaheb Ambedkar: Writings and Speeches*, Vol. 3, Bombay, Maharashtra: Education Department.

———. 1989a. 'Annihilation of Caste', in V. Moon (ed.), *Writings and Speeches*, Vol. 1, pp. 23–96. Bombay, Maharashtra: Education Department.

————. 1989b. 'Evidence before the Southborough Committee', in V. Moon (ed.), *Writings and Speeches*, Vol. 1, pp. 243–78. Bombay, Maharashtra: Education Department.

————. 1989c. 'Untouchables or the Children of India's Ghetto', in V. Moon (ed.), *Writings and Speeches*, Vol. 5. Bombay, Maharashtra: Education Department.

————. 1990a. 'Who were the Shudras? How they came to be the Fourth-varna in the Indo-Aryan society?', in V. Moon (ed.), *Writings and Speeches*, Vol. 7, pp. 9–227. Bombay, Maharashtra: Education Department.

————. 1990b. 'The Untouchables. Who were they and why they became untouchables?', in V. Moon (ed.), *Writings and Speeches*, Vol. 7, pp. 237–382. Bombay, Maharashtra: Education Department.

Austin, G. 2000. *The Indian Constitution: Cornerstone of a Nation*. New Delhi: Oxford University Press.

Bagchi, A.K. 2002. *The Developmental State in History and in Twentieth Century*. New Delhi: Regency.

Baxi, U. 2002. 'The (im) Possibility of Constitutional Justice', in Z. Hasan, E. Sridharan, and R. Sudharshan (eds), *India's Living Constitution: Ideas, Practices, Controversies*, pp. 31–63. New Delhi: Permanent Black.

BCC (Mandal Commission). 1990. *Report of the Backward Classes Commission II*. New Delhi: Akalank Publishers.

Constituent Assembly Debates (henceforth CAD) Official Report. Fourth Reprint 2003. New Delhi: Lok Sabha Secretariat.

Chatterjee, P. 1997. *State and Politics in India*. New Delhi: Oxford University Press.

Collins, H. 2003. 'Discrimination, Equality and Social Inclusion', *The Modern Law Review*, 66(1): 16–43.

Corbridge, S. and J. Harriss. 2005. [Second edn]. *Reinventing India: Liberalization, Hindu Nationalism and Popular Democracy*. New Delhi: Oxford University Press.

Centre for Women's Development Studies (CWDS). 2012. *Towards Equality: Report of the Committee on the Status of Women in India*. New Delhi: CWDS.

Dirks, N. Castes of Mind. 2001. *Colonialism and the Making of Modern India*. Princeton and Oxford: Princeton University Press.

Fraser, N. 1989. *Unruly Practices: Power, Discourse and Gender in Contemporary Social Theory*. Minneapolis: Minnesota Press.

Galanter, M. 1984. *Competing Equalities: Law and the Backward Classes in India*. New Delhi: Oxford University Press.

Ghosh, R. and A.K. Pramanik (eds). 1999. *Panchayat System in India: Historical, Constitutional and Financial Analysis*. New Delhi: Kanishka Publishers.

Government of India (GoI). 1955. *Report of the Backward Classes Commission* (3 volumes). New Delhi: GoI.

————. 2002. *The Scheduled Castes and the Scheduled Tribes (Prevention of Atrocities) Act 1989.* (GoI: Ministry of Social Justice and Empowerment, 19th report.

————. 2006. *Sachar Committee Report: Social, Economic and Educational Status of the Muslim Community of India.* Prime Minister's High Level Committee, GoI.

Harriss, J. 2012. 'Reflections on Caste and Class, Hierarchy and Dominance', in 'Caste Matters', *Seminar*, 633 (May): 19–22.

Jaffrelot, C. 2003. *India's Silent Revolution: The Rise of the Lower Castes in North India.* London: Hurst & Co.

Jan Sahas and UNICEF. 2009. *Exclusion and Inclusion of Dalit Community in Education and Health. A Study.* Bhopal: A Jan Sahas Social Development Society and UNICEF.

Joshi, S. 2005. *Fractured Modernity: Making of a Middle Class in Colonial North India.* New Delhi: Oxford University Press.

Kabeer, N. 2008. *Social Exclusion: Two Essays.* New Delhi: Critical Quest.

Kaviraj, S. 2001. 'Democracy and Social Inequality' in F. Frankel, Z. Hasan, R. Bhargava, and B. Arora (eds), *Transforming India: Social and Political Dynamics of Democracy,* pp. 89–119. New Delhi: Oxford University Press.

————. 2012. 'The Empire of Democracy: Reading Indian Politics through Tocqueville' in P. Chatterjee and I. Katznelson (eds), *Anxieties of Democracy: Tocquevillean Reflections on India and USA,* pp. 20–49. New Delhi: Oxford University Press.

Lukes, S. 2005. [2nd edn]. *Power: A Radical View.* Hampshire and New York: Macmillan.

Marquand, D. 2004. *Decline of the Public: The Hollowing Out of Citizenship.* Cambridge: Polity Press.

Ministry of Women & Child Development (MWCD) and Ministry of Human Resource Development (MHRD). 1988. *National Perspective Plan for Women.* New Delhi: MWCD & MHRD.

Nanda, B.R. 2004. *Jawaharlal Nehru: Rebel and Statesman.* New Delhi: Oxford University Press.

Nehru, J. 1961. *The Discovery of India.* London: Asia Publishing.

Omvedt, G. 1993. *Reinventing Revolution: New Social Movements and the Socialist Tradition in India.* New York: M.E. Sharp.

Parkin, F. 1979. *Marxism and Class Theory: A Bourgeois Critique.* New York: Columbia.

Phillips, A. 2004. *Which Equalities Matter?* London: Polity.

Rao, B. Shiva. 2006a. *The Framing of India's Constitution. Select Documents. Vol. I* (revised, updated, and edited by Subhash C. Kashyap). Delhi: Universal Law Publishing Company.

———. 2006b. *The Framing of India's Constitution. Select Documents. Vol. II* (revised, updated, and edited by Subhash C. Kashyap). Delhi: Universal Law Publishing Company.

———. 2006c. *The Framing of India's Constitution. A Study, Vol. V* (revised, updated, and edited by Subhash C. Kashyap). Delhi: Universal Law Publishing Company.

Rudolph, L. and Rudolph, S. 1967. *The Modernity of Tradition.* Chicago: Chicago University Press.

Sarkar, S. 2002. 'Indian Democracy: The Historical Inheritance', in A. Kohli (ed.), *The Success of India's Democracy*, pp. 23–46. Cambridge: Cambridge University Press.

Teltumbde, A. 2011. 'Dalit Capitalism and Pseudo Dalitism', *EPW*, XLVI (10): 10–11.

Tilly, C. 1999. *Durable Inequality.* Berkeley: University of California Press.

Turner, B. 1986. *Equality.* England and New York: Ellis Horwood Limited.

United Nations (UN). 1979. *Convention on the Elimination of all Forms of Discrimination against Women* (CEDAW). Geneva: UN.

Verma, V. 2011. *Non-discrimination and Equality: Contesting Boundaries of Social Justice in India.* London: Routledge.

Vijaybaskar, M. and A. Wyatt (2013). 'Economic Change, Politics and Caste', *Economic and Political Weekly*, 30 November, XLVII (48): 103–11.

Weiner, M. 2002. 'The Struggle for Equality: Caste in Indian Politics', in A. Kohli (ed.), *The Success of India's Democracy*, pp. 193–225. Cambridge: Cambridge University Press.

West, C. 1982. *Prophesy Deliverance. An Afro-American Revolutionary Christianity.* Philadelphia: Westminster.

PART I

THEORETICAL PERSPECTIVES

1

Social Exclusion and Poverty
Linkages, Consequences, and Policies

Sukhadeo Thorat and Nidhi Sadana Sabharwal

Why does the poverty of excluded groups continue to be high? Literature on Indian poverty, extensive as it is, has indeed enriched our understanding on the magnitude and causes of poverty. While it is quite rich in some respects, in some other respects, it offers a limited insight. The causes for slow rate of improvement in the poverty of social groups of scheduled castes and tribes compared with their counterparts from higher castes and the persistent gap between them and the rest is something which has remained relatively less explored. One of the reasons is the aggregate nature of the poverty analysis and hesitation to recognize the heterogeneous character of the poor in terms of their social belonging. It is now clear that the poor are not a homogenous category, particularly with respect to causes of poverty. There are poor within poor, and some persons belonging to certain social groups are poorer than others. These are invariably the groups which faced exclusion from equal opportunity to resources—economic and political—that others enjoy. They happen to be excluded and indigenous groups. It is now recognized that while the persistent poverty of excluded groups has roots in common factors that caused poverty among all the poor (including the poor from the excluded group and the rest); however, the channel through which the poverty of the excluded groups is aggravated is different than their poor counterpart from non-excluded groups. Unlike the poor from the non-excluded groups, the persons from excluded groups suffered from unfair exclusion from access to rights and entitlements, which results in denial of equal rights and opportunities and induced more poverty among them.[1] The exclusion is based on the group identity of persons such as caste, ethnicity, gender, religion, and other identities. Exclusion involved denial of access to income-earning assets and capital (agricultural and non-agricultural enterprises and business), employment, education, health services, and governance. The lack of access to income-earning assets like agricultural land and non-farm production/business results in low income. The lack of access to education and skills reduces the employability of poor persons. Similarly, poor access to health services affects their health, which in turn reduces productivity as well as employment. Poor education, skill, and health result in low earning from casual employment.

People need the opportunity to participate fully in the benefits of the development process if they are to flourish and realize their potential. However, excluded groups in society are excluded from opportunities that are open to others, because they are discriminated against on the basis of their caste, ethnicity, religion, gender, or other identity (DFID 2005: 3). Thus the people who are excluded are not just like the rest of the poor. They are also disadvantaged by who they are or where they live, and as a result are locked out of the benefits of development. Social exclusion deprives people of choices and opportunities to escape from poverty and denies them a voice to claim their rights and induces more poverty: 'Social exclusion makes it harder to access the opportunities. Social exclusion explains why excluded groups of people remain poorer than others, have less food, die younger, are less economically or politically involved, and are less likely to benefit from services.' (DFID 2005: 6)

Therefore, addressing the poverty of discriminated groups in Indian society requires an approach that would be similar to that of rest of the poor in some respects, but in some other respects, would be necessarily different from the one used for the rest of the poor. In the case of the poor from the excluded group, the focus has to be on not only addressing the outcome of past exclusion, which resulted in less access to resources and human capital among them, but also ensure equal and non-discriminatory access to rights and entitlements in the present through legal safeguards and affirmative action policies. The excluded groups cover a large portion of India's population, which include schedule castes, schedule tribes, other backward castes, nomadic and de-notified tribes, some religious minorities, and women.

In this context, this essay discusses the framework to understand and to deal with the poverty of excluded groups. It considers the groups that faced caste discrimination, that include the lower castes—scheduled castes, and the backward castes.[2] The framework could be applied to similar groups facing discrimination in Indian society. The essay discusses four interrelated issues: Firstly, it attempts to bring clarity on the concept of social exclusion in general and the one related to institution of caste in particular. Secondly, it discusses the concept and indicator of market and non-market discrimination. Thirdly, it discusses the consequences of exclusion in economic spheres that include market and non-market institutions, government schemes, and political institutions on poverty. Finally, it discusses the policies to address the problem of exclusion and poverty.

Social Exclusion: Concept and Features

In the current literature in social science, there is a general agreement on the core features of social exclusion, its principle indicators, and its consequences on human poverty. The social exclusion is defined as 'the inability of an individual to participate in the basic political, economic, and social functioning of the society, due to denial of equal access to opportunities imposed by certain groups of society upon others' (Buvinic 2005: 5).

The concept of social exclusion has three distinguishable features. First, is that it involves denial of equal rights to persons from a group due to identity. So the denial of equal rights to a group that others enjoy is the first and important characteristic of exclusion. The second characteristic is that the denial of equal rights applies to the group as a whole. So the group characteristic is important as it implies that all individuals belonging to a particular group are denied equal rights irrespective of their individual attributes. The groups' focus of social exclusion, recognizes that people are excluded because of ascribed rather than achieved features, beyond individual agency or responsibility (Buvnic, 2005: 5). A third characteristic is that exclusion is embedded in social relations and it is through social interrelation that groups are wholly or partially excluded from full participation in the society in which they live (Sen 2000). A fourth and final characteristic is that in so far as social exclusion involves denial of rights and entitlements, it impoverishes the excluded groups and induces high poverty among them. The negative outcome of social exclusion, however, would depend crucially on the degree to which the economic, social, and political processes are exclusionary and discriminatory in their outcomes. Thus, exclusion is reflected in the inability of individuals from the discriminated groups to interact freely and productively with others, and this also inhibits their full participation in the economic, social, and political life of the community. Incomplete citizenship or denial of civil rights (freedom of expression, rule of law, right to justice), political rights (the rights and means to participate in the exercise of political power) and socio-economic rights (right to property, employment, and education) are the key dimensions of an impoverished life of excluded people (World Bank 2006).

Distinction between Individual Exclusion and Group Exclusion

Although we have mentioned the group characteristic of social exclusion, this feature needs further clarifications, as it is the most misunderstood aspect of social exclusion. A clear distinction needs to be drawn between the exclusion of a group from that of exclusion of an individual. The social exclusion essentially refers to the processes through which a group as a whole is completely or partially excluded on the basis of group identities from full participation in the society, economy, and polity in which they subsist. Theoretically speaking, in the case of group exclusion, all persons belonging to a particular social/cultural group are excluded because of their cultural (group) identity, and not due to their individual attributes. On the other hand, exclusion of an individual is fundamentally different from the exclusion of a group. Individuals (both from excluded and non-excluded groups) often get excluded from access to economic and social opportunities for various reasons specific to them (and not because of their group, social/cultural identity). For instance, individuals may be excluded from employment due to lack of the requisite education qualification. Individuals may face exclusion in access to education due to lack of minimum qualification and merit, or their inability to cover the high cost of education. An individual may also be excluded from access to input and consumer markets due to lack of income and purchasing power or may not receive credit due to lack of security. On the other hand, in the case of the group exclusion, social and cultural identities—such as caste, ethnicity, religion, gender, colour, and race—become a reference point for exclusion and discrimination, and exclude all persons bearing those features. Thus while group exclusion is due to the ascribed features of a group, the exclusion of an individual is due to the individual attributes (Thorat and Newman 2009). As we shall see later, this particular feature has a significant implication for policy.

Social Exclusion, Inequality, and Poverty: The Indian Context

In India, social exclusion revolves around societal institutions that exclude, discriminate, isolate, and deprive some groups on the basis of group identities such as caste, ethnicity, religion, gender, race, colour, regional identity, and similar identities in different magnitudes and varied forms.

The groups that suffered from social exclusion and discrimination associated with the institution of caste include former untouchables—(SCs) and OBCs. The former untouchables and OBCs who converted to Islam, Christianity, Sikhism, and Buddhism also suffered from discrimination and exclusion in some forms, if not in the same form from which their counterparts in the Hindu religion suffered. These include SCs and OBCs in the Muslim, Christian, Sikh, and Buddhist fold.

The social exclusion of SCs is closely associated with the institution of caste. The Hindu social order, namely, the caste system is governed by six principles: artificial division of the Hindu population in five groups called caste through the institution of endogamy, assignment of rights in advance by birth to each of these castes, and making it fixed and hereditary without freedom of change, unequal assignment, and entitlement of rights among the caste groups. The rights are also assigned in a graded (or hierarchal) manner, as one moves down in caste hierarchy the rights reduce in number. The system provides a societal mechanism of social ostracism in terms of social and economic penalties to enforce the system, and finally, support from some religious principles to the caste system.

The principle feature of pre-determined and fixed social and economic rights for each caste, with restrictions for change, implies forced exclusion of one caste from the civil, economic, and educational rights that other castes enjoy. Exclusion in civil, educational, and economic spheres is, thus, internal to the caste system and a necessary outcome of its governing principles. The core governing principle of the caste system is, however, not inequality alone, but graded inequality, which implies unequal entitlement of rights to various castes. With the entitlement to rights being hierarchically unequal, every caste (except the higher castes) suffers from a degree of denial and exclusion. But all suffering castes do not suffer equally. Some suffer more and some less. The loss of rights is not uniform across caste groups. As one moves down the caste hierarchy, the rights and privileges are also reduced, but duties and obligation towards higher castes increase. By implication, castes located at the bottom of the caste hierarchy, namely the untouchables, suffer the most. The OBCs follow closely. The OBCs have probably not suffered from the practice of untouchability or from residential and social isolation as much as the SCs, but historically, they too, have faced exclusion in education, employment, and certain other spheres.

The untouchables and OBCs converted to Islam, Christianity, Sikhism, and Buddhism also suffered from some form of discrimination as some elements of the Hindu caste system have been carried forward in case of these low-caste converts. The lower-caste converts do face discrimination, though not in the same forms and manifestations as the Hindu low castes. In fact, the problem of former untouchables converted to Sikhism and Buddhism, and of the OBCs converted to Islam has been recognized and the reservation policy has been extended in a selective manner to them. But the problems of the former untouchables converted to Christianity and Islam have not yet been addressed.

Nature and Forms of Caste Exclusion

The nature of social exclusion involved in the caste system needs to be understood properly. The inter-caste relations involved in the institutions of caste and untouchability are both exclusionary and inclusionary in nature at the same time and cover all spheres of social, cultural, religious, economic, and political participation. The low caste, particularly the untouchables, are excluded from the right to property, education, certain occupations, and civic rights. However, they are obliged to perform some duties for the high castes, and to that extent there is an inclusion of theirs. Their inclusion is mainly in labour on the farm and some non-farm work, community work, and in occupations dubbed as impure and polluting. The obligations and duties, however, are governed by exploitative and unequal relations of social participation. Viewed from this perspective, the concept of caste-based social exclusion can be conceptualized with reasonable clarity by using Amartya Sen's definition. Sen draws a distinction between unfavourable exclusion and unfavourable inclusion. Unfavourable exclusion is a complete exclusion or denial to members of certain (excluded) groups from having access to property and other rights, which are unrelated to normal terms and conditions of exchange and fair access. Unfavourable inclusion involves selective inclusion but with differential treatment. Sen observed:

> Indeed many problems of deprivation arise from unfavourable terms of inclusion and adverse participation, rather than what can be sensibly seen primarily as a case of exclusion as such. For example there are reasons to complain about exploitative conditions of employment, or of deeply unequal terms of participation, the immediate focus is not on exclusion at all but on the unfavourable nature of the inclusion involved—it is, of course, possible to make the rhetoric of social

exclusion cover unfavourable inclusion or even exclusion from acceptable arrangements of inclusion.

Thus, Sen goes on to add that,

> it is however very important to distinguish between the nature of a problem where some people are being kept out (or left out) and the characteristics of different problems where some people are being included—may even be forced to be included-in deeply unfavourable terms. More positively, we have reason to take full note both of deprivations that arise from unfavourable exclusion and those that originate in unfavourable inclusion. (Sen 2000: 28–9).[3]

Using the concept of unfavourable exclusion and unfavourable inclusion to the caste, we could capture the exclusion involved in the caste system in economic, social, and political spheres in the following manner:

a. Complete exclusion or denial (unfavourable exclusion) to lower castes by higher castes, in employment, in private and public.

Complete exclusion or denial (unfair exclusion) to lower castes in sale and purchase of factors of production (like agricultural land, non-land capital assets (required for business), and various services and inputs required in production processes, in sale and purchase of consumer goods, and private housing transacted through market channels.

Complete exclusion or denial (unfavourable exclusion or denial) to lower castes in accessing social needs like education, health services, food, and other services transacted through non-market channels, by the government and government-approved agencies.

Complete exclusion or denial (unfavourable exclusion) to lower castes in accessing the goods and services supplied under government schemes in food/nutrition, health, education, and employment and similar areas by the government and government-approved agencies.

Complete exclusion or denial (unfavourable exclusion) of lower castes from civic rights and public services and amenities such as drinking water bodies, public roads, private transport and buses, religious places, and other common property.

Complete exclusion or denial (unfavourable exclusion) of lower castes from institutions of governance such as village panchayats and other institutions of governance.

b. Selective inclusion (unfavourable inclusion) of lower castes with unfavourable terms and conditions, reflected in differential price charged or received for goods and services (different than market prices). This may include price of input factors and consumer goods, price of factors involved in production such as wages to human labour, price for land or rent on land, interest on capital, and rent on residential houses.

This may also include price or fee charged by public institutions for services such as water, electricity, and other goods and services.

c. Selective inclusion (often forced) bound by caste/ethnic obligations and duties reflected, firstly, in over-work, loss of freedom leading to bondage, and attachment, and secondly, in differential treatment at the place of work.

d. Exclusion in certain categories of jobs and services of the former untouchables who are involved in so-called unclean or polluting occupations (such as scavenging, sanitary jobs, leather processing, etc.). This is in addition to the general exclusion or discrimination that persons from these castes would face on account of being low-caste untouchables.

Selective inclusion (unfavourable inclusion) of lower caste to civic rights and public services and amenities such as drinking water bodies, public road, private transport and buses, religious places, common property with unequal treatment.

Selective inclusion (unfavourable inclusion) of lower castes to institutions of governance such as village panchayats and other institutions of governance.

Identifying Exclusionary Behaviour in Market and Non-market Spheres

After having developed an insight about the exclusion in the institution of caste, we now try to address the question of identification of exclusionary behaviours or experience by the untouchables and other low castes. We use the concept of unfavourable exclusion and unfavourable inclusion to define the indicators of exclusionary behaviour.[4]

Market Discrimination

We first discuss the concept of economic exclusion. Economic exclusion operates mainly through various markets as people as producers/business person's procure inputs (including labour input) and services necessary for production and business from the market, including credit. Economic exclusion also operates through sale of products, goods, and services.

A typology of the market would include (a) labour/employment markets; (b) land markets—for agricultural and non-agricultural use; (c) credit markets; (d) input markets (needed in any production and business activity); (e) markets in services necessary for production and businesses; (f) products and consumer markets in goods and services; (g) housing markets; (h) markets in health services and others.

Two criteria: We may use two main criteria to measure the incidence of discrimination in the market. These criteria relate to (a) access to market for purchase or sale, (b) prices charged for labour, factor inputs, goods and services, and (c) terms and conditions of market and non-market exchanges. These criteria are:

Unfavourable Exclusion—Exclusion may be practised through complete exclusion or denial to members of certain groups from having an access to various market and non-market exchanges such as in hiring labour, in sale and purchase of factors inputs, in supply of credit, in sale and purchase of product and consumer goods, and in supply and demand of social services, which are unrelated to normal terms and conditions of exchange.

Unfavourable Inclusion—Selective inclusion but with differential treatment. Discrimination may be practised though selective access to market and non-market transactions, but with unequal treatment reflected in prices charged for factor inputs, goods, and services to certain groups; and

Labour market: In light of the above criteria, discrimination in the labour market as a concept can be conceived as:

a.   Complete exclusion or denial of certain social groups in hiring/
     employment by higher castes, which is unrelated to productivity;
b.   Selective inclusion or hiring, but with unequal wages, that is,
     lower wages (lower than market wages or the wages given to work-
     ers from non-discriminated groups) unrelated to productivity;
c.   Unfavourable inclusion (often forced) bound by caste and other
     obligations and duties reflected in, firstly, overwork, loss of free-
     dom leading to bondage, and various types of attachments and
     secondly, in differential treatment in the workplace; and
d.   Exclusion in certain categories of jobs and services of those low
     caste persons who are involved in so called unclean or polluting
     occupations (such as sanitary jobs, leather processing jobs, etc).
     This is in addition to the general exclusion or discrimination that
     persons from these groups would face.

Thus, exclusion or discrimination in the labour market may be conceived in terms of: (a) complete exclusion of discriminated groups
from employment, that is, employment discrimination; (b) selective
inclusion in employment, but with an unequal treatment reflected in
lower wages unrelated to productivity, that is, wage discrimination;
(c) selective inclusion with unequal hiring terms and conditions with
respect to hours of work and other terms; (d) differential behaviour
towards low caste employees in the workplace; (e) compulsory or
forced work associated with traditional caste-related obligations
involving loss of freedom; and (f) exclusion of low castes from certain
types of jobs due to notions of pollution and purity.

Land market: In case of the land market, excluded groups may
experience discrimination in the form of denial in (a) sale and purchase of land for agricultural and non-agricultural usage (for pro-
duction/business location and residential housing); and (b) prices
paid and received by discriminated persons in the event of sale and
purchase.

Discrimination may also persist in leasing of land by the discriminated groups for agricultural use and for renting of residential houses.
Discrimination in lease markets may be practised either in the form of
denial to lease agricultural land and residential houses or by charging
higher prices or rents on leased land for agricultural use or on renting

of houses for residential purposes compared to other social groups for identical services.

Credit market: Discrimination in credit markets may take the form of denial of credit to the discriminated persons and in the event of them being given credit, they may be charged higher interest rates. Besides, it may also be practised in other terms and conditions for repayment of loan and mortgage.

Factor input markets: The other form of discrimination may be in input factor markets. These include material inputs and services required in the production processes and businesses. Discrimination may either be in terms of denial of such inputs, or in the event of purchase by discriminated persons, they may be required to pay higher prices than those paid by the others for purchasing identical inputs and services. The other terms and conditions may be biased towards discriminated producers and business persons.

Product and consumer goods markets: The discriminated persons may face discrimination in sale and purchase of products and consumer goods (manufactured or produced by them). Like input markets, discrimination in the consumer goods market may take the form of denial in purchase from and sale to discriminated business persons. Discrimination may also be experienced by discriminated persons as they may be charged higher prices for the goods that they purchase and alternatively, low prices for the goods that they sell. Discrimination in the consumer goods market will put them at a disadvantageous position.

Non-farm businesses: Discrimination in the non-farm business may take the form of discriminatory access to initial permission or licence for setting up business, supply of necessary services requirement in the business such as land, electricity, water, and other services. This may involve complete denial or supply at unequal terms and conditions. The persons from discriminated groups may face discrimination in accessing these services in terms of the requirement to pay higher price/fees. Discrimination may take shape in terms of refusal by high castes to give buildings or space for starting of businesses by entrepreneurs from the discriminated groups. They may also face discrimination in acquiring various inputs and material that they require in their manufacturing processes either in terms of complete denial or supply of this input and material or supplying them at a higher price and on unfavourable terms and conditions.

They may face discrimination in sale of products and goods produced by them or put on sale. The discrimination may take the shape of denial by high-caste persons to buy the goods and services from the discriminated producers and business persons.

Non-market Transactions: Publicly Supplied Goods and Services

Non-market transactions may include several public goods offered by government and public institutions. These may include (a) social needs like education, food-security related schemes like mid-day meals, health services, public roads, electricity and drinking water, fair price shops in consumer goods, and other services; and (b) common property resources in the villages like irrigation, grazing lands, forests, etc.

Non-market transactions include goods and services that are supplied by the government and/or state supported public organizations and agents at fixed prices decided by the government/public bodies, and not by the market mechanism. Individuals from discriminated groups may face discrimination in access to these services.

The social exclusion through the non-market channel will take effect, if there is complete denial of access to the services offered by government and government approved public institutions or if there is access, it is with unequal terms and conditions.

Educational institutes: Discrimination in education may occur inside the school which may operate in various spheres such as discriminatory behaviour of teachers towards the students from certain social groups in various manners, in relation between the students, participation in the cultural and corporate life in the school, seating arrangements inside the classrooms and discriminatory access to the facilities in the school such as mid-day meals, drinking water, supply of books and uniforms, scholarships provided by the government, and occasional health services. This discrimination in multiple spheres and forms not only affects the social psychology of the discriminated students but also leads to poor academic performance, a withdrawal attitude, and ultimately, in the heavy drop-out rate from schools.

Public and private health services: Discrimination in the sphere of public health service providers and the private health providers may operate in the following manner:

(a) Complete denial of certain social groups, for example, the untouchables.

    i. In admission to the primary health centre in the villages and by the private health providers,

    ii. Access to primary health centres and private health centres but with differential treatment

- in standing arrangements—being ignored and kept waiting for long or asked to come at the end,
- in health check-up and treatment,
- in the delivery of the medicine,
- in visits to houses by doctors and medical practitioners,
- in private health doctors and hospitals.

Access to civic amenities: Discrimination in civic amenities may take the form of denial of access to public sources of water such as taps in their localities, drainage in the localities of the discriminated groups, and provision of electricity and other village-level amenities.

Participation in village panchayats: Discrimination in participation in village panchayat of members belonging to excluded groups may be practised in terms of not permitting them to participate effectively in decision-making and also providing unequal treatment in the office of the panchayat.

Common property resources at village level: Common property resources at the village level generally includes water tanks, grazing land and forest resources to which all persons in the villages should have an equal access. In case of discriminated groups, they may face complete denial of access to resources, or if they have access, it may be given at differential terms and conditions.

How does Social Exclusion Cause Poverty? Discussion of the Processes

After having brought some clarity on the concept of social exclusion and indicators, we now discuss the likely consequences of discrimination in market and non-market institutions on poverty and channels through which social exclusions operate and aggravate poverty for excluded groups.

The labour and other market discrimination involves denial of equal economic rights and entitlements to the persons from discriminated groups. The consequences of economic discrimination, not only negate the provisions of equal opportunity and the principle of non-discrimination, but also create fairly serious consequences on access to income earning capital assets like agricultural lands and non-land assets, employment, social needs like education and health, housing and other needs, which induce lower income and high poverty among discriminated groups.

The adverse consequences of discrimination in the labour market are fairly obvious. The denial to employ and/or deny giving jobs in certain categories of works results in higher unemployment and under-employment among the discriminated groups. Lower wages reduce their wage earnings and compulsory involvement in works due to traditional caste and other obligations make them liable to exploitation and often unpaid labour.

The consequences of discrimination in other markets through denial of access to land, credit, factor inputs, products and consumer goods, restrictions on sale of products, consumer goods, and services, and differential treatment in terms of prices paid in purchase of capital goods, inputs, and services are equally adverse. Further, various types of restrictions on the purchase of income earning capital assets and non-land assets reduce the ownership of these assets and increase the incidence of assetless persons among the discriminated groups. Also, restrictions on the purchase of inputs and services affect the scale, viability, and profit of the firms and businesses.

Price discrimination under which the discriminated groups are required to pay higher prices for inputs and services may affect costs, competitiveness, and profitability of firms and businesses owned by discriminated groups.

The most adversely affected businesses owned by discriminated groups are likely to be ones dealing in consumer goods, in which the restrictions on purchases by higher castes/or majority religion from the low castes/minority persons may be more pronounced and persuasive due to the notions of purity and pollution and various stereotypes. Such restrictions affect the magnitude of sale of consumer goods and incomes of businesses owned by the discriminated groups.

Finally, discriminatory access to social needs like education, health services, food security schemes, and housing, will lead to lower education levels, lower access to food and public housing.

Likely Consequences of Social Exclusion in Market and Non-market Institutions on Assets, Income, and Poverty

In order to bring further insight on the consequences of social exclusion on poverty, we will discuss the case of each individual market separately.

I) Markets in sources of livelihood and income-earning capital assets

- agricultural land,
- non-farm business, and
- employment

II) Social needs

- education and skill development,
- public and private health,
- participation in village panchayat

Agricultural land markets: The consequences of discrimination in agricultural land markets may operate through the restrictions faced by the discriminated groups in purchase of land for agricultural use. This may also operate through denial of land to discriminated groups through leases for agriculture purposes. The denial faced by discriminated groups in the purchase of land for agricultural use may result in low ownership of agricultural land and landlessness and higher dependence on wage labour. This also results in increased dependence of discriminated groups on wage labour, low income, and ultimately, in high poverty.

Discrimination in lease markets may be practised either in the form of denial to lease out agricultural land, or leasing low quality land or by charging higher rents on leased land for agriculture use, to the persons from discriminated groups (as compared to other social groups).

The result on poverty due to denial in leasing of land for agricultural use will result in landlessness, higher dependence on wage labour, and low income. When higher rent is charged from the discriminated group, this form of discrimination will increase their per acre cost of production, lower the agricultural profits, result in low income, and lead to high levels of poverty. Leasing lower quality of land will result in low agricultural productivity, low profits, and income.

Non-farm businesses: Discrimination in the non-farm business may take the form of discriminatory access to initial permission or licence for setting up business, supply of necessary services required in the business such as land, electricity, water, and other services. This may involve complete denial or supply at discriminatory terms and conditions. The persons from discriminated groups may face discrimination in accessing these services in terms of requiring to pay higher price/fees. Discrimination may take a shape in terms of refusal by high castes to give building or space for starting of business by entrepreneurs from the discriminated groups. They may also face discrimination in acquiring various inputs and material that they require in their manufacturing process either in terms of complete denial or supply of this input and material or supplying them at a higher price and on unfavourable terms and conditions.

They may face discrimination in the sale of products and goods produced by them or put on sale. The discrimination may take the shape of denial by high caste persons to buy the goods and services from the discriminated producers and business persons. The consequences of the discrimination will affect the business of discriminated groups in the following manner:

(a) Discrimination through complete denial or discriminatory access with differential terms and conditions may discourage the potential business persons from discriminated groups to start the business which will lead to lower ownership of businesses by persons from some discriminated groups.
(b) Differential treatment in terms of receiving services with a higher price and on unfavourable terms and conditions may lead to higher cost of production and of goods and services put on the sale. This will lead to reduction of sales and lower profit margins and ultimately, in the non-viability of the business.

Credit markets: Discrimination in credit markets may take the form of denial of credit to the discriminated persons. And if they are given access to credit by private lenders, it may be on unequal terms in the form of high interest and other unfavourable terms and conditions of repayment. This would result in a lack of availability of credit for production and business activities. This may lead into low ownership of business, higher dependence on wage labour, low income, and high poverty. In the event of their being charged higher interest rates for loans that they might have taken, it would result in a higher cost of loans, making entrepreneurial ventures unprofitable. This would lead to lower income and high poverty.

Factor input markets: The other form of discrimination may be in input factor markets. These include material inputs and services required in the farm production and (non-farm) businesses. Discrimination may either be in terms of denial of such inputs and in the event of purchase by the discriminated groups; they may be required to pay higher prices than those paid by the others for purchasing identical inputs and services. This will lead to higher business cost, lower profits, and, relatively higher cost of production putting them at a disadvantage with respect to other producers. This may induce the exit from the production and business.

Products and consumer goods markets: The discriminated persons may face discrimination in sale of products and consumer goods. Like input markets, discrimination in product and consumer goods market may take the form of denial in purchase from discriminated business persons. Discrimination may also be experienced by persons as they may be required to sell goods and services at lower prices. The low sale, or higher transaction cost for sale may reduce their volume of sale. The higher transaction cost (through sale at places away from the markets where their identity is known) is likely to reduce their profit margin, which results in low income and exit from the business and production activities. This may push them back to wage labour. This contributes toward continuing poverty amongst the excluded groups.

Labour market: The adverse consequences of discrimination in the labour market manifests in poor terms of engagement (hours, pay, and work conditions). The denial of employment in general, and in certain categories of work results in higher unemployment and under-employment amongst the discriminated groups. Lower wages reduce their wage earnings and compulsory involvement in certain categories of work due to traditional caste obligations, makes them liable to exploitation and often unpaid labour. Consequently, excluded groups are over-represented among the poor. Poverty is likely to be caused because of forced labour, which is an extreme manifestation of discrimination in the labour market. Workers from the excluded groups may be vulnerable to this form of discrimination that results in the practice of debt bondage. The system of bondage due to debt may operate when wage-workers from the excluded groups are recruited by labour intermediaries who—through wage advances and other manipulations—induce them into an artificial debt that they cannot repay. Long hours of work may not be sufficient to repay this debt, thus trapping the workers into greater debt and a longer debt repayment period. This system perpetuates the poverty or extreme poverty of the workers belonging to excluded groups.

Non-Market Institutions

Common property resources: The denial of access to common property resources at the village level such as water tanks, grazing land, and forest resources will affect the fodder and drinking water for animals and consequently, less income because of less access to forest resources. In the case of fodder, the reduced access to grazing land may compel the discriminated group to buy fodder from the market that will increase their cost and reduce income. Similarly, reduced access to forest resources will reduce their income and also have consequences for their other needs, such as fuel needs, etc.

Publicly supplied social needs and services: The social exclusion through non-market channels will take effect if there is complete denial of access to services offered by government and government supported public institutions or access with differential terms and conditions.

Non-market transactions include goods and services supplied by the government and/or state supported public organizations and agents at fixed prices. These publicly supplied services include education, health facilities, drinking water, and other civic amenities like public roads, electricity, public housing, and village level common property resources like canals, tank water, grazing lands, and forests.

School education institutions: Discrimination in school in a village setting may take the form of denial of access to education and skill development and/or discriminatory treatment in school. This may reduce the quality of human resources and reduce the employability for quality jobs and force them to fall back on low earning manual wage labour in farming and non-farming activities. Specifically, denial of access to education leads to high illiteracy, low functional literacy, and high dropout rates, limited skill development, and low human capital. Impact of limited skill development and low human capital due to discrimination in education may cause high representation in menial jobs, low wages, low income and ultimately high poverty.

Public and Private health services: Discrimination in the sphere of public health service providers and private health providers may operate through denial of admission in the primary health centre in villages and /or through discriminatory access to primary health centres and private health providers which may take the following forms:

- separate standing lines,
- being ignored and kept waiting for long,
- discrimination in health check-up and treatment, including the avoidance of physical touch,
- discrimination in the delivery of medicine,
- avoidance of visits to houses by public and private doctors and medical practitioners.

Lower access to public health services and private health services affects the health status, increases the number of days fallen ill, lowers the days of employment, and ultimately, affects the income levels negatively. Denial of access to public health services or improper services leads to the dependence on private health services providers with expensive medical treatment. This results in borrowing money for treatment, high debt, and ultimately affects the income levels.

Political participation: Discrimination in participation in the village panchayat is likely to result in lack of effective power in decision making in the village panchayat in deciding the use of public funds on poverty, reducing programmes, civic amenities like drinking water, electricity, drainage, and public housing.

Provision of safe drinking water, civic amenities, and common property resources: Denial of access to safe drinking water and other civic amenities is likely to result in poor health, increase the number of days fallen ill, lower the days of employment, and ultimately, impact the income levels negatively.

Policies: Insight from Theories

Selective exclusion in market and non-market institutions, exclusion in accessing civil rights and in participation in political institutions is something that is faced by the low caste untouchables. Continuing denial of equal rights in many spheres if not all, brings a different dimension to the problem of excluded groups of untouchables. Given a negative outcome of exclusion, reducing exclusion is necessary, as it is likely to enhance access to economic, civil and political resources, and help reduce poverty and inter-group inequalities.

How to overcome discrimination has been the central concern in economic theories. Three main theoretical approaches have emerged in economic literature. The first is the Gary Baker theory of taste-based discrimination. In this theory, white employers can dislike hiring black workers, and white workers can have a similar dislike of working with blacks. In both cases the results are that black workers will receive less pay, and will work in different jobs, than white workers (Akerlof and Rachel E. Kranton 2010). The second one is the statistical discrimination theory proposed by Kenneth Arrow. According to this theory, white employers discriminate against black employees, not because of their own desire or taste for discrimination, but because they think that blacks, on average, have low skills. The view about the skill and productivity are determined not by taste, but based on the general view about the black worker. Employers often cannot assess the skill of individual workers and therefore they make their hiring decision based on the average skills in a population, which invariably are discriminatory in judgement.[5] The third theoretical approach is the identity theory by Akerlof and Kranton.[6] Akerlof and Kranton argue that while discrimination still persists, the taste and statistical theories cannot help us understand many patterns. In their opinion the limitation of the taste theory is that while it recognized the non-economic motive, basic tastes are assumed to be universal and any variation is attributed to idiosyncratic differences and personal experiences. By and large, tastes are not assumed to vary with social context. Akerlof and Kranton developed an identity theory, and brought the influence of social context and norms into economic decisions by the individuals. The social categories and norms constitute the identity. People's identity defines who they are—their social category and different norms for behaviour are associated with different social categories. Individual pecuniary and non-pecuniary motivation and tastes and preferences are influenced by social context and norms. In so far as identity theory brings the social context (that is who they are) and norms (and how should they behave or relate with others) in economic decision-making by individuals, this changed the economists' old presumption that tastes and preferences are individual characteristics independent of social context. The identity is brought into economic analysis—identity and norms into action. The identity theory maintained that there are social categories, there are norms for how someone in that social category should or should not behave, and that norms affect behaviour.

Thus the theory has three main elements: First, it associates individuals with a particular social category or identity. Second, it specifies the prevailing norms and ideals for these categories. And finally, it posits individual gains and losses from different decisions, given identities, and corresponding norms. It maintains that identity utility which is the gain when action conforms to norms and ideals, and loss in so far as they do not. These gains and losses, combined with the standard concerns of economic analysis, will then determine what people do. According to the authors, this 'socially framed conception of individual decision-making should help economists working at various levels to construct sturdier accounts of the economy' (Akerlof and Kranton 2010: 13–20).

In its application to race and poverty, identity theory explains racial discrimination in terms of what authors call oppositional identity. The behaviour of whites towards blacks is determined by different codes or norms. These norms or code perpetuate a distinction between us and them. Thus, white Americans think of black Americans as them rather than included in all of us (Akerlof and Kranton 2010: 100). This division of us and them based on the norms is what authors call oppositional identity—with the expression of opposition and differences. The oppositional identity results in discrimination, which explains the poverty of blacks through a theory of identity, discrimination, and black poverty.

These theoretical strands have their policy implications. The taste theory predicts that in highly competitive markets, discrimination will prove to be a transitory phenomenon as there are costs associated with discrimination to the firms/employers which result in a lowering of profits. Firms/employers who indulge in discrimination face the ultimate sanction imposed by the markets. This proposition of market–power hypothesis sees the resulting erosion of profits as a self-correcting solution for eliminating discrimination. The taste theory recommends promotion of market competitiveness and the statistical discrimination theory perfects information to reduce market discrimination. However, it is argued that there are several reasons why economic discrimination might persist over longer periods. Firstly, even if the markets are sufficiently competitive, market discrimination will continue to persist if all firms discriminate because they would face identical cost, revenue, and profit frontiers. The persistence of decades of labour-market discrimination in high-income countries attests to the resilience of market discrimination to market forces. Secondly, in reality, not all markets are competitive. Indeed, in most of the economies, the markets are imperfect and governed by oligopolistic and monopolistic market situations, which often empower the firms to discriminate at will. Similarly, the imperfect information theory which argues for perfect information as a solution to elimination of discrimination has its limitations, as discrimination is found to persist in situations of perfect information. The identity theory's position deviates from the taste and statistical theories of discrimination.

The identity theory recognized that discrimination and occupational segregation persists despite competitive market forces. In the context of gender discrimination, identity theory maintains that the real problem is the norms that stipulate that men and women should do particular jobs, irrespective of their individual tastes and abilities. Therefore, what is required is the social movement and government intervention rather than a competitive market place to erode the discrimination against women (Akerlof and Kranton 2010: 94). The government intervention necessarily is in the form of laws to prohibit discrimination and provide safeguards against it, programmes for the change of norms, and other positive government interventions.

Therefore, correcting discrimination would require the following steps:

First is the civil society movement/efforts to change the norms and ideologies which shape the behaviour of the people for discrimination through social activism and reform of the education system that would instil the principles of non-discrimination, equality, democracy, and justice in thought and action—this would essentially mean education for good citizenship.

Second is the law banning discrimination, and legal safeguards against the practice of discrimination.

Third is the positive action for facilitating a fair access and share in resources and opportunities to discriminated groups in various market and non-market institutions, including political institutions. The positive steps would include instruments like affirmative action policies and groups, focus empowerment measures. It calls for positive action in land, labour, and capital markets, in product markets, and social needs such as education, housing, and health. Beside it is equally necessary to have participation in the institutions of governance, like legislature and policy-making, implementing, and monitoring bodies. Central to this view is the exposition that discriminated groups face discrimination in transactions through market and non-market channels and in institutions of governance; in that regard positive affirmative steps are necessary.

Empowerment and equal-opportunity policies: In a discussion on the reservation policy in India, it is often argued that since poverty is the main problem of discriminated groups, the general policy of economic and educational empowerment which is used for all poor should be adequate enough for discriminated groups as well and avoid the use of special policy for the poor from discriminated groups. This argument suffers from limitations as it is based on an inadequate understanding of the problem of discriminated groups such as untouchables and OBCs. While the policy of general economic and educational empowerment is necessary for all the poor (including the poor from excluded groups), the poor from discriminated groups need additional support to compensate for denial of rights in the past, the consequences of which are reflected in inter-caste disparities. But more importantly, the additional and supplementary policies are essential for excluded groups to provide safeguards against discrimination in the present and ensure equal access to markets and non-market institutions and institutions of political governance.[7]

The general pro-poor policies are, of course, needed both for poor from the excluded groups and the non-excluded groups. The policy of economic empowerment is expected to enhance the access to income-earning assets and the human capabilities of individuals from excluded and non-excluded groups. For instance, improved access to income-earning assets will improve the capacities to partake in production and business activities. Education and skill development are expected to increase employability and enable access to jobs. While the capacity enhancement will result in to gains to the persons from non-excluded groups, this may not necessarily convert into gains easily for individuals from excluded groups. The capacity enhancement may not yield a positive outcome for discriminated individuals due to discrimination in various markets and non-market institutions. They may fail to realize positive outcomes of their assets and human resources. For instance, even if the employability of the excluded individuals may improve on account of education and skill but they may face difficulties in accessing jobs due to discrimination in employment (which persons from non-excluded groups will not). Similarly, even if the excluded persons gain in ownership of agricultural land or private enterprise, these may not get converted into positive gains due to discrimination that they may face in the input and product market. Similarly, discriminated individuals may face discrimination in accessing education, public health service, and government schemes in food, nutrition, health, employment, housing, and also in participation in panchayat and other political institutions (Thorat and Newman 2009).

The discriminated groups, therefore, require supplementary or additional policy (in addition to general policy for all) in the form of legal safeguards against possible discrimination in market and non-market transactions and positive actions (in the form of reservation or similar measures) to ensure a fair share in market and non-market institutions and institutions of political governance. In the absence of legal and positive measures, the excluded groups may not benefit despite empowerment. It is precisely for this reason that the policies of general economic empowerment (pro-poor policies) are supplemented by equal-opportunity policies such as reservation policies—and similar policies in many countries—not only to improve their access to income-earning assets and education and skill, but also to ensure a fair share in enterprises, business, employment, education, housing, etc., through affirmative action policies. The complementary nature of these two policies will ultimately help the historically discriminated groups not only in their capability enhancement, but also to receive a fair share in the economic and social progress of the country.

Notes

1. See World Bank 2013. This report provides the cross comparison on the Human Development of Excluded and Indigenous Communities.
2. Caste groups are selected for analysis because of a clear structural nature of discrimination and availability of primary and secondary data.
3. Sen also discussed two other types of exclusion namely Active and Passive Exclusion, and Constitutional and Instrumental, which can be applied to the exclusion of other excluded groups and communities.
4. For a detailed discussion, see Thorat and Sabharwal 2010.
5. For various theories of economic discrimination, see Darity 1995.
6. This is a recent contribution and an important one which is built up on the earlier theories but makes a fresh addition to Akerlof and Kranton (2010). On the role of identity, see Darity, Mason, and Stewart (2006: 283–305).
7. For a detailed discussion on the issue, see Thorat and Newman 2009 and Thorat and Kumar 2008.

References

Akerlof, G.A. and R.E. Kranton. 2010. *Identity Economics: How Our Identities Shape Our Work, Wages and Wellbeing*. New Jersey: Princeton University Press.

Buvinic, M. 2005. 'Social Exclusion in Latin America', in M. Buvinic, J. Mazza, and R. Deutsch (eds), *Social Exclusion and Economic Development*, Maryland: Johns Hopkins University Press and Inter-American Development Bank.

Darity, W. Jr. 1995. *Economics and Discrimination*, Vol. 1, Aldershot, UK: An Elger Reference Collection.

Darity, W.A. Jr., P.L. Mason, and J.B. Stewart. 2006. 'The Economics of Identity: The Origin and Persistence of Racial Identity Norms', *Journal of Economic Behaviour and Organization*, 60 (July): 283–305.

Department for International Development (DFID). 2005. DFID Policy Paper: 'Reducing Poverty by Tackling Social Exclusion'. United Kingdom: DFID.

Sen, A. 2000. 'Social Exclusion: Concept, Application, and Scrutiny', Social Development Papers No. 1, Office of the Environment and Social Development. Manila: Asian Development Bank.

Thorat, S. and N. Kumar. 2008. *In Search Of Inclusive Policy: Addressing Graded Inequalities*. Jaipur: Rawat.

Thorat, S. and K. Newman. 2009. *Blocked by Caste: Economic Discrimination in Modern India*. New Delhi: Oxford University Press.

Thorat. S. and N. Sabharwal. 2010. *Caste and Social Exclusion: Issues Related to Concept Indicators and Measurements*. New Delhi: UNICEF.

World Bank. 2006. *World Development Report – Equity and Development*. Washington DC: World Bank.

———. 2013. *Inclusion Matters: The Foundation For Shared Prosperity*. Washington DC: World Bank.

2

The Promise and Challenge of Non-discrimination
Developing an Ethics of Political Action

Vidhu Verma

There is wide agreement about the normative concept of equality in the fight against hierarchies, privileges, and injustices in the contemporary world, but when we explore the meaning it is very complex. This is partly because by now a large literature on equality advocates a range of philosophical issues that help us to focus on the scope of our principles and also reflect on several other values such as a commitment to non-discrimination, liberty, democracy, and citizenship rights. Formal equality models have developed with the assumption that inequality can be overcome by treating people in an identical manner and by providing them equality of access to resources and other primary goods. Public justifiability of major institutions rests upon including this principle of equal treatment as it attacks the world of cruelty, stigma, and humiliation and limits state action to promotion of citizenship rights at the same time.

The ideal of non-discrimination, including formal equality before the law, is a fundamental value of democratic societies. Despite the centrality of this ideal many impediments remain to its realization. One limitation has been the differing political and legal interpretations of the concepts of non-discrimination and equality of opportunity. The liberal approach is that discrimination stems from the personal prejudices of individuals and results in some kind of harm to others. This view originating with J.S. Mill was that use of the law in a free society is limited to prevention of harm. It also placed limits on the state's interventions into social spheres. Marxists claim that capitalism uses divisions among the working classes to maintain power over them. Many conceptualized discrimination as an institutional problem generated by a complex web of systemic practices that can be overcome by rectifying the unequal distribution of wealth and power. B.R. Ambedkar firmly believed that caste-based inequality would not be rectified without transforming the socio-political reality and the empirical practices embedded in our social structures. Further, it was in the power of the state and its legislative instruments to initiate and control social change. Those who endorsed more substantive models of equality focused on equality of result requiring unequal treatment, if possible, to have an equal impact; this was taken forward by arguing for special protections or positive discrimination for disadvantaged groups. There is also a difference in context: certain countries in the West began dismantling formal legal impediments to slavery, exclusion of married women and suffrage much earlier followed by anti-discrimination legislation in the 1970s and positive duties to promote equality laws in the early twenty-first century. In Britain, the Equality Act of 2010 extends protection to the following characteristics: age, disability, gender reassignment, race, religion, or belief, sex, sexual orientation, marriage or civil partnership, pregnancy and maternity.[1] The trajectory of these laws has been applauded, some also calling the recent changes as the 'fifth generation of equality and anti-discrimination laws'.

In India, although there are legislations that cover several kinds of discrimination, there is no anti-discrimination law that would address various dimensions of social inequalities emerging today. One of the reasons is that an individual justice model rests on an anti-discrimination principle, which besides questioning classifications, also implicates notions of individual right, merit, and achievement in the context of markets.[2] Secondly, protective measures for marginalized groups existed for a long time in the presidency and princely areas of South India. Since the constituent assembly debates, the effects of history and institutional nature of discrimination were addressed by legislation specifically related to reservations in public employment and education for disadvantaged groups.[3] As the market becomes a key player in the Indian economy, civil rights and questions of discrimination emerge in an energized way in the new context. A key part of the court's constitutional architecture is the emergence of disadvantaged categories from grounds prohibited in Article 15, and further developed with the idea of legitimate and illegitimate classifications (*State of West Bengal* v. *Anwar Ali 1952*). Despite the exhaustive list of provisions in the constitution, in the absence of an anti-discrimination code, there is no statutory definition of discrimination that takes into account different manifestations of discrimination and its impact. The Indian constitution covers grounds of religion, race, caste, sex, place of birth, or any of them but it clearly ignores disability, sexual orientation, and age or discrimination of denotified, nomadic, and semi-nomadic tribes. There are numerous regulations for combating discrimination against scheduled castes (SCs) and scheduled tribes (STs) and for promoting constitutional guarantees for religious minorities but there are no statutory protections against religious discrimination.[4]

Nevertheless in the seminal case of the Naz Foundation, the Delhi High Court declared that the Indian penal code violated constitutional equality as it criminalized consensual acts of adults (European Commission 2012). More recently, statutes dealing with discrimination faced by people with disability have been applied in court cases like the Disabilities Act of 1995. A sexual harassment bill now protects women employees. But instead of a law on indirect discrimination as developed in the US, Canada, or South Africa, the interpretation of the general equality guarantee in Articles 14–17, focuses on reservation policies and rationality of classification. Protection against intersectionality is vague as an individual has to see that his or her claim fits into the discrete grounds mentioned in the constitution. The Menon Committee Report in 2008 proposed a new framework of the Equal Opportunity Commission with extensive authority to investigate and gather data but the government has not taken any concrete steps so far (Ministry of Minority Affairs 2008). To secure the constitutional promise of equality and achieve full equality of opportunity for vulnerable groups, a discrimination legal framework is needed in India in the near future. Given the ambiguity surrounding these concepts and limited success of legislation related to the promise of non-discrimination, this chapter examines some of the legal and social pressures hindering the comprehensive operation of such ideals.

Preliminaries

I present a few preliminaries regarding the distinct themes that emerged during this research. To begin with, the objective of this chapter is not merely to engage in debates over the correct theory or of the reach and scope of non-discrimination. It is part of a wider research that I am doing about a transition from the negative philosophical element, at the core of discrimination, as negating the idea of human species characterized by 'durable inequalities' to a critical reflection that engages with social structures that enable production of subjectivities (Tilly 1999). The story of discrimination is an account of human dispositions and social practices that lead to injury, difference, otherness, egoism, suffering, and exclusion from juridical orders. A study of these psychological forces that erupt into politics is educative as it directs attention towards motivations for subsequent hostility to institutional forms that have often been a vehicle for sustaining structures of domination. Second, this research alerts us to the way discrimination as a distinct issue is ignored in theories that emphasize justice in distribution of goods as exclusion from resources and public institutions. Many times these distributions will be determined in battles for public goods such as education, health, recognition, and representation. Those who are subordinated and victims of discrimination have their own perspective of these battles; they are subject to systematic disadvantages which need to be addressed by the state. But these calls for inclusion in institutions may also end up defeating demands for recognition thereby creating new group identities. Thus, understanding struggles against discrimination is one way of providing access to transformative views on politics. The emphasis on non-discrimination also highlights that justice is not only about maldistribution of goods; certain discriminations, prohibitions, deprivations are part of interlocked acts like ill-treatment by police, bonded labour, vulnerability to violence, and unemployment. Hence justice is not only restricted to spheres of exchange but also deeply embedded in intimacy, emotions, power, and domination in everyday relations. The resistance to such discriminatory practices might not always result in better distribution of goods but might lessen the humiliations and injuries inflicted on subordinate groups. Thirdly, the essay grapples with the problem of 'passive injustice' raised by Judith Shklar, as 'refusal of both officials and private citizens to prevent acts of wrongdoing when they could and should do so'. She defines it as more than habitual indifference to misery of others as it is specifically 'civic failure to stop private and public acts of injustice' (Shklar 1990: 35). The question is whether a justice deficit can be addressed by overcoming indifference to the lives and dignity of others? Does combating discrimination unsettle and challenge traditional theories and institutions? Can these values for combating discrimination be justified by robust moral commitments drawn from liberal political theory or do they collapse due to transactions based on market justice?

In what follows, I will try to address some of these questions by examining the traditional formulations of non-discrimination in liberal political theory that have come under critical scrutiny from several quarters, including difference theorists. Certain key features of the state—including representative government, a mixed economy, a developed system of social welfare, a meritocratic educational system—that define the institutional framework of liberal democracies are critiqued in these interventions. For many difference theorists, making sense of these efforts to overcome injustices specific to group disadvantage, has become increasingly necessary as these have over the past decades transformed the grammar of justice. In liberal democracies the focus on cultural recognition, self-respect, and difference has expanded the meaning of social justice well beyond distribution of goods that is tied to class-based politics. At the same time there is clearly a common ground to injustices faced by groups: the exclusionary force of nation-state citizenship that must be overcome by enacting policies that are best addressed by deepening democracy. A second development following from the above is that class stratification is no longer seen as the only source of inequality; disparities are seen to arise due to other non-class factors like caste, gender, region, and community. Visible inter-group economic disparities that demonstrate pressing varieties of injustices in society are increasingly seen to be of the elderly, religious minorities, women, disabled, and sexual minorities.

While there are serious problems is their conceptualizations, the attack on liberal egalitarians is not helpful as difference theorists do not view policies of affirmative action as part of implanting distributive justice between groups as we do in India today. Against this backdrop, this chapter offers an approach in which discrimination embodies a specific kind of social injustice faced by members by virtue of belonging to disadvantaged groups. It is useful to use the term oppression as a normative concept to name injustice perpetuated through social institutions, practices, and norms. Oppression differs from many other kinds of injustices like exploitation but subsumes within it actions related to discrimination. Towards developing these arguments, in the first section, I examine the promise in the idea of non-discrimination and equality of opportunity in the writings of liberal and difference theorists. The second section explains how the equal treatment principle defines the problem narrowly as direct discrimination. But in so far as anti-discrimination law deviates from that standard, it is clear that the social problem is regarded as one involving structural or systematic disadvantage for groups. Two policies commonly used are anti-discrimination laws and affirmative action to counter these inequalities. How substantial are these policies in changing the characterization of equality debates? To what extent can reservation policies challenge the dominance of existing capital formation and market system to call into question the unequal distribution of income and wealth? The way in which we eventually define the role of grounds of discrimination and how we determine why discrimination is considered bad on normative grounds is also examined in the third section. Although inequalities can emerge due to different reasons (choice, desert, social positions) it is arguments within justice discourse that question why certain kinds of inequalities (based on discrimination) should not exist. The final section examines the grounds for wrongful discrimination and values it violates in a larger moral theory in order to develop an ethics of political action.

The Promise of Equality and Non-discrimination: Legal and Constitutional Issues

Laws relating to non-discrimination provide clear examples of how classification of persons based on race, caste, and religion are clearly prohibited. The promise of the principle of non-discrimination is that it prevents the state, employers, housing authorities, health providers, and other civil society organizations from denying opportunities because of any attributes that groups share. The core moral idea behind this is that each has a chance to carry out his or her good without being inhibited in this pursuit by prejudice or bias.

But are non-discrimination laws only about equality of opportunity? Most political theorists are so vague about what equality of opportunity actually amounts to that when seen synonymously with non-discrimination it can begin to look like an empty term. Alan H. Goldman views it as a 'chance to attain some goal or obtain some benefit' (Goldman 1979: 88). John Rawls attempts to address this problem of ambiguity and of the harms to individuals condoned by utilitarianism when he proposes equality as applied to the respect which is owed to persons irrespective of their social position.[5] It is defined by the liberty principle in which each person is to enjoy equal civil and political rights—the right to vote, to run for office, due process, free speech, mobility, etc., (Rawls 1973: 61; 511). In principle this means that equality of opportunity is about access to important social institutions that should be open to all on universalistic grounds, especially by achievement and talent (Turner 1986: 35). It is similar to a 'conception of careers open to talents' that requires the elimination of arbitrary discrimination on grounds of race, gender, etc., by either state or private agents (Rawls 1973: 72). Consequently, inequalities of income and prestige are justified as there is fair competition in the awarding of the offices and positions; people's fates are determined by the choices they make rather than their social circumstances; and an individual's performance and the choices he or she makes are not due to any morally arbitrary factor such as the race, class, or sex they belong to.

In Rawls' reading, an equality of opportunity is 'unstable' and the injustice of this system lies in the way distribution of shares is strongly influenced by social and natural contingencies such as accident or good fortune. Hence there is a need to correct these 'arbitrary' factors by asserting a 'fair equality of opportunity' where all should have a 'fair chance' to compete for social advantages; 'in all sectors of society there should be roughly equal prospects of culture and achievement' and 'those with the same abilities and aspiration should not be affected by their social class' (Rawls 1973: 72–3). Rawls proposes a second conception of equality in the distribution of goods as defined by the structure of organizations and distributive shares. However, while distribution of income and wealth need not be equal it must proceed on the principle that social and economic inequalities are to be so arranged that they yield the greatest benefit to the least advantaged and at the same time 'positions of authority and offices of command must be accessible to all, that is, as the ideal of equality of opportunity' (Rawls 1973: 61). In short, Rawls conceded that fair equality of opportunity has to mitigate the influence of social contingencies and natural fortune by imposing the basic structure as condition on the social system. When the administration of the institutions of the basic structure is distorted by prejudice or bias, Rawls regards this as a violation of formal justice. Building on this we can argue that institutional discrimination or bias exists when administration or enforcement of the rules and procedures of a major social institution, labour market, or criminal justice system is regularly distorted by the prejudice or bias of those who exercise authority within the institution (Rawls 1973).

It is clear that equality should demand more than what opportunity can give but it is not easy to agree on a particular set of demands. Over the years, scholars have found problems with Rawls' conceptualizations. Amartya Sen argues that a basic weakness of primary goods discussed by Rawls is that they cannot adequately deal with the pervasive inter-individual differences among people. An opportunity can be of no use for various reasons or there may be no gain in using it. Equality concerned with comparison of different persons' opportunities and deprivation of opportunities moves us in the direction of the idea of poverty as capability deprivation (Sen 2004). R.J. Arneson attempts to amend Rawls' principle by emphasizing the need to accept two conditions: persons with the same talent and same ambition should have the same prospects of competitive success; and education and socialization processes should be unmarred by bigotry and unfairness (Arneson 1999: 77–112). Baker argues against the key assumption found in liberal egalitarians that there 'will always be major inequalities between people in their status, resources, work and power' and thus the main challenge is reduced to a 'fair basis for managing these inequalities, by strengthening the minimum to which everyone is entitled' (Baker et al. 2004: 24).

So, though Rawls presents a critique, it nonetheless remains a weak version of equality of opportunity since his theory upholds equal consideration of essential interests that are protected by rights, notably the right to property, talents and skills, and above all, the right to a restricted self-ownership. His analysis ignores the impact of the market on natural disabilities that might require some additional resources or compensation for them. Fair equality of opportunity assumes that people are mostly functional over a normal life span. The impact of disease or disability on welfare or equality has been mostly overlooked, along with issues of dependency in what would count as a robust philosophical perspective on social justice (Nussbaum 2006).

One of the earliest debates in the American context, to address some of these worries of the principle of non-discrimination that controls the equal protection clause for individuals, was raised by Owen Fiss (1976: 107–77). This principle was too thin and superficial as it was an interpretation of equality as a formal and procedural value. By requiring equal treatment of individuals without addressing differences in their levels of social disadvantage, it is unable to condemn past discrimination. The remedies that liberal egalitarians have historically looked to are articulated within the framework of individual rights that are poorly suited to address the discriminations of groups. Thus the value of equality that the American constitution expresses should be understood as 'equality of status' and the unfairness to be addressed consists of the practices that affect the status of groups.

Like other difference critics, Anne Phillips and Nancy Fraser, Iris Marion Young contests the three principles on which equality is narrowly framed within liberal egalitarianism: equal treatment, non-discrimination, and atomistic notion of the good (Young 1989). Besides focusing on issues of 'status' as a discrete entity from economic and political positions, a central theme is the relationship between equality and difference. Iris Young critiques notions of social equality that are equated with the elimination or transcendence of group differences in what is broadly known as an 'assimilationist ideal' (Young 1989: 195). She claims that where 'differences in capacities, culture, values and behavioural styles exist among groups, but some of these groups are privileged, strict adherence to a principle of equal treatment tends to perpetuate oppression or disadvantage' (Young 1989: 251). She sharpens some of the points made by Fiss in her works when she identifies status inequality as a 'structural situation where a group of individuals stands in a relatively disadvantaged position on parameters of occupational respect and reward, residence and autonomy'.[6] On any reasonable conception of justice, even fair equality of opportunity cannot trump people in positions where they repeatedly suffer disadvantages in access to benefits, or where they are stigmatized in direct interactions.

Enormous differences seem to separate liberal egalitarians from difference theorists in their justifications yet they converge in affirming the fundamental equality of human rights and civil rights, and a more positive role for the state. John Rawls even accepts civil disobedience to rectifying what we may call structural injustices or injustice in the institutional rules of society's basic structure in a near-just state. But rectifying historical illegitimacy of the resource-deficient position of marginalized groups is different from contesting wrongful conduct in the history of state's subjection of social groups due to their stigmatized social identities. Thus the differences revolve around the way the former ignore the causes of structural inequality or the institutional context that determine the pattern of these distributions. In all this the legitimacy of altering state institutions to achieve greater equality of material conditions is highly contested through ideas on luck, desert, and entitlement. In a spirited critique, Anderson clarifies that the proper aim of 'egalitarian justice is not to eliminate the impact of brute luck from human affairs, but to end oppression' (Anderson 1999: 288). The attempt of a revitalized philosophical liberalism to grapple with claims for socio-economic distribution and recognition in relation to group claims has given rise to a shift from viewing equality as equal treatment of individuals to concerns about social groups 'incorporating analyses of the systems and structures that constitute and perpetuate the inequalities under consideration in the first place' (Squires

2008: 47). Despite these worries about arguments challenging premises of liberal theory, to ensure 'fair' equality of opportunity, two contrasting policies have been pursued: Anti-discrimination laws and affirmative action for disadvantaged groups.[7]

Anti-Discrimination Laws: Definition and Scope

In an elementary sense, discrimination means to differentiate, but in this chapter, I refer primarily to social discrimination which makes differences between persons on a categorical basis. It refers to conduct that makes some kind of distinction between persons that rests on social devaluation, or is viewed as a 'source or sign of incompetence or inferiority' (Shelby 2007). Examples would be when an employer rejects candidates from a group like SCs, a landlord refuses to rent rooms to a single woman, or when a police officer beats up a person who is from a sexual minority group. These should be distinguished from classifications made by governments for a variety of reasons based on physical characteristics like age for appointment and retirement in certain kinds of jobs.

Anti-discrimination laws are founded on the principle that likes should be treated alike. They question any measure which on its face makes distinctions or discriminates directly by treating another person less favourably on the grounds of say caste, race, or gender (Morris 1995: 199). Laws against discrimination seek to 'suppress categories of social judgment' or 'neutralize widespread forms of prejudice that pervasively disadvantage persons based on inaccurate judgments about their worth or capacities' (Post 2001: 7).

The distinction between direct and indirect discrimination is tenuous but for the purpose of my argument discriminatory behaviour manifests in several ways; at direct, indirect, institutional, or structural levels. Direct discrimination is about treating individuals on the basis of their salient group identities that are described as an inferior social category. These can occur and can be face-to-face type of interactions through five gradations of negative human conduct: verbal antagonism, avoidance, segregation, physical attack, and extermination. Some scholars extend this to include lists of behavioural expressions of inequality as discriminatory acts, including avoidance that reflects discomfort, rejection, or even hostility to disadvantaged groups.[8]

Discriminatory speech might not be directed to a victim but might be about the conditions of the group as well. Slurs, for example, typically characterized as a form of hate speech, are used to humiliate group members with reference to a descriptive feature. The fact is that any public discussion involves communication and if groups are labelled, this makes up the discriminatory character of the discourse.

However, in most societies, institutions including laws, customs, religion, and education, work to reinforce existing prejudices and discrimination. For example, caste divisions have influenced the behaviour of members through control over rewards and penalties. To the extent that discrimination is intrinsic to the caste system, it conferred on Dalits a specific and subordinate status; that of being marked as members of a group judged inferior, not worthy of sharing meals with others, and not virtuous enough to be entrusted with public or private authority. While most of the legal supports of inequality of castes have been removed, inequality of social status remain. More recently the labour market, and lending practices in loans and mortgages are seen to be highly prejudiced towards certain minorities (Thorat and Attewell 2007). But this distinction might not be always very clear in the Indian context. For example, institutional discrimination based on caste discrimination in selection of personnel for example, is enforced by individual members of the institution who have a stake in sustaining these practices. Moreover, direct discrimination often goes to strengthen group cohesion as well as boundaries that are entrenched within institutions. A study done in UK reports caste-based bullying and abuse, caste discrimination in access to education, and discrimination in work in respect of recruitment, promotion, task allocation, and dismissal. Significantly the evidence relies on the testimony of lower castes or those associated with low castes like the Ravidassias, Valmikis, Ambedkarite Buddhists, and religious minorities like Christians (Metcalf and Rolfe 2010).

The problem with prejudice which underlies the legislation on direct discrimination is that it reduces such acts to individual aberration and suppresses recognition of institutional and structural dimensions of discrimination. To begin with, it ignores the metaphysical presuppositions of purity and pollution inherent in the caste system that legitimize cognitive beliefs and associations. It also seems to suggest that since discrimination is due to a mistaken belief that people are different, differences do not exist, making it difficult to address differences which result from social and economic causes (Bacchi 1996: 18–19). There is often a shift in focus from the perpetrators to the objects of prejudice producing a preoccupation with just what it is about these people which causes others to perceive them as different. The model, therefore, casts the victims of discrimination as the problem. They are labelled disadvantaged which becomes almost an explanation of their social location. As Didi Herman explains, anti-discrimination law constructs a 'classification of identities' or categories of person who are in some way lesser than the unstated norm. It is not surprising that the 'anti-discrimination laws contribute to a low sense of self-worth in victims of discrimination' (Didi 1994: 45).

Thus the analysis reveals that non-discrimination is a restricted concept for understanding group related injustices. Young shares her scepticism to contest the claim that discrimination is the primary injustice that disadvantaged social groups suffer; from her perspective it tends to focus attention on the perpetrator and a particular action, policy, or atrocity rather than on victims and their situation. Identifying group-based injustice with discrimination tends to put the onus on the victims to prove a harm is done case by case (Young 1989: 196). If one focuses on discrimination as the primary wrong groups suffer then the more profound wrongs of exploitation, marginalization, powerlessness, and violence that we still suffer go unaddressed.

Due to the inadequacies of the direct discrimination model many of its related issues make their way into the discursive and political domain. Indirect discrimination occurs 'when someone applies unjustifiable standards which people of one sex or race find it harder to comply with than people of another, to the detriment of someone' (Gardner 1996: 355). One discriminates indirectly by marking some origin in a person, causing the same effect as direct discrimination: by applying on an individual some assumptions about members of a disadvantaged social group (Morris 1995).

Laws against indirect discrimination are an achievement of the American Supreme Court, which as early as in 1971 decided that discrimination also comprised seemingly neutral practices, which did not differentiate on grounds of race, sex, religion, or national origin as such. Yet it had a significantly adverse or disparate impact on a protected group and could not be justified by business necessity or job-related practice. The concept was adopted in UK anti-discrimination legislation and case-law in the mid-1970s. It was understood to occur when an apparently non-discriminatory requirement or condition which applied equally to everyone could only be met by a considerably smaller proportion of people from a protected group and which could not be justified on grounds unrelated to the protected ground.

The recognition of what has been called structural discrimination opens the door to examining a wide range of employment-related practices. It raises questions about the impact of deeply entrenched institutional practices on oppressed groups. On this view, acts of discrimination are seen to emanate from collective agents through public laws and organizational relations in government agencies, religious bodies, universities, or corporations. Hence, discrimination is possible through ideological strategies of control and domination of marginal groups. However, organizations and their rules are a function of agents of institutions and they act as those official powers enable them to do so. By defending everything structural or organizational, it is increasingly difficult to find someone to be held responsible for the discrimination; it also leads to assertions that since the practices at issue are part of an organization's systems of operation, good personnel practices are all that are required to update administrative procedures (Bacchi 1996: 20). Thus, both overt rules of institutions and their everyday practices must be subject to critical scrutiny.

Affirmative Action, Group Claims, and Politics of Transformation

In contrast to anti-discrimination laws, affirmative action refers to a range of positive programmes directed toward certain disadvantaged groups to redress their inequality. While affirmative action encompasses measures that allocate goods—admissions in universities, public employment, or business loans—to increase the proportion of members of under-represented groups, anti-discrimination laws only require that action should not be motivated by prejudice or bias (Brest and Oshige 1995: 862). Anti-discrimination legislation in the USA, Canada, India, and Australia, for example, are either specific acts condemning different grounds of discrimination most often caste, racial or sexual discrimination, or are about restrictions in entry points in the labour market.

In the past 20 years, the debate about affirmative action policies has occupied a great deal of the attention of policy-makers, legal experts, and political theorists. The goal of affirmative action policies is to 'erase' deeply entrenched group-based disparities, contribute to diversity in institutions or in terms of corrective and distributive justice (Galanter 1984: 563). Despite this broad understanding, affirmative action policies vary substantially across countries, regarding which individuals are within the beneficiary groups, the form of the programmes involved, level of the norms from which they derive, and their domain of implementation. Thomas Weisskopf makes a distinction between 'preferential boosts' and 'quotas'. The former add explicit or implicit points for being a member of a target group whereas quotas are fixed allotments designated for members of the target group. In the USA, it is about preferential boosts but in India, Malaysia, and even Brazil it takes the form of quotas or reservations (Weisskopf 2004: 16).

I endorse Richard Wasserstrom's view that affirmative action is an issue of distributive justice. There is at present he argues 'a maldistribution of power and authority along racial and sexual lines that is part of the social structure'. He claims that the redistribution of positions creates a new social reality 'one which more clearly resembles the one captured by the conception of the good society' (Wasserstrom 1980: 56). They undo the effects of institutions and practices that make preferential treatment for certain groups as central to their existence. By their operation they directly alter the composition of institutions by increasing the number of people from discriminated social groups in positions of power and authority.

For Nancy Fraser, group injustices are related to socio-economic maldistribution of resources and recognition when groups are either misrepresented or ignored by the majority culture. In her attempt to resolve the dilemma on 'discrimination', Fraser suggests a distinction between affirmative and transformative remedies for injustice arguing for the superiority of the latter. By affirmative remedies she means remedies aimed at 'correcting inequitable outcomes of social arrangements without disturbing the underlying framework that generates them'. By transformative remedies in contrast she means 'remedies that aim at correcting inequitable outcomes precisely by restructuring the underlying generative framework' (Fraser 1997: 23). It follows that even if strong affirmative action programmes existed in most institutions; however, they would have only a minor effect in altering the basic structure of group oppression. Iris Young is very critical of the terms of the affirmative action debate that 'accept the basic structure of the division of labour and the basic process of allocating positions'. Thus because this debate is restricted to the distribution and redistribution of positions, broader structural questions about justice in the definition of positions and how admission to them is determined rarely get raised in public (Phillips 2004: 1–19). Such an interpretation of affirmative action resolves the problem of dominance of a set of cultural attributes; in its attempts to understanding biases and their standards it ignores the specific differences of oppressed groups.

The Indian Case

The current recognition of group claims in Western political theory represents a temporary departure from the ideal to mitigate social inequalities among individuals. At issue is the coherence and incorporation of groups as appropriate subjects of liberal justice that raise further questions about their rights, harms, and benefits. The institutional preoccupation with individual distributive equality in liberal theory can be deeply uneasy with plural and sometimes conflicting concerns that bear on our understanding of group justice.

While groups are forged around various differences, the urge to make group-interest claims as central to public policies like affirmative action is not as acceptable as in India, a point I will elaborate later in this chapter. So far I argued that while more concerned with fate of social groups, difference theorists and their critiques of affirmative action grossly underestimate the significance of policies of quotas or reservations. Reservations are an attempt to promote equality of opportunity in the context in which many institutional practices work to impede the development of equal consideration and equal treatment. These practices include a variety of discriminations such as informal networks of recruiting, hiring, hostile working environment. In order to overcome them, policies attempt to level the playing field. They undo the effects of institutions and practices that make preferential treatment for certain groups as central to their existence.

The Indian debates on discrimination have evolved over the years and share many historical connections with other countries given the sustained exposure to colonial rule and western values. The dominant constitutional tradition in the USA neither defines any backward groups nor explicitly provides for quotas for such groups as the emphasis is clearly on individual rights in contrast to India's constitution that identifies groups eligible for quotas. The essential motive of most anti-discrimination laws, including the fourteenth amendment, is to break barriers to equality of opportunity and equality of treatment. Although heavily modelled on an individual rights framework, most Western democracies responded to group claims only after their citizens had acquired substantive political and social rights.

Like the USA, the debate on discrimination policies in India developed against the background of minority rights. India's 'pursuit of equality through group preference' is an instance of using law to reshape recalcitrant social patterns (Galanter 1984: xvii). The purpose of compensatory discrimination in favour of historically deprived groups is to recompense both for historic deprivations and to offset present handicaps.

During debates in the constituent assembly, most participants argued that discrimination draws from stereotypes and prejudices in society; it was not simply a matter of individual behaviour that should be condemned but should be seen as an issue of collective and of state responsibility. The idea of debt owed to scheduled castes that had suffered due to discrimination was widespread, and therefore made grounds for the reservation policy extending its scope to future generations.

Secondly, positive discrimination in favour of under-represented groups in the USA arose in the 1960s in response to the civil rights movement focusing primarily on the 'egregious pattern of social injustice done to African Americans' (Weisskopf 2004: 19). It developed through executive orders and congressional state legislative endorsements to promote equality in work places, hiring practices, and university admissions. The history of reservation polices for groups goes back much further in India than in the USA since they begin in the late nineteenth and early twentieth centuries. Groups or communities defined in ethnic or religious terms were salient under British rule, subsequently, community identity has been more important in India. Consequently, quota-based schemes over the years reserve seats or opportunities for such candidates in contrast to 'preferential boosts' in the American experience. Unlike the USA, there is no national enforcement mechanism for reservation policies in India even though Ministry of Social Justice and Empowerment (SJE) plays an important role in allocating funds. Recently, affirmative action has been questioned in the USA as many immigrant groups (Latinos or Hispanics from Puerto Rico, Cuba, Central and South America; Asian Americans from Japan, China, India) become beneficiaries, the most famous case being that of Alan Bakke who sued the University of California for denying him admission. In 2003, the Supreme Court reversed some of these rulings against affirmative action in the sphere of education in the Michigan cases (Weisskopf 2004: 16). Summarizing, the affirmative action provisions in India use the rationale of systemic group disadvantage principle and have grounds on which discrimination is prohibited in the legal domain. These provisions are modified to accommodate the historical basis of discrimination against Dalits as it has left behind a trail of barriers and prejudices that makes it difficult for them to effectively participate in the democratic process.

Wrongful Discrimination: Legal and Ethical Issues

A major critique of non-discrimination laws has also been that it diverts attention from relations of domination and exploitation. The relation of formal equality between individuals conceals the reality of class exploitation. Another dimension of Marxist theory is the debate on morality and justice that has raised the issue of whether we can ever see morality as independent of the interests of the ruling class or class relations of our society. Norman Geras, however, claims that concepts in Marxist theory are critical because they not only permit a comprehension of capitalist exploitation but also 'envisage a state of affairs in which there is no exploitation' (Geras 1986: 86). In Herbert Marcuse's words they contain 'an accusation and an imperative' (Marcuse 2009: 63). The principle reflection on problems of resource distribution has been central to classical Marxism but its stand on moral theory has been contestable (Wood 1972: 244–82). Alienation in Marxist theory is closest to capturing the estrangement and powerlessness in individuals because of their membership of the proletariat class. With the rise of identity politics and displacement of class, many moral concepts like injustice, domination, violence, humiliation, and misrecognition have been investigated highlighting the experiences that go with subject location. How does the concept of discrimination furnish the theoretical tools to grasp the manner of the interface between various structural processes in our society? How does combating discrimination give rise to support for the ideals of equality, justice, and fraternity?

Borrowing from the philosopher, John Rawls, one might argue that in liberal theory there is an 'overlapping consensus' on eliminating the concept of discrimination which assures the development of principles of justice which otherwise might be based on inconsistent beliefs (Rawls 2005). However, I argued above there have been disagreements in the theory of disparate impact that breaks down this consensus over what constitutes prohibited discrimination. Legal theorists in the USA have appealed for the 'disparate impact' doctrine or for a results-test rather than an intent-test of discrimination famously articulated by the Supreme Court in the Griggs case.[9] Arguments for this inspired by utilitarianism usually rely on statistical analysis to prove that a policy may seem neutral but actually has disproportionate effects on a social group that is protected. In short, a policy should be found discriminatory if it results in the disproportionate exclusion of certain groups.

The relationship between discrimination against a protected group and evidence that members of certain groups are disproportionately excluded from a benefit or burden has been the subject of many debates. Would a distinction between candidates on a standardized test that excludes more members of an untouchable social group than others on religion be indicative of discrimination based on caste? Would a company policy that asks for minimum number of days in office place be a burden upon pregnant women? Philosophical reasons exist for arguing against disparate impact drawn from the right-wing idea that violation of one's act must be specific and intentional; background economic and social structures are not evidently or directly based on denial of access to anybody. Hence if certain groups fail in a standardized test or pregnant women fail to work for the required days in office it is no discrimination if they fall behind.

Article 15 of the Indian constitution, discussed in the earlier section, prohibits on grounds of certain enumerated categories such as religion, race, caste, sex, place of birth, or any of them. By choosing the word 'ground' the constitution makes the motive of policies or rules irrelevant. Instead the grounds on which classifications are made are enough to declare a policy discriminatory. The reason for focusing on grounds was that debates in the constituent assembly argued against prejudices, untouchability, and historical discrimination that had targeted groups on the basis of these classifications. In this way the Indian constitution limits the cases of disparate impact by enforcing grounds as the basis for discrimination. I argued that affirmative action is to a large extent in India to remedy the effects of disparate impact on groups. Hence although equality of opportunity is similar to non-discrimination, the latter goes beyond the requirement of equal treatment of individuals in the Indian context. Laws relating to non-discrimination clearly prohibit classifications of persons based on race, caste, and religion, 'neutralize widespread forms of prejudice that disadvantage persons based on inaccurate judgments about their worth or capacities' (Post 2001: 39). But these laws leave open the question as to how these practices relate to a given society's basic arrangements, to caste hierarchies, formative beliefs, and its cognitive presuppositions.

The second aspect of discriminatory practices that I now turn to is the grounds on which they violate certain core values which we cherish. In liberal theory there have been debates about whether a consequentialist account of what makes discrimination impossible can be based on a harm-based account. What makes discrimination wrong is that it causes some harm to the group. With a few exceptions, proponents, however, have devoted insufficient attention to the question of what harm is, or what dimensions of individual liberty it can protect. The harm-based account supports the claim that it is logically possible for discrimination not to be bad when nobody is harmed by it. Raz points out that 'one harms another when one's action makes the other person worse off than he was, or is entitled to be' (Raz 1986: 414). This leaves open the question as to how these practices relate to a given society's basic arrangements, to its structure of institutions and formative beliefs. What emerges is that anti-discrimination statutes drawing from liberal theory of harm principle are weak. I now turn to examine more specifically how in liberal theory an autonomy-based understanding of discrimination is advanced as a more persuasive moral foundation for combating anti-discrimination positions.

John Gardner claims that what sets apart legitimate from illegitimate discrimination on various grounds is that the latter unfairly impairs a person's autonomy (Gardner 1989). He also argues that both direct and indirect discrimination restricted valuable choices and may therefore be prohibited by the liberal state. Along such lines, Joseph Raz has defended an 'autonomy-based doctrine of freedom' according to which positive freedoms or broadly, the capacity for autonomy should be promoted. The argument on autonomy challenges the claim that the harm principle, which is about diminishing an individual's range of possibilities, could be grounds for wrongful discrimination.[10]

A person must have options for developing abilities and for which he points out three requirements: non-domination, adequate capacities, and range of choices. An additional requirement is that autonomy must mean many morally, even incompatible, forms of life be available to the person. Drawing from this notion, Raz argues that toleration is adequate to overcome limitations of others in pursuit of different virtues, and it implies, the suppression or containment of an inclination or the desire to persecute, harass, harm or react in an unwelcome way to a person. However, it now seems that by asserting that the state should provide options and conditions for citizens where they cannot provide for themselves, what is doing the work is a theory of distributive justice rather than the harm principle to which I turn to later in the section.

Due to the problems in liberal political theory, a set of scholars have argued that what makes discrimination impermissible is because certain actions and practices disrespect properties in individuals in virtue of which they are stigmatized as having a lower moral status.[11] Certainly there is much that makes dignity appealing as Sandra Fredman argues that it also creates a substantive underpinning to the equality principle as it considerably 'enhances rather than diminishes the status of individuals' (Fredman 2012: 20–1). Dignity has been introduced into the statutory definition of sexual harassment by the EU (European Union Charter of Fundamental Rights) law and applies across a wide range of characteristics including age, disability, gender reassignment, race, religion or belief, sex and sexual orientation.

There are many difficulties in defining dignity as they are different conceptions of what the intrinsic worth of the individual human being consists in; and it fails to distinguish slavery and forced labour from non-cognitive forms of discrimination like stereotypes and prejudice. Even if it is included in a constitution, the state's views of dignity could be at odds with an individual's ideas on what is good for them. These disagreements lead Hepple to point out that we cannot rely exclusively on dignity as an aspect of equality as it is not sufficiently sensitive to conflicts with individual liberty and autonomy (Hepple 2008). For McCrudden dignity seems to be open to judicial interpretation 'increasing rather than decreasing judicial discretion' (McCrudden 2008: 655).

A number of scholars like Axel Honneth take on the central theme of dignity by relying on the idea of misrecognition understood as the negative valuation of a cultural group. Misrecognition is a form of disrespect internalized by individuals impairing their self-esteem and inhibiting their capacities for self-development and autonomous agency. He views the idea of recognition as a constituent element of justice rather than an egalitarian distribution of resources defined in Nancy Fraser's work. Increasingly identities are shaped by perceptions and judgements of others and acts of misrecognition and non-recognition can constitute forms of injustice. In this way, the negative experiences of injuries, sufferings, and injustices lead to elaborate positive ideals. He places recognition as love at the centre of his psychology of the subject.[12]

Habermas proposes toleration based on mutual recognition and mutual acceptance of divergent world views as a political virtue. But he is of the view that the norm of equal inclusion must be universally recognized within a political community before we can expect tolerance from one another. A shared standard of non-discrimination first provides the main reason for toleration. As a general rule the question of toleration arises only after discrimination is eliminated (Habermas 2003: 2–12).

All these theorists summon the need for additional commitments apart from an attack on discrimination; an account of dignity, respect, toleration, and the human need for recognition. Clearly, normative theorists working to define the grounds for wrongful discrimination are not in agreement. For Judith Shklar any overlapping consensus on concepts like discrimination should not be expected as it ignores the actualities of modern societies. She considers aversion to cruelty as the most peculiar trait of liberalism. Clearly, cruelty is an unacceptable insult to human dignity that violates freedom but the challenge is to affirm a diversity of freedoms to pursue conceptions of the good of our own choosing and design. Nevertheless, the viability of Shklar's conception is dependent upon the ability to defend liberalism as a project to bring forth kindness. The relationship between cruelty and liberal politics is a perilous terrain as similar kinds of worst acts—genocide, terrorism, humiliation, exploitation, and brutalization—are part of liberal societies. Indeed it could be argued that the penal system, punishment and security agencies along with the right to property for the few remain quintessentially cruel. Shklar's other argument is that injustice is similar to human ills like misfortune, tragedy, and disappointment following from her main claim that there is no ground for distinguishing injustice from misfortune or bad luck. By seeing roots of injustice largely in individual acts, not in patterns of social positions produced by social processes she raises the question of removing injustices by those who do not even recognize them.

***

I began the chapter by discussing the limitations of the formal equality doctrine that have led scholars, theorists, and policy-makers to search grounds for substantive equality. From the discussion we can argue that as long as we confine ourselves to the liberal theories of justice, we will be unable to arrive at a moral ground to identify wrongful discrimination as they are multiple dimensions and overlapping claims. Reflecting on similar concerns, Amartya Sen views the main tasks of a theory of justice to 'reduce injustice' rather than aiming only at the characterization of institutions in perfectly just societies. While criticizing the foundational role of institutions in promoting social justice he argues that the 'presence of remediable injustice may well be connected with behavioural transgressions rather than with institutional shortcomings' (Sen 2009: ix). The two problems of institutional design and personal conduct require two different kind of principles labelled 'dualism' (Murphy 1999: 254).

Rawls' principles of justice do not apply to everyday choices but only to the design of institutions that depend on the coercive powers of the state to enforce those principles. G.A. Cohen argues that the basic structure on its own is not capable of making corrections for all possible patterns in individual choice. If justice is to be secured 'people have to make decisions contrary to their own interests, they have to choose actions that will promote justice' (Cohen 2008: 16). Thus for fulfilling the promise of non-discrimination, and for substantive equality to be really implemented, an 'egalitarian ethos in society' must prevail. Those who accept the social and political ideal of equality will have compelling reasons to question institutions that are indifferent to social and economic inequalities and promote discrimination.

The debates in India are instructive in this regard as the historically close connection between languages of law, politics, and morality have searched for grounds for identifying wrongful discrimination. The discursive domain points to a strong relationship between stigma, denied opportunity and their historical significance as instruments of disenfranchisement and disadvantage. This has a lot to do with the classification of some groups as unworthy in our society. Summarizing the debate, I argue for the need to demonstrate the inadequacy of thinking about justice as distribution or justice as recognition; from exclusively as a matter of goods in circulation or about denial of cultural goods, and more in terms of how interlocking systems of oppression can through spheres of intimacy, power, and domination heap humiliations upon groups. Reflecting on these concerns B.R. Ambedkar spoke about the need for developing fraternity in an ideal society where there 'should be many interests consciously communicated and shared' and 'should be varied and free points of contact with other modes of association' which he called social endosmosis. Democracy which was another name for fraternity, was not merely a form of government, but 'a mode of associated living, of conjoint communicated experience' (Ambedkar 1989: 57). Cass Sunstein explains the moral aspects of indirect discrimination which he terms the 'anti-caste principle': 'The motivating idea is that without good reason, social and legal structures should not turn differences that are both highly visible and irrelevant from the moral point of view into systematic social disadvantages' (Sunstein 1994: 2410–45). Hence social processes through structures that turn differences into disadvantages are morally wrong as are face-to-face interactions that use grounds to promote classification as a basis for derogatory treatment.

Notes

1. Beginning in 1965 many restrictions on discrimination in employment, education, and services can be noted in Britain in the form of the Equal Pay Act of 1970, the Sex Discrimination Act 1975 and Race Relations Act 1976.
2. I have developed this account of a group justice model in Verma (2011).
3. Article 14 draws on the fourteenth amendment of the American constitution (Rao 2006: 184–5).
4. For relations between discrimination and denial of liberty, see Kannabiran (2012: 16).
5. Liberal egalitarianism as found in the writings of John Rawls and Ronald Dworkin provides philosophical justification for recommending an interventionist role for the government to promote political liberties and greater social and economic equality. For this essay I use the term 'difference theorists' for a wide spectrum of scholars—Iris Young, Nancy Fraser, and Anne Phillips.
6. I.M. Young provides an excellent synopsis of the dilemmas in *Issues in Legal Scholarship*, 2002, 2(1).
7. The argument excludes a substantial chunk of discrimination law scholarship, particularly those like Crenshaw who reject traditional liberal constraints on the law as preventing real change in matters of race and gender (Crenshaw 1988).
8. (Graumann and Kallmeyer 2002). A variety of names are used to identify the low castes in India which are very problematic. For example, the term 'untouchable' itself is derogatory and reinforces prejudice.
9. *Griggs* v. *Duke Power Co.*, 401 U.S. 424 (1971), was a court case argued before the Supreme Court of the United States on 14 December 1970. It concerned employment discrimination and the adverse impact theory and was decided on 8 March 1971. Available at http://finduslaw.com/griggs-v-duke-power-co-1971-401-us-424-91-sct-849.
10. (Raz 1986: 156). Raz distinguishes personal autonomy, which is based on unconstrained choices from moral autonomy that closely related to the ideal that people should make their own lives. Autonomy is a distinct moral ideal; it is not a precondition for self-realization which

consists in the development to the full extent of all valuable capacities a person possesses.

11. The primacy of individual dignity as the foundation for equality of human beings is mentioned in the constitution of South Africa. It locates the state as 'founded on values of human dignity, the achievement of equality and the advancement of human rights and freedom' (cited in Fredman 2012: 20).

12. Nancy Fraser takes justice as distribution of material goods as a distinct paradigm of justice, and views the role of misrecognition as enforcing status hierarchies that preserve the power of dominant groups and impede the equal participation of subordinate groups in democratic society.

References

Ambedkar, B.R. 1989. 'Annihilation of Caste', in V. Moon (ed.), *Writings and Speeches*, Vol. 1, Bombay: Education Department.

Anderson, E. 1999. 'What is the Point of Equality?', *Ethics*, 109(2) January.

Arneson, R. J. 1999. 'Against Rawlsian Equality of Opportunity', *Philosophical Studies*, 93(1): 470–87.

Bacchi, C. L. 1996. *The Politics of Affirmative Action. Women, Equality and Category Politics*. London: Sage.

Baker, J., K. Lynch, S. Cantillon, and J. Walsh. (eds). 2004. *Equality: From Theory to Action*. New York: Palgrave.

Brest, P. and M. Oshige. 1995. 'Affirmative Action for Whom?', *Stanford Law Review*, 47(5): 862.

Cohen, G.A. 2008. *Rescuing Justice and Equality*. Cambridge: Harvard University Press.

Crenshaw, K. 1988. 'Race, Reform and Retrenchment: Transformation and Legitimation in Anti-discrimination Law', *Harvard Law Review*, 101(7).

Didi, H. 1994. *Rights of Passage: Struggles for Lesbian and Gay Legal Equality*. Toronto: University of Toronto Press.

European Commission. 2012. *Report on Comparative Study of Anti-discrimination and Equality Laws of the US, Canada, South Africa and India*. Luxembourg: European Commission.

Fiss, O. 1976. 'Groups and the Equal Protection Clause', *Philosophy and Public Affairs*, 5(2) 107–77.

Fraser, N. 1997. *Justice Interruptus: Critical Reflections on the 'Post socialist' Condition*. London and New York: Routledge.

Fredman, S. 2012. *Discrimination Law*. Clarendon: Oxford.

Galanter, M. 1984. *Competing Equalities: Law and the Backward Classes in India*. Berkeley: University of California Press.

Gardner, J. 1989. 'Liberals and Unlawful Discrimination', *OJLS*, 9(1): 1–22.

———. 1996. 'Discrimination as Injustice', *OJLS*, 16(3): 355.

Geras, N. 1986. *Literature of Revolution*. London: Verso.

Goldman, A.H. 1979. *Justice and Reverse Discrimination*. New Jersey: Princeton University Press.

Graumann, C.F. and W. Kallmeyer. 2002. *Perspectives and Perspectivation in Discourse*. Philadelphia and Netherlands: John Benjamin Publishers.

Habermas, J. 2003. 'Intolerance and Discrimination', *I.CON*, 1 (1): 2–12.

Hepple, B. 2008. 'The Aims of Equality Law', *Current Legal Problems (CLP)*, 61,(1): 1–22.

Kannabiran, K. 2012. *Tools of Justice*. New Delhi: Routledge.

Marcuse, H. 2009. *Negations: Essays in Critical Theory*. London: Mayfly Books.

McCrudden, C. 2008. 'Human Dignity and Judicial Interpretation of Human Rights', *European Journal of International Law*, 19 (4): 655.

Metcalf, H. and H. Rolfe, 2010. *Caste Discrimination and Harassment in Great Britain*. London: National Institute of Economic and Social Research.

Ministry of Minority Affairs. 2008. *Report on Equality Opportunity Commission: What, Why and How?* New Delhi: Government of India.

Morris, A.J. 1995. 'On the Normative Foundations of Indirect Discrimination Law: Understanding the competing models of discrimination law as Aristotelian forms of justice', *OJLS*, 15(2): 199–228.

Murphy, L.B. 1999. 'Institutions and the Demands of Justice', *PPA*, 27(4): 254.

Nussbaum, M.C. 2006. *Frontiers of Justice: Disability, Nationality, Species*. Oxford: Oxford University Press.

Phillips, A. 2004 'Defending Equality of Outcome', *Journal of Political Philosophy*, 12(1): 1–19.

Post, R. 2001. *Prejudicial Appearances. The Logic of American Antidiscrimination Law*. Durham: Duke University Press.

Rao, S. 2006. [Second edn Subhash C. Kashyap]. *The Framing of India's Constitution: A Study*, Vol. 5, pp. 184–5. Delhi: Universal Law Publishing Co.

Rawls, J. 1973. *A Theory of Justice*. Oxford: Oxford University Press.

———. 2005. *Political Liberalism*. USA: Columbia University Press

Raz, J. 1986. *The Morality of Freedom*. Oxford: Clarendon.

————. 1988. 'Autonomy, Toleration and the Harm Principle', in S. Mendus (ed.), *Justifying Toleration*, pp. 155–75. Cambridge: Cambridge University Press.

Sen, A. 2004. *Social Exclusion. Concept, Application, Scrutiny*. New Delhi: Critical Quest.

————. 2009. *The Idea of Justice*. London: Allen Lane.

Shelby, T. 2007. 'Justice Deviance and the Dark Ghetto', *PPA*, 35(2): 126–60.

Shklar, J. 1990. *Faces of Injustice*. CT: Yale University Press.

Squires, J. 2008. 'Equality and Difference', in Dryzek, J., S.B. Honig, and A. Phillips, (eds) *Oxford Handbook of Political Theory*. p. 47. Oxford: Oxford University Press.

State of West Bengal v. *Anwar Ali. All India Report (AIR)* 1952 *Supreme Court Report (SCR)* 284.

Sunstein, C. 1994. 'The Anticaste Principle', *Michigan Law Review*, 92: 2429.

Thorat, S. and P. Attewell, 2007. 'The Legacy of Social Exclusion: A Correspondence Study of Job Discrimination in India', *Economic and Political Weekly*, 42(41): 4141–5.

Tilly, C. 1999. *Durable Inequality*. Berkeley: University of California Press.

Turner, B. 1986. *Equality*. New York: Ellis Horwood Limited.

Verma, V. 2011. *Equality and Non-discrimination: Contesting Boundaries of Social Justice*. London: Routledge.

Wasserstrom, R. 1980. *Philosophy and Social Issues: Five Studies*. Notre Dame: University of Notre Dame Press.

Weisskopf, T. 2004. *Affirmative Action in the United States and India. A Comparative Perspective*. London: Routledge.

Wood, A. 1972. 'The Marxian Critique of Justice', *PPA*, 3(3): 244–82

Young, I.M. 1989. *Justice and the Politics of Difference*. New Jersey: Princeton University Press.

————. 2002. 'Status Inequality and Social Groups', *Issues in Legal Scholarship*, 2(1). ISSN (Online) 1539–8323, DOI: 10.2202/1539-8323.1019, August 2002.

3

Political Economy and Discrimination against Dalits

Anand Teltumbde

Discrimination may be defined as a practice that excludes, disadvantages, or merely differentiates between individuals or groups of individuals on the basis of some ascribed or perceived trait. Most philosophical, political, and legal discussions of discrimination proceed on the premise that discrimination is morally wrong and, in a wide range of cases, ought to be legally prohibited (Altman 2011). Following them, most countries have constitutional or statutory provisions outlawing discrimination (Osin and Porat 2005). Despite all this, discrimination is widely practised all over the world. Discriminatory traditions, policies, ideas, practices, and laws exist in every part of the world, even where discrimination is generally looked down upon. In countries, where discrimination is legally banned on some grounds, discrimination still takes place on other grounds not covered by the law. Against the general trend, in some countries, discrimination is legal or even official government policy as in the case of the countries having a state religion where people of other religions are discriminated against. After the transfer of power in 1947, the constitution of India prohibited discrimination on grounds of religion, race, caste, sex, gender, or place of birth. India also has been a signatory to the six core international human rights treaties.[1] Despite it, discrimination on all these bases continues till this day to the extent that India may be the best exemplar of what discrimination is. Discrimination not only affects people's opportunities, their social resources, self-worth and motivation, and their engagement with wider society, it entails great loss to the society itself.

Why do people discriminate against others? The clichéd answer to this question is that people are prejudiced. Prejudice is the inflexible and irrational attitudes and opinions held by members of one group about another. Sociologists and psychologists tried to fathom the source of these prejudices and found them in psychological processes of people (Whitley and Kite 2010: 243). According to them, prejudice stems from subconscious attitudes that cause a person to ward off feelings of inadequacy by projecting them onto a target group. Fundamentally, the source of prejudice is low self-esteem of people. By hating certain groups, people are able to enhance their sense of self-worth and importance. They use certain people as scapegoats—particularly those without power, whom they can afford to use as such—to reduce their anxiety and uncertainty by attributing complex problems to a simple cause: 'Those people are the source of all my problems' (Zgourides and Zgourdias 2000: 101). Beyond a person's psychological realm, the social scientists have identified some social processes contributing to prejudice and discrimination such as socialization (process of imbibing values, beliefs, attitudes from parents, and thereafter media, etc.), conforming behaviours (the pressure to conform to views of families, friends, and associates lest one should lose social support), economic benefits (expectation of gain in competitive situations and social stress), authoritarian personality (induced by early socialization by which one develops rigid attitude), ethnocentrism (evaluating others' cultures by one's own cultural norms and values), group closure (groups keeping clear boundaries between themselves and others) and the conflict theory (in order to preserve distinctive social status, power, and possessions, privileged groups resorting to suppress underprivileged groups) (Sechrist and Stangor 1996: 167–87).

Thus the discussion on discrimination largely focused on certain prejudices produced by psychological processes within individuals or social processes that induce and reinforce them. It may be axiomatic to say that these processes are not self-generative and are the product of the political economy that shapes and in turn is shaped by these processes. Unfortunately, this discussion largely proceeds in the manner as though the entire matter belonged to the 'superstructure', to use a Marxian metaphor. Particularly, in the context of the Indian caste system which entails huge discrimination against the people at the lowest rung of the caste hierarchy called Dalits, this has been a big problematic because of a certain stereotype about the system itself. The caste system is viewed as ordained by and rooted in the Hindu religious scriptures. Ambedkar diagnosed caste as being rooted in Hindu religious scriptures and had adopted the exit strategy as he thought, the Hindus would never be ready to discard their scriptures. The remedies to escape this discrimination are conceived on the basis of this erroneous understanding. Since the scriptures might not be discarded, the solution is proposed in terms of religious conversion, supplemented by measures such as affirmative action and constitutional safeguards. The very fact that these remedies have not worked, as the huge evidence of increasing atrocities, which could be considered as precipitation of the pervasive discrimination against Dalits and experiential output in Dalit literature, there is a need to take a hard look at this understanding of the caste system. It will necessarily lead to the understanding of the contemporary castes. Insofar as discrimination is an experiential matter of the discriminated, one can easily observe that while the traditional discrimination against Dalits still persists in the vast countryside, the new institutional structure that evolved during post-colonial decades has immensely contributed to it.

Character of the Caste System

All ancient societies display some kind of stratification and therefore India's varna system, dividing Indian society into four varnas is not an exception. However, the caste system, which perhaps came into existence as nomadic tribes began settling for agriculture without undergoing any structural change mainly due to the rich natural endowment of the Indian subcontinent and were embedded into the varna system, imbibing the latter's hierarchical notions, has been unique to India. The varna system seems to have remained an ideological device because nowhere does one come across its classical hierarchy of four varnas, namely, *brahmin*, *kshatriya*, *vaishya*, and *shudra*. The caste system, rather, has been more authentic and more real. The number of castes strung within each varna in a fluid hierarchy, each closed by the rules of endogamy and exogamy, laden with the notion of purity and pollution mapping the entire society do not have any parallel in the world. The continuum of hierarchy the castes constitute across varnas extends to the people who are formally outside the pale of the varna system. The rights and duties of castes were inversely proportional to their hierarchical placement. The system integrity is maintained through rigid enforcement of social ostracism (a system of social and economic penalties) in case of default. But more than this punitive provision, the internalization of the logic of the system by all has been more effective in its survival.

The logic of the caste system stems from the religious belief in karma (acts), dharma (duties) and *punarjanma* (rebirth). This belief held that the birth in a particular caste was due to one's karma in a previous birth and one could get a better caste in the next birth by following one's own dharma (caste rules). The systemic property that helped the system equilibrium was fluidity of hierarchy within a varna, stemming from the sheer numerousness of castes, which led each caste to be in perpetual contention with the caste in its vicinity for claiming superior status without challenging the macro structure, the real source of hierarchy. This secular dynamics overwhelmed religious anchors of the caste system and imparted it its autonomic character. The closed village system sustained it largely undisturbed. The old castes died, collapsed into one another, and new castes were born all through history with the rise of new vocations, without denting the macro structure. This feature has been the most consequential in lending the caste system its amazing longevity.

Castes were best suited to a closed village system and were threatened by urbanization and trade. While there were spells of urbanization and trade in ancient India with the emergence of empires that for a major part patronized the non-caste ideologies of Jainism and Buddhism (Darian 1977: 226–38), it appears, the life-world of castes managed to survive unscarred. The changes in political economy entailing changes in the caste system began showing up only from medieval times with the advent of Muslim rule in the country (1150 AD). Muslim rule brought in advanced feudalism from central Asia and caused certain changes in its configuration in terms of the large scale exodus of lower castes into Islam, the emergence of numerous new castes, lowering of statuses of traditional high castes, etc. Whether these changes brought in by the political economy under the Muslim rule, made the caste system more rigid or more fluid,[2] there is no doubt that the practice of caste discrimination was duly impacted. However, when the higher caste people also converted to Islam, either under force or for greed of money and power, they brought in the caste practices to the new religious society and infected it permanently. At the official level however, Muslim kings, and the Muslim ruling elites more generally, in collaboration with so-called upper caste Hindus, supported the caste system and the oppression of the so-called 'low' castes, both Hindus and Muslims. Mullahs toeing the line of the kings refused to allow so-called low or *razil* castes, both Hindus and Muslims, to be educated or even to enter their courts, which was preserved as a monopoly of the 'high' caste Hindus and Muslims (Falahi 2008).

More pronounced changes occurred during the colonial rule that followed. Having faced the catastrophic mutiny of 1857, which had heavy religious overtones against the perceived British interference with the customs and traditions of the Hindus, the British rulers had decided to make a strategic use of caste and communal divisions to their best advantage. In the guise of anthropological investigations, they began to rigidify castes from their fluid state as the life-world of people (Bayly 2001: 263; Sharma 2002). The institution of the census in 1872 enumerating nationality, race, tribe, religion, and caste further concretized caste and communal identities of people. It gave the localized castes a pan-Indian identity, ignited agitations for caste superiority and variously reinforced caste consciousness (Dirks 2001; Bhagat 2006: 119–34; Hobson 2006). On the other hand, the Christian missionaries that entered the subcontinent in the wake of colonial campaigns had opened the doors of education to the lower castes, which was later followed by the colonial administration. The education made the lower castes aware of the unjust and oppressive system they lived in. The advent of the British rule had brought in the ethos of Western liberalism and with it the institutional structure of governance in India signifying equality before law, and the sense of rights and obligations. It opened up a new horizon before the lower castes that reassured them of the possibility of their liberation from caste bondage. The British rule additionally had brought many job opportunities to Dalits, which were multiplied by the coming of capitalist development in the country, leading to the rise of a tiny class of literate and economically independent urbanite Dalits away from the caste-ridden villages. This class assumed a vanguard role in variously articulating Dalit emancipation and launching a movement for socio-cultural reforms in the community. When with the dawn of the twentieth century, politics began unfolding along communal lines; these socio-cultural movements were transformed into a political force by Dr B.R. Ambedkar, the legendary leader of the Dalits, accomplishing many institutional provisions against discrimination and for development of Dalits.

Traditional Forms of Discrimination

Both the varna and the caste system being ascriptive birth-based systems ordaining prestige and privileges according to the hierarchical positions of castes are inherently discriminatory. The discrimination occurred at the interface of varna division. For example, in a village setting, while Shudra peasants faced discrimination from the upper-caste landlords, they discriminated against Dalits as landless labourers. The discrimination within a caste cluster belonging to a varna also existed but it was relatively of a milder nature, basically due to fluidity of the hierarchies. The discrimination assumed forms of social and cultural exclusion and economic exploitation. It was naturally most pronounced in the case of Dalits who were placed lowest in the hierarchy. They were totally excluded from all social and cultural spheres as untouchables and in some instances, as unapproachable and even unseeables. They lived in ghettos at a distance on the western part of the village such that winds flowing over them would not pollute the high-caste village. They had their separate water source, separate gods, separate panchayat, and so on. In the event they came across a high-caste Hindu, they were supposed to pay obeisance to her/him, irrespective of age. They had to make way for her/him standing aside at a distance with lowered head such that their shadows do not pollute her/him and mean disrespect by having an eye contact. In no case could they touch the high caste. They sat separately in a rare event of village gathering. They were supposed to perform all unclean menial tasks such as dragging dead animals, scavenging dirt and faeces, besides many other tasks as ordered by the high castes. Their womenfolk were treated as the property of the upper castes. While the system was mostly internalized by all as the life-world, which blocked any conflictual occurrence, any failing in observance of this caste code brought them disproportionate punishment. In return they received food and grains from each household within a jajmani system, a system of interdependence in a village.[3]

Although Dalits lived a segregated life, they were divided into many castes with a similar notion of hierarchy as others. Each caste lived within its mini-ghetto inside the outcaste village. They too observed various kinds of exclusions among themselves, including untouchability. They, too, did not marry across castes, and even subcastes. This seclusion and caste practices had become an integral part of peoples' lives as a natural order, none feeling ordinarily anything odd in them. Economic exploitation was also inbuilt in this essentially feudal system. Although the jajmani system was universal in rural India, which ensured subsistence of occupationally specialized castes, it did not apply to all families. Where jajmani or jajmani-like systems operated, implying a unified, conflict-free, reciprocal, and hierarchically weighted system of interrelated castes, it made up only part of the total village economy. Whether it was a jajmani system or any other, there must have been some system which took care of subsistence needs of Dalits and did not let them die of hunger. Neither the caste system nor the forms of discrimination against Dalits were static and they changed over time. The shashtras (scriptures) like *Manusmriti*, prescribed harsh punishments even for minor transgression of the caste boundaries. Much of the scriptural prescriptions were for Shudras and not for the avarna Dalits, who probably had not yet entered the transactional arena. The dictates of *Manusmriti* moreover, were never fully operated and were meant only to create a scare in the minds of people against violation of the caste code, under the influence of the Shraman ideologies (Teltumbde 2010: 18).

Without any authentic details of the societal structure in those days, it may be assumed that Dalits lived completely segregated lives, toiling all their lives for the upper castes. By the medieval times, some castes within Dalits gained a certain role in administration like village errand men (messengers), security, escorts, and such like for which they were gifted some lands called *vatani* or *panchami* lands. A few of such people accumulated savings, bought additional lands and became quite rich. One finds such rich individuals in the majority Dalit castes in every region. Such economic upliftment occurred for a few households, but it did not spell any improvement in their social and cultural status; the majority of Dalits anyway remained outcaste labourers.

Since most social transactions were banned for them, they had developed their own caste infrastructure that supplied them goods and services. They had their own water source, own panchayats, own gods, own priest, their own doctor, own barber, and so on. Since there was no development of self-worth there was no defiance of the caste code and therefore no manifest retribution. The ritualistic hold being strong, the fear of pollution protected their women from being sexually abused by the upper castes. The discrimination was ritually ordained which did not forbid having good relations on secular terms. The remains of this practice could still be seen in the interior villages, where the Dalit and caste Hindu families could have intimate friendly relations without violating the rules of purity and pollution. Since everybody observed the ritualistic practices, there was no occasion for violent clashes. Any minor aberration was referred to the concerned caste panchayat, which adjudicated it.

Post-1947 Political Economy

The entire thrust of the new rulers was to get the country onto a path of rapid capitalist development as the big bourgeois willed. However, the political condition at that time was far from congenial for such a goal to be openly pursued and hence they covered it with a socialist veneer. It was helped by the Fabian image and charisma of Jawaharlal Nehru who headed the first post-colonial all-party government. He gave a vision of a 'secular, democratic, republican, and civil-libertarian political structure' for the Constitution[4] which was to be created by an elitist body as the Constituent Assembly.[5] Congress under Gandhi had mastered this gigantic camouflage. Gandhi, who actually represented the interests of business people, however, presented himself as a pro-poor native, advocating rural industry, and opposing machine-production.[6] He was unconvinced about the virtues of capitalism but was not against it as much as he was against socialism.[7] If one takes stock of his entire public life, right from his days in South Africa, and his voluminous writings, he comes out as a strategist extraordinaire who acutely modelled himself in order to appeal to the masses of poor people but has always been with imperialists or rich barons like the Birlas and Bajajs. He just wanted them (the rich) to be the trustees and take care of the interests of poor, under his idea of trusteeship, his answer to socialism.

One of the first economic steps the government had taken was to declare the central planning for development, shocking the world that newly freed India would go the Soviet way (Staley 2006; *The Economist* 2012). It was a deliberate camouflage. When Nehru declared the first Five-Year Plan when the constituent assembly was still on the job of making a constitution, he adopted the figures from a document called Bombay Plan, which was prepared by the eight big business leaders of the country as early as January 1944, when few had a premonition about the transfer of power and the form in which it would happen (Sanyal 2010). The Bombay Plan had presented a blueprint of 15 years' investment to double the GDP and treble the per capita income. Nehru had not accepted the Plan in public but had surreptitiously adopted it for the first Five-Year Plan. Not only the first plan, the second as well as the third plans of free India, also can be seen conforming to the investment plan contained in the Bombay Plan, corrected only for the different way the country was bifurcated from what the Bombay Plan makers had perhaps assumed (Sanyal 2010). The logic, the camouflage, and the time clearly showed the subtle plan of the government to push for capitalist development in the manner wanted by the capitalists.

Having given a pro-capital push, the government unfolded its plan for the vast rural area. Pretending to address the issue of peoples' hunger for land, the government announced land reforms. It appeared to meet crucial aspirations of the vast majority of people built up during the freedom struggle, but the government drove it in very different ways. Taking cover under the fact that land was a state subject, the government asked states to legislate a plethora of convoluted laws and to carry out land reforms. The resultant outcome of which was calibrated action, wherein lands were distributed to the erstwhile tenants belonging to the farming (Shudra) castes, keeping the untouchables, who might have actually tilled the land, high and dry. These land reforms resulted in vacating the villages of the upper caste landlords, making the erstwhile tenants owners of lands, who would soon constitute a class of rich farmers, reducing Dalits to be the landless labourers utterly dependent on rich farmers for farm wages.

Under the alibi of increasing agricultural productivity to mitigate acute food shortage, the government soon adopted a capitalist strategy of the Green Revolution, based on high-yielding seeds and capitalist inputs. It was concomitant to the strategy of capitalist development of the country, and therefore, primarily in the interest of bourgeoisie. The strategy soon transformed the entire rural economy into a market economy comprising the input market, output market, implement market, service market, credit market, etc., thus demolishing the traditional relations of interdependence in the traditional jajmani system. The huge surpluses accrued through enhanced agricultural productivity flowed as an investment into nearby towns in cold storages, oil mills, ginning factories, transport business, contracting business etc., that hybridized the class of rich farmers with bourgeois interests. The Congress had carved out the class of rich farmers to be its important ally in the rural area, which it had initially been. But with their economic empowerment, their own political aspirations began rising, leading to the rise of regional parties that began gradually to capture local power structures up to the state. The process intensified competition in electoral politics inaugurating a new era of coalition politics. The rich farmers with their caste ties with the most populous shudra band of castes, overcame the class contradiction between them and the shudra poor, on the one hand, and on the other, became a formidable adversary to Dalits who were reduced to be the rural proletariat utterly dependent on them. The class contradictions between them soon started manifesting through the fault lines of caste into gory atrocities, unleashed by upper caste collectives on Dalits in a celebratory mode. It began with Kilvenmeni in Tamil Nadu in 1968 and continued through 1980, to further escalate after

1990s. The rising statistics of atrocities are solely attributed to these changes in the political economy.

During the colonial times, the untouchables were granted reservation of seats in legislatures as a result of concerted pleadings by Dr Ambedkar with the Simon Commission and thereafter, in the Round Table Conferences of 1930–32. The Poona Pact signed between Gandhi and him, which *inter alia*, stressed the historical discrimination against the untouchables by the caste Hindus, which became a part of the Communal Award, conceded the demand for political reservations. The other reservations, mainly, the reservations in public services and in educational institutions (along with other measures) for the promotion of their education' were granted at the instance of Dr Ambedkar, as a member of the Viceroy's Executive Council in 1943. The overall rationale revolved around the lack of 'representation' and the 'historical discrimination'. When the constitution was adopted on 26 January 1950, the practice of untouchability was declared illegal (Article 17). In the entire section dedicated to 'Fundamental Rights,' the Indian constitution prohibited discrimination based on religion, race, caste, sex, and place of birth (Article 15[1]). In response to a Supreme Court judgment outlawing quotas in school admissions that came soon thereafter, the first Amendment to the Constitution, *inter alia*, inserted a clause in Article 15 allowing the union and state governments to make 'any special provision for the advancement of any socially and educationally backward classes of citizens or for the Scheduled Castes and Scheduled Tribes' on 18 June 1951. Similarly, Article 16, calling for 'equality of opportunity in matters of public employment', contained clauses permitting the 'reservation of appointments or posts in favour of any backward class of citizens which, in the opinion of the state, is not adequately represented in the services under the state' and another allowing 'reservation in matters of promotion' for SCs and STs. What began as an exception had thus become general and then open-ended.

The reservations were granted during the colonial times only to the untouchables, who were 'scheduled' together on the concrete criterion of untouchability. But after independence, a separate schedule was created for the tribals as the 'scheduled tribes' which did not have such a definitive criterion like untouchability to identify.[8] The 'exception' was thus diluted into 'general' because the tribals, though backward, were not socially ostracized with the stigma of untouch-ability. It did not remain confined only to them but was extended potentially to any community that was 'socially and educationally backward', thus making it totally open-ended, left to the will of the state (read the ruling classes). The reservations, which emerged as an instrument for 'social justice' to an exceptional section of the population during colonial rule was forged into a political weapon to be wielded as necessary by the ruling classes to divide people asunder. The backwardness in a backward country like India could not constitute a criterion for making an exception to the general egalitarian principle. There is no doubt that the state had a special obligation towards a majority of people but it did not have to be only reservations. The pro-people policies the state could adopt to empower them would have even eliminated the need for reservation but the state, instead, had decided the opposite: pro-elite policies and reservations to weaken the people.

The constitution had a plethora of other provisions, displaying its commitment to the development of the SCs and STs. It provided for the SC/ST Commission (under Article338) as one of the three constitutional regulatory institutions, along with the Comptroller and Auditor General of India and the Election Commission. In the face of it all, this was nothing short of 'revolutionary measures'.[9] The constitution thus appeared to have taken due cognizance of caste based discriminations and provided a number of safeguards to promote the interests of the scheduled castes. In keeping with the constitutional provisions the state has also promulgated legislations to prohibit untouchability and protect Dalit communities from dis-abilities arising out of it, such as:

- The Untouchability Offences Act, later reformulated as the Protection of Civil Rights Act 1955, and rules, 1977
- The Scheduled Caste/Scheduled Tribe (Prevention of Atrocities) Act 1989 and rules, 1995
- Bonded Labour (System) Abolition Act, 1976
- Employment of Manual Scavengers and Construction of Dry Latrines (Prohibition) Act, 1993
- Devadasi System Abolition Acts in the states of Andhra Pradesh, Maharashtra, and Karnataka.

- Child Labour (Prohibition and Regulation) Act, 1986
- Minimum Wages Act, 1948
- Equal Remuneration Act, 1976
- Land Reforms Acts

Besides the Indian constitution, discrimination is also banned by the Universal Declaration of Human Rights by the United Nations. It is significant that having played a leading role in the formation of this institution, India neither mentioned casteism as a source of discrimination, nor Dalits as victims of discrimination in the Universal Declaration of Human Rights. It may also be noteworthy that India brought the issue of discrimination of people of Indian origin in South Africa in 1946 and had argued for the inclusion of 'descent' as a source of discrimination during the drafting of the International Convention on the Elimination of All Forms of Racial Discrimination (ICERD) (A/C.3/1306 of UNGA 3rd Committee), but vehemently argued against the inclusion of caste discrimination under descent in the World Conference against Racism, Racial Discrimination, Xenophobia and Related Intolerance in 2001. Caste is not listed in the UN treaties like ICERD, ICCPR (International Covenant on Civil and Political Rights), CEDAW (Convention to Eliminate All Forms of Discrimination Against Women) or CRC (Convention on the Rights of the Child), nor did the Dalit concerns inform UN Human Rights discourse for almost five decades. As a result, caste-based discrimination went into a black-hole for almost five decades and the issues of untouchability and caste discrimination that victimizes about a sixth of the world population did not come into the purview or debate of building universal human rights mechanisms.

Current State of Discrimination

Despite all kinds of noble intentions and display of concerns and commitment in the constitution over the last six decades, caste hierarchy, discrimination, and untouchability continue to be an integral part of the social, economic, cultural, and religious life of India. While the classical caste discriminations essentially continue unabated, the newer forms of discriminations attributable to the new institutions ordained by the constitution have been added to them.

Dalits are predominantly a rural people, their urbanization being only 19 per cent as against over 30 per cent for the rest. The persisting difference between them and others on almost all developmental parameters, testifying to the discrimination against them, is still stark. For instance, only 28 per cent of the SC population in the rural area earned their income from self-employment compared to 56 per cent for the non-SC population. In the urban areas too, the access of SC households to self-employment (27 per cent) is far lower than that for the others (35.5 per cent). Dalits predominantly continue to be landless labourers; the incidence of landlessness in them has been only increasing over the years. The landless and near landless (that is those owning less than one acre) put together account for nearly 70 per cent of the total SC households in 1991 (NSS 1992), which had gone up to 75 per cent in just a decade (NSS 2000). The lower access to capital assets has led to an exceptionally high proportion of wage labour among the SCs. In rural areas 60 per cent of SCs work as agricultural labour compared to 52.34 per cent from non-SC communities. In urban areas 69.48 per cent of SCs work as casual labour compared to 60.6 per cent of non-SCs. The studies also show that 61 per cent of all bonded labour comes from the SC households (Namala 2006: 24–5). There are discrepancies in unemployment rates as well as wage earnings of Dalits and non-Dalits. The NSS data show that the CDS-based (Current Daily Status) unemployment rates for SCs was about 5.0 per cent as compared to about 3.5 per cent for workers from other communities in rural and urban areas. In 1999–2000 the average weekly wage earning of an SC worker (at 1993–94 prices) was Rs 174.50 compared to Rs 197.05 for others (NCDHR and IIDS 2005). The high incidence of wage labour is associated with a high rate of under and unemployment and low wage earning; consequently, the SCs suffer from low income and high incidence of poverty as compared to others. In 1999–2000, 35.43 per cent of SCs were below the poverty line (BPL) compared to 21 per cent among others in the rural areas. The respective BPL figures in urban areas were 39 per cent and 21 per cent (NCDHR and IIDS 2005). As per the data on monthly per capita expenditure (MPCE) for 1999–2000, the MPCE for SCs in rural areas was

Rs 418.51 compared to Rs 577.22 for others and Rs 508.79 for SCs compared to Rs 1,004.75 for others in urban areas. The 2011 data shows that overall literacy rate among SCs was 54.69 per cent compared to 82.14 per cent among others. The same for females was 41.9 per cent and 65.46 per cent respectively. The dropout rate of SC children by high school is as high as 80 per cent, which according to many scholars is due to discrimination of various forms in the schools (Nambissan and Sedwal 2002).

The discrimination suffered by the SCs is also shown by various surveys and field studies. The much publicized field study of Action Aid in 2000 shockingly revealed that the practice of untouchability in its various forms, ranging from the crudest to sophisticated, was prevalent in 50 to 70 per cent of villages.[10] This study was fairly extensive, covering 11 states and 514 villages relating to the practice of untouchability in the 'secular public sphere' defined as an area of public life that is neither directly associated with the state, nor with the purely individual or religious-cultural aspects of community life. The study includes within its purview the practice of untouchability, access to secular resources, and discrimination within spheres like access to water resources, public thoroughfares, modes of public (but not state-owned) transport, and other village-level services and amenities like tea shops, barbers, or washermens' services, and so on. Within the scope of the 'secular public sphere', the practice of untouchability is categorized into residential segregation, denial of access, and discriminatory treatment in basic public services, and discriminatory restrictions on public behaviour. Information from the study on the practice of untouchability in economic and market spheres is also referred to in the report.

Under the traditional economic framework of the caste system, the occupation and economic rights (including property rights) of each caste are fixed and therefore, involved forced exclusion of one caste from the occupations of another. The untouchables were particularly excluded from access to all sources of livelihood, except manual labour and service to other castes. The exclusion of untouchables was multiple and comprehensive, covering almost all economic spheres, which continues even today.

Discrimination in labour markets refers to a situation of unequal treatment of the workers possessing the same productivity in hiring or in wage payment due to non-economic factors such as race, colour, or gender, or caste (Banerjee and Knight 1985). Dalits are often discriminated against in hiring for jobs, in sale and purchase of agricultural land, or non-land capital assets and various other inputs, consumer goods, social services like education, housing, and health, including common property resources (such as water bodies and grazing land), etc. Significant discrimination is noted in prices received or charged from Dalits in the markets, depending on whether they are sellers or buyers. The Action Aid study brings to the fore the nature and magnitude of discrimination in labour markets, input markets, consumer markets, and in access to common property resources.

Dalits constitute a majority in the child labour in India, which is estimated in the wide range of 10 to 100 million. Children from migrant and bonded families have a preponderance in child labour. Dalit women face triple discrimination: as a labourer, as a woman, and as a Dalit; 89.5 per cent of Dalit women participate in some productive labour outside their homes (Indira 1994: 193–207). More than 94 per cent of Dalit women workers are employed in the unorganized sector. Of this 81.5 per cent work in the agricultural sector and of this group 50 per cent are wage labourers. In urban areas Dalit women fill unorganized, self-employed sectors such as hawkers, scrap collectors, municipality contract workers, garbage collectors, petty traders, and domestic servants. They earn their livelihood in wage work: domestic workers, construction workers, earthwork, beedi rolling, agarbatti making, candle making, garment and jari work, and embroidery work. All these are characterized by low wages, irregular work, absence of social security, sexual harassment, and dependency on the whims of middlemen and employers. The strong caste and patriarchy systems deny them just and equal wages, fair share in economic distribution, maternity benefits, health care, security or protection of property rights. Descent-based discrimination results in the violent appropriation and sexual control over Dalit women by men of dominant caste evident in the systematic rape of Dalit women and the tradition of forced prostitution in the name of religion through the Devadasi system.[11] Though this system was abolished on statutes, it still continues in many parts of the country. In keeping with the work and descent-based discrimination, which accords Dalits the most unclean and polluting occupations and Dalit women the worst of the lot, more Dalit women and girls work as *Safai Karmacharis* as compared to Dalit men. Again, the abominable practice of manual scavenging stood abolished on the statues without any dent on reality. There still exist over 1.3 million manual scavengers in the country, engaged with even the public sectors like municipalities, municipal corporations, and Indian Railways with no signs of stopping this shameful practice.

To cap it all the government adopted neoliberal reforms in 1991, which are nakedly elitist without any space for the 'non-competitive' poor and downtrodden. All the discriminations that came in the Action Aid Report were noted during its initial period of these reforms. They have only worsened with the passage of time. If inequality is taken as the key contributing factor in discrimination, it has been admittedly galloping at unprecedented rates all over the globe. Dalits being the poorest, the impact of these policies on them have to be anything but bad.

***

The pre-colonial caste system was largely informed by rituals as ordained by the *Dharmashastras*. It approximated to its classical form of a continuum of hierarchy, making discrimination also correspondingly hierarchical. Under capitalism, the ritualistic basis of the caste system has been significantly weakened making the *dwija* castes that adopted it initially, to collapse into a single group. Their internal differences reflect only cultural inertia which is overcome without much resistance. With the capitalist transformation of the agrarian sector during the early years of the post-1947 period and consequent enrichment and empowerment of the newly created class of rich farmers in the countryside within the shudra castes, the shudra bandwagon also got hitched to this dwija block, effectively reducing the caste system to its primordial divide between Dalits and non-Dalits. In the pre-colonial times the discrimination happened along ritualistic lines along the entire hierarchy and hence in a diffused manner, which moreover was largely internalized. In the post-colonial period, due to collapse of the hierarchy, the entire discrimination is concentrated at the interface between Dalits and non-Dalits. With the accelerated rise in inequality due to neo-liberal policies during the last two decades, this discrimination has only been rising.

There have been qualitative changes, too, in the caste configuration during the colonial times, particularly during its last phase. The rise of the anti-caste movements of the lower castes demolished the hegemony of the upper castes. The internalization of discrimination by the victims coming through millennia was dispelled, its space having been filled by the resentment of the victims for their historical oppression and exploitation by the upper castes. Besides Dalits, who were of course, the worst victims of the caste system, the Shudras, who were once clubbed with them as working class (by the pioneers of the non-brahmin movement like Phule) had become turncoats to this spirit, identifying with the upper castes vis-à-vis Dalits. By the 1960s, with the empowerment of a section of Shudras along with the baton of brahminism coming into their hands, the estrangement between Dalits and them hardened. Unlike the upper castes, who were ensconced in a modern urban economy with tenuous considerations for castes, their material interests were thickly entangled with Dalits who supplied them labour. The cultural deficit of Shudras, made the resultant discrimination ever more problematic for Dalits. The lean ritualistic difference between them and the Dalits was now replaced by the strong material contradiction between the capitalist farmers and the Dalit labourers, invariably giving rise to wage disputes. It was this dispute that ignited the Kilvenmeni massacre, inaugurating a new genre of atrocity. In pre-colonial times, there was no possibility of this class of atrocity but during post-colonial times it became a commonplace phenomenon.

As seen before, all the forms of discrimination are still intact after 60 years of the constitutional operation. There is a significant incidence of the crudest form of untouchability being practised in many parts of the country. The yawning gap in developmental parameters for Dalits and non-Dalits still persists and is closing, if at all, at the most imperceptible pace. In earlier times they were mutely accepted but today they are quite prone to flare up into a caste clash. In addition to the pre-colonial or classical discrimination, new forms of discrimination have been added. They are more subtle and sophisticated but far more damaging and devastating. The system of reservations as such meant by design to benefit increasingly fewer individuals has stigmatized the entire Dalit community. It has created a perception that Dalits were unduly pampered, notwithstanding that more reservations than theirs are extended to others, including those afflicted by such perceptions. The resultant grudge pervades the entire countryside which can flare up into disproportionate reaction with a spark of any minor cause. In the actual spheres of reservations, the discrimination that follows is far more strategic and sophisticated. Dalits are discriminated in indeterminate ways sometimes: negatively, discriminating against capable but assertive Dalit employees and positively discriminating in favour of incapable but pliant Dalit employees. The essence of discrimination lies in the practice of discounting Dalit worth, whether it is a farm labourer or a highly educated Dalit. Unless, the Dalit individual overtly exhibits her unquestioned submission to the powers that be, she has to suffer this discount. A Dalit with the same qualification as a non-Dalit is sure to suffer a cascading lag vis-à-vis the latter. A recent study done to test out discrimination on account of caste and community in the job market verily proves it (Thorat, Attewell, and Rizvi 2009). Another study conducted on the placement pattern in a hallowed place like IIM, Ahmedabad, also revealed that the Dalit students generally get placed at 19 and 35 per cent salary discount in domestic and foreign jobs respectively, compared to their non-Dalit counterparts.[12] This is just the initial placement; she has to meekly endure a series of discriminations in postings, promotions, and transfers during her entire life until she gets totally demoralized and is reduced to being deadwood.

The aggravation of discrimination during the post-1947 period can mainly be attributed to the short-sighted elitist policies of the government in favour of the entrenched classes. The caste discrimination can be logically abolished by annihilating the caste system. However, all the policies of the government directly or indirectly promote caste consciousness in people. It has intrigued to rejuvenate castes by making them part of the modern institutional framework under the garb of social justice to the victims. Instead of realizing its follies and huge cost to the nation, it has persisted with its elitist attitude and adopted a neo-liberal policy package that theoretically eliminates the entire discourse of discrimination. The accumulated damage has already been huge and difficult to overcome by the government. The only way to work in the direction would be to restore a voice to the people, in the truest spirit of democracy, so that they would exercise their creative faculties to stem the rot and recover the damage to the nation.

Notes

1. These treaties are: (i) The International Covenant on Economic, Social and Cultural Rights, (ii) The International Covenant on Civil and Political Rights, (iii) The Convention against Torture and Other Cruel, Inhuman or Degrading Treatment or Punishment, (iv) The International Convention on the Elimination of All Forms of Racial Discrimination and the Convention on the Elimination of All Forms of Discrimination against Women, (v) The Convention on the Rights of the Child and (vi) Convention on the Rights of Persons with Disabilities and Optional Protocol.

2. Some scholars say that the caste system got rigidified during the Muslim rule (Smith, 2001: 66) but some say that 'Muslim rule did not substantially disrupt the class and caste system, although it may have become more fluid than it previously was', (Duiker and Spielvoger 2005: 221).

3. Under the jajmani system, the family or families entitled to certain services from certain persons are called *jajman* (*yajman*) and the persons rendering those services are called *kameen* of the Jajman. The first detailed study of jajmani tradition in India was made by William H. Wiser in his book, *The Indian Jajmani System*. Oscar Lewis, observed that the jajmani system prevails in all regions though there are minor local differences (Lewis 1958: 56).

4. See Objective Resolution in the Constituent Assembly moved by Jawaharlal Nehru on 13 December, 1946. http://parliamentofindia.nic.in/ls/debates/facts.htm. Accessed 10 October 2013.

5. The constituent assembly consisted of 385 members, of which 292 were elected by the elected members of the provincial legislative assemblies while 93 members were nominated by the princely states. To these were to be added a representative each from the four chief commissioners, provinces of Delhi, Ajmer-Marwar, Coorg, and British Baluchistan.

6. Interestingly, his entire affair was funded by the industrialist, Ghanashyam Das Birla of Calcutta, who owned mills besides several other businesses. See 'Birla Family and Mahatma Gandhi', Part I. Available at http://gandhiking.ning.com/profiles/blogs/birla-family-and-mahatma-gandhi-part-i-1. Accessed: 10 October 2013; Also see, (Allan 1986).

7. Jawaharlal Nehru lamented that Gandhi put up with capitalism but considered socialism as an inherently violent system. See (Nehru 1936: 8).
8. The aftermath is visibly disastrous because some extremely well off communities that managed to get themselves into the schedule have monopolized the entire reservations, keeping the real tribals away.
9. Statement of Rajesh Prasad, Indian Representative in the thematic discussion on descent-based discrimination before CERD on 8 August 2002.
10. See Action Aid, People's Report on Untouchability in Rural India. See (Shah *et al* 2006). This percentage refers to a percentage of villages in which a particular form of untouchability prevailed. In sum, all villages may have practised some or the other form of untouchability.
11. Dedicating girls to a deity is a part of the customary practice of India and continues today. 'The powerful section of society brought this custom into vogue to exploit the ritual and religious pretext since the divine prostitutes ultimately become sex objects of dominant caste persons of groups', (*Report on the Prevention of Atrocities against Scheduled Caste*, NHRC 2004: 60).
12. (Chakravarty and Somanathan 2008: 45–60). Also see, for the discrimination in salaries for degree holders and technical personnel (Madheswaran 2006: 349–72).

References

Allan, R. 1986. *The Emissary: G. D. Birla, Gandhi and Independence.* London: Collins Harvill.
Allen, T.J. and Sherman, J.W. 2011. 'Ego Threat and Intergroup Bias: A Test of Motivated-Activation Versus Self-Regulatory Accounts', in *Psychological Science.* Available at http://pss.sagepub.com/content/early/2011/02/10/0956797611399291.
Altman, A. 2011. [Spring edition]. 'Discrimination', in Edward N. Zalta (ed.), *The Stanford Encyclopedia of Philosophy.* Available at http://plato.stanford.edu/archives/spr2011/entries/discrimination/. Accessed: 10 October 2013.
Banerjee, B. and J.B. Knight. 1985. 'Caste Discrimination in the Indian Urban Labour Market', in *Journal of Development Economics*, 17 (3: 277–307.
Bayly, S. 2001. *Caste, Society and Politics in India.* New Delhi: Cambridge University Press.
Bhagat, R.B. 2006. 'Census and Caste Enumeration: British Legacy and Contemporary Practice in India', *Genus*, LXII (2): 119–34.

Chakravarty, S. and E. Somanathan, 2008. 'Discrimination in an Elite Labour Market? Job Placements at IIM, Ahmedabad', *Economic & Political Weekly*, November 1, pp. 45–60.

Commander, S. 1983. 'The Jajmani System in North India: An Examination of its Logic and Status across Two Centuries', *Modern Asian Studies*, 17(2): 283–311.

Darian, J. C. 1977. 'Social and Economic Factors in the Rise of Buddhism', *Sociological Analysis*. 38(3): 226–38.

Dirks, N.B. 2001. *Castes of Mind: Colonialism and the Making of Modern India*: New Jersey: Princeton University Press.

Duiker, W. J. and J.J. Spielvoger. 2005. *The Essential World History*. Boston: Wordsworth.

Falahi, M.A. 2008. Caste and Social Hierarchy Among Indian Muslims: M.A. Falahi (Interview). Available at http://www.dalitmuslims.com/2008/08/caste-and-social-hierarchy-among-indian.html. Accessed: 4 October 2013.

Fuller, C.J. 1989. 'Misconceiving the grain heap: A critique of the concept of the Indian Jajmani System', in M. Bloch and J. Parry (eds). *Money and the Morality of Exchange*, pp. 33–63. Cambridge: Cambridge University Press.

Hobson, K. 2006. 'Ethnographic Mapping and the Construction of the British Census in India', http://www.britishempire.co.uk/article/caste-system.htm.

Indira, M. 1994. 'A Study of Landless Labour', in C. Chakrapani and S. Vijaya Kumar, (eds). *Changing Status and Role of Women in Indian Society*. New Delhi: MD Publications.

Lewis. O. 1958. *Village Life in Northern India*. Illinois: University of Illinois Press.

Madheswaran, S. 2006. 'Caste Discrimination in The Indian Urban Labour Market: An Econometric Analysis', *ISEC, Springer*, 53(3): 349–72.

Namala, A. 2006. 'Children and Caste-based Discrimination: Policy Concerns', A UNICEF-IIDS Paper. Kathmandu: UNICEF-IIDS.

Nambissan, G.B. and M. Sedwal, 2002. 'Education For All—The Situation of Dalit Children in India', in R. Govinda (ed.), *India Education Report: A Profile of Basic Education*. New Delhi: Oxford University Press.

National Campaign on Dalit Human Rights (NCDHR) and Indian Institute of Dalit Studies (IIDS). 2005. *Report on Dalits' Access to Rights*. New Delhi: NCDHR and IIDS.

Nehru, J. 1936. *An Autobiography*. London: The Bodley Head.

National Human Rights Commission (NHRC). 2004. *Report on the Prevention of Atrocities against Scheduled Caste*. New Delhi: NHRC.

National Sample Survey (NSS). 1992. *NSS Land holding survey*. New Delhi: GoI.

———. 2000 *NSS Employment/Unemployment survey, 1999–2000*. Delhi: GoI.

Osin, N. and D. Porat (eds). 2005. *Legislating Against Discrimination: An International Survey of Anti-Discrimination Norms*. Leiden: Martinus Nijhoff.

Rudner, D. W. 1994. *Caste and Capitalism in Colonial India: The Nattukottai Chettiars*. Berkeley: University of California Press.

Sanyal, A. 2010. 'The Curious Case of the Bombay Plan', *Contemporary Issues and Ideas in Social Sciences*, June. Available at journal.ciiss.net/index.php/ciiss/article/download/78/75. Accessed: 10 October 2013.

Sechrist, G.B. and C. Stangor. 1996. 'Prejudice as Social Norms' in C.S. Crandall and M. Schaller (eds), *Social Psychology of Prejudice: Historical and Contemporary Issues*, pp. 167–87. Lawrence: Lewinian Press.

Shah, G., H. Mander, S. Deshpande, and A. Baviskar. 2006. *Untouchability in Rural India*, New Delhi: Sage Publications.

Sharma, U. 2002. *Caste*. New Delhi: Viva Books.

Smith, V.A. 2001 [fourth edn]. *The Oxford History of India*. New Delhi: Oxford University Press.

Staley, S.R. 2006. 'The Rise and Fall of Indian Socialism: Why India embraced economic reform'. Available at http://reason.com/archives/2006/06/06/the-rise-and-fall-of-indian-socialism. Accessed: 10 October 2013.

Teltumbde, A. 2010. *Persistence of Caste: The Khairlanji Murders and India's Hidden Apartheid*. London: Zed Books.

The Economist. 2012. 'Economic Planning in India: Tales of the unexpected'. Available at http://www.economist.com/node/21547800. Accessed: 10 October 2013.

Thorat, S., P. Attewell, and F.F. Rizvi. 2009. 'Urban Labour Market Discrimination', Working Paper Series, Vol. 3, No. 1, New Delhi: Indian Institute of Dalit Studies.

Whitley, B.E. and M.E. Kite. 2010. *The Psychology of Prejudice and Discrimination*. Belmont: Wadsworth Cengage Learning.

Wiser, W.H. 1936. *The Indian Jajmani System*. Lucknow: The Lucknow Publishing House.

United Nations. 2006. *The Core International Human Rights Treaties*. New York and Geneva: United Nations Publications.

Zgourides, G.D. and C.S. Zgourdias. 2000. *Cliffs Quick Review: Sociology*. Foster City: IDG Books.

PART II

COMPARATIVE PERSPECTIVES

4

The Architecture of Discrimination Law[*]

Tarunabh Khaitan

> If on the road a shoe falls off my horse, and I come to a smith to have
> one put on, and the smith refuses to do it, an action will lie against
> him, because he has made profession of a trade which is for the public
> good, and has thereby exposed and vested an interest of himself in
> all the King's subjects that will employ him in the way of his trade.
> If an innkeeper refuses to entertain guests where his house is not full,
> an action will lie against him and so against a carrier, if his horses
> are not loaded, and he refuses to take a packet proper to be sent by a
> carrier...[1]

This is Chief Justice Holt's summary in 1701 of the English common
law duty on the providers of certain public utilities. It is perhaps one
of the earliest examples of something akin to the anti-discrimination
principle in the common law tradition. Although relied upon by a
famous black cricketer as late as in 1944 to successfully challenge a
London hotel's refusal to accommodate him (because of objections
made by some of its white guests),[2] it lacks key features of contemporary discrimination law: the salience of groundsand groups (See
Khaitan 2013). The duty in English law protected everyone who was

willing and able to pay for the service, irrespective of the grounds on which the inn-keeper (or the carrier, etc.) refused to serve. A person who was turned away because of the colour of her eye, or the first letter of her first name, or on no ground at all, would still have a remedy. It also protected everyone to the same extent, irrespective of the group they belonged to. But what we now understand as discrimination law has at its core the protection of certain definite grounds—race, sex, religion, age, disability, sexual orientation, and so on—and the groups that these grounds classify us into. Contemporary discrimination law also has a much wider scope and imposes duties on many more actors than the old common law duty on public utilities.

Rules enacted in the second half of the nineteenth century in India and the United States are much closer to what we have come to regard as discrimination law. This is hardly surprising, for these two regions witnessed the most pervasive and entrenched forms of prejudice and disadvantage faced by caste and racial groups respectively. While the American focus was on a constitutional guarantee of equal protection under the Fourteenth Amendment, the emphasis in Indian discrimination law was decidedly towards affirmative action for 'low' caste groups in education and employment—[3] an emphasis that continues to this day.

This chapter will provide an overview of the architecture of discrimination law as it has developed since these early beginnings in other common-law democratic jurisdictions. This architecture is best understood as framed around three issues. First, the protégés of discrimination law need to be identified. The early duties in India and the United States protected disadvantaged caste and racial groups respectively. Contemporary discrimination law has a much wider scope. Who is entitled to the protection of discrimination law is perhaps the most central (and controversial) issue in this area of law. This question will be explored in the first section. Secondly, jurisdictions need to decide who the duty bearers are. All of these aforementioned measures relate to state action. However, the unsuccessful attempt by the US Civil Rights Act of 1875 to impose anti-discrimination duties on private persons gave rise to an enduring controversy about who can be legitimately required to shoulder these duties. The responses of the chosen jurisdictions to this question will be presented in the second section. Finally, the scope of the duty has to be determined.

The early attempts focused on what we would now refer to as direct discrimination or affirmative action. But in the last few decades, new tools have been invented, as discrimination law becomes increasingly sophisticated. Controversies relating to whether discrimination law should only regulate acts or also omissions, whether the causative event for triggering the duty is harm to the victim or fault of the perpetrator or both, and the interrelationship between different duties when they conflict will be outlined in the third section. How Indian discrimination law currently fits within this framework is outlined in (Table 4.1) at the end of the chapter.

These questions are interrelated rather than insular. Our answer to any of them has an impact on all the others. Different groups of potential defendants may shoulder the obligation to refrain from discriminating to different extents. Similarly, not all the protégés of anti-discrimination law are protected to the same extent. What results, therefore, is a complicated web of interrelationships. Obviously, there are other aspects to the practice of discrimination law—mainly matters of detail—which will not be captured by these questions.[4] In particular, the issue of appropriate enforcement mechanisms will be entirely overlooked.

Protectorate

Discrimination law protects persons—especially groups of persons defined by certain personal characteristics that are technically called grounds. Groups disadvantaged by these grounds are protected more than those advantaged because of them. But, at least with respect to certain grounds like disability and age, we are all potentially subject to ground-based disadvantage. Because of the ground-sensitive nature of its protection, we can elliptically say that grounds constitute the protectorate of discrimination law. Every duty that discrimination law imposes—prohibition on direct and indirect discrimination and harassment, provision for reasonable accommodation, provision for affirmative action—is sensitive to grounds. A state could, of course, prohibit harassment per se, rather than merely sexual or racial harassment. It could also—and many states do—provide material benefits whose distribution is not sensitive to grounds protected by discrimination law: provisions for minimum wages, fuel allowance, bus passes etc are good examples. These norms, however, are not norms of discriminationlaw, for the simple reason that they are not sensitive to grounds (just as we would not consider *Lane* v. *Cotton* as a discrimination law case either).

Grounds are personal characteristics that are protected by discrimination law in the sense that disadvantaging people on the basis of these grounds is usually prohibited and advantaging them on these grounds is sometimes required. The (dis)advantaging may be direct or indirect. It is direct when the protected grounds are relied upon directly. It is indirect when the apparent ground is not protected, but is a proxy for a protected ground such that any benefit or burden distributed on the basis of the unprotected apparent ground (say educational qualification) gets distributed in a manner that implicates the protected ground (say race). Thus, the list of apparent grounds on which discrimination is prohibited is potentially limitless, for any such ground may be a proxy for a protected ground under certain circumstances. But these apparent grounds do not matter for their own sake—they matter because they act as proxies for protected grounds in these circumstances (Fishkin 2014: 246f). Directly protected grounds are therefore key to our understanding of discrimination law.

Section 9(3) of the South African constitution, for example, prohibits discrimination 'against anyone on one or more grounds, including race, gender, sex, pregnancy, marital status, ethnic or social origin, colour, sexual orientation, age, disability, religion, conscience, belief, culture, language and birth'. Comparable provisions can be found in statutory as well as constitutional provisions in other jurisdictions.[5] Given the importance of the list of protected grounds, it is no surprise that judges and legislators have faced a growing (and often successful) clamour in the last couple of decades for expanding the list of protected grounds—candidates such as weight (Kristen 2002: 7), physical appearance (Post et al. 2001), and genetic identity (Silvers and Stein 2002: 1341) are offered as 'analogous' to the ones alreadylisted.[6] Fiss famously called this phenomenon the 'proliferation of the protectorate' (Fiss 1974; McCrudden 1991 and 2004). Commentators and law-makers have struggled to evolve principled criteria which can be employed to determine these claims. Judgments from jurisdictions that have an open-ended list of protected grounds[7] are perhaps the most instructive in this regard. When invited to determine whether a candidate ought to be added to this list, judgesin these jurisdictions appear to be applying the following two cumulative requirements that a ground must satisfy in order to be protected by discrimination law:

(i) It must be a ground that classifies persons into groups with a significant advantage gap between them, and
(ii) It must either be immutable or it must constitute a fundamental choice.

Groups

Let us consider the first condition first. Sex is a protected ground because there is a significant advantage gap between women and men. All protected grounds divide persons into groups with a significant advantage gap between them: protected groups suffer relative disadvantage in comparison to cognate groups (that is, that is, different groups defined by the same ground, such as men and women). Instead of adopting a blinkered view of disadvantage as economic alone, courts have usually been sophisticated in unpacking the notion of relative group disadvantage. They have recognised that disadvantage may be political, socio-cultural, material—more often, a complex combination of these different facets of disadvantage. Affluent members of racial minorities may have overcome material disadvantage, but are likely to remain saddled with political and socio-cultural disadvantage, which can be even more difficult to shake off. As Justice Wilson insisted in *Andrews*, the 'place of the group in the entire social, political and legal fabric of our society' was relevant to determining whether it should be protected.[8]

Political disadvantage is evidenced by factors such as the numerical strength of a group as an electorate (foreigners,[9] people living with HIV/AIDS,[10] and gay and lesbian people[11] have been protected because of their numerical insignificance in the electoral process); the quantity and quality of actual representation of the group in the offices of state;[12] and the nature and the degree of attention paid by state institutions to the group in question.[13] Political disadvantage can be a cause, as well as an effect, of other forms of disadvantage. The socio-cultural disadvantage that women face in our societies leaves them underrepresented in and under-catered for by our public institutions. On the other hand, the important role of political power in material distribution means that politically disadvantaged groups may also fail to secure fair distribution of society's resources.[14]

Socio-cultural disadvantage is usually (although not exclusively) indicated by the prevalence of prejudice against and (certain) stereotypical assumptions about the members of a group. Prejudice (or bias) is 'a judgment that those with a certain trait are morally less worthy than others merely by virtue of possessing that trait'. For example, prejudice against Dalits signifies a belief that a person is less deserving morally because of her 'lower' caste status. This is a categorical preference against certain groups of people, simply based on who they are. A person's belief in his moral superiority can spring not just from caste—religion, sex, sexual orientation, race and various other attributes have been, and still are, the bases for prejudice in our societies. Stereotypes (or proxies) do not entail such categorical judgments about persons (Timmer 2011: 707). Instead, they involve a judgment—rightly or wrongly—that a person with a certain trait is quite likely to possess other, descriptively relevant, traits. When the judgment is accurate, the correlation between the traits could be due to biological factors (for example a woman is likely to live longer than a man), socio-cultural factors (for example a woman is more likely to quit her job to accommodate her husband's career than the other way around), or because of the reaction of others (for example a black cop is likely to be more effective than a white cop in policing a black neighbourhood). The stronger the statistical correlation, the more accurate a stereotype will be. Often, stereotypes are inaccurate, such that there is little evidence for the supposed correlation (for example the belief that the poor are lazy). Fuelled by anecdotal rather than statistically significant evidence, inaccurate stereotypes are often attempts to rationalize prejudices.[16]

Apart from being accurate or inaccurate, stereotypes can also be positive, neutral, or negative, depending on the desirability of the correlative trait. The assumption that women are caring is a positive stereotype, and that men are violent is negative. Things get complicated because these traits may be objectively positive or negative, and still be subjectively judged differently in any given society. It may be, for example, that caring is seen as a sign of weakness, whereas

a proclivity to violence is seen as strength. Furthermore, even positive stereotypes which a society correctly views as positive can have
disadvantageous effects—assumptions about women's care-giving
nature results in them being saddled with most of the child-rearing
responsibilities while men can focus on their career advancement.

Groups against whom prejudices or subjectively negative stereotypes are widespread in a society aremore clearly disadvantaged
socio-culturally. They affect the members' ability to take pride in
their membership of a group, especially in cases where such membership partly constitutes personal identity. Positive stereotypes that
have negative effects can also contribute to social disadvantage, as
also other forms of disadvantage. In fact, socio-cultural disadvantage
generally has a causal relationship with other facets of disadvantage.
It may result in political disadvantage for two reasons. First, political
officials, as members of the society, may often share the prejudices
and negative stereotypes prevalent in society, which are then gets
reflected in official acts. The second reason is that even if public
officials themselves do not hold these beliefs, the fact that they are
responsible electorally to those who do gives them an incentive to
act on these prejudices or stereotypes. It is for this reason that Justice
O'Connor applied 'a more searching form of rational basis review'
when a law was designed to harm 'a politically unpopular group'.[17]
The implication seems to be that the group faces such a degree of
social hostility that acting against them may accrue political divi-
dends for public officials. Similar causal connections can sometimes
be drawn between socio-cultural disadvantage and material disadvantage. The socio-cultural disadvantage of a group is often the cause
of hostility and violence against, and boycotts and ghettoization of,
its members—factors that render them materially disadvantaged.[18]

The third indicator of disadvantage is material disadvantage.
While primarily determined by economic indicators like income
and wealth, it can be given a broader interpretation to include access
to education and employment,[19] freedom from private and public
violence and hostility,[20] longevity, and health, among other factors.
to identify these groups.[21] These factors indicate the socio-economic
security of the material status of a group.[22]

On similar lines, the criteria for 'backwardness' evolved by the
Second Backward Classes Commission to determine eligibility for

affirmative action programmes in India include 'social factors' ('classes considered socially backward by others', dependence on manual labour, etc.), 'educational factors' (school attendance, drop-out, and matriculation rates) and 'economic factors' (value of assets, loans owed, and proximity to drinking water facilities) (Mandal 1980). Although economic factors were accorded relatively low weight, they 'were considered important as they directly flowed from social and educational backwardness. This also helped to highlight the fact that socially and educationally backward classes are economically backward also' (Mandal 1980).

The disadvantage we are concerned with is relative—it is the gap between the protected and the cognate groups that counts. It may well be, of course, that a protected group is also disadvantaged in some absolute sense—that it may fall below any absolute threshold of well-being necessary to live a decent life. But it seems that for judges to protect a particular ground, relative disadvantage between any two groups defined by that ground would suffice. Thus, a group need not be entirely excluded from the political process—the fact that it is a political minority will be sufficient. No doubt men bear the burden of social stereotyping too—it is enough that, on the whole, women face a significantly greater degree of social disadvantage. 'Backward classes' in India may not be poor in absolute terms—relative material disadvantage is all that is required. That said, the advantage gap between relevant groups must be significant rather than trivial. Hence our first condition that makes a ground eligible for the protection of discrimination law: it must classify persons into groups with a significant advantage gap between them. Notice that the relative disadvantage of a group (say women) makes the entire ground (sex) eligible for protection, at least in a prima facie sense. We will see shortly that sometimes the duties imposed by discrimination law do apply asymmetrically such that disadvantaged groups are given a greater degree of protection.

Grounds

The second, additional, requirement that judges have insisted upon is that a candidate ground must either be immutable or it must constitute a fundamental choice (See generally, Wintemute 1995) if it is to be protected. These requirements together amount to a demand that the ground be normatively irrelevant, that is, our possession of these grounds should not affect how successful our lives are.

Immutability of a characteristic has been the most frequently used rationale, especially in cases involving racial classifications. In Korematsu, the US Supreme Court noted that the appellant 'belongs to a race from which there is no way to resign'.[23] Courts have understood 'immutability' broadly, at least inasmuch as they include not only characteristics that cannot be changed, whether a characteristic is mutable,[24] but also those whose initial acquisition itself was not based on a choice made by the possessor. Apart from race, first place.[25] Other characteristics that have been protected for immutability-based reasons include sex,[26] marital status of one's parents,[27] place of residence of young children,[28] and citizenship.[29]

Judicial reliance on immutability as the sole test for selecting a protected characteristic has been severely criticized (Yoshino 1998: 510–15, 530–6). It has been shown that it tends to be biased towards protecting corporeal grounds, that is, that is, i.e. those defined by nature, for example race, sex, etc. Non-corporeal or social grounds like religious status, linguistic identity, marital status, sexual orientation, etc, which are more easily hidden and (arguably) changeable, are less favourably treated.[30] These behavioural grounds manifest themselves to the outside world only through behaviour or conduct. In High Tech Gays, Judge Brunetti held that homosexuality is behavioural, 'hence [it] is fundamentally different from traits such as race, gender, or alienage'.[31] Thus, the argument goes, homosexuals should not be part of the protectorate. Reacting to these types of cases, Sunstein rhetorically asked if the discovery of an accessible race-altering drug could have any implication on the protection of race (Sunstein 1994: 2410, 2443). Feminists have also raised the same concerns, arguing that the immutability test can be (and has been) used to deny protection to pregnancy, since pregnancy is (assumed to be) within the control of a woman (Kessler 2001: 371). Furthermore, immutability is in any case a matter of degree—even one's sex can be changed, while gender is reasonably mutable, to the extent that it is possible to distinguish sex from gender.[32] Even grounds such as caste and race can be hidden, if not changed.

The judicial reaction to these criticisms was two-fold. One way in which courts reacted to this problem was by distinguishing between 'strict' and 'effective' mutability:

It is clear that by 'immutability' the Court has never meant strict immutability in the sense that members of the class must be physically unable to change or mask the trait defining their class. People can have operations to change their sex... the Supreme Court is willing to treat a trait as effectively immutable if changing it would involve great difficulty...[33]

There are other similar cases where courts have been satisfied with effective immutability, where changing the trait would impose significant personal costs.[34] Obviously, these costs are more than mere economic ones, and include psychological and social costs as well (Gibson 1991: 772, 786-7).

Once this is accepted, it is easy to see how effective immutability merges with fundamental choice, for 'immutability may describe those traits that are so central to a person's identity that it would be abhorrent for government to penalize a person for refusing to change them, regardless of how easy that change might be physically.'[35] This explicit recognition of fundamental choice alongside immutability as an alternative basis for protection of a ground was the second judicial response to the criticisms against the immutability test. Thus, while grounds such as marital status, pregnancy, and religious status are (to an extent) a matter of choice and could be changed, such change is usually impossible without significant personal costs to the individual.[36] When judges were already protecting characteristics over which we lack effective control, protection for characteristics that constitute a fundamental choice merely lay further along the same spectrum, rather than in a separate category altogether. By protecting grounds constituting fundamental choice, discrimination law resists assimilationist demands that those carrying these grounds must convert (that is, that is, give up), pass-off (that is, that is, hide), or cover (that is, that is, not-flaunt) their chosen characteristic (Yoshino 2001–2002: 769).

To be plain, the choice in question is important because it is fundamental to the person whose choice it is.[37] Justice L'Heureux-Dubé in *Miron* equates marital status to religion and citizenship: they may be matters of choice, but involve such fundamental personal judgments that legal outcomes should not depend on the failure to make a particular choice.[38] Justice O'Regan echoed the point in *Harksen*, where she held that 'the decision to enter into a permanent personal relationship with another is a momentous and defining one'.[39]

In addition to being fundamental, the choice should be valuable (or, at least, not-without-value). In *Nyquist*, for example, while rejecting the justification offered by the State that the law giving scholarships to citizens but not permanent resident aliens was intended to encourage naturalization, the majority held that resident aliens pay their full share of taxes and often provide leadership in many spheres of community life, and that the state is not harmed in providing them equal benefits.[40] Thus, the second requirement for eligibility for protection is that the ground in question must be an effectively immutable trait or constitute a valuable fundamental choice. Examining these alternative features—immutability and fundamental choice—through the lens of 'choice' makes them appear contradictory. We seem to be protecting grounds over the possession of which we have no choice, and also grounds that constitute a fundamental choice. But that is the wrong lens to examine these selection criteria. It is clear that judges have used these criteria to identify grounds that are normatively irrelevant. When a ground is immutable, possessing it is not generally immoral. When a ground represents a valuable fundamental choice, it is positively valuable, rather than merely not-immoral.

The shape of the protectorate of discrimination law is not symmetric.[41] While a ground may be protected, the protection offered to all its cognate groups is not necessarily the same. The question is whether women alone are protected from sex discrimination, or also men; and, when both are protected, whether they are protected to the same degree. There are three mutually incompatible positions a jurisdiction could adopt on the question of symmetrical protection of groups: (i) completely symmetric protection, where the cognate and the protected groups are offered exactly the same degree; or (ii) completely asymmetric protection, where only the protected group gets any protection at all; or (iii) largely asymmetric protection, where both groups benefit, but protected groups benefit more than cognate groups.

The prohibition on direct discrimination usually applies symmetrically for most grounds. There are, however, exceptions. The most stable exception common to all jurisdictions is the asymmetric protection of disability: only a disabled person can bring a claim of discrimination, an able-bodied person cannot claim disability discrimination. Even though the actual prohibition on direct discrimination is usually symmetric, members of cognate groups who lose out because of the operation of a justified affirmative action measure are deemed not to have suffered direct discrimination. Thus, all jurisdictions under study adopt the third position by providing largely asymmetric protection for most grounds, and completely asymmetric protection for some grounds (mainly disability).

To summarize, the scope and shape of the protectorate of discrimination law is determined by a complex interaction between two factors: grounds and groups. Its scope is determined by two cumulative requirements for protecting a ground: that it must classify persons into groups with a significant advantage gap between them, and that it must either be immutable or constitute a fundamental choice. The shape of the protectorate is largely asymmetric, in favour of greater protection for protected groups and less so for cognate groups.

Duty-bearers

Having looked at the protectorate of the duties of discrimination law, it is time to examine who the bearers of the duties imposed by discrimination law are. Unlike typical duties in criminal law or the law of torts, the duties of discrimination law are not borne by everyone. Instead of a universal approach, the law identifies specific types of persons to shoulder its burdens. In many respects, discrimination law has expanded beyond what the lay model would characterize as discriminatory. In respect to the question currently under consideration, however, the law is more restrained: it refuses to regulate certain types of conduct that laypeople would view as discriminatory. At the start of this chapter, we looked at the English common law duty on the providers of certain public utilities—innkeepers, blacksmiths, common-carriers—to refrain from discrimination (although this prohibition on 'discrimination' was not ground-sensitive in the contemporary sense). However, when the US Congress sought to extend legal protection to ground-sensitive discrimination by private persons in 1875, it hit a judicial roadblock. The Civil Rights

Act of 1875 had declared that had declared that 'all persons within the jurisdiction of the United States shall be entitled to the full and equal enjoyment of the accommodations, advantages, facilities, and privileges of inns, public conveyances on land or water, theaters, and other places of public amusement; subject only to the conditions and limitations established by law, and applicable alike to citizens of every race and color, regardless of any previous condition of servitude.' The US Supreme Court struck it down as unconstitutional, asserting that the 14th Amendment governed state action alone.[42] Discrimination law has come a long way from this nineteenth-century controversy. As far as the practice of discrimination law is concerned, it is no longer contentious that anti-discrimination duties apply to public as well as private persons—, that is, in 'vertical' as well as 'horizontal' relationships respectively. The debate has shifted to the determination of which private persons

In most jurisdictions, constitutional as well as statutory provisions impose the anti-discrimination duties and license affirmative action.[43] The legal source of the duties usually has implications for who the duty-holder is. In general, duties imposed by constitutions and bills of rights apply only to the 'state' or 'public authorities',[44] whereas statutory obligations tend to apply to public as well as private bodies. The two exceptions to the general rule regarding constitutional texts are South Africa[45] and the European Union—[46] constitutional texts of both these jurisdictions have provisions that are worded broadly enough to impose non-discrimination obligations not merely on public authorities but also on private bodies, although these horizontal constitutional duties are normally given effect to by statutes. Constitutional provisions are framed vaguely, and usually guarantee a right to equality—the right against discrimination is usually understood to be an aspect of this right in all jurisdictions. Judges have interpreted the duties corresponding to these rights in relation to (but not necessarily mirroring) the more specific duties imposed by statutes.[47] Although applicable usually to the state, judges have sometimes given these constitutional duties 'indirect' horizontal effect (not to be confused with 'indirect discrimination').[48] They have done so by exercising their law-making powers to develop the common law in light of constitutional principles. The Canadian Supreme Court has, for example, held that:

Where ... private party 'A' sues private party 'B' relying on the common law and where no act of government is relied upon to support
the action, the Charter [of Rights and Freedoms] will not apply....
this is a distinct issue from the question whether the judiciary ought
to apply and develop the principles of the common law in a manner consistent with the fundamental values enshrined in the Constitution. The answer to this question must be in the affirmative. In
this sense, then, the Charter is far from irrelevant to private litigants
whose disputes fall to be decided at common law.[49]

The House of Lords went a step further by suggesting that:

'the time has come to recognise that the values enshrined in articles 8
and 10 [of the Human Rights Act] are now part of the cause of action
for breach of confidence.... The values embodied in articles 8 and 10
are as much applicable in disputes between individuals or between an
individual and a non-governmental body ... as they are in disputes
between individuals and a public authority.'[50]

Even in the context of anti-discrimination law, the House of Lords
has used its interpretative power under section 3 of the Human Rights
Act to give indirect horizontal effect to the right against discrimination in the context of a landlord–tenant relationship.[51] Comparably,
the US Supreme Court has held that the judiciary, as an organ of
the state, is constitutionally prohibited from enforcing private discriminatory contracts.[52] It appears, therefore, that a constitutional
prohibition on discrimination by the state has implications for the
anti-discrimination duties of private persons. It is better to consider
the state's refusal to enforce discriminatory contractual terms as flowing from its constitutional obligations qua state. This is because the
law does not prohibit non-state bodies from agreeing upon such
terms—unlike the activities that we are going to examine shortly. It
simply refuses to extend the contract enforcement services that the
state normally provides to discriminatory contractual terms.

Statutory (non-constitutional) duties identify certain types of
persons as the duty-bearers—usually employers,[53] landlords,[54] associations,[55] retailers,[56] service-providers,[57] educational institutions,[58]
and so on. These duties apply irrespective of whether these are state
institutions or non-state. So, the state—wearing its employer or
service-provider hat—carries these statutory duties in addition to

its constitutional anti-discrimination obligations. The duty-bearers under statutory regimes tend to be limited in three different senses. First, the sectors of human activity to which these duties apply are limited. Second, within these sectors, these duties apply unidirectionally. Finally, these statutory duties are not comprehensive, in that they govern some but not all activities of these duty-bearers.

The sectoral limitation essentially means that statutory duties in discrimination law operate in sectors such as employment, health care, provision for goods and services, education, etc. All these sectors are quasi-public inasmuch as they exclude deeply personal areas of human relationships—such as friendships and romantic relationships. It is, of course, possible to discriminate against protected groups in one's choice of friends or romantic partners—but the law tends not to regulate discrimination in deeply intimate and personal spheres. The state, on the other hand, must never discriminate: constitutional provisions are not limited to specified sectors as statutory regimes are (admittedly, it is difficult to think of examples of intimate and personal activities that the state could perform).

Second, statutory duties tend to be unidirectional, in the sense that they attach to employers but not employees or independent contractors,[59] to providers of goods and services but not to consumers,[60] to landlords but not tenants.[61] Another way of understanding this point is to reimagine the protectorate as consisting of specific groups such as consumers, employees, patients, students, tenants, citizens/subjects.[62]

Finally, unlike constitutional duties, statutory duties are not comprehensive. Constitutional duties are comprehensive in the sense that they apply to all state action.[63] It is not just certain functions that the state must discharge without discrimination. Instead, whatever the state does must be done while respecting its anti-discrimination duties. As Bamforth rightly notes, 'highly significant anti-discrimination issues nowadays arise in the context of the criminal law, police practice, judicial review (particularly in the context of immigration law), family law and property law' (Bamforth 2004: 693–5). Statutory duties, on the other hand, burden the duty-holders only when they perform certain specified functions. For example, section 29 of the UK Equality Act 2010 forbids a service-provider from discriminating in providing services. This third qualification is slightly different from, and applies in addition to, the sectoral limitation we have already discussed.

Employers usually carry anti-discrimination duties only when they do things in their capacity as employers—decisions about recruitment, terms of employment, pension, dismissal, etc. An employer is usually free to discriminate—even on protected grounds—in choosing his friends, in determining which suppliers to buy goods from, in patronizing restaurants for workplace parties, etc.[64]

The scope and weight of the duties of discrimination law vary depending on who the duty-bearer is. We will see in the next section that the state generally shoulders a heavier burden of these duties than private persons—especially when it comes to affirmative action duties. But even amongst private persons, the duty is heavier on those with greater power. For example, the UK Equality Act 2010 makes exceptions for landlords with 'small premises',[65] while the South African Employment Equity Act 1998 imposes mandatory affirmative action duties only on 'designated employers'—apart from public bodies, this category includes private employers who employ more than 50 employees or have an annual turnover above a fixed threshold.[66]—Title VII of the US Civil Rights Act only applies to employers who have 15 or more employees workers.[67] Although controversial amongst theorists, it is clear that the law is sensitive to at least some concerns relating to costs and affordability.

The Duties

The third step towards understanding the overall structure of discrimination law is to examine the shape and scope of the duties that it imposes. Contemporary discrimination law prohibits direct and indirect discrimination and harassment, requires reasonable accommodation, licenses (or mandates) affirmative action. In this section, I will explain the broad contours of each of these concepts. Before we do that, it is worth noting that there are significant differences between jurisdictions over the use of these terms—for example, reasonable 'accommodation' is reasonable 'adjustment' in British law. 'Direct' discrimination (or 'disparate treatment') was simply called discrimination, until the need to distinguish it from 'indirect' discrimination (or 'disparate impact') arose. Scholars disagree on the proper characterization of 'affirmative action'—depending on whether or not they approve of it, people characterise it as 'positive discrimination', 'positive action', 'reverse discrimination', 'compensatory discrimination', etc. Based on the form it takes, specific affirmative action measures are referred to as 'quotas', 'reservations', 'preferential treatment', 'outreach', 'access programmes', 'diversity programmes', 'indirect affirmative action', 'positive duties', and such like. I do not intend the terms to settle any ideological disputes by the choice of labels.

Most non-lawyers would associate a prohibition on discrimination primarily with a prohibition on direct discrimination. Direct discrimination (or 'disparate treatment') entails unfavourable or less favourable treatment 'on the ground of' a protected characteristic (such as race, sex, religion) or, sometimes, a combination of such characteristics (to deal with intersectional or multiple ground discrimination faced by, say, black women).[68] The first thing to note is that direct discrimination is used to characterise some form of 'treatment'—this may be an act or an omission. In other words, the norm against direct discrimination is an action-regarding norm—it makes essential reference to something done (or the failure to do something)—as opposed to a situation-regarding norm (Holmes 2005: 175). Contrary to what the American label 'disparate impact' implies, we will see shortly that the norm against indirect discrimination is also an action-regarding norm.

Second, the treatment must be 'on the ground of' (or 'because of', 'based on', 'for a reason related to') a protected characteristic. Some causal connection between the protected ground and the treatment in question is required. Opinions diverge on whether this is an objective standard or a subjective one. In the United States, courts have held that this connection is established only if a discriminatory motive, purpose, or intention on the part of the discriminator has been proved.[69] This subjective approach probes the mental state of the perpetrator in order to determine whether the causal requirement has been satisfied. A somewhat broader subjective approach—where the causation requirement is satisfied by proof of conscious as well as sub-conscious intention—has been endorsed by Lord Nicholls in the UK.[70] On the other hand, in the landmark *James* v. *Eastleigh Borough Council* case, Lord Goff considered that 'cases of discrimination ... can be considered by asking the simple question: would the complainant have received the same treatment ... but for his or her sex?'[71] This objective 'but-for' formula was motivated by a desire to avoid 'complicated questions relating to concepts such as intention, motive, reason or purpose'.[72]

In *James*, there was an exact correspondence—rather than a mere correlation—between the actual ground on which the distinction was made (pensionable age) and a protected characteristic (sex). Cases where the objective test is satisfied but the (broader) subjective test isn't will be rare. Notice that the required intention/purpose/motive is only to use the protected ground in some way—the law does not require the intention to be malicious. A subjective intent under Lord Nicholls's standard can usually be inferred from any distinction that directly relies on a protected ground. Cases where a protected ground is not directly relied upon to make a distinction are far more likely to involve indirect discrimination rather than direct discrimination à la James.

Third, while discrimination law sometimes requires proof of unfavourable treatment, at other times the claimant must show less-favourable treatment. In other words, sometimes the claimant has to show relative disadvantage owing to the treatment in comparison with a similarly situated real or hypothetical comparator, at other times non-relative disadvantage will suffice. The traditional position in most jurisdictions has been to insist upon the comparator analysis[73] —unsurprising given the assumption about the ties between discrimination and equality. Often the case turns on the choice of the appropriate comparator,[74] making the issue of comparators extremely controversial.

Apart from the difficulties in choosing the right comparator, an insistence on a comparator raises problems in cases where there is no appropriate comparator.[75] The prime example is that of discrimination based on the ground of pregnancy. In Turley, for example, a pregnant woman was recognised as 'a woman, as the Authorised Version of the Bible accurately puts it, with child, and there is no masculine equivalent.'[76] Other courts, in their desperation to find a comparator, have compared pregnancy with sickness.[77] The inadequacy of such fantastical comparisons forced courts (and legislators) to seek a non-comparative approach.[78] The non-comparative approach to pregnancy discrimination has also been extended to disability discrimination[79] and cases where multiple grounds are involved or intersectional discrimination has been claimed.[80] In other areas, although comparators are technically required, different jurisdictions place a varying degree of emphasis on this requirement. For example, in *Shamoon*, Lord Nicholls urged that:[81]

> [T]ribunals may sometimes be able to avoid arid and confusing disputes about the identification of the appropriate comparator by concentrating primarily on why the claimant was treated as she was. Was it on the proscribed ground ... or was it for some other reason?

There is some recognition that the comparator analysis is only a means to determine the causation question. Similar rulings expressing a general scepticism over the requirement of a comparator for proving direct discrimination have been made in Canada.[82] The South African Promotion of Equality and Prevention of Unfair Discrimination Act 2000 gives an entirely non-comparative definition of discrimination.[83] It is in recognition of these trends that Principle 5 of the 'Declaration of Principles of Equality' developed by the Equal Rights Trust defines direct discrimination in a manner which embraces the comparative as well as the non-comparative approach:

Direct discrimination occurs when for a reason related to one or more prohibited grounds a person or group of persons is treated less favourably than another person or another group of persons is, has been, or would be treated in a comparable situation; or when for a reason related to one or more prohibited grounds a person or group of persons is subjected to a detriment.[84]

Finally, whether and to what extent direct discrimination can be justified depends on the protected characteristic concerned and whether the norm is constitutional or statutory. There are significant jurisdictional variations too. Constitutional anti-discrimination clauses almost always permit the justification of direct discrimination, although the standard that must be met is often quite high.[85] In statutory contexts, jurisdictions differ more significantly. The US Civil Rights Act of 1964 permits limited justification of direct discrimination.[86] Canadian and South African statutes also permit the justification of direct discrimination, although the justificatory standard is quite high.[87] In the UK, direct discrimination cannot normally be justified in an adjudicative context, although there are numerous legislative exceptions to this prohibition.[88] For certain grounds, such as age, the UK allows the justification of direct as well as indirect discrimination. What remains of the blanket prohibition has been criticized by some judges who have called for some form of justification for direct discrimination.[89] The overall consensus seems to allow limited justification of direct discrimination; it also agrees that the standard of review for justifying direct discrimination is higher than that for justifying indirect discrimination.

Indirect discrimination (or 'disparate impact' as it is called in the US) involves an apparently neutral practice or policy which puts persons belonging to a protected group at a particular disadvantage.[90] The concept was first developed in the landmark American case *Griggs* v. *Duke Power Company*. The US Supreme Court held that the requirement of an educational qualification which disproportionately disqualified blacks from employment would violate Title VII of the Civil Rights Act of 1964 unless the requirement could be justified on the touchstone of business necessity.[91]

Like direct discrimination, indirect discrimination is an action-regarding norm. It is triggered by some provision, policy, practice, or criterion that the alleged discriminator applies (or seeks to apply) to the complainant. Of course, indirect discrimination is established if and only if a situation-regarding criterion—disproportionate impact on a group—is also satisfied (Holmes 2005: 175, 184). But a mere statistical disproportionality in, say, a workforce, will not amount to indirect discrimination unless it can be linked to some action, such as a provision or a policy.[92]

Second, the connection between the protected ground and the act in question is different from that in the case of direct discrimination. Instead of the decision being based on a protected characteristic, it should have a disproportionate impact on a protected group. For example, in *Griggs*, the decision had a disproportionate impact on blacks, a protected group. Indirect racial discrimination in *Griggs* was direct discrimination on the ground of educational qualification. However, educational qualification is not a protected ground, while race is. The claimant is not required to prove any discriminatory intention, motive, or purpose on the part of the employer. The apparent ground of discrimination could be anything whatsoever, what is moot is its connection with a protected ground in the context of a given case. Thus, the list of apparent grounds on which discrimination is prohibited is potentially limitless, for any such ground may be a proxy for a protected ground under certain circumstances. But these apparent grounds do not matter for their own sake. They matter because—and only because—they are proxies for protected grounds in these circumstances.

Thirdly, although indirect discrimination is structurally comparative, the nature of the comparator analysis is very different from that used in direct discrimination cases. The comparative analysis for indirect discrimination involves groups rather than individuals. Section 19(2)(b) of the UK Equality Act 2010 requires that the offending measure must put 'persons with whom [the claimant] shares the characteristic at a particular disadvantage when compared with persons with whom [the claimant] does not share it'. This usually avoids the need to find an individual 'appropriate comparator'—a search that has plagued direct discrimination jurisprudence. There are, of course, controversies surrounding comparison in indirect discrimination too—but they are of a different character. The first problem is the determination of the relevant pool within which the two comparator groups are to be identified. In the case of employment discrimination, for example, should the relevant pool be the entire population of the jurisdiction, or only the pool of persons qualified to perform the job in question, or simply the workforce of the employer? We will often arrive at different conclusions about whether a policy disproportionately excludes women in comparison to men depending on our relevant pool. The second controversy surrounds the extent of disproportionality required for it to count as indirect discrimination. For example, section 1(1)(b)(i) of the UK Sex Discrimination Act 1975 required proof of the fact that 'the proportion of women who can comply with [the requirement or condition] is considerably smaller than the proportion of men who can comply with it'.[93] Following developments in EU law, the UK Equality Act 2010 has now replaced this standard by only insisting on proof of 'particular disadvantage'.[94] Related to this is the issue of whether a claimant needs to provide statistical evidence to prove disproportionate impact, or whether a rule of thumb assessment of likely impact will suffice.[95]

Fourth, indirect discrimination is almost always justifiable. The discriminator is entitled to show that the discriminatory policy is a necessary and proportionate tool to pursue a sufficiently important objective. Although the standard required to justify indirect discrimination is usually quite high, it tends to be less exacting than justifying direct discrimination. This, along with the fact that the two forms of discrimination are considered to be mutually exclusive,[96] has led to expansionary pressures on the scope of direct discrimination. from claimants, and a concomitant backlash from defendants. These difficulties in clarifying the boundary between direct and indirect discrimination motivated the Canadian Supreme Court to reject the bifurcated approach and adopt instead a common legal response to either form of discrimination.[97] This strategy has not found favour in any of the other jurisdictions so far.

The usual remedy for unjustified indirect discrimination is a change in the offending rule, practice or policy—either the abandonment of the rule in favour of a new, non-discriminatoryone, or the retention of the old rule but with exceptions to accommodate the disadvantaged minority. In the absence of discriminatory intent, it is rare for damages to be awarded for indirect discrimination.[98]

Reasonable accommodation (or 'reasonable adjustment') is yet another facet of anti-discrimination law. Section 20 of the UK Equality Act 2010 imposes three requirements that amount to 'reasonable adjustments' in the context of disability:

> arequirement, where a provision, criterion or practice of A's puts a disabled person at a substantial disadvantage in relation to a relevant matter in comparison with persons who are not disabled, to take such steps as it is reasonable to have to take to avoid the disadvantage.
>
> a requirement, where a physical feature puts a disabled person at a substantial disadvantage in relation to a relevant matter in comparison with persons who are not disabled, to take such steps as it is reasonable to have to take to avoid the disadvantage.
>
> a requirement, where a disabled person would, but for the provision of an auxiliary aid, be put at a substantial disadvantage in relation to a relevant matter in comparison with persons who are not disabled, to take such steps as it is reasonable to have to take to provide the auxiliary aid.

'Reasonableness' must be seen as a limit to the accommodation that can be sought. The considerations that go into deciding whether an adjustment is reasonable are similar to those that determine whether an instance of indirect (or, sometimes, direct) discrimination can be justified. The right to reasonable accommodation under the Americans with Disabilities Act 1990 is available only to a 'qualified individual with a disability',[99] which is defined as 'an individual with a disability who, with or without reasonable accommodation, can perform the essential functions of the employment position that such individual holds or desires.'[100] There is no logical reason why reasonable accommodation should be limited to disability alone. Meenan argues that 'the reasonable accommodation approach of disability law could be applied to physiological changes associated with ageing'(Meenan 2007: 278, 283). Although not characterised as such, flexible working hours and parental leave provisions are examples of reasonable accommodation for women, who bear the brunt of childcare duties. So is a provision for flexible holidays to accommodate diverse religious festivals. In fact, sections 7(e) and 8(h) of the South African Equality Act require 'steps to reasonably accommodate the needs' of persons on the basis of their race and gender respectively. Here is an example of a development that is ground-sensitive in most jurisdictions, but one that is sensitive to different sets of grounds in each of them. Almost all jurisdictions provide for reasonable accommodation for disability discrimination. But some also allow it for religion, others for sex, and Canada and South Africa for all grounds. The ground-sensitivity of reasonable accommodation does not seem to be stable, and I will therefore assume that the jurisdictions are moving towards allowing it for discrimination based on any ground.

Each of the aforementioned jurisdictions envisages the failure to provide reasonable accommodation (in certain specified contexts) as a distinct wrong in discrimination law. Conceptually, however, it is difficult to imagine a case where a failure to provide reasonable accommodation will not also amount to indirect discrimination (and, sometimes, even direct discrimination, if we follow the broader understanding of this concept as envisaged in *James* v. *Eastleigh Borough Council*). This failure will always result in a protected group being disproportionately disadvantaged or even entirely excluded.[101] Thus, the duty to provide reasonable accommodation can be thought of as a form of remedy for discrimination—one that works by requiring exceptions to the general norm instead of a change in the norm itself. Indeed, in *Simpsons-Sears*, the Canadian Supreme Court accepted that reasonable accommodation was an available remedy for all forms of indirect discrimination:

Where there is adverse effect discrimination on account of creed, the offending order or rule will not necessarily be struck down. It will survive in most cases because its discriminatory effect is limited to one person or to one group, and it is the effect upon them rather than upon the general workforce which must be considered. In such cases, there is no question of justification raised because the rule, if rationally connected to the employment, needs no justification; what is required is some measure of accommodation. The employer must take reasonable steps towards that end which may or may not result in full accommodation. Where such reasonable steps, however, do not fully reach the desired end, the complainant, in the absence of some accommodating steps on his own part such as an acceptance in this case of part-time work, must either sacrifice his religious principles or his employment.[102]

The conceptual difference between the Canadian approach and that of other jurisdictions boils down simply to the fact that Canada permits discrimination to be remedied by creating exceptions to the discriminatory norm in all cases where it is possible. Other jurisdictions normally require the offending rule to be replaced by a non-discriminatory rule, except where the retention of the offending rule with exceptions is specifically authorized. The difference is significant: although it is easier to create exceptions than to reformulate general rules, the former also give the impression that a certain group is getting 'special treatment' and may be more controversial for that reason. Furthermore, the availability of a separate cause of action for reasonable accommodation in jurisdictions other than Canada allows litigants to avoid having to prove the onerous requirements for establishing indirect discrimination. These practical distinctions aside, what emerges from our discussion is the notion that the right to reasonable accommodation is best understood as a secondary right that one becomes entitled to upon breach of the primary right against direct or indirect discrimination. Secondary rights are therefore parasitic on primary rights. This understanding also shows the poverty of the simplistic approach that divides anti-discrimination duties on the basis of whether they are negative (do not discriminate) or positive (provide reasonable accommodation), and of the concomitant discomfort with reasonable accommodation duties as if they represent a startling departure from 'traditional' anti-discrimination duties (Karlan and Rutherglen 1996: 1).

We have seen that the duty to refrain from direct and indirect discrimination, and the duty to provide reasonable accommodation are usually subject to the justification defence—although some jurisdictions do not permit this for direct discrimination. For this reason, we will fail to fully understand those duties without first understanding this concept. Justification usually entails a means-end analysis where the law tests the desirability of the objective sought to be achieved, and the proportionality and necessity of the discriminatory means employed. This is often expressed as the need to demonstrate that the protected characteristic is a necessary 'bona fide occupational qualification'. The degree to which the discriminator is morally culpable and the degree to which the victim is harmed are relevant to this analysis. The intensity of judicial scrutiny of the justification defence is sensitive to the nature of the duty infringed, the protected ground in question, and the nature of the discriminator (especially whether it is a public or a private person and the degree to which it is able to bear the cost of non-discrimination).

Anti-discrimination legislation also tends to prohibit harassment 'based on' a protected characteristic, and also victimization of (or retaliation against) a complainant for having made the complaint.[103] The Equal Rights Trust defines harassment thus:

'Harassment constitutes discrimination unwanted conduct related to purpose or effect of violating the dignity or creating an intimidating, hostile, degrading, humiliating or offensive environment'.[104]

Harassment cannot be justified, perhaps because of the significant extent to which the harasser is morally culpable. This is also the reason why direct discrimination is often not justifiable, or is more difficult to justify—although the moral culpability of the direct discriminator is often less evident than that of the harasser.[105] Justification may be possible if the defendant failed to protect the claimant from harassment by a third person (for whom the defendant is legally responsible, as is an employer for the behaviour of his subordinates), especially if she can show that the harassment took place despite the reasonable steps she had taken to prevent it.

In addition to regulating discriminatory harassment, jurisdictions can, and do, prohibit harassment per se. This prohibition may constitute a criminal offence, and usually requires proof of intent. This harassment, which need not be ground-based, is not a part of discrimination law.

Finally, there is the issue of affirmative action. The term covers a wide variety of measures designed to benefit a protected group. The extent to which they actually achieve this purpose is a matter of empirical investigation and will depend on a number of contextual factors. What is essential is that their chief purpose is to benefit a group that is, in some sense, disadvantaged. Section 15 of the South African Employment Equity Act, for example, requires affirmative action in favour of 'designated groups'—section 1 defines 'designated groups' to mean 'black people, women and people with disabilities'. Similarly, Article 15(4) of the Indian Constitution permits 'any special provision for the advancement of any socially and educationally backward classes of citizens'.[106] It is, of course, possible that a group is wrongly characterised as disadvantaged—this mischaracterization may even be insidious. What is important is that even in such cases, those undertaking the measure will feel compelled to insist that the beneficiary group is actually disadvantaged. No one advocates 'affirmative action' measures for groups they openly acknowledge not to be disadvantaged. Some may object to the characterization of affirmative action as part of 'discrimination law'(See Abram 1986: 1312). Admittedly there are important distinctions between affirmative action and the other concepts examined above. What is also clear is that the practitioners—lawyers, judges, litigants, legislators—all assume that there is an essential connection between affirmative action and discrimination. Several references in the discussion that is to follow allude to anti-discrimination statutes that regulate ground-basedaffirmative action. At least insofar as the practice is concerned, discrimination and affirmative action seem to be inseparable. Because the practice is so unequivocal, theorists must not be too quick to deny this connection.

Affirmative action measures come in a variety of shapes and sizes.[107] In their broadest usage, they can be remedial or non-remedial. Remedial measures, understood narrowly, are those measures that benefit the same particular persons who suffered disadvantage due to discrimination. They respond to specific acts of direct or indirect discrimination against particular persons and are usually undertaken by the discriminator who caused the disadvantage in the first place. A good example is found in the facts of *Ricci* v. *DeStefano*, where a city discarded the results of a promotional test because no black fire-fighter passed it, and conducted a new test.[108] The city was worried that the original test may have been indirectly discriminatory. Its cancellation and the institution of a new test was therefore a remedial affirmative action. The city lost the case because it failed to show that the original test would have amounted to unjustified indirect discrimination. While this ruling is controversial for several other reasons, it does not cast doubt on the fact that at least in cases where discrimination has been or can be established, affirmative measures may be taken to stop or remedy it. This category of affirmative action measures in fact concerns the question of appropriate remedies, and is likely to be less illuminating for our purposes the notion that discriminatory acts sometimes require affirmative action to be remedied is pedestrian.

We are mainly concerned with non-remedial affirmative action measures. These measures are not designed to remedy specific acts of discrimination against particular persons, although they may well aim to remedy past discrimination against a group generally.[109] Even so, the beneficiaries need not have suffered the past discrimination personally, and the person or body undertaking the affirmative action measure may not be responsible for this past discrimination. Non-remedial affirmative action measures come in a variety of shapes and sizes. They could range from light-touch transparency-increasing measures (such as requiring the publication of the diversity profile of a workforce) to very demanding measures (such as quotas). They can be entirely voluntary, or imposed through public procurement contracts, or statutorily mandated. They can be direct, in that they directly allocate benefits to a protected group; or they can be indirect, in the sense that they are facially neutral (that is, that is, not based on a protected ground) but are designed to primarily benefit a protected group. A good example of such indirect measures is the Texan 'Top Ten Percent Law'. In 1996, the US Court of Appeal Fifth Circuit had declared direct affirmative action programmes for racial minorities unconstitutional.[110] Following this ruling, Texas enacted the Top Ten

Percent Law, requiring that 'each general academic teaching institution shall admit an applicant for admission to the institution as an undergraduate student if the applicant graduated with a grade point average in the top 10 percent of the student's high school graduating class'.[111] Increasing the intake of underrepresented minorities was the announced target of this measure, and it did succeed in increasing the number of racial minorities being admitted to Texan Universities.[112] Thus, a facially neutral policy relied on the lack of racial diversity in the high school system to increase the access of racial minorities to higher education. It is an indirect affirmative action measure because it does not rely upon race directly in order to achieve its intended objective, which is to disproportionately benefit racial minorities.[113]

We can now see the entire range of duties imposed by discrimination law—duties to refrain from direct and indirect discrimination and harassment, duties to provide reasonable accommodation, and duties to undertake positive action. These duties do not, in themselves, require the conferment of a substantive benefit (such as education, housing, employment, etc) to all members of a protected group. They control the manner in which certain allocative decisions can be made. As a result of their operation, some, but not all, members of protected groups will get access to these scarce tangible benefits. Together, these duties determine the scope of the protection of anti-discrimination law.

***

This chapter and its predecessor should have made it clear that discrimination law is unusual and complex. It protects all of us, but to varying degrees depending on the context. In particular, its protection depends on the sensitivity of the impugned act or omission to certain personal characteristics called grounds, and our membership of a protected group. This sensitivity to grounds is what distinguishes discrimination law from other welfare measures such as legal guarantees to food, healthcare, housing, etc. Any theory of discrimination law must account for this ground sensitivity generally, and explain the basis on which the protected grounds are selected. It must also justify the role that relative group disadvantage plays in determining the protection afforded.

Anti-discrimination duties are imposed not on members of advantaged groups, but on certain categories of persons which primarily include the state, employers, and providers of goods and services. These duties are imposed unidirectionally—on the employer but not the employee, on the service-provider but not the consumer, etc. Again, the scope of the duties vary depending on who the duty-holder is (especially whether it is a public or a private body) and the context where the duty is applicable. Theoretical explanations must help us understand these peculiarities.

Finally, the duties that discrimination law imposes do not guarantee access to any substantive benefits that flow from the sectors it regulates, including employment, health care, education, housing, etc. A theoretical account must tell us what interest it is, then, that discrimination law protects, and why can its infringement sometimes be justified. Some of these duties give rise to concomitant rights, others don't. An intention to discriminate is relevant for evidential or remedial reasons, but is generally not essential to prove discrimination. The role of comparators, at least in the context of direct discrimination, is shaping into a similar framework.

These are some of the central features of the doctrine of discrimination law in the chosen democratic, culturally-conversant, English-speaking, doctrine-swapping, common-law jurisdictions. These features gloss over important matters of detail, where the practice in these jurisdictions is significantly divergent. Even with respect to these core features, there are issues on which a chosen jurisdiction is an outlier. But there is remarkable consensus on most of the core issues identified in this chapter, even in theatypical jurisdictions.

Appendix: Overview of Discrimination Law in India

Duty / Ground	Direct Discrimination		Indirect Discrimination[i]		Reasonable Adjustment[ii]		Affirmative Action[iii]		Harassment[iv]
	Public Sector	Private Sector	Public Sector	Private Sector	Public Sector	Private Sector	Public Sector	Private Sector	
Sex	Prohibited[v]	Prohibited in employment[vi]	Unclear	Unclear	Provision in certain specified contexts[vii]	Provision in certain specified contexts[viii]	Permitted generally,[ix] mandated in certain contexts[x]	Not prohibited	Prohibited[xi]
Caste	Prohibited[xii]	Prohibited in certain contexts[xiii]	Unclear	Unclear	No provision	No provision	Permitted generally, mandated in certain contexts[xiv]	Not prohibited	Prohibited in certain contexts[xv]
Religion	Prohibited[xvi]	Prohibited in very limited contexts[xvii]	Unclear	Unclear	No provision	No provision	Unclear[xviii]	Not prohibited	Not prohibited
Tribe	Prohibited[xix]	Not prohibited	Unclear	Unclear	No provision	No provision	Permitted generally, mandated in certain contexts	Not prohibited	Prohibited in certain contexts[xx]

	Prohibited in certain contexts xxi	Not prohibited xxii	Prohibited in certain contexts xxiii	Not Prohibited xxiv	Limited provisions xxv	No provision	Mandated in certain contexts xxvi	Not prohibited	Not prohibited
Disability	Prohibited in certain contexts xxi	Not prohibited	Prohibited in certain contexts xxiii	Not Prohibited	Limited provisions xxv	No provision	Mandated in certain contexts xxvi	Not prohibited	Not prohibited
Sexual Orientation	Not prohibited xxvii	Not prohibited	Not prohibited	Not prohibited	No provision	No provision	Not prohibited	Not prohibited	Not prohibited
Gender Identity	Prohibited xxviii	Not prohibited	Unclear	Unclear	No provision	No provision	Mandated in certain contexts xxix	Not prohibited	Not prohibited
Linguistic Identity	Prohibited xxx	Not prohibited	Unclear	Unclear	No provision	No provision	Not prohibited	Not prohibited	Not prohibited

(Contd.)

Notes: i. The concept of 'indirect discrimination' is woefully underdeveloped in the Indian context. One of the few references to it in the constitutional context was made by the Delhi High Court in the now-overruled judgment in *Naz Foundation v. Union of India* 160 (2009) DLT 277[93]. The draft Equal Opportunities Commission Bill also mentions 'indirect discrimination'.

ii. There does not appear to be any general duty to provide reasonable accommodation under any law. The Table mentions some specific measures that may be provided in certain contexts.

iii. Although affirmative action by the state is usually permitted under the Indian constitution, there is vast jurisprudence on the extent to which it is permissible, and also on the question of identification of legitimate beneficiaries.

iv. The Delhi High Court has suggested that constitutional prohibitions on discrimination include a prohibition on harassment: see *Naz Foundation v. Union of India* 160 (2009) DLT 277, para 93. However, the High Court judgment was overturned by the Supreme Court in *Suresh Kumar Koushal v. Naz Foundation* (2014) 1 SCC1.

v. Articles 14, 15(1), 16(2) of the Constitution, ss 4, 5 of the Equal Remunerations Act, 1976.

Appendix: *(Contd.)*

vi. ss 4, 5 of the Equal Remunerations Act, 1976.

vii. S 48 of the Factories Act 1948, s 12 of the Plantation Labour Act 1951, s 14 of the Beedi and Cigar Workers (Conditions of Employment) Act 1966, etc., provide for crèches in certain contexts. S 4(3) of the Maternity Benefits Act 1961 prohibits an employer from requiring work that may interfere with the pregnancy or affect the health of a pregnant woman. S 5, Maternity Benefits Act 1961 grants a right to paid maternity leave.

viii. Same as footnote vii.

ix. Article 15(3), Constitution of India. Unlike SCs, STs and OBCs, women (in general) do not get the benefits of reservations in public employment.

x. Articles 243D and 243T reserve seats for women in local government. A Constitutional Amendment Bill pending before Parliament mandates reservation of seats for women in central and state legislatures.

xi. Vishaka v. State of Rajasthan AIR 1997 SC 3011.

xii. Articles 14, 15(1) and (2), 16(2), 17, 29(2) of the Constitution; Caste Disabilities Removal Act 1850; Protection of Civil Rights Act 1955. Although the Caste Disabilities Removal Act was passed by the colonial state to facilitate religious conversions, it was amended by independent India in 1951 and has potential for application beyond its initially intended objective.

xiii. The Caste Disabilities Removal Act 1850 prohibits the enforcement of any legal disability following 'loss of caste'; Article 15(2) and 17 of the Constitution and the Protection of Civil Rights Act 1955 prohibit certain discriminatory practices.

xiv. See Articles 15, 16, 243D, 243T, 330, 332 and 335 of the Constitution of India.

xv. S 3(x) of the Scheduled Castes and the Scheduled Tribes (Prevention of Atrocities) Act 1989 criminalizes one who 'intentionally insults or intimidates with intent to humiliate a member of a Scheduled Caste or a Scheduled Tribe within public view'.

xvi. Articles 14, 15(1), 16(2), 29(2) of the Constitution.

xvii. The Caste Disabilities Removal Act 1850 prohibits the enforcement of any legal disability following conversion; Article 15(2) of the Constitution prohibits discriminatory denial of access to shops and other public places.

xviii. It may be possible to provide affirmative action to religious groups if they constitute an 'other backward class'.

xix. Even though Articles 15(1) and 16(2) do not expressly mention tribal status as a prohibited ground, such discrimination will surely fall foul of the general provision in Article 14.

xx. S 3(x) of the Scheduled Castes and the Scheduled Tribes (Prevention of Atrocities) Act 1989 criminalizes one who 'intentionally insults or intimidates with intent to humiliate a member of a Scheduled Caste or a Scheduled Tribe within public view'.

xxi. (Arguably) under Article 14 of the Constitution; also Persons with Disabilities Act 1995.

xxii. In *Dalco Engineering v. Padhye* (2010) 4 SCC 378, the Supreme Court held that the Persons with Disabilities Act 1995 does not apply to the private sector.

xxiii. Ss 44-46 of the Persons with Disabilities Act 1995 appear to prohibit indirect discrimination on public transport, roads and buildings, without expressly using the term 'indirect'.

xxiv. In Dalco Engineering v. Padhye (2010) 4 SCC 378, the Supreme Court held that the Persons with Disabilities Act 1995 does not apply to the private sector.

xxv. S 38(1)(d) of the Persons With Disabilities Act 1995, for example, makes provision for the 'creation of a non-handicapping environment'. A proposed amendment to the Act seeks to introduce a general right to 'reasonable accommodation' by stating that its denial amounts to discrimination.

xxvi. See s 43 of the Persons with Disabilities Act 1995.

xxvii. Koushal v. Union of India (2014) 1 SCC 1.

xxviii. National Legal Services Authority v. Union of India 2014 (5) SCALE 1.

xxix. National Legal Services Authority v. Union of India 2014 (5) SCALE 1 [60].

xxx. Articles 14, 29(2) of the Constitution.

Notes

    * This chapter is based on material from Khaitan (2015), chapter 3.

1.   *Lane* v. *Cotton* [1558–1774] All ER Rep 109 KB, 114. The quotation is from a dissenting opinion, but the statement of law contained therein is not contested by the majority.

2. *Constantine* v. *Imperial London Hotels* [1944] KB 693. See also, *Rothfield* v. *The North British Railway Company* [1920] SC 805; Kline (1917-18: 123; 1919: 109); Avins (1968: 1–7).

3. (Galanter 1978). In footnote 1 on page 1821, Galanter cites an affirmative action policy dating back to 1895.

4. (Bamforth, O'Cinneide, and Malik 2008: 19–23). Other questions include the possibility of justifying impermissible discrimination in certain contexts, any exceptions from the protection, clash between anti-discrimination and other rights, non-legal remedies, etc.

5. See Canadian Charter, SA Promotion of Equality Law, ECHR, Canadian Human Rights Act.

6. See generally, *Law* v. *Canada* [1999] 1 SCR 497 [39], [62]-[75]. US 14th Amendment is an exception, in that there are no specified grounds—all protected grounds have been determined by judicial interpretation.

7. For example, Canadian Charter of Fundamental Rights and Freedoms, s 15.

8. *Andrews* v. *Law Society of British Columbia* [1989] 1 SCR 143[51]. See also, *R.* v. *Turpin* [1989] 1 SCR 1296 [52]; *Egan* v. *Canada* [1995] 2 SCR 513[180].

9. Apart from their numerical insignificance, foreigners often do not have the right to vote. Graham v. Richardson 403 US 365 (1971), 372. See also In *Re Griffiths* 413 US 717. *Sugarman* v. *Dougall* 413 US 634; Examining Board of Engineers v. Flores de Otero 426 US 572; *Andrews* v. *Law Society of British Columbia* [1989] 1 SCR 143[31], [51].

10. *Hoffmann* v. *South African Airways* 2001 (1) SA 1 [28].

11. *National Coalition for Gay and Lesbian Equality* v. *Minister of Justice* 1999 (1) SA 6 [25] and fn 32.

12. *Frontiero* v. *Richardson* 411 US 677 (1973) 686 fn 17: although women were not a numerical minority, they 'are vastly underrepresented in this Nation's decision making councils. There has never been a female President, nor a female member of this Court. Not a single woman presently sits in the United States Senate, and only 14 women hold seats in the House of Representatives. And ... this

underrepresentation is present throughout all levels of our State and Federal Government.' See also, *Watkins* v. *United States Army* 875 F2d 699, 727: the 'very fact that homosexuals have historically been underrepresented in … political bodies is itself strong evidence that they lack the political power necessary to ensure fair treatment at the hands of government'.

13. *Frontiero* v. *Richardson* 411 US 677 (1973) 685: In the past, women could not 'hold office, serve on juries, or bring suit in their own names, and married women traditionally were denied the legal capacity to hold or convey property or to serve as legal guardians of their own children'—even the right to vote was denied to them for long. See also *United States* v. *Virginia* 518 US 515, 531. See generally, *United States* v. *Carolene Products* 304 US 144, 153 (1938), footnote 4, per Justice Stone: 'prejudice against discrete and insular minorities may be a special condition, which tends seriously to curtail the operation of those political processes ordinarily to be relied upon to protect minorities, and which may call for a correspondingly more searching judicial inquiry.'

14. For an analysis of the institutional implications of political disadvantage, see J.H. Ely (1980).

15. Most of the insights in this paragraph are borrowed from Alexander (1992).

16. (Choudhry. 2000: 145, 156). '…Irrational proxies are so tightly linked to prejudice that discrimination relying on the former is tantamount to discrimination motivated by the latter.'

17. *Lawrence* v. *Texas* 539 US 558, 580.

18. See, for example, *R.* v. *Turpin* [1989] 1 SCR 1296[52].

19. 'The result of being responsible for children makes it more difficult for women to compete in the labour market and is one of the causes of the deep inequalities experienced by women in employment': *President of RSA* v. *Hugo* 1997 (4) SA 1 CC [38]. 'In the private sphere, homosexuals continue to face discrimination in jobs, housing and churches': *Watkins* v. *United States Army* 875 F2d 699, 724. See also, *Frontiero* v. *Richardson* 411 US 677 (1973) 686; *Harksen* v. *Lane* NO 1998 (1) SA 300 CC[63]; *Hoffmann* v. *South African Airways* 2001 (1) SA 1[28].

20. The South African Constitutional Court has taken notice of incidents of societal hostility and threats faced by aliens as evidence of their disadvantage: *Larbi-Odam* v. *Member of the Executive Council for Education* 1998 (1) SA 745[20]. See also, *Watkins* v. *United States Army* 875 F2d 699, 724: 'it is indisputable that homosexuals have

historically been the object of pernicious and sustained hostility' and that 'reports of violence against homosexuals have become commonplace in our society'. See further, *Egan* v. *Canada* [1995] 2 SCR 513[182]; *M* v. *H* 171 DLR (4th) 577 [64], [69].

21. Sen criticizes the focus on income as the primary focus in analysing inequality (Sen 1992: 28–30).

22. *Regents of the University of California* v. *Bakke* 438 US 265, 395-6.

23. *Korematsu* v. *United States* 323 US 214 (1944) 243. See also, *Fullilove* v. *Klutznick* 448 US 448, 496: Justice Powell said that 'Racial classifications must be assessed under the most stringent level of review because immutable characteristics, which bear no relation to individual merit or need, are irrelevant to almost every governmental decision'. See also *R.* v. *McKitka* [1987] BCJ No 3210 [20]. Sunstein also talks of the 'accident of birth' being irrelevant morally: Cass R. Sunstein, 'The Anticaste Principle' (1994) 92 *Michigan Law Review* 2410, 2434; likewise, Justice Murphy noted the 'accident of race or ancestry' while reluctantly concurring with the racial classification: *Hirabayashi* v. *United States* 320 US 81, 111.

24. *Korematsu* v. *United States* 323 US 214 (1944) 243: the appellant 'belongs to a race from which there is no way to resign'; *Fullilove* v. *Klutznick* 448 US 448 (1980) 496: 'Racial classifications must be assessed under the most stringent level of review because immutable characteristics, which bear no relation to individual merit or need, are irrelevant to almost every governmental decision.'; *Andrews* v. *Law Society of British Columbia* [1989] 1 SCR 143 [75]: 'The characteristic of citizenship is one typically not within the control of the individual and, in this sense, is immutable. Citizenship is, at least temporarily, a characteristic of personhood not alterable by conscious action and in some cases not alterable except on the basis of unacceptable costs.'

25. *R.* v. *McKitka* [1987] BCJ No 3210 [20]: 'the enumerated categories of s 15 all tend to reflect ... how, when and where we come into this world, matters over which we have no control.'; *Hirabayashi* v. *United States* 320 US 81 (1943) 111: 'The difference between their innocence and his crime would result, not from anything he did, said, or thought, different than they, but only in that he was born of different racial stock.'; *Weber* v. *Aetna Casualty & Surety Company* 406 US 164 (1972) 175: 'no child is responsible for his birth and penalizing the illegitimate child is ... unjust'.

26. *Frontiero* v. *Richardson* 411 US 677 (1973) 686: Sex is determined 'solely by the accident of birth'.

27. '[N]o child is responsible for his birth and penalizing the illegitimate child is ... unjust': *Weber* v. *Aetna Casualty & Surety Company* 406 US 164, 175. See also *Mathews* v. *Lucas* 427 US 495, 505; *Clark* v. *Jeter* 486 US 456, 461; *Milne* v. *Alberta* [1990] 5 WWR 650 [37]. In Plyler, a law denying educational benefits to children of unlawful immigrants was held to be 'directed against children, and imposes its discriminatory burden on the basis of a legal characteristic over which children can have little control': *Plyler* v. *Doe* 457 US 202, 220.

28. In San Antonio, the dissenting opinion of Justice Marshall held that classification 'between the schoolchildren of Texas on the basis of the taxable property wealth of the districts in which they happen to live' was a basis upon which the 'individual has no significant control' *San Antonio Independent School District* v. *Rodriguez* 411 US 1 (1973), 96.

29. *Larbi-Odam* v. *Member of the Executive Council for Education* 1998 (1) SA 745 [19]. See also, *Andrews* v. *Law Society of British Columbia* [1989] 1 SCR 143 [75]: 'The characteristic of citizenship is one typically not within the control of the individual and, in this sense, is immutable. Citizenship is, at least temporarily, a characteristic of personhood not alterable by conscious action and in some cases not alterable except on the basis of unacceptable costs.'

30. (Yoshino 1998: 495–8) This distinction between corporeal and social characteristics must be taken with a pinch of salt. Almost all 'corporeal' characteristics are mediated by socio-cultural norms to some extent. Clothing, contact lenses, artificial colour, high-heeled boots, and make-up are capable of masking our 'corporeal' characteristics like sex, eye-colour, hair-colour, height, and physical appearance respectively. See also (Butler 1999: 10-11) 'If the immutable character of sex is contested, perhaps this construct called "sex" is as culturally constructed as gender; indeed, perhaps it was always already gender, with the consequence that the distinction between sex and gender turns out to be no distinction at all.'

31. *High Tech Gays* v. *Defense Industrial Security Clearance Office* 895 F2d 563, 573. See also *Miron* v. *Trudel* [1995] 2 SCR 418 (Canada) [28], [57]; *R.* v. *Baig* [1990] BCJ No 203 (British Columbia County Court, Canada); *Delisle* v. *Attorney General of Canada* [1999] 2 SCR 989 (Canada) [44].

32. See Butler 1999: 10–11, quoted in note 30.

33. *Watkins* v. *United States Army* 875 F2d 699.

34. Justice Mokgoro seems to have effective mutability in mind when she says that 'citizenship is a personal attribute that is difficult to change':

Larbi-Odam v. *Member of the Executive Council for Education* 1998 (1) SA 745[19]. *Corbiere* v. *Canada* [1999] 2 SCR 203 [13]: 'what these grounds have in common is the fact that they often serve as the basis for stereotypical decisions made not on the basis of merit but on the basis of a personal characteristic that is immutable or changeable only at unacceptable cost to personal identity'. See also, *Egan* v. *Canada* [1995] 2 SCR 513 [5]: Justice La Forest considered sexual orientation to be either 'unchangeable or changeable only at unacceptable personal costs'.

35. *Watkins* v. *United States Army* 875 F2d 699, 726. See also Yoshino (2001–2002: 769).

36. *Miron* v. *Trudel* [1995] 2 SCR 418 [97]-[98]. See also, *Harksen* v. *Lane* NO 1998 (1) SA 300 CC [92]: 'the decision to enter into a permanent personal relationship with another is a momentous and defining one'; *Harksen* v. *Lane* NO 1998 (1) SA 300 CC[123]-[124]: classifications on the basis of marital status degraded the 'moral citizenship (independence and self-fulfilment) of persons who happen to be married'; *Watkins* v. *United States Army* 875 F2d 699, 726: 'allowing the government to penalize the failure to change such a central aspect of individual and group identity would be abhorrent to the values animating the constitutional ideal of equal protection of the laws'; *Andrews* v. *Law Society of British Columbia* [1989] 1 SCR 143[19]: 'Distinctions based on personal characteristics attributed to an individual solely on the basis of association with a group will rarely escape the charge of discrimination'.

37. See *Brooks* v. *Canada Safeway Ltd.* [1989] 1 SCR 1219 (Canada) [31].

38. *Miron* v. *Trudel* [1995] 2 SCR 418 [97]-[98].

39. *Harksen* v. *Lane* NO 1998 (1) SA 300 CC [92].

40. *Nyquist* v. *Mauclet* 432 US 1, 12.

41. See generally, Fiss (1976: 107); Abram (1986: 1312); Yoshino (1988: 485).

42. *United States* v. *Stanley* (The Civil Rights Cases) 109 US 3 (1883).

43. See generally, Bamforth (2004: 693–701).

44. See, for example, the 14th Amendment to the Constitution of the United States ['No state shall ... deny to any person ... the equal protection of the laws']; Article 14 of the European Convention for the Protection of Human Rights and Fundamental Freedoms, read with Protocol 12 ['No one shall be discriminated against by any public authority ...']; Article 15 of the Constitution of India

['The state shall not discriminate against any citizen ...']; Article 15 of the Canadian Charter of Rights and Freedoms ['Every individual is equal before and under the law and has the right to the equal protection and equal benefit of the law without discrimination ...'].

45. Section 8(2) of the Constitution of the Republic of South Africa: 'No person shall be unfairly discriminated against...'

46. Article 19 of the Consolidated version of the Treaty on the Functioning of the European Union, Official Journal C 115, 09/05/2008 P. 0001 - 0388: The European Union ... 'may take appropriate action to combat discrimination based on sex, racial or ethnic origin, religion or belief, disability, age or sexual orientation.' See also, Article 21(1) of the Charter of Fundamental Rights of the European Union: 'Any discrimination based on any ground ... shall be prohibited.'

47. *Washington* v. *Davis* 426 US 229 (1976).

48. See generally, Hunt (1998: 429–35); Bamforth (1999: 159, 168–70).

49. *Retail, Wholesale and Department Store Union* v. *Dolphin Delivery Ltd* [1986] 2 SCR 573[39].

50. *Campbell* v. *MGN Ltd* [2004] UKHL 22[17].

51. In *Ghaidan* v. *Godin-Mendoza* [2004] UKHL 30, a private landlord was not allowed to take possession of a flat from the surviving same-sex spouse of the deceased tenant. The House of Lords interpreted the law governing landlord-tenant relationship to protect same-sex as well as opposite-sex couples.

52. *Shelley* v. *Kramer* 334 US 1 (1948).

53. S 39 UK Equality Act; 42 USC § 2000e-2, s 7 Canadian Human Rights Act.

54. UK Equality Act s 33; 42 USC § 2000a; s 6 Canadian Human Rights Act.

55. UK Equality Act s 101.

56. S 29 read with s 31(2) UK Equality Act; s 5, Canadian Human Rights Act.

57. UK Equality Act 2010 s 29; s 5 Canadian Human Rights Act.

58. UK Equality Act ss 85, 91; 42 USC § 2000c-1.

59. It is possible for an employer to be vicariously liable for the discriminatory acts of an employee: s 110 UK Equality Act.

60. *Mingeley* v. *Pennock* [2004] EWCA Civ 328, [2004] ICR 727 (CA).

61. For a general treatment of this argument, see McCrudden (1982: 303).

62. Constitutional duties prohibit the state from discriminating against all citizens/subjects, even when it is a consumer of goods and services

rather than the provider, and not just when it is a landlord but also when it is a tenant.

63. See, for example, the 14th Amendment to the Constitution of the United States ['No state shall ... deny to any person ... the equal protection of the laws']; Article 14 of the European Convention for the Protection of Human Rights and Fundamental Freedoms, read with Protocol 12 ['No one shall be discriminated against by any public authority ...']; Article 15 of the Constitution of India ['The state shall not discriminate against any citizen ...']; Article 15 of the Canadian Charter of Rights and Freedoms ['Every individual is equal before and under the law and has the right to the equal protection and equal benefit of the law without discrimination ...'].

64. The one exception to these differences between constitutional and statutory duties is found in the South African Promotion of Equality and Prevention of Unfair Discrimination Act 2000, which prohibits all forms of unfair discrimination by all persons—public and private—in all contexts, perhaps due to the bitter legacy of apartheid.

65. Schedule 5 paras 3-4.

66. Section 13 read with section 1, South African Employment Equity Act 1998.

67. 42 USC § 2000e (b).

68. Canadian Human Rights Act s 3.1, UK Equality Act s14, *Corbiere* v. *Canada* [1999] 2 SCR 203[61].

69. *Washington* v. *Davis* 426 US 229 (1976), 240, 2048.

70. *Constable of West Yorkshire Police* v. *Khan* [2001] UKHL 48, [29]; *Nagarajan* v. *London Regional Transport* [2000] 1 AC 501, 511-2.

71. *James* v. *Eastleigh Borough Council* [1990] 2 AC 751, 774.

72. *James* v. *Eastleigh Borough Council* [1990] 2 AC 751, 774.

73. UK Sex Discrimination Act 1975 s 1: 'In any circumstances relevant for the purposes of any provision of this Act, other than a provision to which subsection (2) applies, a person discriminates against a woman if—(a) on the ground of her sex he treats her less favourably than he treats or would treat a man...'

74. See *Auton* v. *British Columbia* [2004] 3 SCR 657 Supreme Court of Canada.

75. It is also alleged that insisting on a comparator encourages assimilation of minority cultures (especially religious and queer cultures). Because the relevant comparator is invariably an idealised member of the majority community, it is claimed that such comparisons normalize majority values and make them aspirational (even

when there may not be anything intrinsically wrong with minority values).

76. *Turley* v. *Allders Department Stores Ltd* [1980] ICR 66, 70. See also, *Geduldig* v. *Aiello* 417 US 484 (1974).

77. *Hayes* v. *Malleable Working Men's Club* [1985] ICR 703, 708: 'the proper approach is to ask whether pregnancy with its associated consequences is capable of being matched by analogous circumstances such as sickness applying to a man...'

78. *Dekker* v. *Stichting* (VJV- Centrum) Plus C-177/88 [1991] IRLR 27; C-32/93 *Webb* v. *EMO Air Cargo* [1994] ECR I-03567 [24-5]. See also, Paul Lewis, 'Pregnant Workers and Sex Discrimination: the Limits of Purposive Non-Comparative Methodology' (Spring 2000) The International Journal of Comparative Labour Law and Industrial Relations 55, the United States Pregnancy Discrimination Act 1978 and United Kingdom Equality Act 2010 s 18.

79. UK Equality Act 2010, s 15: although this provision is entitled 'discrimination arising from disability' and treated distinctly from 'direct discrimination' in the statutory scheme, it is best understood as an instance of direct discrimination.

80. *Hassam* v. *Jacobs* [2009] ZACC 19.

81. *Shamoon* v. *Chief Constable of the Royal Ulster Constabulary* [2003] UKHL 11 [11].

82. *R.* v. *Kapp* 2008 SCC 41 [22]; *Withler* v. *Canada* [2011] SCC 12 [2], [60].

83. s 1: '"discrimination" means any act or omission ... which directly or indirectly—(a) imposes burdens, obligations or disadvantage on; or (b) withholds benefits, opportunities or advantages from, any person on one or more prohibited grounds'.

84. Declaration of Principles of Equality (Equal Rights Trust 2008).

85. In the United States, this standard is famously sensitive to the protected ground involved. Race discrimination gets 'strict scrutiny' while gender gets 'intermediate scrutiny'. See generally, Suzanne Goldberg, 'Equality Without Tiers' (2004) 77 Southern California Law Review 481.

86. 42 USC § 2000e-2(e) (2013).

87. Canadian Human Rights Act 1985, s 15; SA Employment Equity Act 1998, s 6(2).

88. UK Equality Act 2010, s 15, schedules 5, 7, 9, 11, 16 and 18.

89. *R. (on the application of E)* v. *Governing Body of JFS* [2009] UKSC 15 [9]: 'there may well be a defect in our law of discrimination. In contrast to the law in many countries, where English law forbids direct discrimination it provides no defence of justification.'

90. See, *Griggs* v. *Duke Power Co* 401 US 424; section 703 of Title VII of the US Civil Rights Act of 1991. See also, section 19(2) of the UK Equality Act 2010: 'a provision, criterion or practice is discriminatory in relation to a relevant protected characteristic of B's if

(a) A applies, or would apply, it to persons with whom B does not share the characteristic,
(b) it puts, or would put, persons with whom B shares the characteristic at a particular disadvantage when compared with persons with whom B does not share it,
(c) it puts, or would put, B at that disadvantage, and
(d) A cannot show it to be a proportionate means of achieving a legitimate aim.'

91. *Griggs* v. *Duke Power Co* 401 US 424 (1971).
92. *Wards Cove Packing Co* v. *Atonio* 490 US 642 (1989), 656.
93. Emphasis mine.
94. UK Equality Act 2010 s 19(2)(b).
95. *Wards Cove Packing Co* v. *Atonio* 490 US 642 (1989), C-237/94 *O'Flynn* v. *Adjudication Officer* [1996] 2 CMLR 103 ECJ.
96. *R. (on the application of E)* v. *Governing Body of JFS* [2009] UKSC 15 [57].
97. *British Columbia (Public Service Employee Relations Commission)* v. *BCGEU* [1999] 3 SCR 3.
98. UK Equality Act s 124(4)&(5), 42 USC § 1981a.
99. 42 USC 12112(a).
100. 42 USC 12111(8).
101. See also, Section 21(2), UK Equality Act 2010.
102. *Ontario Human Rights Commission* v. *Simpsons-Sears Ltd* [1985] 2 SCR 536 [23]. See also, Canadian HRA s 15(2).
103. See, for example, sections 14 & 14.1 of the Canadian Human Rights Act 1985.
104. Principle 5, Declaration of Principles of Equality (Equal Rights Trust 2008).
105. *R. (on the application of E)* v. *Governing Body of JFS* [2009] UKSC 15 [9]: 'Nothing that I say in this judgment should be read as giving rise to criticism on moral grounds of the admissions policy of JFS in particular or the policies of Jewish faith schools in general, let alone as suggesting that these policies are "racist" as that word is generally understood.'
106. Also see UK Equality Act 2010 s 158 and Canadian Employment Equity Act 1995 s 2.

107. These distinctions are adapted, with significant modifications, from McCrudden (2011: 157).
108. *Ricci* v. *DeStefano* 557 US 557 (2009).
109. See *Canadian National Railway* v. *Canadian Human Rights Commission* [1987] 1 SCR 1114.
110. *Hopwood* v. *Texas* 78 F 3d 932 (1996) US Court of Appeal 5th Circuit.
111. Texas Education Code § 51.803 (1997).
112. *Fisher* v. *University of Texas at Austin* 631 F 3d 213 (2011) US Court of Appeals 5th Circuit 224.
113. On indirect affirmative action, see generally, Sabbagh (2011: 470).

References

Abram, M.B. 1986. 'Affirmative Action: Fair Shakers and Social Engineers', *Harvard Law Review*, 99(6): 1312–16.

Alexander, L. 1992.'What Makes Wrongful Discrimination Wrong? Biases, Preferences, Stereotypes and Proxies', *University of Pennsylvania Law Review*, 141(1): 149–219.

Avins, A. 1968. 'What is a Place of "Public? Accommodation?', *Marquette Law Review*, 52(1): 1–7.

Bamforth, N. 1999. 'The Application of the Human Rights Act 1998 to Public Authorities and Private Bodies', *Cambridge Law Journal*, 58(1): 159–70.

Bamforth, N. 2004. 'Conceptions of Anti-Discrimination Law', *Oxford Journal of Legal Studies*, 24(4): 693–716.

Bamforth, N., C. O'Cinneide and M. Malik. 2008. *Discrimination Law: Theory and Context* (Text and Materials). London: Sweet & Maxwell.

Butler, J. 1999. *Gender Trouble: Feminism and the Subversion of Identity* (10th anniversary edn.). London: Routledge.

Choudhry, S. 2000. 'Distribution vs. Recognition: The Case of Anti-Discrimination Laws', *George Mason Law Review*, 9(1):145–77.

Ely, J.H. 1980. *Democracy and Distrust: A Theory of Judicial Review.* Cambridge, Mass.: Harvard University Press.

———. 1976. 'Groups and the Equal Protection Clause', *Philosophy and Public Affairs* 5(2): 107–177.

Fishkin, J. 2014. *Bottlenecks: A New Theory of Equal Opportunity.* USA: Oxford University Press.

Fiss, O. 1974. 'The Fate of an Idea whose Time has Come: Anti-discrimination law in the Second Decade after Brown v. Board of Education'. *University of Chicago Law Review,* 41(4):742–73. UK: Aldershot.

Galanter, M. 1978. 'Who are the Other Backward Classes?: An Introduction to a Constitutional Puzzle' *Economic and Political Weekly,* 13(43/44): 1812–28.

Gibson, D. 1991. 'Analogous Grounds for Discrimination Under the Canadian Charter: Too Much Ado About Next to Nothing', *Alberta Law Review*, 29(4): 772–91.

Holmes, E. 2005. 'Anti-Discrimination Rights Without Equality', *Modern Law Review*, 68(2): 175–94.

Hunt, M. 1998. 'The "Horizontal Effect" of the Human Rights Act', *Public Law,* 423–436.

Karlan, P. and Rutherglen, G. 1996. 'Disabilities, Discrimination, and Reasonable Accommodation', *Duke Law Journal*, 46(1): 1–41.

Kessler, L. 2001. 'The Attachment Gap: Employment Discrimination Law, Women's Cultural Caregiving, and the Limits of Economic and Liberal Legal Theory', *University of Michigan Journal of Law Reform*, 34(3): 371–469.

Khaitan, T. 2008. 'Transcending Reservations: A Paradigm Shift in the Debate on Equality', *Economic and Political Weekly*, XLIII(38): 8–12.

———. 2013. 'Prelude to a Theory of Discrimination Law', in D. Hellman and S. Moreau (eds), Philosophical Foundations of Discrimination Law. UK: Oxford University Press.

———. 2015. A Theory of Discrimination Law. UK: Oxford University Press.

Kline, B. 1917–18. 'The Origin of the Rule Against Unjust Discrimination', *University of Pennsylvania Law Review* 66 (3/4): 123–156.

———. 1919. 'The Scope of the Rule Against Unjust Discrimination by Public Servants', *University of Pennsylvania Law Review*, 67(2): 109–135.

Kristen, E. 2002. 'Addressing the Problem of Weight Discrimination in Employment', *California Law Review*, 90(1): 57–109.

Mandal. B.P., 1980. Report of the Second Backward Classes Commission. New Delhi: Government of India.

McCrudden, C. 1982. 'Institutional Discrimination', *Oxford Journal of Legal Studies*, 2(3): 303–367.

McCrudden. C. 1991. 'Introduction' in C. McCrudden (ed), *Anti-Discrimination Law*. Aldershot, UK: Ashgate/Dartmouth.

———. 2004. 'Introduction' in C. McCrudden (ed.), *Anti-Discrimination Law* (2nd edn,). Aldershot, UK: Ashgate/Dartmouth.

———. 2011. 'A Comparative Taxonomy of "Positive Action" and "Affirmative Action" Policies', in R. Schulze (ed.), *Non-Discrimination in European Private Law*, pp.157–80. Tübingen, Germany: Mohr Siebeck.

Meenan, H. 2007. 'Age Discrimination—Of Cinderella and The Golden Bough' in H. Meenan, *Equality Law in an Enlarged European Union:*

Understanding the Article 13 Directives, pp. 278–312. Cambridge, United Kingdom: Cambridge University Press.

Post, R.C., K. Anthony Appiah, Judith Butler, Thomas C. Grey and Reva B. Siegel. 2001. *Prejudicial Appearances: the Logic of American Antidiscrimination Law*. Durham: Duke University Press.

Sabbagh, D. 2011. 'The Rise of Indirect Affirmative Action', World Politics, 63(3): 470–508.

Sen, A. 1992. *Inequality Reexamined*. Oxford: Clarendon Press.

Silvers, A. and M.A. Stein. 2002. 'An Equality Paradigm for Preventing Genetic Discrimination', *Vanderbilt Law Review*, 55 (5) 1341–95.

Sunstein, C.R. 1994. 'The Anticaste Principle', *Michigan Law Review*, 92 (8): 2410–55.

Timmer, A. 2011. 'Towards an Anti-Stereotyping Approach for the European Court of Human Rights'. *Human Rights Law Review*, 11(4): 707–38.

Wintemute, R. 1995. *Sexual Orientation and Human Rights: The United States Constitution, the European Convention, and the Canadian Charter*. Oxford: Clarendon Press.

Yoshino, K. 1998. 'Assimilationist Bias in Equal Protection: The Visibility Presumption and the Case of "Don't Ask, Don't Tell"', *Yale Law Journal*, 108 (3): 485–571.

———. 2001–2002. 'Covering', *Yale Law Journal*, 111: 769.

5

Elements toward a Comparative Analysis of Affirmative Action Policies

Daniel Sabbagh

Broadly defined, affirmative action encompasses any measure that allocates goods—such as admission into selective universities or professional schools, jobs, promotions, public contracts, business loans, rights to buy, sell or use land...through a process that takes into account individual membership in designated groups, in order to increase the proportion of members of those groups in the relevant population, where they are currently underrepresented as a result of past or present (illegitimate) discrimination by state authorities or private agents.[1] 'Unlike traditional welfare policies grounded in distributional equity, affirmative action takes its moral force from a corrective justice ideal' (Pager 2007: 289–356): it targets a specific type of disadvantage arising from the illegitimate use of a morally irrelevant characteristic of individuals in the allocation of scarce resources. Yet these measures, which may result from constitutional mandates, statutes, administrative regulations, court orders, or voluntary initiatives, go beyond anti-discrimination strictly conceived, insofar as they do not require evidence of discrimination on an individual basis. Their goal is to counter deeply entrenched social practices that reproduce group-structured inequality even in the absence of intentional discrimination, by producing positive externalities beyond their individual recipients. They usually benefit groups 'with whose position and esteem in society the affiliated individual may be inextricably involved'.[2]

Beyond this most general definition, affirmative action policies vary substantially across countries, regarding the identification of their intended beneficiaries (ethnic, racial, or religious groups (or castes) held to be economically and/or socially disadvantaged, aboriginal peoples, women, the handicapped, war veterans...), the form of the programmes involved (quota/non-quota), the level (constitutional, legislative, administrative) of the legal norms from which they derive, and their domain of implementation.[3] They also vary in the explicitness with which and the extent to which group membership operates in the decision-making process. In this respect, at least three different types of affirmative action may be identified:

The first one is indirect (yet intentional) affirmative action, that is, policies that are apparently neutral but actually designed to benefit disadvantaged groups and that might be construed as 'disparate impact' discrimination if the distribution of their costs among groups affected by them were just the opposite of what it is. In the case of gender, an example would be a requirement in hiring and promotion decisions to take into account experience in looking after children and to ignore seniority.[4] In the case of race and ethnicity, an example would be the French formally 'color-blind' yet arguably 'race-oriented' policies under which residents of educationally and/or economically disadvantaged areas benefit from the additional input of financial resources allocated by the state to those areas as a whole, since some of the criteria used for delineating the latter (the rate of failure in high school, the unemployment rate, and the percentage of residents under 25 years old) are correlated with ethnic (African) origin (Sabbagh 2004: 246–58). In that case a 'substitution strategy' is being used, under which what looks like the secondary effect of a formally neutral principle of allocation is at least in part the reason why that principle has been adopted in the first place, given the perceived illegitimacy and/or unlawfulness of pursuing the decision-maker's true objective in a more straightforward manner (Elster 1992: 116–20).

The second kind of affirmative action consists in outreach measures and other proactive policies designed only to bring a more diverse range of candidates into a recruitment (or promotion) pool. In that case, group membership is explicitly taken into account, but in a limited way: it is allowed to enter the picture only within the preliminary process of enlarging the set from which individuals will eventually be selected, not at the selection level itself. An example in British law would be the section of the 1976 Race Relations Act allowing employers to grant 'persons of a particular racial group access to facilities or services to meet the special needs of persons of that group in regard to their … training…'.[5]

The third kind of affirmative is positive discrimination, that is, measures that grant an advantage to the members of designated groups in the final decision over the allocation of scarce goods through more or less flexible policy instruments (compulsory quotas, aspirational 'goals' or 'targets', or simple tie-break rules). In that case, an applicant from one of the designated groups (DGA 1) will be selected for a position (for which he or she is minimally qualified) in spite of there being at least one applicant from a non-designated group whose qualifications were deemed to be higher. 'Higher' means that if another applicant from a designated group (DGA 2) had come up with exactly the same qualifications as the applicant who was not selected, the person in charge of making the selection would have selected him/her instead of DGA 1 (Nagel 1973: 348). In other words, group membership is the key factor triggering the outcome: DGA1 succeeds in obtaining the position that he/she applied for and would have failed but for his/her being identified as a member of a designated group. As a general matter, positive discrimination can thus can be criticized for being in conflict with two distinct principles more or less widely embraced in the different societies under consideration: the meritocratic principle, according to which the most qualified applicant for a position should always be selected, and the principle of 'color (gender/caste/religion….)-blindness', under which it would always be intrinsically wrong to draw distinctions on the basis of such characteristics—for state authorities at least.

Because, as a matter of fact, this third type of affirmative action is the main subject of current political and legal controversies, the following developments will focus on it exclusively. More specifically, by broadening the spectrum of comparison beyond a couple of unavoidably idiosyncratic cases,[6] my goal is in part to identify some common trends that obtain despite major differences in national models of citizenship among countries that have set up affirmative action programmes (sections first and second). This comparative inquiry should also help one to assess the importance of numbers in accounting for the diverging patterns that do persist—at least in democratic settings where the majority group is bound to be the politically dominant one (third section).

The Political Origins of Affirmative Action as a Strategy for Conflict Management in Deeply Divided Societies

With the important exceptions of Brazil and of India—where reservations themselves and, most of all, their extension to a broader group of beneficiaries over time are the factor that has led to substantial protest and violence by urban upper-caste youth in northern states (Jaffrelot 2006: 184–5)—, the common feature of the contexts in which affirmative action policies of the positive discrimination variety have been set up is the existence of a risk of mass violence threatening the very legitimacy of the state. Those are countries that could believe themselves to be on the brink of civil war, or at least had experienced some serious unrest. Affirmative action, then, was partly understood as a last-resort device designed to deal with a major crisis or prevent the occurrence of an impending one, in circumstances where the preservation of the social compact itself seemed to be at stake. As explained by Justice Albie Sachs of the South African Supreme Court, countries that introduce affirmative action 'do so not to meet widely proclaimed human rights standards but, sadly, because the social and economic costs of change are outweighed by the social and economic costs of policing the status quo. Put bluntly, affirmative action has frequently come about as a rushed and forced response to what have been called race riots' (Sachs 2006: ix).

The United States is a case in point. As shown by John David Skrentny, the emergence of American positive discrimination programmes was the somewhat paradoxical outcome of a reversal in law and policy that took place in a remarkably short span of time, during the second half of the 1960s (Skrentny 1996: 67–110).

Indeed, not only did the Congress fail to provide such programmes with a constitutional foundation—unlike in India, Malaysia, or South Africa; it had also enacted a statute—the 1964 Civil Rights Act—which seemed to preclude their coming into existence. Now covering private employers with 15 or more employees, federal, state, and local governments, educational institutions, employment agencies, and labour unions, that statute prohibited discrimination on the basis of race, colour, religion, sex, and national origin. One of its key provisions was its Title VII, which declared it 'an unlawful employment practice for an employer...to fail or refuse to hire or to discharge any individual or otherwise to discriminate against any individual with respect to his compensation, terms, conditions, or privileges of employment, because of such individual's race, color, religion, sex or national origin'.[7] Thus, even though the motivating force behind the introduction of the bill on the legislative agenda was most certainly to end the discrimination suffered by blacks, whites were also protected from all kinds of race-based discrimination in employment. Furthermore, section 703 (j) of Title VII explicitly stated that employers would not be required

> to grant preferential treatment to any individual or to any group because of the race, color, religion, sex, or national origin of such individual or group on account of an imbalance which may exist with respect to the total number or percentage of persons of any race, color, religion, sex, or national origin ... in comparison with the total number or percentage of persons of such race, color, religion, sex, or national origin in any community, State, section, or other area, or in the available work force in any community, State, section, or other area.

Yet the first affirmative action programs were to be implemented only a few years later.

While no single factor entirely accounts for this dramatic policy innovation, the atmosphere of emergency created by the unprecedented wave of race riots that major American cities (New York, Los Angeles, Detroit...) faced between 1964 and 1968—with several hundred deaths as a result—clearly played an important role. During that period, as Doug McAdam has argued, 'the level of open defiance of the established economic and political order was as great

... as during any other in th[e] country's history, save the Civil War'
(McAdam 1982: 182). In this highly unstable political context, the
federal government basically accepted as accurate black leader A.
Philip Randolph's warning that 'the Negro ghettoes in every city
throughout the nation [were] areas of tension and socio-racial
dynamite, near the brink of similar explosions of violence'.[8] The
objective of reducing the unemployment of young urban African
Americans—understood as the underlying cause of that violence—
now seemed compelling enough to justify considering new and more
radical measures that would have been dismissed (and actually had
been dismissed) as illegitimate and/or illegal a few years earlier. To
be sure, the National Advisory Commission on Civil Disorders—a
commission set up by President Johnson to investigate the causes
of the riots and chaired by the governor of Illinois, Otto Kerner—
mentioned neither racial quotas nor even more flexible goals. Yet,
although the means necessary for implementing its prescriptions
were left unspecified, the seriousness of the crisis and the breadth
of the commitment needed to prevent other riots from occurring
were now clear. Thus, it should come as no surprise that the causal
relationship between those outbursts of racial violence and the introduction of affirmative action programmes was most immediately
perceptible in the field of law enforcement. The contrast between
the racial distribution of the police force—from which blacks and
Hispanics were almost completely absent—and that of the urban
population living in its area of intervention did look like a recipe for
further trouble. Therefore, one of the main recommendations submitted by the Kerner Commission was to 'increase substantially the
recruitment of Negroes in the Army National Guard'. That blacks
made up only 1.15 per cent of its members in August 1967 was
viewed as a 'deficiency [to] be corrected as soon as possible' (Lawson
1984: 1237). From then on, some kind of affirmative action beyond
outreach was clearly on the agenda.

   In the United States the role of interracial strife in creating for political elites a new decision-making environment that proved conducive
to the introduction of race-based positive discrimination was made
particularly visible by the existence of a contradictory prescription of
'color-blindness' apparently enshrined in a statute enacted only a few
years earlier. Yet a similar dynamic has been operating in many other

countries. In Malaysia, it is commonly acknowledged that the riots of May 1969 between Chinese and Malay residents of Kuala Lumpur, which resulted in a death toll of several hundred persons (most of them Chinese), prompted not only a markedly authoritarian turn of the Malaysian political system—reflected in the declaration of emergency, the suspension of Parliament, and the transfer of power to the National Operations Council—, but also the introduction in 1971 of a 'New Economic Policy' (NEP) extending affirmative action from the public to the private sector, under the notion that the key to restoring some minimal inter-communal harmony lay in reducing the income and wealth gap between the politically dominant Malays and the economically successful Chinese. Similarly, in Northern Ireland, in contrast to the theoretically non-compulsory nature of 'positive action' programmes for private employers in mainland UK, continued violence and the need to defuse the tension sustained by persistent discrimination on a religious basis has opened the way for the emergence of a stronger affirmative action regime. Thus, in accordance with the Fair Employment Act of 1989, all public authorities and private sector employers with more than 10 employees are required to register with the Fair Employment Commission—now the Equality Commission—and periodically submit reviews on the religious composition of their workforce; when the workforce is unbalanced, the employer is under an obligation to consider implementing an affirmative action programme, which will generally include goals and timetables.[9] Also, in what so far remains the only example of a mandatory quota in UK law, section 46 of the Police (Northern Ireland) Act 2000 requires equal numbers of Catholics and non-Catholics to be appointed to the Police Service from a pool of qualified applicants.[10] Even in France, where according to the prevailing legal doctrine colour-blindness has been constitutionalized,[11] the most blatant violation of that rule occurred during the Algerian War of Independence, as an ultimately unsuccessful attempt to legitimize the colonial order by co-opting its subjects in greater numbers.[12] The existence of a causal link between the occurrence or the likelihood of violence disruptive of the current political order and the introduction of affirmative action programmes—a link observed in otherwise strikingly different cultural and legal environments—is thus hard to deny.

Expansion as a Structural Feature of Affirmative Action Regimes

While in theory the goal of special treatment for members of disadvantaged groups is to make the need for it disappear as rapidly as possible, as a practical matter those programmes are difficult to dislodge. Although affirmative action usually has been conceived and justified as a temporary measure,[13] it tends to become permanent in democratic societies, where benefits once given cannot easily be withdrawn. Insofar as the resilience of policies and institutions is determined by the effects they produce, and in particular by the benefits they provide to those who will then be led to support them, there is no guarantee that states will ever have enough leeway to end affirmative action once the policy has achieved its goal, assuming that moment can be identified in a non-arbitrary way. In many cases affirmative action programmes have even expanded in scope, either embracing more groups or spreading to wider realms for the same groups—or both.

In the United States, for instance, affirmative action almost immediately spread from one unquestionably oppressed group (native-born blacks) outward to other groups with arguably a lesser need for remedial treatment (other ethno-racial minorities whose size was just about to increase dramatically as a result of immigration reform—Hispanics and Asians—as well as women),[14] without much thought being given to the consequences that might be expected from that extension of the policy's range. It was the exceptional experience of African Americans and the impulse to remedy the injustice inflicted upon them that permitted the principle of affirmative action to be (imperfectly) legitimized in the first place and subsequently to be picked up by other groups who would not have been able to make the original claim (Skrentny 2006: 1762–1815). Yet, even if it had been 'politically feasible and socially desirable' to cast affirmative action as a corrective measure predicated upon the sui generis nature of the African American experience and exclusively designed to undo the harm suffered by members of that particular group as far as possible, the Supreme Court held it could not legitimately do so. The reason was that this would require a comparative assessment of the degrees of victimization experienced by all groups with potential claims for affirmative action benefits, an assessment involving a 'kind of variable sociological and political analysis (...) [that] does not lie within judicial competence'.[15] Instead, the Court has conditioned the use of race-based affirmative action on enhancing the diversity of viewpoints represented in higher education,[16] an argument safer from this institutional, self-legitimizing perspective, but which clearly does not help prevent the policy from being extended to an ever-broader set of groups—quite the contrary. Finally, affirmative action also spread from its beginnings in the requirements of the federal government on public contractors to universities, state and local governments, private employment, and the policies of regulatory agencies in granting licences (not an exhaustive list). And while in some domains the Supreme Court did make the policy's conditions of validity more restrictive over time,[17] in others—such as higher education—it confirmed the constitutionality of affirmative action provided the programmes remain suitably informal (Sabbagh 2007).

Similarly, in India the extension of quotas in university admissions and government employment (although not in the field of electoral representation) from Scheduled Castes (SCs)[18] and Scheduled Tribes (STs)[19] to the more numerous (52 per cent of the Indian population in 1980) and somewhat better-off other low castes is certainly striking. This transformation of the national affirmative action regime into one benefiting ascriptive (non-gender) groups that make up a majority of the population—like in Malaysia and South Africa—is all the more noticeable as it had to overcome some protracted, large-scale resistance from different quarters over a period of several decades.

Affirmative action began under British colonial rule as a set of programmes designed for the advancement of the 'untouchables', first in the field of education—a network of special schools was established for their benefit as early as 1892—then in the civil service and political representation, with reserved seats for them on the provincial legislative councils and in the central legislative assembly from 1919 onwards (Jaffrelot 2006: 174–5). As noted by Frank de Zwart, initially 'the British motive for starting these programs was to promote representative bureaucracy for purposes of effective government, not socio-economic equality' (De Zwart 2000: 244). Besides, only in south India—where members of the upper castes were only about 5 per cent of the population and were, therefore, not in a position to oppose the rising tide of caste-based reservations as effectively as in the north—did strong anti-Brahmin movements lead to the extension of affirmative action benefits to the lower castes (other than SCs) before independence (Jaffrelot 2006: 181).

After independence, the 1950 Indian constitution—inspired by the emancipatory vision of its chief architect, Dr B.R. Ambedkar—retained the principle of affirmative action for the most disadvantaged groups (SCs and STs) by mandating the reservation of a proportional number of seats for them in the federal[20] and state[21] legislative assemblies and enabling states to set aside a population-linked share of government jobs and places in educational institutions for their benefit. Also, while it officially abolished untouchability[22] and prohibited discrimination on grounds of religion, race, caste, sex, and place of birth,[23] it provided for the possible extension of quotas to groups other than SCs and STs in its Article 15(4): 'Nothing in this article [stating a general antidiscrimination principle] ... shall prevent the State from making any special provision for the advancement of any socially and educationally backward classes of citizens or for the Scheduled Castes and the Scheduled Tribes'. Yet, while the principle of affirmative action was constitutionally sanctioned, the ratios to be used, and even the definition of the relevant groups—in the case of these 'Other Backward Classes' (OBCs)—were left for state governments to determine, and by no means was it pre-ordained that caste should be their defining feature. Aside from the cases of SCs and STs, both the constituent assembly and successive parliaments after independence expected the criteria of 'backwardness' to be defined in economic terms and dismissed the recommendations of the different Backward Classes Commissions that caste be relied on for that purpose for about 40 years (Jaffrelot 2006: 177–9). Although the OBCs had been granted affirmative action benefits in some individual states and provinces, it was not until the beginning of the 1990s that the 1978 proposal by the Mandal Commission to add a national 27 per cent quota in government jobs for OBCs to the existing 22.5 per cent quota for SCs (15 per cent) and STs (7.5 per cent) was adopted and received the imprimatur of India's Supreme Court.[24]

Finally, there has been a progression in the domains where reservations have been provided—from admission to state colleges and professional schools for SCs and STs to appointments to the state and central administrative services and, eventually, access to almost any position in the public sector. Thus, the Central Educational Institutions (Reservation in Admission) Act of 2006 extended the 27 per cent reservation for the OBCs to all government-funded institutions of higher education, a law whose constitutionality the Indian Supreme Court upheld in April 2008.[25] As economic liberalization under the direction of the International Monetary Fund and the World Bank's Structural Adjustment Programme and its attendant privatization of government sector jobs have drastically reduced the reach of affirmative action since the beginning of the 1990s, bringing the private sector under the purview of the reservation policy is also being debated.

In short, as suggested by juxtaposing those condensed summaries of the historical development of the US and Indian affirmative action regimes, whether or not the political legitimacy of the policy has been buttressed by an explicit authorization for its enactment being inserted into the constitution itself, in cases where initially the groups that are supposed to benefit from it were stigmatized numerical minorities, one witnesses an increase in the number of beneficiaries and/or policy areas covered. That a similar expansion also takes place in countries where affirmative action has been constitutionalized in more specific terms and benefits numerical majorities is, therefore, hardly surprising.

Affirmative Action for Politically Dominant yet Economically Disadvantaged Groups

In most countries where the beneficiaries of affirmative action (women excepted) are or originally were minority groups, the legal validity of a programme of this kind will depend upon whether it meets a set of formal requirements. The most important of those is that the outcome of the decisional process by which scarce goods are being allocated should not be exclusively determined by group membership. Thus, in the 1963 *Balaji* v. *State of Mysore* decision, the Indian Supreme Court, while not objecting to the use of caste as a criterion for the identification of backwardness, held that it could not be the only factor considered for that purpose. This holding is similar to the 1978 *Regents of the University of California* v. *Bakke* decision of the US Supreme Court allowing race to be taken into account in university admissions as long as it is treated as one among many potentially 'diversity'-enhancing features, to be weighed against all the others.[26] In the same vein, the European Court of Justice has opposed schemes for appointment or promotion under which women were to be automatically preferred to men[27] yet approved of 'a tie-break rule giving preference to women where women and men are equally qualified, as long as an equally qualified male had the opportunity to establish that a reason specific to his case should tilt the balance in his favour'.[28] In contrast, in Malaysia and South Africa, two developing countries and former British colonies where the disadvantaged groups that receive the benefits of affirmative action are numerical majorities, because there is no seriously threatening challenge to the legitimacy of positive discrimination as a matter of principle, programmes that qualify as such, unsurprisingly, are more extensive, more explicit, and less subject to formal constraints. This pattern common to Malaysia and South Africa stands as the product of a conjunction of demographic, economic, and legal factors.

On the demographic side, it is certainly significant that, as a result of the shift that saw the Malay population expanding and Chinese numbers contracting following the secession of Singapore from the Federation of Malaya in 1965, in Malaysia those who benefit from affirmative action—the ethnic Malays, also called bumiputeras ('sons of the soil'), and other indigenous groups—now comprise 65 per cent of the estimated 27.5 million population, while the Chinese are 26 per cent and the Indians nearly 8 per cent.[29] Similarly, in post-apartheid South Africa, according to figures from 2011, 'blacks' (including 'Africans', 'Coloureds' and 'Indians/Asians') made up 90.6 per cent of the estimated 51.8 million population, and whites 8.9 per cent.[30]

On the economic side, in both cases the extent of group inequality that affirmative action aimed at reducing was especially impressive. In Malaysia, in 1970 the mean household income for Malays was 172 dollars per month, as against 304 dollars for Indians and 394 dollars for Chinese. Among those classified as poor, 74 per cent were Malays, and among all Malays 65 per cent were poor—compared to 26 per cent of Chinese and 39 per cent of Indians. Whereas foreigners held 63.3 per cent of capital and non-Malay Malaysians 34.3 per cent,

Malays held only 1.6 per cent (Crouch 1996: 21). In South Africa, in 1995, whites—12.9 per cent of the population—had 58.6 per cent of total personal income, whereas Africans—who made up 76.2 per cent of the population—received 29.3 per cent of income share (Van der Westhuizen 2002: 127). In 1998, whites made up 86 per cent of managers still; Africans were 6 per cent, and Coloureds and Indians were 4 per cent each (Jain, Sloane, and Horwitz 2003: 35). The racial wage differential was also substantial: in the mid-1990s, the average wage of an African worker was one-fifth of that of a white one, although half of that discrepancy was explained by differences in education and location (Schultz and Mwabu 1997: 1).

On the legal side, because the marginalization of the bumiputeras through their relegation in the rural component of the economy was then widely understood as resulting from the large-scale immigration of the Chinese and Indians encouraged by the British as part of their standard divide-and-rule policy, special rights for Malays were entrenched in the 1957 Federal Constitution of Malaysia as a necessary step toward the eradication of the old colonial order. Under this new 'social contract', the non-Malay minorities, in return for being granted citizenship based on the principle of jus soli, agreed to have privileges conferred on the Malays in order to uplift their economic position. As a result, Article 8(5) makes clear that the general principle of non-discrimination on the basis of 'religion, race, descent, gender, or place of birth' enshrined in Article 8(2) does not ban provisions for the advancement of Malays; and Article 153(2) goes into an unusual level of detail by specifying that those provisions will consist in

> reservation[s] for Malays and natives of any of the States of Sabah and Sarawak of such proportion as ... may [be] deem[ed] reasonable of positions in the public service ... and of scholarships ... and other similar educational or training privileges or special facilities given or accorded by the Federal Government and, when any permit or licence for the operation of any trade or business is required by federal law, then, subject to the provisions of that law and this Article, of such permits and licences.

Also, in another remarkable extension of the affirmative action principle, Article 89 empowers state authorities to reserve areas of land for exclusive bumiputera ownership. Last but not least, in the aftermath of the 1969 riot, the 1948 Sedition Act was revised so as to make it illegal to question 'any matter, right, status, position, privilege, sovereignty or prerogative established or protected by the provisions of...Article...153...of the Federal Constitution'.[31] In Malaysia, criticizing affirmative action thus constitutes a criminal offence punishable by up to 3 years in jail[32]—a provision with no equivalent in any other country.

In South Africa the 1996 constitution was also designed to forestall any argument as to the permissibility of positive discrimination for members of disadvantaged groups, with a view to avoiding legal controversies of the kind that were then unfolding in the United States. Section 9 (2) thus states that 'to promote the achievement of equality, legislative and other measures designed to protect or advance persons, or categories of persons, disadvantaged by unfair discrimination may be taken'.[33] Section 9 (3) indicates that 'the state may not unfairly discriminate directly or indirectly against anyone on one or more grounds, including race, gender, sex, pregnancy, marital status, ethnic or social origin, colour, sexual orientation, age, disability, religion, conscience, belief, culture, language and birth'.[34] Section 9 (5) makes clear that, in some cases, discrimination may be considered 'fair', and the 1998 Employment Equity Act confirms that 'affirmative action' measures by 'designated employers' vis-à-vis members of 'designated groups' fall under this rubric.[35]

In Malaysia, in the aftermath of the events that made curbing group inequality appear more urgent than ever, the constitutional status of affirmative action provided the central government with an already familiar set of policies whose scope would then be substantially enlarged for the sake of political stability. Thus, in a major departure from the laissez-faire economic approach that had guided Malaysian development since independence, in 1971 the government launched the 'New Economic Policy' (NEP), which basically extended the principle of reservations for bumiputeras from the public to the private sector. It had two primary objectives: to reduce and eventually eradicate poverty; and to promote 'the restructuring of society so as to eliminate the identification of race with economic function',[36] with a view to making the distribution of the workforce in each economic sector reflect the racial composition of the population by 1990.[37] To this end, in addition to providing credit, training, and business sites to Malay businessmen, the government has acquired shares in private corporations on behalf of bumiputeras, with a view to reaching an objective of 30 per cent bumiputera corporate ownership (Abdullah 1997: 189–221). The project of bringing about a radical, large-scale social transformation, which arguably underlies affirmative action policies even in liberal democracies (Sabbagh 2007: 97–101), was thus made strikingly—and unusually—explicit.

Similarly, some of the specific features of the South-African brand of affirmative action reflect a particularly high level of commitment to the policy. Thus, not only does the 1998 Employment Equity Act provide that 'every designated employer must, in order to achieve employment equity, implement affirmative action measures for people from designated groups ... [in order] to ensure their equitable representation in all occupational categories and levels of the workforce'; in addition, the law explicitly states that those measures 'include preferential treatment'.[38] Furthermore— and most distinctively—under Section 20 (5) of the Act a designated group member's lack of the necessary qualifications is not a sufficient reason for hiring a non-designated group member instead: the employer 'may not unfairly discriminate against a person solely on the grounds of that person's lack of relevant experience',[39] the only legitimate matter of concern being the applicant's 'capacity to acquire, within a reasonable time, the ability to do the job'.[40] By rejecting the very criterion of merit as conventionally defined by the current level of qualification, South African law thus embraces a conception of affirmative action that responds most directly to historical circumstances in which the majority of the population, defined by race, was systematically deprived of opportunities to gain expertise relevant to managerial positions. This is evidence of the comparatively high degree of legitimacy that the principle of affirmative action still has in that country, a fact largely explained by the obviousness of the causal link between current group inequality and the recently dismantled and morally discredited apartheid regime. In this case, affirmative action most visibly partakes of a simultaneously corrective and prospective strategy geared toward the de-racialization of power and the structural transformation of the polity in an egalitarian direction, in line with the reference in the Preamble of the 1993 Interim Constitution to the 'crea[tion] of a new order'[41] and the Postamble's definition of this document's ultimate purpose as being no less than the 'reconstruction of society'.[42]

***

At the end of this preliminary and highly condensed comparative overview of affirmative action policies and their legal underpinnings in states faced with the challenge of overcoming major societal cleavages, the following tentative conclusions may be drawn. Positive discrimination exists in numerous jurisdictions. As a general matter, it is found in countries where economic inequalities track boundaries between groups defined on the basis of largely immutable traits such as race, ethnicity, or caste—at least in part as a result of prior action by state authorities—and where such inequalities are plausibly understood as undermining the legitimacy of the existing political order. Over time, there is also a tendency for the policy to target more groups and/or to spread to new decisional domains. Still, beyond these two structural features, some positive discrimination regimes are more far-reaching and more explicit than others. This is, no doubt, explained in part by the fact that, in those cases, affirmative action benefits the—ethnically or racially defined—majority holding political power. It is also explained by the greater scale of the problem to be dealt with and the arguably greater risk involved in the failure to solve it, in the context of a recent and still imperfectly stabilized regime change.

As for the consequences of affirmative action, they can be examined from at least two different perspectives. One may consider either the policy's immediate quantifiable objectives—did it entail an increase in the proportion of jobs, public contracts, and admission offers at selective universities obtained by the targeted groups over a period of time, and to what extent?—or its contribution towards the ultimate goal of facilitating the integration of minority groups into society at large, beyond the distribution of those specific resources. However, that second goal is not always present to the same degree. In Malaysia, for instance, reducing the inequality in the distribution of social goods between groups is clearly not conceived as partaking of the more utopian project of abolishing group boundaries within the nation-state. Giving communities their proportional share of some social benefits is not supposed to lead to the blurring of the lines that keep them separate from each other in other, non-allocative spheres. In the United States and in France, on the other hand, the connection between policies equalizing patterns of economic distribution and the ideal of societal integration is much stronger.

That distinction is relevant to the key question of how to define the preconceived social outcome the attainment of which would justify the termination of affirmative action programs. In the first case—that of Malaysia—the proportionality criterion provides an obvious standard, generally acknowledged as such. In the second case—that of the United States—proportional representation is emphatically rejected as a distributive principle, even though it arguably operates at the policy-making level covertly, by providing the benchmark against which 'discrepancies' and 'deficiencies' will be identified and compensated for. Yet, at the end of the day, one may argue that the ultimate goal of affirmative action will be reached only when it will not occur to anyone to check on the percentage of African American students or employees anymore. For if the reference to eye-colour—as the prototypical example of a physical characteristic as non-salient as race should eventually become, according to the colour-blind ideal—is such a familiar feature of the affirmative action debate, it is less because we know that there is no correlation between that socially unimportant trait and the position held by individuals in the economic and occupational hierarchy than because no one would even think of undertaking an empirical investigation designed to investigate whether there is one. In this respect, at least in countries where the ideal of societal integration is the strongest, one of the many paradoxes of affirmative action arguably lies in this attempt to organize the disappearance of the policy's own conditions of possibility.

Notes

1. As a general matter, discrimination consists of practices that impose a relative disadvantage on persons based on their perceived membership

in a salient social group. In this descriptive, morally neutral sense, to classify an action as discrimination leaves open the question of whether it can be justified (Singer 1978). Also, it is analytically useful to distinguish 'discrimination in contract'—'the unequal treatment of otherwise like persons...in the execution of formal transactions'—from 'discrimination in contact'—'the unequal treatment of persons...in the associations and relationships that are formed among individuals in the informal, private spheres of life'. This is so because 'ending discrimination in contract can [not]...ensure equality of developmental opportunity' when 'discrimination in contact' persists (Loury 2002: 95, 99).

2. US Supreme Court decision, *Beauharnais* v. *Illinois* (343 US 250 (1952)), p. 263.

3. While in the United States, Canada, South Africa, Malaysia, and Northern Ireland affirmative action programmes cover both the public and the private sectors, in India the entire sphere of private employment is excluded from reservations.

4. See the European Court of Justice decision, *Badeck and others* v. *Hessische Ministerpräsident*, Case C-158/97, 2000. http://www.lex. unict.it/eurolabor/en/documentation/sentenze/causa158-97en.htm. Accessed 02 May 2015.

5. Race Relations Act (1976), part VI, section 35. http://www.statutelaw.gov.uk/content.aspx?ActiveTextDocId=2059995. Accessed 02 May 2015.

6. For another—-more polemical—attempt in this direction, see Sowell 2004.

7. Civil Rights Act (1964), Title VII, section 703 (a). http://www.eeoc. gov/policy/vii.html. Accessed 02 May 2015.

8. Quoted in Skrentny (2006: 77).

9. Fair Employment (Northern Ireland) Act 1989, Section 31 http:// www.opsi.gov.uk/acts/acts1989/Ukpga_19890032_en_1. Accessed 02 May 2015.

10. See the 2002 decision by the Northern Irish High Court in the Matter of an Application by Mark Parsons for Judicial Review (NIQB 46) (rejecting a challenge to that quota).

11. Article 1 of the French Constitution of 1958 provides that 'the Republic ... ensures the equality of all citizens before the law, without any distinction of origin, race, or religion'. Available at http://www.legifrance. gouv.fr/html/constitution/constitution2.htm. Accessed 02 May 2015.

12. Between 1958 and 1960 affirmative action measures for Algerian-born French Muslims including straight quotas—were enacted through executive orders (ordinances) so as to promote their integration into

selected components of the civil service and public administration; see Shepard 2011: 291–2.

13. In India, the original reservations specified in the constitution of 1950 were set to expire 10 years later; yet they have since been extended by amendment several times for additional 10-year periods. In Malaysia, preferences for Malays enshrined in the 1957 constitution were supposed to remain in place for a period of 15 years only and be repealed in 1972—but they were not. On the US case, see the Supreme Court decision *United Steelworkers* v. *Weber*, 443 US 193 (1979), p. 208.

14. In 1967 Executive Order 11375 expanded the coverage of the 1965 Executive Order 11246 on affirmative action to include women. Available at http://www.dotcr.ost.dot..gov/documents/ycr/eo11375.htm. Accessed 02 May 2015.

15. *Regents of the University of California* v. *Bakke*, 438 U.S. 265 (1978), p. 297.

16. *Grutter* v. *Bollinger*, 539 U.S. 306 (2003).

17. 'Minority set-asides' are a case in point: see *Adarand Constructors, Inc.* v. *Pena*, 515 US 220 (1995).

18. According to the 2011 Census, SCs are 16.2 per cent of the Indian population. http://censusindia.gov.in/Census_Data_2001/India_at_glance/scst.aspx. Accessed 02 May 2015.

19. According to the 2011 Census, STs are 8.2 per cent of the Indian population. Available at http://censusindia.gov.in/Census_Data_2001/India_at_glance/scst.aspx. Accessed 02 May 2015.

20. The Constitution of India, Article 330. Available at http://www.servat.unibe.ch/icl/in00000.html. Accessed 02 May 2015.

21. The Constitution of India, Article 332. Available at http://www.servat.unibe.ch/icl/in00000.html. Accessed 02 May 2015.

22. The Constitution of India, Article 17. Available at http://www.servat.unibe.ch/icl/in00000.html. Accessed 02 May 2015.

23. The Constitution of India, Articles 15 (1) and 16 (2). Available at http://www.servat.unibe.ch/icl/in00000.html. Accessed 02 May 2015.

24. *Indra Sawhney* v. *Union of India*, All Indian Reporter 1993 S.C. 477 (India). The reason why the OBCs—52 per cent of the Indian population—were granted a quota almost twice smaller than their proportion is that in an earlier decision, *Balaji* v. *State of Mysore* (All India Reporter 1963 SC 649), the Supreme Court had capped at 50 per cent the percentage of goods to be distributed through reservations by any single decisional unit—and a proportional quota of 22.5 per cent of government jobs and university spots had already been introduced for SCs and STs (who then represented 15 per cent and 7.5 per cent of the

Indian population respectively). Thus, the 3,743 castes identified in the Mandal report as making up the OBCs for all practical purposes were to receive only what was left of the 50 per cent available for reservation after the SC and ST quotas had been taken into account. The SCs and STs had their own separate reservations; they did not have to compete for reserved seats against the more numerous and frequently more affluent and influential OBCs. Similarly, in the *Indra Sawhney* decision, in order to address the concern that the benefits of reservations were not distributed evenly throughout each backward group but instead were monopolized by persons at the socio-economic top of the group, the Supreme Court emphasized the necessity of combining caste and class for ascertaining whether a specific individual ought to be eligible for such benefits. It thus ruled that OBC membership only created a rebuttable presumption that a member needs affirmative action (*Indra Sawhney* v. *Union of India*, pp. 558–60) and it directed the government to adopt an economic means tests in order to screen out those advanced backward class members—the so-called 'creamy layer'—who did not need government assistance, thus defusing a major issue of contention. However, this disaggregation of the group of potential affirmative action beneficiaries according to class criteria and the restriction that follows, often discussed but never implemented in the United States, apply only to the OBCs; SCs and STs remain out of reach of this newly enforced trimming process. In this respect, too, and in sharp contrast with the US affirmative action regime—in which policy-makers and judges alike have avoided answering the question of whether minorities benefiting from the policy might have differential needs for it—members of the groups generally considered as the most disadvantaged are being granted a compensatory advantage also in relation to the other beneficiaries of the programmes involved.

25. *Ashoka Kumar Thakur* v. *Union of India and Others* etc., 6 SCC 1 (10 April 2008).

26. *Regents of the University of California* v. *Bakke*, pp. 315-18.

27. *Kalanke* v. *Freie Hansestadt Bremen*, case C-450/93 (1995).

28. *M. H. Marshall* v. *Southampton and South-West Hampshire Area Health Authority*, C-271/91, European Court of Justice (1993).

29. See http://www.state.gov/r/pa/ei/bgn/2777.htm. Accessed 02 May 2015. According to the 1970 census, at about the time when the New Economic Policy was introduced, the bumiputeras and other indigenous groups already made up 55.5 per cent of the Malaysian population, while Chinese were 34.1 per cent, and Indians 9 per cent (Crouch 1996: 14).

30. Available at http://www.southafrica.info/about/people/population.htm. Accessed 02 May 2015.
31. Sedition Act 1948 (Act 15), section 3(1) (f). Available at http://www.agc.gov.my/agc/oth/Akta/Vol.%201/Act%2015.pdf). Accessed 02 May 2015.
32. Sedition Act 1948 (Act 15), section 4(1) (d).
33. Constitution of the Republic of South Africa, Act No.108 of 1996, Chapter 2, section 9(2). Available at http://www.gov.za/documents/constitution/1996/96cons2.htm#9). Accessed 02 May 2015.
34. Constitution of the Republic of South Africa, Act No.108 of 1996, Chapter 2, section 9(3) (emphasis added)
35. Employment Equity Act, No. 55 of 1998, section 6(2). Available at http://www.workinfo.com/Free/Sub_for_legres/data/equity/Act551998.htm. Accessed 02 May 2015.
36. Official Website of the Economic Planning Unit, Prime Minister's Department (Malaysia), introduction. Available at http://www.epu.jpm.my/new%20folder/development %20plan/2nd%20opp%20content/2nd%20outline(chap%204-i).htm. Accessed 02 May 2015.
37. Initially, the clustering of the different groups in distinct occupations was remarkable: the Chinese were concentrated in urban commerce and in tin-mining communities, the Indians in rubber plantation labour, and the Malays in the rice-farming peasantry.
38. Employment Equity Act, Section 15(3). Under this same Section, quotas are excluded, however. In this respect the South African case stands as an exception to the otherwise observable pattern connecting the constitutionally sanctioned nature of affirmative action with the use of this most rigid instrument (Malaysia, India) and the absence of an explicit constitutional authorization for the policy with the prevalence of supposedly flexible goals—like in Canada and the United States.
39. Employment Equity Act, Section 20(5).
40. Employment Equity Act, Section 15(3), Employment Equity Act, Section 20(3) (d).
41. Constitution of the Republic of South Africa Act 200 of 1993. Available at http://www.justice.gov.za/trc/legal/sacon93.htm). Accessed 02 May 2015.
42. Constitution of the Republic of South Africa Act 200 of 1993, "National Unity and Reconciliation" Section.

References

Abdullah, F.H. 1997. 'Affirmative Action Policy in Malaysia: To Restructure Society, to Eradicate Poverty', *Ethnic Studies Report*, XV(2): 189–221.

Crouch, H.A. 1996. *Government and Society in Malaysia*. Ithaca (NY): Cornell University Press.

De Zwart, F. 2000. 'The Logic of Affirmative Action: Caste, Class and Quotas in India', *Acta Sociologica*, 43(3): 244.

Elster, J. 1992. *Local Justice: How Institutions Allocate Scarce Goods and Necessary Burdens*. Cambridge: Cambridge University Press.

Jaffrelot, C. 2006. 'The Impact of Affirmative Action in India: More Political than Socioeconomic', *India Review*, 5(2): 173–89.

Jain, H.C., P.J. Sloane and F.M. Horwitz. 2003. *Employment Equity and Affirmative Action: An International Comparison*. Armonk (NY): M.E. Sharpe.

Lawson, S.F. (ed.), 1984. 'Letter from the Kerner Commission to President Johnson', in *Civil Rights during the Johnson Administration, 1963–1969*, Frederick: University Publications of America, [microfilm, Yale University library], part 1, reel 10, frame 1237.

Loury, G. 2002. *The Anatomy of Racial Inequality*. Cambridge (Mass): Harvard University Press.

McAdam, D. 1982. *Political Process and Development of Black Insurgency, 1930–1970*, Chicago: The University of Chicago Press.

Nagel, T. 1973. 'Equal Treatment and Compensatory Discrimination', *Philosophy and Public Affairs*, 2(4): 348.

Pager, S.A. 2007. 'Anti Subordination of Whom? What India's Answer Tells Us about the meaning of Equality in Affirmative Action', *University of California at Davis Law Review*, 41(1): 289–356.

Sabbagh, D. 2004. 'Affirmative Action at Sciences Po', in H. Chapman and L.L. Frader, (eds). *Race in France: Interdisciplinary Perspectives on the Politics of Difference*, pp. 246–58. New York: Berghahn Books.

———. 2007. *Equality and Transparency: A Strategic Perspective on Affirmative Action in American Law*. New York: Palgrave Macmillan.

Sachs, A. 2006. 'Foreword' in Elaine Kennedy-Dubourdieu, (ed.), *Race and Inequality: World Perspectives on Affirmative Action*, p. ix. Aldershot: Ashgate.

Schultz, T.P. and G. Mwabu. 1997. 'Labour Unions and Distribution of Wages and Employment in South Africa', Discussion Paper No. 776, Economic Growth Centre: Yale University, p. 1. Available at http://www.econ.yale.edu/growth_pdf/cdp776.pdf. Accessed 02 May 2015.

Shepard, T. 2011. 'Algeria, France, Mexico, UNESCO: A Transnational History of Anti-racism and Decolonization, 1932–1962', *Journal of Global History*, 6(2): 273–97.

Singer, P. 1978. 'Is Racial Discrimination Arbitrary?', *Philosophia*, 8(2/3), pp. 185–203.

Skrentny, J.D. 1996. *The Ironies of Affirmative Action: Politics, Culture, and Justice in America*, pp. 1762–1815. Chicago: The University of Chicago Press.

―――. 2006. 'Policy-Elite Perceptions and Social Movement Success: Understanding Variations in Group Inclusion in Affirmative Action', *American Journal of Sociology*, III(6): 77; 1762–1815.

Sowell, T. 2004. *Affirmative Action Around the World: An Empirical Study*. Yale: New Haven University Press.

Van der Westhuizen, J. 2002. *Adapting to Globalization: Malaysia, South Africa and the Challenges of Ethnic Redistribution with Growth*. Westport: Praeger.

PART III

STRUCTURAL DISCRIMINATION

6

Mindset, Memoirs, and Untouchability

Veracity beyond Conventional Structures

Narender Kumar

The conception of untouchability has been associated with the present-day Dalits/Scheduled Castes or vaguely known as ex-untouchables. Untouchability, a socio-cultural practice indicating towards bias or prejudice on the basis of considerations of pollution associated with them remains a social reality. Prejudice may be defined as an antipathy based on faulty and inflexible generalization directed towards a group as a whole or towards an individual because s/he is a member of that group which may be felt or expressed in different social settings. Explaining about the prejudicial behavior Allport divided it in five stages: 1) Verbal antagonism; 2) Avoidance; 3) Discrimination; 4) Physical attack; and 5) Extermination (Allport 1954). Dalits have been facing prejudices leading to all five types of prejudicial behaviour from verbal antagonism to extermination. Verbal antagonism could be in terms of rude and abusive language with direct confrontation from the offender to the victim. Avoidance may be used in the form of alienation with physical and psychological hurt.

Discrimination may be in terms of treating people differently due to their membership of a social group other than the one to whom the offender belongs. Sometimes it may physically allow participation in the societal activities but does not make him/her complete part of such participation. Physical attack may be direct hurt to the body of the victim without physical elimination. Extermination refers to the physical elimination of the victim. Among these, verbal antagonism, physical attack, and extermination have the physical form of untouchability, and avoidance and discrimination are more of a psychological untouchability.

After the legal abolition of untouchability by the constitution of India in 1950, it was believed that Untouchability will be what is called as a 'thing of the past', more so with the introduction of modernity and democracy by the constitution. Nevertheless, it is difficult to abolish the structured social realities but legally and one of the important scholars studying structures, Bourdieu states the following: 'The structures constitutive of a particular type of environment . . . produce *habitus*, systems of durable, transposable dispositions, structured structures predisposed to function as structuring structures, that is, as principles of the generation and structuring of practices and representations.... [T]he practices produced by the *habitus* [are] the strategy-generating principle enabling agents to cope with unforeseen and ever-changing situations' (Bourdieu 1977: 72).

Thus structures are not merely producing continuities of a particular kind but they themselves become producers of structures to cope up with emerging situations in different times and spaces. One cannot write with confirmation due to lack of studies that constitutional provisions bear no impact on the structure of untouchability, at least in its physical or manifest form, as its severity was widespread and too common to be popularly considered even a menace that needed abolition.

As there is the inevitability of change and transformation in every process so has there been in this case. The way the parliament of India has been enacting the laws against untouchability by modifying the existing legal rules, itself reveals the transformative nature of untouchability. Within five years of Article 17 for the abolition of untouchability coming into force, with the adoption of the constitution of India, a comprehensive law known as Untouchability

Offences Act (UOA) 1955, was legislated to contain various forms of untouchability prevalent in the society that was not apparently included in Article 17 in the absence of elaboration of the offences being committed. The UOA elaborated various forms of untouchability and the relevant punishment for the crimes perpetuated by the non-Dalit offenders.

However, lacunae and loopholes in the formulation and implementation of the law in arresting the commission of atrocities based on untouchability forced the government to introduce a major overhaul by modifying and renaming the UOA as the Protection of Civil Rights Act (PCRA) in 1976. Despite various measures adopted to improve the socio-economic conditions of the SCs and STs they remained vulnerable and subjected to various offences, indignities, humiliations, and harassment with continuing atrocities, more so when they started asserting their rights according to the constitutional mandate (Mendelsohn and Vicziany 1998).

The normal provisions of the existing laws like, the PCRA and Indian Penal Code were again found inadequate to check these atrocities continuing the gross indignities and offences against SCs and STs. Recognizing these, the parliament passed the 'Scheduled Caste and Scheduled Tribe (Prevention of Atrocities) Act', 1989 and Rules, 1995. The statement of objects and reasons mentioned while moving the bill in the parliament, reads:

> …despite various measures to improve the socioeconomic conditions of SCs & STs, they remain vulnerable. They are denied a number of civil rights; they are subjected to various offences, indignities, humiliations and harassment. They have, in several brutal incidents, been deprived of their life and property. Serious atrocities are committed against them for various historical, social and economic reasons.

Thus objectives of the Act clearly emphasized the intention of the government to deliver justice to these communities through pro-active efforts to enable them to live with dignity, self-esteem, and without fear or violence or suppression from the dominant castes. The practice of untouchability, in its overt and covert form was made a cognizable and non-compoundable offence, and strict punishment provided for any such offence.

Contemporary Laws and Untouchability

If we look into the data of the National Crime Records Bureau, it reflects that despite the Prevention of Atrocities Act (PAA), the number of atrocities committed against the Dalits is on the rise. In this light, a review study of the PAA 1989 was recently conducted by a civil society organization, namely, National Campaign on Dalit Human Rights[1] mentioning the following:

> Discriminatory practices till now not included in the Act must be listed hereafter, Dalits and Adivasis are subjected to wide range of 'Untouchability'-based discriminatory practices as for example, social disabilities based on 'Untouchability', discrimination in educational institutions and mid-day meal scheme, discrimination in access to public goods & services, discrimination in employment, discrimination in labour organization, discrimination in the private corporate sector, etc......when Dalits and Adivasis protest against such practices and simultaneously assert their rights, there is a likelihood of dominant castes committing atrocities against them.

However, the change in the laws has not been able to contain the incidents of untouchability as the number of atrocities is multiplying with the passing of years and decades. Nevertheless, we also cannot confirm that the law has not contained the atrocities as sometimes it is argued that the increase in the level of consciousness among the Dalits might also be instrumental in the increase of atrocities as more and more people affected are going to register the cases that might not have been the case previously.

In spite of various changes in the law dealing with the untouchability offences, the focus has remained on physical untouchability, reflecting physical denial of access to public spaces, and it has been addressed in a way as if the untouchability as practice subsists in a traditional set-up and has rural-centric connotations. The study of the urban domain and the modern institutions like the bureaucracy, academic institutions, etc. has not attracted sufficient attention of social scientists vis-à-vis discrimination that is reflected in the practice of changing forms of untouchability in the case of Dalits after they started occupying positions in public institutions. The modern institutions may not deny the entry of Dalits but these might produce institutional discrimination. Institutional discrimination takes place when there is negative or unfair treatment meted out by an institution as a consequence of the structure, organization, or practices of that particular institution (Sampson 2008: 726). By looking into the practices of various institutions, scholars and policymakers have struggled to indentify the effects and significance of various forms of discrimination in the multi-ethnic, multicaste, and multiracial societies, which are not only based on equality in theory, but equally eulogize and accept differences, yet so often accept and at times promote both individual and institutional discrimination. The institutional discrimination may be more difficult to detect and address as compared with individual discrimination simply because here the practices, policies, and structures are in question and have their own complications. These institutions may be public or private, namely, governments or government agencies, schools, or public universities, on the one hand and businesses, private colleges or universities, corporations, or media outlets on the other. Another study of institutional discrimination in the US against the blacks describes how the federal and state governments have had large roles in creating and maintaining residential racial segregation as the Federal Housing Administration employed practices that disadvantaged Blacks with the practice called 'red-lining' to determine risks associated with loans made to borrowers in specific neighborhoods exited (Seitles 1996: 1–30). Yet another study on disabled persons reveals how there exists institutional discrimination against the disabled persons, asserting, 'negative attitudes and discriminatory practices which effectively deny basic human rights to disabled people ingrained in the core institutions of our society' (Barnes 1991).

In this essay, we look into the discrimination prevalent in the bureaucratic and academic institutions against ex-untouchables. Though the institutional discrimination approach should explain it, it may not be adequate to understand the issue at hand, the way in which the selected instances have been narrated in the autobiographies and otherwise. The institutional discrimination approach does look into the issues of structural discrimination when there is unequal treatment against individuals due to their association to a group in the absence of specific rules and regulations in favour of the discriminated groups or lack of special provisions for them and when discrimination takes place due to the general policy of equality but it may not make us understand the issue of discrimination when the special policy in existence gets implemented and still there is a prevalence of discrimination. It means that there are two situations: 1) there is a general policy of equality but discrimination continues to take place, then the approach of institutional discrimination addresses the problem; and 2) there is a special policy to address the institutional discrimination and Dalits become part of the institutions of bureaucracy and academics, but they continue to face the discrimination, then the institutional approach may not address the issue of discrimination as the discrimination has effectively been addressed by the institutions by adopting the special provisions, in our case by adoption of the reservation policy. As we are taking instances from the autobiographies, the question of subjectivity and objectivity also becomes significant. There are criticisms of the autobiographies as these revolve around the self and the individual, as the individual possesses the choice of narrating those events of life which s/he thinks significant and secondly, there is the glorification of self and recording of an individual's achievements (Rajkumar 2010). Nevertheless, Dalit autobiographies are generally narratives, which are more of pain, sorrow, grief, and discrimination and less of self-glorification and, individual's achievements. Thus despite being subjective, the narratives signify objectivity as the larger social reality remains embedded in discriminative practices.

As the discrimination of ex-untouchables goes beyond the institutional discrimination approach so it may not be adequate to explain and understand it. The kind of narratives discussed in this essay thus need added perspectives for explanation as we need to look into the circumstantial evidence as well as the documents referred to bring to the forefront the issues of discrimination. Here we shall be taking four instances from the autobiographies and other written documents. Though the present essay relates to the discrimination inside governmental or public institutions, it may not purely be termed as a reflection of institutional discrimination. As mentioned earlier, in institutional discrimination, there is an inherent tendency to discriminate due to the absence of implicit rules and regulations in favour of the discriminated groups but in our case, the Dalits who had joined the public institutions with the help of the reservation policy got discriminated against and thus it may not be understood within the framework of institutional discrimination, as it was not the institution, as such, that discriminated against them but the individuals in the institution who were instrumental in discriminating against them.

The psychological literature[2] in the US vis-à-vis discriminated groups, particularly the blacks, could be helpful in understanding the position of ex-untouchables in India as the former suffer from race and the latter from considerations of caste/untouchability. This phenomenon has also been understood in terms of subtle prejudice marked by unconscious beliefs and associations affecting the attitudes and behaviours of members of an in-group (whites) towards members of the out-group (blacks or Hispanics). Here, members of the in-group face an internal conflict that results in a disconnect between the societal rejection of racist behaviours and the societal persistence of racist attitudes (Dovidio and Gaertner 1986). Another study (Blank, Dabady and Citro 2004) mentions that despite people's good intentions, their racially biased cognitive categories and associations may persist in society and subsequently, in the institutions resulting in a modern and subtle/sophisticated form of prejudice that continues to shape people's cognitive, affective, and behavioural responses. Subtle forms of discrimination of race or in our case, untouchability are indirect, automatic, ambiguous, and ambivalent in modern institutions like bureaucracy and academics. However, 'subtle' does not mean trivial or inconsequential; subtle prejudice can result in major adverse effects.

In the case of ex-untouchables, various efforts to deal with untouchability have primarily focused on physical untouchability and almost completely ignored the less discussed and unrecognized form of untouchability that has been termed as notional untouchability by Ambedkar that goes beyond manifest and explicit forms of discrimination and thus is more of an implicit and subtle nature (Ambedkar 2005, 2014). It physically permits the entry of this group into the public spaces or institutions explicitly through special provisions and policies, making their access possible but with limited sharing. The persons of dominant sections consciously or sub-consciously may adhere to the societal norms and rules of discrimination in which prejudice plays a crucial and determining role. Thus biased cognitive categories may persist in society and consequently, in the public institutions resulting in a modern and subtle/sophisticated form of prejudice that might persistently shape individuals' cognitive, affective, and behavioural responses towards a particular group.

Ambedkar cautioned against a partial understanding of the concept of untouchability and remarked that 'An individual may not be treated as an untouchable in the literal sense of the term on account of various circumstances. None the less outside the scope of such compelling circumstances he does continue to be regarded as an impure person by reason of his belonging to the untouchable class' (Ambedkar 2005: 492–3). Thus despite an untouchable having been allowed access to public spaces earlier denied to them, the social groups already occupying these spaces consider the entry of the untouchables inept and unwarranted as they look at an ex-'untouchable' with prejudice and thus the concept of untouchability without roping in of notional form produces partial understanding.

To prove his observation Ambedkar, taking an excerpt from the census superintendent of Bihar and Orissa in his census report of 1921, quoted:

In places like Jameshpur where work is done under modern conditions men of all castes and races work side by side in the mill without any misgivings regarding the caste of their neighbours. But because the facts of everyday life make it impossible to follow the same practical rules as were followed a hundred years ago, it is to be supposed that the distinctions of pure and impure, touchable and untouchable are no longer observed. A high caste Hindu will not allow an untouchable to sit on the same seat, to smoke the same hookah or to touch his person, his seat, his food or the water that he drinks (Ambedkar 2005: 492–3).

The excerpt reveals that not only Ambedkar, but also the census officials collecting data on the socio-economic conditions of the various social groups, observed this phenomenon. Responding to the observations of the census official, Ambedkar in the same write-up remarked:

If this is a correct statement of the facts of life then the difference between untouchability in its literal and notional sense is a distinction which makes no difference to the ultimate situation; for as the extract shows untouchability in its notional sense persists even where untouchability in its literal sense has ceased to obtain. This is why I insist that the test of untouchability must be applied in its notional sense (Ambedkar 2005: 492–3).

On similar lines, Ambedkar while writing on the 'Problem of Discrimination' referred, 'There is another form of discrimination which though subtle is nonetheless real. Under it a systematic attempt will be made to lower the dignity and status of a meritorious Untouchable...A Hindu singer would be described as a great Indian singer. If the same person happens to be an Untouchable he would be described as an Untouchable singer...(Ambedkar 2014: 109).

Nevertheless, one needs to explain why the notional untouchability persists despite changing conditions of the society. Reflecting on this, a recent work brings contemporary debate into focus and mentions that '...various studies prove beyond doubt that all efforts to eradicate untouchability have not substantially shaken core beliefs of people in many parts of the country which has an impact in the public domain' (Verma 2012: 85). The core beliefs of people, though being practised in society, are fundamentally ingrained in the mind consciousness in favour of the practice of notional untouchability.

While looking into the debates inside the Indian parliament,[3] it was observed that during discussion on atrocities on Dalits, parliamentarians would time and again bring in the inability of the laws to restrain the atrocities. The more parliament discussed the issue, the higher the cases of atrocities committed and in addition the need was realized to discuss the issue. In such circumstances, they would always invoke changing the 'mindset' of the individuals in particular and the society in general. This changing of the mindset makes us investigate the issue of untouchability deeper which provides the basis for the atrocities against the Dalits in contemporary India as well, forcing us to look into why despite various changes, be it constitutional, legal, social, political, cultural, economic, etc., the discrimination continues not only in older or traditional forms but in more nuanced forms in the public institutions like bureaucracy, and educational institutions; and in urban settings away from the rural areas. Moreover, such forms of discrimination faced by ex-untouchables are difficult to capture and comprehend. Thus untouchability is not only physical but also notional in nature where mind consciousness comes to the forefront.[4]

Of late, society in general is becoming more rational and wants to avoid physical untouchability as the surroundings do not permit the practice of physical untouchability and there obviously is fear of the law. However, the real challenge is to abolish the notional untouchability, that is, the basis or foundation for untouchability. It further implies that the efforts to abolish untouchability in its true sense will be futile unless and until there is a change in the mindset signifying that physical untouchability may be abolished in most of the forms but abolishing notional untouchability or getting rid of the mindset that practises untouchability due to the prejudices might remain a challenge.[5]

To substantiate how notional untouchability has been playing its role, despite institutional discrimination having been addressed, we look into four cases in diverse settings and different periods, including colonial and post-colonial times, wherein we could argue that untouchability does not stay confined to traditional structures of society, that is, in the social and cultural spheres but also in the so-called modern settings such as bureaucracy and academic institutions, which are supposed to be beyond the structures of the practice of untouchability. These structures might allow physical entry to the ex-untouchables/Dalits as institutional discrimination got absolved with their entry into these institutions due to the reservation policy but they do face discrimination and capturing such discrimination in 'secular', 'modern', and 'democratic' structures is not only difficult but also a challenge. Critics might argue taking the untouchability argument too far. Nevertheless, the prevalence of untouchability in subtle forms of prejudice and its consequences might tell a different story.

In the subsequent discussion, we explain notional untouchability which is difficult to capture and more difficult to fight against in the absence of legal safeguards and this absence is complicated further by non-recognition of such attitudes by the civil society itself, thus making the individuals coming from the untouchability associated groups vulnerable. These are four cases, two each from the bureaucracy—higher and lower, and another two from academics—higher and lower levels. The cases have been cautiously selected from different locations namely tehsil headquarters, district headquarters, the state capital, and national capital to capture all locations. The cases are also in different periods, namely, from the early twentieth, mid-twentieth, late twentieth, and current twenty-first century. These are cases in diverse locations and manifest that the mindset that has habituated to discriminate and humiliate in its historical, societal, and cultural setting does not stop to involve itself even in the new circumstances, turning the legal and constitutional mandates insignificant for bringing equality and justice in the society.

An Untouchable's Entry as *Talati*[6] in a Town of Gujarat 1936[7]

This incident has been narrated by Ambedkar in one of his writings, wherein an untouchable young man was appointed as the *patwari* (village record-keeping official). This explains how a young untouchable was treated in the 1930s after the adoption of the reservation policy in jobs[8] in the new space called tehsil office away from his colony as well as the village, which are supposedly considered the domains of untouchability practices. This is not a narrative of a single incident but the continuous practice of untouchability against the official by the fellow employees inside the office, a modern organization.

On Entering the Public Office as Official

As soon as the person entered the office, his social status of an untouchable troubled him in the 'modern' and 'secular' setting. The untouchable was appointed as a *talati* and as he entered with his credentials, the dealing hand, a clerk from a non-SC background, came to know about the social status in advance and asked the young man, 'Who are you?' The young man replied, 'Sir, I am a Harijan.' The clerk retorted, 'Go away, stand at a distance. How dare you stand so near me? You are in office; if you were outside I would have given you six kicks, what audacity to come here for service.' However, looking at the official papers in his hands, the clerk asked him to drop his certificates and the appointment order on the floor so that the clerk could pick them up without inviting the wrath of his seniors as there was always a fear of punishment of disobeying the rules in colonial

India—the British may not tolerate hindering the official work as the rule of law was their concern. The young man dropped the papers and joined the office.

Struggling for Drinking Water Inside the Office

The problems of the young untouchable who was allowed to enter the office with grudges of social stigma did not end with entering the institution. The day-to-day life was equally difficult for him. There was a common pot for the officials in the office but the untouchable official was not allowed to drink the water from it and experienced a lot of difficulty in getting water to drink. The waterman in-charge of the cans of water used to keep those in the verandah. He was to serve the water to the officials but in his absence people could take water on their own which was not allowed for this new entrant. He could not touch the cans as it would pollute the water and he had to depend on the mercy of the waterman. For him, a small and rusty pot was kept that would not be touched by others. Interestingly, in the absence of the waterman, he would not get the water as the waterman had to pour the water in his pot and others would not do it on two accounts; one, it was not their duty and second—and more important—was that why should someone get polluted by pouring water in an untouchable's pot? The matter did not end there but even on the days of his presence in the office, the water-man used to slip away when he saw that the untouchable official coming to take water. He wrote in his memoir letter, 'the days on which I had no water to drink were by no means few.' It shows that the prejudices of non-untouchable might be detrimental and play havoc for the Dalits in the non-traditional socio-cultural settings as well.

Being Humiliated while Engaging in Routine Office Work

It was not only the non-official interaction that was prejudiced but even while finishing official work he had to suffer the humiliation and wrath of other persons/colleagues. One day the senior talati/patwari called him to a village office where he was doing some work with the headman. The untouchable young man went and wished them, 'Good morning' without any response from them. And he was kept standing for a long time.

After standing at the door for 15 minutes, he sat on a chair nearby as he was feeling tired due to the journey that he covered to reach the village office from the tehsil headquarters. As both senior talati and headman noticed that he had sat on the chair, they went out of their official room quietly. After some time a large crowd gathered there and rounded up the young man. The crowd was led by the librarian of the village library to whom the chair officially belonged. The librarian began abusing the young man asking the *ravania* (village servant), 'Who allowed this dirty dog of a *bhangi* to sit on the chair?' The ravania unseated him, forcing him to sit on the ground. The crowd entered the village office and hurled abuses, some even began saying they should cut him to pieces with a sharp-edged weapon.

> I implored them to excuse me and to have mercy upon me. That did not have any effect on the crowd. I did not know how to save myself. But an idea came to me of writing to the *mamlatdar* (higher officer) about the fate that had befallen me and telling him how to dispose of my body in case I was killed by the crowd.

He wrote to the mamlatdar[9]

> 'Sir
>
> Be pleased to accept the humble salutations of Parmar Kalidas Shivram. This is to humbly inform you that the hand of death is falling upon me today. It would not have been so, if I had listened to the words of my parents. Be so good as to inform my parents of my death.'
>
> The librarian read what was written and asked him to tear the paper off and the crowd showered innumerable insults saying, 'You want us to address you as our talati? You are a bhangi and you want to enter the office and sit on the chair'. The young man had to regret his action and promised to give up the job. That convinced the crowd to leave him.
>
> This was the mix of physical and notional untouchability as the young man was asked to stand away by the clerk; asked to put his papers on the ground; was not allowed to sit on the official chair; abuses were hurled on him reminding him of his identity. It was notional

in the sense that 1) his identity was known; 2) he did not wear dirty clothes as nobody mentioned that his attire was filthy; and 3) all this was happening in the official set-up, supposed to be free from the practice of untouchability.

On Being an IAS Officer at District Headquarters in Uttar Pradesh (1964)[10]

This is the memoir of an ex-untouchable who entered the highest level in the civil administration known as the Indian Administrative Services in republican India around the mid-twentieth century. His location was the district headquarters in Uttar Pradesh. But his social status hindered the performance of his duties and not only his attendant but even his superiors behaved with him in a manner that was not deserved by him in the non-rural, that is, urban, and non-traditional organizational setting, that is, the bureaucracy. One day he decided to quit the highest administrative position that was achieved with a whole lot of difficulties associated with his poverty and various discriminations heaped against him in village life. Thus instead of facing humiliation at the hands of both subordinates and superiors equally, he parted with his earned position, where institutional discrimination was not at play.

Facing the Attendant's Wrath

The official was posted in Meerut of Uttar Pradesh. His peon was a Brahmin. The peon would not bring or take the IAS officer's cup of tea despite it being his official duty and when he had been doing the same for all other officers. Rather he would call a Dalit to give this official the cup of tea and take it back. The peon/attendant was not only prejudiced about serving tea to his superior but did not keep his glass of water with other glasses lest those got 'polluted'.

Restricting Performance of Duty

After his posting at Meerut, he was transferred to another district known as Lalitpur. Here a case of the practice of physical untouchability came before him in which a barber denied a hair-cut to a Dalit and was put behind bars for six months as per the rule by this official for practising untouchability. This became an issue frustrating the fellow junior employees and they started making efforts to get him transferred from the position, complaining about his intrepidness in dealing with the untouchability offences while abiding by the rules and regulations and accomplishing his duty according to the law of the land.

Even the junior officials started reporting to the higher officials with a phrase that 'one Chamar officer has come to teach Brahmins, needs to cut to size'. Intervening in the matter, the chief secretary asked this official to appear before him, and when the Dalit official appeared before his superior, he received him with contempt and said, 'You are super-sensitive and not settling down'. On this, the ex-untouchable officer said he was doing his duty. However, the superior insisted that he should behave properly and transferred him to another district.

Facing Demotion Instead of Promotion

This official was then transferred to another district. The transfer would have been fine which was within the jurisdiction of the higher officials but he was demoted to the post of additional district magistrate from that of a district magistrate. The officer writes in his memoir 'Perhaps I was the first and last IAS to have been taught a lesson by demoting in such a way.'

This case also proves that the untouchable official faced both physical and notional untouchability inside the modern organization, namely bureaucracy, as even his peon would not serve him water and tea but would call a Dalit to serve him water and tea. Even keeping his glass was considered to having a polluting effect so the official was not only given a separate glass for water and tea but it was kept away from the other personnels' glasses of water and tea, reminding us of the practice of a 'separate tumbler system' in some parts of the country even today. Secondly, the junior officials of a non-Dalit background could not tolerate it when he started to implement the law against the untouchability practice of the barber. The prejudice was so pressing that they took it as if the ex-untouchable official was teaching them a lesson while abiding by rules and regulations. The mix of both physical and notional untouchability made the official resign from his job earned with a lot of hardships. This might show the lack of self-esteem in the official but one needs to understand psychologically how difficult it would have been to quit such a job, due to the practice of untouchability, both physical and notional.

On Becoming a Professor in the State Capital of Rajasthan (1989–1991)[11]

The lived experiences of a Dalit official at the district headquarters were narrated, and now we narrate about the prejudiced mindset in the state capital of Rajasthan.[12] Not only is the setting changed from the town to the state capital but also from the bureaucracy to an academic institution, that is, the University, which is supposed to be the learning ground against for opposing societal norms of discrimination against any social group.

Experts' Comments and Selection to the Post of Professor

The teacher with an ex-untouchable background applied for the position of professor in the University of Rajasthan located in Jaipur, its capital city. He had published extensively despite being in a college in a relatively backward district. After going through the bio-data of this person, one of the experts observed,

> ....though the candidate belongs to [the] reserved category, he has to his credit publication of a large number of research papers and standard works in spite of serving in Government College, Banswara, which has [a] lack of library facilities ...in Government Colleges, we do not have the senior faculty members with whom we can share and interact academically....Therefore, if an opportunity is given to such candidates they would prove more useful to the University (Shyamlal 2001: 114).

These comments convinced the selection committee to appoint him to the post. But worse had to come after this.

Struggle for the Statutory Right of Headship of the Department

After an appointment as professor, another position that remains to be achieved in the academic hierarchy is that of the head of the department. The professor of Dalit origin was being denied the right of headship due to the prejudiced mindset of the colleagues practising untouchability in the 'modern' setting. According to the convention, on expiry of the headship of a person, the next one in seniority was/is appointed so it was the turn of the new Dalit incumbent. As he was to be appointed the head, the colleagues in the department started secret and informal confabulations with the university authorities to appoint another colleague, who was not from the department but appointed in another department—the Social Sciences Research Centre, University of Rajasthan.

The new incumbent met the vice-chancellor and apprised him of his statutory right but the university administration did not take it seriously and when he lost his hopes to get justice from the university administration, he approached the Rajasthan High Court against the university for depriving him of his legitimate right.

The university had to prepare a detailed reply for the High Court that clearly stated that 'it has decided to issue appointment orders of Professor Shyamlal as head of the department in due course of time'. And just a day before the expiry of the incumbent's tenure, the university issued orders for his appointment as head of the department. He writes that two issues emerged out of this episode, one 'my fighting zeal against injustice played a very important role and proved supreme' and two, 'my reputation as a teacher was established and it prepared a background for my future relationship....'

This case is different in nature from the other two cases narrated earlier as those were associated with the bureaucracy but this refers to academics. This shows that even if a Dalit earns merit on his own qualities then also the hardships of being elevated at higher positions are rendered futile. One needs to ask whether a non-Dalit professor will be forced to approach the judiciary for positions which are time-bound and need to be occupied according to the seniority in accordance with the statutes. This again is the instance of not institutional discrimination but of the mindset.

On Becoming a College Teacher in the Capital of India (1999–2005)[13]

Universities are supposed to be reflections of a progressive, secular, and democratic culture, inculcating human values among the students. However, if one looks at the callousness with which the Delhi University academics, who did not allow implementation of the legally mandated reservation policy for the SCs and STs, for almost 50 years since the constitution came into force, tells a story of the notional form of untouchability.

SC/ST Entry as Teachers' Perceived to Desecrate Goddess Saraswati's Clothes

In 1996, the university administration through its Academic Council accepted implementing the reservation policy after forceful persuasions from the Parliamentary Committee for SCs/STs. While discussing the matter, some members leading a group of academics even went to the extent of saying, 'The clothes of mother goddess Saraswati will be desecrated, if reservation policy is adopted'.[14] If this has been the level of prejudice among the teachers sitting in the capital of the country then one can easily imagine what would be happening in the colleges and universities in the towns, districts, and states' capitals and above all, how they would be dealing with the students coming from an 'untouchable' background and what message would they be giving to the students about democracy, justice, equality, and secular values, and could we expect a change of attitude among the common students towards their disadvantaged fellow beings?

Writing on the issue, a former principal of a Delhi University college and human rights activist remarked that one of the arguments advanced by teachers including well-known 'Marxists' and 'progressive' faculty members is that academic standards will suffer if SC/ST teachers are appointed...no one has however, said a single word about the increasingly and alarming falling standards in spite of the fact that the academic community has always been dominated and controlled by the upper and forward castes (Pal and Bhargava 2010: 245).

Getting Dues through the Scheduled Castes Commission's Intervention

In this background of Delhi University academics, a Scheduled Caste young man applied for an ad-hoc position in a college and was interviewed in November 1998. Interestingly, this college which had around 100 teachers did not have till then even a single teacher from amongst the Dalits/adivasis. After waiting for a month for the appointment letter, he approached the National Commission for Scheduled Castes and Scheduled Tribes to intervene in the matter and got his due right as he fulfilled all the requisite conditions of getting an appointment as ad-hoc lecturer. The Commission's intervention forced the college to send a letter of appointment on the same day, giving the person an opportunity of teaching in a college of the national capital that did practise untouchability by not allowing even a single teacher to be appointed from the ex-'untouchable' community despite the legal and statutory provisions.

Denying Promotion Despite having Higher Qualifications than the Eligibility Conditions

The same person was confirmed after a permanent position and became eligible for the first elevation (not promotion as the designation was to be the same but the pay scale was to be increased) under the Career Advancement Scheme. The selection committee was constituted for promotion and he was denied the elevation. This was not a simple denial but a denial despite the fact that he had completed his M.Phil, and PhD, published articles in reputed journals, published books and, of course, no complaints of any kind either by the students or by anyone else in the college. On the other hand, teachers from other backgrounds who had completed just a Master's degree which is the basic qualification with the required number of experience, without an MPhil, PhD, published research papers or books were elevated before and after his denial. Surprisingly, the promotion at this level had been given on the basis of just screening of the applications and for him a proper interview was conducted.

Teachers' Elections as Respite

This denial made the teaching community of the college and the university at large angry and the Delhi University Teachers Association (DUTA) pitched in as its election was also near and it was an issue that could affect not only the Dalits but also all teachers. The teachers of diverse backgrounds anticipated and protested that if today a person who by chance belongs to a scheduled caste is denied this first level of elevation, then in future anyone of them could be the victim of the personal and flimsy choices of the selection committees.

University Administration Acknowledges Prejudice

This case became so popular that various newspapers kept reporting about it and a fortnightly devoted to academic news kept reporting in almost every edition about the developments and it reported that the college administration has given an issue to the contestants of the DUTA elections on a platter. When the matter was reported to the university administration, it intervened by pointing out the following to the college principal:

- The constitution of the selection committee was in violation of the rules and regulations of the university since the senior-most member of the department of political science of your college was not a member of the committee. A separate communication seeking an explanation is being sent to you in this regard by the University of Delhi.
- The recommendations of a selection committee cannot be accepted in part and since the selection committee transgressed its mandate by recommending that the candidate be asked to appear before another interview in six months the decision and recommendations of the selection committee are invalid.
- The governing body of the college erred in turning down the recommendations of the selection committee without assigning any reasons whatsoever.

The selection process may thus be started afresh; and the college is advised to ensure that the process is carried out without prejudice, free of external pressures and consistent with the above observations.[15]

What comes out of the letter may be sufficient to show how a mindset prejudiced against someone on societal norms could play havoc not only for him or her but also waste the time and energy of the people/officials around. One needs to understand how the principal constituted an erroneous selection committee by incorporating someone who did not deserve to be on the committee, but who would abide by his wish against the candidate's initial promotion.

In a huff, the selection committee also committed a mistake by asking the candidate to appear before it after six months instead of one year that is mandated by the ordinance of the university in case the promotion was denied at the first instance.

Though the governing body acknowledged the fault of the selection committee, it did so without assigning any reasons, and so that effectively was of no consequence.

One wonders what would have been the corollary, if the mistakes of the college principal constituting an erroneous selection committee and the rules of the university ordinance were not faulted by the principal and the selection committee. Secondly, if the DUTA elections were not around the corner, would the academic community have come for the rescue of this denial of the promotion with same vigour and force that continued for seven months? Thirdly, what if the candidate would have accepted a fortune and not got support from the colleagues? Fourthly, what if the university administration would not have noticed the gross violation and not written to conduct the proceedings without prejudice?

***

In this essay we tried to explore the practice of discrimination against the ex-untouchables of India in the modern institutions of bureaucracy and academics, which may partially be understood with the approach of institutional discrimination but not adequately explain the nature of discrimination/untouchability discussed in these cases. This form is primarily a consequence of what is popularly known as a sub-conscious mind that generally is a product of the seeds/*sanskaras* which get implanted primarily unconsciously by parents, ancestors, schooling, and society.

By looking into the four instances, first from the lower bureau-cracy, second of higher bureaucracy, third from higher academic levels and fourth of lower academic level; and these being in the tehsil headquarters, district headquarters, state capital and national capital, respectively, we have tried to explain that the subtle forms of discrimination/untouchability are located more in the modern insti-tutions and away from conventional structures. The first instance of the early twentieth century of the young untouchable *talati* shows a mix of physical and notional untouchability, where he was discriminated against not only physically but also notionally as the young man was asked to stand away by the clerk; to put his papers on the ground; not allowed to sit on the official chair; and abuses were hurled on him reminding him of his identity. It was also of a notional form as his identity was invoked again and again and all this was conspiring in the official set-up supposed to be free from the practice of untouchability.

The second case of the IAS officer also proves that the untouch-able official faced both physical and notional untouchability inside the modern organization, namely the bureaucracy as even his peon, whose consciousness got nurtured in a way that he would practise physical untouchability by not serving him water and tea, and keep-ing his glass with other glasses for non-Dalit officials was considered to have a polluting effect. Practising notional untouchability on their part, the junior officials of a non-Dalit background could not toler-ate it when he implementing the law against untouchability practice against the barber. The prejudice was so high that they took it as if the untouchable official was teaching them a lesson while perform-ing his duty by implemented rules and regulations on the subject. Finally, with the intervention of a higher level official, they were able to get him transferred and that culminated in his resignation. The physical untouchability practised by the IAS officer's attendant may not be possible in contemporary changed circumstances in the state of Uttar Pradesh but notional untouchability may not be ruled out.

The third and fourth instances primarily depict notional untouch-ability as both the Dalits were allowed to enter the university and college as institutions, though with contempt and thus faced discrim-ination. If one looks at these incidents then one realizes the higher institutes of teaching-learning, which are supposed to be bastions of transformation in society are also not independent of untouchability practices, though in subtle form, even in the locations of state capital and national capital. Writing on similar lines, Verma maintains that 'it is not just economic differences but also hereditary life chances based on hierarchy and those which generate gradations of ritual impurity that are unfair for various groups' (Verma 2012: 44). One may only hope that as the physical untouchability is on the decline in the rural areas. Similarly, the subtle forms of discrimination that Ambedkar termed notional untouchability, which is independent of economic prosperity, might also decline from the so-called modern institutions located in the urban settings and elsewhere.

Notes

1. On the completion of 20 years of the Prevention of Atrocities Act 1989, the National Campaign on Dalit Human Rights (New Delhi) published a comprehensive report 'Atrocities against the Dalits and Adivasis...Proposed Amendments for effective monitoring and implementation' revealing lacunae in addressing various emerging forms of untouchability practices, which have not been adequately addressed by the existing laws and are more of a subtle or notional kind than of physical.
2. Studies such as McConahay (1986), Katz and Hass (1988), and Fiske (1998).
3. For a detailed discussion see Kumar (2004: Chs 3 and 4).
4. A Buddhist scholar, Thich Nhat Hanh, in his book *Understanding Our Mind* (2006) explains that the mind consciousness has broadly two components. The first has occurrence on occasions like when the eyes see structures/forms; the ears hear sounds; the tongue tastes; the nose smells or the skin touches. These are purely the components of the physical world where the eyes which see structures/forms develop a kind of consciousness; the ears on hearing sounds develop another kind of consciousness; the tongue after taste develops yet another kind of consciousness; the nose on smelling or the skin on touching develop a consciousness of the physical world. However, the sub-conscious mind functions in non-physical space that may be equated with the 'notional' in Ambedkar's understanding of untouchability. And the notional is the consequence of inherited values from family, parents, schooling, socialization, etc., which are primarily based on assumptions and perceptions.

5. For detailed discussion on untouchability, its origin and consequences see B.R. Ambedkar 2014.
6. Talati/patwari is the official working at the tehsil headquarter and the one who maintains the land records of a cluster of villages.
7. This incident has been documented by Dr B.R. Ambedkar; see Ambedkar 2011.
8. The policy of reservation in jobs was adopted in the light of the Poona Pact in 1932 that granted seats in jobs and educational institutions.
9. Higher official at tehsil (sub-division) headquarters.
10. This incident has been described in the book called *An Untouchable in IAS* written by Balwant Singh as an autobiography and published by the author in 1997.
11. This incident has been narrated by the author in his autobiography (Shyamlal 2001).
12. Of late, Rajasthan has emerged as a hub of atrocities among the Indian states according to the newspapers and government reports.
13. This incident is not yet documented but is based on the experience and documentary evidences of newspapers and official communications.
14. To look at the details please see Pal & Bhargava (2010: 245).
15. A letter was sent to the principal of Motilal Nehru College, New Delhi by the director, University of Delhi South Campus, dated 23 January 2006.

References

Allport, G. 1954. *The Nature of Prejudice*. Reading MA: Addison-Wesley.
Ambedkar, Dr B.R. 2005. *Dr. Babasaheb Ambedkar Writings and Speeches*. Vol. 2. Mumbai: Government of Maharashtra.
———. 2011. *Reminiscences of Untouchability*. New Delhi: Critical Quest.
———. 2014. *Dr. Babasaheb Ambedkar Writings and Speeches*. Vol. 5. Government of India: Ambedkar Foundation, Ministry of Social Justice and Empowerment.
Barnes, C. 1991. *Institutional Discrimination against Disabled Persons: A Case for Legislation*. London: The British Council of Organizations of Disabled People.
Blank, R.M., M. Dabady, and C.F. Citro. (eds). 2004. *Measuring Racial Discrimination*. Washington: The National Academic Press.
Bourdieu, Pierre. 1977. *Outline of a Theory of Practice*. Translated by Richard Nice. New York: Cambridge University Press.
Dovidio, J.F., and S.L. Gaertner (eds). 1986. *Prejudice, Discrimination, and Racism*. San Diego, CA: Academic Press.

Fiske, S.T. 1998. 'Stereotyping, prejudice, and discrimination', in D. Gilbert, S.T. Fiske, and G. Lindzey (eds). *The Handbook of Social Psychology*, (fourth edn) pp. 357–411. New York: McGraw-Hill.

Katz, I., and R.G. Hass. 1988. 'Racial Ambivalence and American Value Conflict: Correlational and Priming Studies of Dual Cognitive Structures', *Journal of Personality and Social Psychology*, 55: 893–905.

Kumar, N. 2004. *Dalit Policies, Politics and Parliament*. New Delhi: Shipra.

McConahay, J.B. 1986. 'Modern Racism, Ambivalence, and the Modern Racism Scale', in J.F. Dovidio and S.L. Gaertner (eds). *Prejudice, Discrimination and Racism*, pp. 91–125. San Diego, CA: Academic Press.

Mendelsohn, O. and M. Vicziany. 1998. *The Untouchables: Subordination, Poverty and the State in Modern India*. Cambridge, UK: Cambridge University Press.

Pal, R.M. and G.S. Bhargava. 2010. *Human Rights of Dalits: Societal Violations*. New Delhi: Gyan Publishing House.

Rajkumar. 2010. *Dalit Personal Narratives: Reading Caste, Nation and Identity*. New Delhi: Orient Blackswan.

Sampson, W.A. 2008. 'Institutional Discrimination', *Encyclopedia of Race, Ethnicity and Society*. Thousand Oaks CA: SAGE.

Seitles, M. 1996. 'The Perpetuation of Residential Racial Segregation in America: Historical Discrimination, Modern Forms of Exclusion, and Inclusionary Remedies', *Journal of Land Use and Environmental Law*, 14(1): 1–30.

Shyamlal. 2001. *An Untold Story of a Bhangi Vice Chancellor*. Jaipur: University Book House.

Hanh, Thich Nhat. 2006. *Understanding Our Mind*. Noida: HarperCollins.

Verma, V. 2012. *Non-discrimination and Equality in India: Contesting Boundaries of Social Justice*. London: Routledge.

7

The World of Work

Gender Discrimination and Rights at the Workplace

Vidhu Verma

Ever since the Supreme Court laid down guidelines in the *Vishaka* case, for dealing with harassment of women at the work place and recognized it as a form of discrimination, debate continues about the scope and definition of sexual harassment.[1] If we look back in history and examine the process through which a persistent and pervasive practice came to be recognized as discrimination, we learn much about the constitution that supported equality of men and women. It was the crucial turning point in our history when the constitution incorporated ideals of equality, social justice, and fraternity as central to our political culture and questioned many aspects of Indian tradition and society. Clearly, this act of recognition of equality by the Indian constitution was a momentous one. For the first time in history, women in India, extracted from law the means to fight certain harassments they were trapped in. However, when we reconsider this development from a historical vantage point, and its moral and legal character, it becomes clear that by appealing to equality we effectively substituted a quasi-juridical notion for a genuinely political vision of a good society. However, conceptions of gender neutrality in law and the rights framework were found to be intrinsically based on domination in which social power excluded those who were different. There were several legislations that were directed to facilitate rights to women but there was no specific legislation dealing with sexual harassment at workplaces: it was only with the *Vishaka* judgment that a new stage was set for judicial activism and the recognition of sexual harassment as a particular form of discrimination.

There is a pressing need for a reappraisal of these developments as important forces have been unleashed that have made us contend with these issues once again. From the late 1990s, economic and political changes through liberalization of the economy have had a profound impact on the lives of women in India.[2] Many more women have been employed as opportunities expanded considerably in cities and emerging towns. Working women, include workers at all levels of skill, from surgeons and airline pilots to bus conductors and manual labourers. Women have made inroads into non-traditional fields such as law, information and communications technology (ICT), and engineering. Since the 1990s, gender index and gender budgeting, have been crucial in many reports of international organizations to document these economic and political changes.[3]

Despite such positive changes, many of these transformations have brought about new kinds of discrimination against women, obstructing their enjoyment of political and social rights (Rao, Rurup and Sudarshan 1996; Kapadia 2002). While there are fewer ways in which women are under legal disabilities compared with men they are still subject to economic and social discrimination.[4] In this scenario, firstly privatization has not been able to address the question of labour laws, social security, health, safety, and transport after state protection has been withdrawn from crucial areas of the economy. Since the paralysing financial crisis and economic downturn, women and children have been hard hit.[5] Moreover, women are concentrated in certain professions like teaching, nursing, and cleaning (horizontal segregation) where at the same time, opportunities for career progression within a company or sector are narrowed down as they often remain in lower categories than men (vertical segregation). Thus despite greater opportunities and diversification of occupations, women are underrepresented in many positions.[6]

Secondly, the present context is deeply marked by a dual, although paradoxical transformation of work: the bipolarization of women's waged work, along with an increased diversification of jobs and functions. The bipolarization creates two groups of women with opposite social and economic profiles as a significant minority of women belonging to the category of executive and intellectual professions have grown with the development of the service sector in personal services, healthcare, and education.[7] Agriculture emerges as the main employer of informal workers that have increased due to male migration to non-farm jobs. The informal sector provides a range of jobs as domestic servant, small trader, artisan, field-labourer, which are unskilled, low-paying, and do not provide any secure benefits. Thus the trend towards a diversification holds in tension bipolarization; on one extreme highly successful skilled professionals (engineers, architects, doctors, professors, managers, lawyers, magistrates) drawing on global discourses of corporate responsibility, professionalism, empowerment, and on the other women workers with very low skills, low wages, and jobs without social recognition or protection.[8]

The ideal that work is the key to women's empowerment in feminist scholarship has little relevance for masses of women who work for wages that cannot liberate them from male domination. Positive benefits have more to do with increased self-esteem and positive participation. Bell Hooks on similar developments in the American context writes:

> If improving conditions in the workplace for women had been a central agenda for [the] feminist movement in conjunction with efforts to obtain better-paying jobs for women and finding jobs for unemployed women of all classes, feminism would have been seen as a movement addressing the concerns of all women. [The] Feminist focus on careerism, [and] getting women employed in high-paying professions, not only alienated masses of women from [the] feminist movement; it also allowed feminist activists to ignore the fact that increased entry of bourgeois women into the workplace was not a sign that women as a group were gaining economic power (Hooks 2000: 100).

This brings me to the third transformation of work sites from clearly defined workplaces, such as factories, plantations, and mines within the boundaries of the state in which labour laws were designed to protect workers based on the relation of employer and employee to a condition where the majority of the workforce is in the informal economy. The discipline present in such workplaces is no longer the same as power is increasingly diffuse, evident in multiple social networking websites. The internet has brought with it an increase in unsolicited mail, which is quite often offensive, and we need an understanding of how this form of sexual harassment affects women and how it can be prevented.[9] The gendered impact of women working in the services industry such as data processing, telecommunications, tourism, finance, insurance, and BPOs, with a specific focus on their flexi-time, gives rise to new challenges for implementing the rights of women.[10] These developments have led us to see sexual harassment as a complex and evolving practice. The law has not kept pace with these developments as the principal limitation is that the law imagines sexual harassment in a traditional workplace setting or single-setting phenomenon, that is, the harassing activity and resulting harms occur in the same protected setting. Given the degree to which cyberspace harassment is targeting women and girls, we need to re-examine our laws. As yet there is no clear conceptualization or understanding of these new sites and activities that sustain sexual harassment.

Even as women surmount many of the restrictions in the public sphere, discrimination remains widespread and systemic in Indian workplaces as enforcement of laws is weak and sexual division of labour well entrenched. The rape and subsequent death of a student in December 2012 sparked a nationwide furore over the lack of implementation of laws dealing with sexual harassment violence.[11] In such cases, although sections of the middle class are more receptive and sympathetic, these sentiments exist against the backdrop of ineffective law. More recently, the alleged gang rape and hanging of two teenage cousins, in a village in Uttar Pradesh has raised many questions regarding women's rights, gender violence, and domination and governance in India.

It is for these reasons that an explicit attention to inequality of opportunities in workplaces between different classes of women, as distinct from adopting a purely gender-sensitive approach is essential to attainment of gender justice.[12] The changing nature of labour markets from permanent workers to casual or daily workers makes women workers, particularly migrant women, more vulnerable to the exploitation of employers, landlords, contractors, and supervisors. The mass of women workers are generally not aware of their legal rights or rights against sexual harassment; even if middle-class women can approach the courts, rules are interpreted according to the employers, as in the case when maternity benefits are viewed as a privilege or concession to women and not as a right.[13]

In this study, I limit myself to rights of women at the workplace, with special attention to the debate on sexual harassment in the Indian context which was seen as a juridical category of crime till 1997, after which the Supreme Court held that sexual harassment in the workplace violated women's rights to equality. It was not, however, until 2013, that the Protection of Women against Sexual Harassment at Workplace Bill was presented to the Indian parliament. The second section seeks to review the contestations, the changing categories and terms of feminist analysis under this Act due to various complaints. I argue that the doctrinal history of harassment points to the power and limitations of legal rights as a strategy for social change: establishing a basis for legal liability can reshape consciousness about working environments but this has not deterred employers and those who harass, from using less formal means of attacking women's rights.

I also argue that the problems with the law against harassment are that it speaks for a specific class of women, along with age, ethnicity, and a level of educational attainment. Many of the regulations emerged from the experiences of the emerging middle-class women who have entered the labour force since the 1960s. Quite often judgments operate within the purview of reform and not conviction for the harms committed. I finally undertake the exercise of locating the voice of Dalit women and their struggles and argue that it is imperative for feminist politics that difference be historically located in the struggle for marginalized women (Kannabiran and Singh 2008: 3). A recent work by Jayshree P. Mangubhai argues that Dalit women bear the 'double burden of subordination due to both their caste and gender'; they are set apart from other caste women 'as polluted and are actively excluded from livelihood resources'.[14] Difficult questions about voice and authenticity that attend the reliance on experience can be countered by contextual analysis; we can gain an understanding not simply of the harms of inequalities but also of the ways in which these harms are reproduced due to structural and ideological features. Any solidarity between Dalit and non-Dalit feminists is often marred by the relative silence of feminists in the face of the politics of collective violence and the structuring of the context of rape cultures Dalit women are trapped in. Cases of coerced sexual conduct are egregious: they are crimes, and hence we must respond to the criminal wrongs perpetrated in these cases. The failure to recognize violence as a critical component of our political modernity or as embedded in linkages between sexuality and labour, raise serious questions for the political praxis of feminism. Tracing the presence of gender inequality, I argue the need for reflecting more on the question of implementation of rights and public policies for different categories of women; if Dalit women's rights are different from other women's groups (Karat 2013), how do new interpretations of the caste/gender question destabilize the assumed meanings of violence, sexuality, or labour in feminist theory?

We begin with India's constitutional history where legal discourse presents a legible template from which to question the role of reason and the rule of law in upholding caste and gender hierarchies. I shall argue that rights against sexual harassment emerged between the era of welfarism and that of neo-liberal reforms and other conditions for its possibility include the institutional and ideological nature of feminist discourse in the late 1980s with the rise of autonomous women's groups. A re-conceptualization of the state laws, institutions, and women's empowerment groups is required, along with an understanding of what it takes to protect the rights of women against discrimination and sexual harassment in the present scenario. Are sexual harassment policies stand-alone policies that are divorced from large policies that target women as a group? Do laws against harassment hold out the promise of gender justice for all classes of women who face discrimination?

Struggles for Gender Equality in the Juridical Sphere: Harassment, Rape, and Violence

Until the early twentieth century, nationalist debates on natural equality and the formal idea of equal opportunity that constituted the 'age of reason' inspired many intellectuals, social activists, and scholars to question prejudice and discrimination. The social reform movements that were mostly in the form of individual revolts against existing social customs of caste, idolatory, and subordination of women took shape under the influence of liberal, scientific, and enlightened thinkers along with Dalit and socialist interventions. The premise upon which most of these movements rested was humanitarianism and moral equality of all human beings; they were structured around affairs which were strictly 'social' in a narrow sense, yet they also encompassed ideas on individualism, rights, duties of the individual to society at large and the idea of progress. A significant factor in the struggle against discriminatory laws was the dichotomy of tradition and modernity, which explained the extraordinary energy with which the colonial intelligentsia raised questions of social reform; for example, abolishing sati, legalizing widow remarriage, raising the age of consent or opposing child marriage. Most of these struggles were concerned with upper-class and middle-class women. During this period discursive representations and constructions of Indian cultures as a barbaric source of women's inequality were attempts to rationalize the political subjugation of India as a civilizing project. Hindu revivalists and social reformers concerned with the changing status of Indian women became trapped in the debate between tradition and modernity. Thus every time a case concerning oppression of women came to the limelight, the whole tradition was brought under attack and defended at the cost of women's rights.

Until well into the twentieth century, women were legally and politically subordinate to men in a host of different ways. The refusal of twentieth-century legislative bodies under the British to accept women as equal citizens was overridden once women associations at the local level and national ones like the Women's India Association, the All India Women's Conference, and the National Council of India, emerged to ask for increased funds for the education of women and for greater representation of women in the legislative council. The negotiation with a discourse of juridical equality began when women's organizations joined the Indian National Congress's claim for universal adult franchise by adopting the idea of inclusion. But then onwards, gender was dismissed as a political category as evident from the writings of leaders like Sarojini Naidu who claimed that giving women the vote, would by no means interfere with separate spheres of men and women, since they were united by nationalism. She treated the preferential treatment to women as an admission of women's inferiority (Kapadia 2002: 14). In general, the Indian women's movement conceived of itself as including and representing women of all religious communities, castes, and classes.[15]

Economic divergences compounded by differences of religion, background, and politics made it difficult to talk of women as a group. How did legal reform contribute to shaping women's lives across classes, castes, and regions? Universalistic positions prevailed for the sake of equality, a principle which soon dominated all debates in the state on women's place in society whereas difference was increasingly irrelevant. In 1939, when the women's subcommittee was created within the National Planning Committee formed by Nehru to evolve the future economic policy of independent India, they rejected the option of women's quotas (Sharma 1998: 26).

Due to the mobilization of women in the Indian national movement they got increasingly involved in the political process that led to the drafting of the constitution. In her interventions on gender representation in the constituent assembly, Renuka Ray argued against reservation of seats for women as 'women have been fundamentally opposed to special privileges'. She claimed that 'women in this country have striven for their rights, for equality of status, for justice and fair-play'. Instead, these reservations were considered 'an impediment to (our) growth and an insult to (our) very intelligence and capacity'.[16]

Juridical equality was conceded but ingrained patterns of discrimination continued.[17] The post-colonial state adopted the main assumptions of modernization theories in the quest for nation-building, economic growth, and equity. An extensive body of literature now views legal approaches as being inadequate and having failed to deliver women their rights. The constitutional form of pluralism based on secular citizenship defined by civic and universalistic criteria also provided equal consideration to communities in the public realm. In the name of freedom of religion, which leaves personal laws alone, women were discriminated against in fundamental ways and denied a host of rights to property, family maintenance, divorce, guardianship, and adoption.

The Committee on the Status of Women in India (henceforth CSWI) in its report *Towards Equality*, published in 1974, surveyed the lives of Indian women to state that the right to 'political equality had enabled women to play their roles as partners and constituents in the political process' (CSWI 2012: 254). Women had been clubbed with children and backward classes of citizens for welfare services as if their discrimination did not have any independent basis. The constitution had said nothing on women's labour or about retention of discriminatory personal laws which denied any independent rights in marriage, property, or productive assets. In the period, following the CSWI Report, the women's movement raised several issues in the public agenda and set them in the political context by pulling them out from welfare mode. The women's movement asked for better laws, state accountability, and distributive justice as there was an escalation in the incidence of crime and violence against women in public and private domains, ranging from female foeticide and infanticide, bride and widow burning, rape, sexual harassment, wife battering, trafficking in women, and prostitution. The emergence of an autonomous women's movement arose in response to the rigid hierarchical structures of the political parties that did not leave any scope for the women members to attain leadership positions.

In the 1990s, women's struggles against the Muslim Women's Bill and sati were intertwined with caste, national, and religious identities in the anti-Mandal agitations and Ramjanmabhoomi movements. The cumulative impact of this politics was further complicated by the Mandal Commission report that gave rise to numerous micro-level caste political formations which were in constant flux, seeking a place amidst shifting political alliances. The issue of overlapping quotas or sub-quotas for disadvantaged groups arose as the women's bill for reservations in parliament was seen to be against the interests of the OBCs, Dalits, and Muslim women.

The Government of India decided to set up gender specific institutions like a National Commission for Women (NCW). The reasons for this can partly be found in the successful politicization of women issues by the women's movements; it was no longer possible for the political parties to ignore women as a political constituency, more especially with the emergence of coalition politics, which required that new constituencies needed to be mobilized. The NCW was particularly active in organizing Parivrik Mahila Lok adalats for resolving problems of women with help of NGOs. In recent years, it has looked into law and legislation to launching programmes of legal awareness, sensitization programmes for police, and for better implementations of laws. The NCW along with the National Human Rights Commission (NHRC) are viewed as major institutions to safeguard the rights of women against sexual harassment.

Despite being subjects of justice, India's overburdened criminal justice system has been unable to provide support to rape, harassment, and sexual assault victims. Sexual violence has devastating effects on survivors and their families. The trajectory of women's legal rights in India is traceable in the way these have been addressed in the women's movements. A crucial Supreme Court judgment in the custodial rape case of Mathura, a young tribal woman in 1979, and later of Maya Tyagi in Baghpat, initiated the anti-rape campaign, and led to the enactment of the criminal law amendment of 1983.[18] The 84th Law Commission Report that dealt with rape and allied offences excluded the relevance of woman's past sexual conduct from a rape trial. It made important recommendations starting a public debate on rape demanded by women's groups and legal experts.

Judicial grappling with gender is instructive not only about the lack of women's rights but also the complex relations between cultural norms and doctrinal developments. It has been more than 15 years since sexual harassment was for the first time recognized by the Supreme Court as a human rights violation and gender-based systemic discrimination. Before 1997, there were laws in the Indian Penal Code (IPC) that could be evoked when a woman is sexually harassed but these were framed as offences that amount to obscenity in public or seen to violate a woman's modesty. Many accused persons in a rape or sexual assault got acquitted or received a minor sentence. Cases of sexual harassment came under a popular category of eve teasing in section 509 of the IPC where it was treated a joke that only trivialized and ridiculed women. Thus before *Vishaka*, women who experienced sexual harassment had to lodge a complaint under section 354 of the IPC that deals with criminal assault of women to outrage a woman's modesty or section 509 that punishes an individual for using words that insult the modesty of a woman. To that extent, the *Vishaka* judgment was a discursive break with categories used in the past as it redefined sexual harassment as a paradigmatic act of violence against women (Baxi 2001).

The public outrage against the 16 December gang rape in New Delhi, 2013 brought all these issues into the limelight; it was unprecedented, but the movement was not geared to fighting a single case. It was an expression of accumulated anger and the shaping of a world view of declining tolerance for gender stereotypes. The Nirbhaya movement, which saw people from different professions and backgrounds pouring onto the streets, was mostly urban: the unevenness of the doctrinal evolution of the law on sexual harassment and its limitations emerged as the idea into making anti-rape laws more stringent and creating a safer urban environment for girls and women.

While there were several attempts made to enact a law on sexual harassment previously, the Sexual Harassment of Women at Workplace (Prevention, Prohibition and Redressal) Bill, 2012 was eventually passed by the Lower House of the Parliament (Lok Sabha) on September 3, 2012, then passed by the Upper House of the Parliament (Rajya Sabha) on February 26, 2013 and received the President's assent on April 22, 2013 (henceforth SHWW).

Sex-discrimination at Workplaces in the Organized Sector

Although it has been a struggle to achieve recognition of sexual harassment as discrimination, it is closely linked to securing rights at work which corresponds to just and favourable conditions related to safety at the workplace, leisure, fair remuneration, decent pay, social security, and abolition of forced labour.[19] The resurgence of the interest in implementing the laws against sexual harassment has drawn into question central tenets of legal jurisprudence in India.[20]

The *Vishaka* PIL case as a writ petition was filed for enforcement of working women and their rights due to the brutal gang rape of a *sathin* (social worker) in Rajasthan. Bhanwari Devi was a grassroots worker of the Women's Development Project trained by the local government to do village-level social work. When as part of a government campaign, she attempted to stop the child marriage of a one-year-old girl in rural Rajasthan, members of the local community retaliated by harassing her and then brutally raping her. Despite facing huge obstacles in recording her statement with the police or for conducting a medical examination, Bhanwari Devi carried on the struggle for justice. The NCW took up the case of providing her security and appointed a special prosecutor to argue her case. Acquitting her rapists in 1995, the Rajasthan state criminal court declared that they were respectable persons of a high caste who could not have raped a woman. The appeal against the acquittals had yet to be decided by the Rajasthan court when five NGOs—Vishaka, Jagori, Kali, Mahila Purnvas Samou, and the Rajasthan Voluntary Health Association—filed a PIL action in 1992 against the State of Rajasthan, its Women and Child Welfare Departments, its department of Social Welfare and the Union of India, in the Supreme Court to challenge sexual harassment at the workplace.

A three-judge bench of the Supreme Court delivered the *Vishaka* judgment on 13 August 1997. Although Bhanwari did not get justice in the case of sexual assault as rape was viewed as a subject matter of a separate criminal action under the IPC section 375, Chief Justice Verma in this case focused on the hazards to which working women may be exposed. Although such incidents resulted in violation of fundamental rights under Articles 14, 15, and 21, it was also a violation of Article 19 which allowed individuals to practice any profession. In the absence of a domestic law and any legislative measures, the contents of international conventions and norms, the Convention on the Elimination of All Forms of Discrimination against Women (CEDAW) were seen as instructive. He also quoted the Beijing statement of principles of the independence of the judiciary (1995) as representing the minimum standards to be observed for maintaining the independence of the judiciary to guide them in the absence of any law (Ghadially 2007).

Chief Justice Verma defined gender equality as protection from sexual harassment, which included the recognition that it was not just a personal injury but violated rights to equality at the workplace. Ahead of its times, to the question, what evil does the law of harassment aim to combat, the judgment reflects on violations of individual dignity. By imposing the onus on responsible persons, accountability was no longer on an individual perpetrator but covered institutions. Providing a utilitarian justification, Justice Verma claimed that it was necessary and expedient from employers in workplaces and institutions to observe guidelines to ensure prevention of sexual harassment of women. Besides, he directed agencies to notify it as an offence, include it in their rules relating to conduct and discipline at the workplace and set up a complaint mechanism.[21]

For all practical purposes, the *Vishaka* guidelines were the law until February 26, 2013, when the Rajya Sabha passed the Sexual Harassment of Women at the Workplace (prevention, Prohibition and Redressal) Act 2012. Under the new law, the definition of sexual harassment follows that of *Vishaka*: as unwelcome, verbal, visual, or physical conduct of a sexual nature that is severe to cause and effect working conditions or creates a hostile work environment. Generally, sexual harassment is a sexually oriented conduct that endangers the victim's job, negatively affects the victim's job performance or undermines her sense of dignity. It also assumes many forms from verbal innuendo leading to sexual assault.

The most important aspect of this law is that it recognizes how sexual harassment causes women not only personal distress and injury but further undermines their right to work. The ambit of the Act is very wide and is applicable to the organized sector as well as the unorganized sector as well as domestic workers who were earlier left out. In view of the wide definition of 'workplace' the statute, *inter alia*, applies to government bodies, private and public sector organizations, non-governmental organizations, organizations carrying on commercial, vocational, educational, entertainment, industrial, financial activities, hospitals and nursing homes, educational institutes, sports institutions, and stadiums used for training individuals. A workplace also covers within its scope places visited by employees during the course of employment or for reasons arising out of employment, including transportation provided by the employer for the purpose of commuting from the place of employment.

Many defects remain. The Act only addresses the protection of women employees and is not gender neutral, hence male employees do not get relief. The definition of sexual harassment does not take into account textual, physical, graphic, or electronic actions due to cyberspace freedoms. This act has to be supported by other laws so that it becomes more meaningful. If allegations are proved, the employer is allowed to deduct from the respondent's salary to pay to the aggrieved women. However there are laws under the Payment of Wages Act 1936 which restrict the deductions that may be made from an employee's salary. Finally, the bill does not cover members of the armed forces even though these are still heavily dominated by men, and women are at a disadvantage in these areas. According to the guidelines, the employer is responsible for both preventing sexual harassment and taking action on complaints. The organization has to have a complaint mechanism in place, which should be well publicized among employees. It is also the employer's responsibility to initiate criminal proceedings where needed and provide all support mechanisms. The increasing number of complaints filed in the courts and in the National Commission for Women (NCW) are a testimony to the lack of the proper implementation of the *Vishaka* guidelines by the employer and the general ineffectiveness of the complaint committees. Some of these cases are discussed in the following sections.

Legal Context of Sexual Harassment Cases in India

Clearly sexual harassment may occur in a single encounter or as a series of incidents but it basically defines the condition of the working environment.[22] The persistence of the problem despite awareness and institutional effort suggests various patterns: complaints are rare because the victims come forward only when they think the situation is serious enough to warrant such an action as they fear reprisals. Going ahead with a trial requires the complainants to intensify their injury or to place for scrutiny their own sexual relationships and behaviour. It is not surprising to note that grounds for legal action are very rare as harassment for long was interpreted within the criminal code procedure; judges treated harassing behaviour as isolated and idiosyncratic or as inappropriate for legal intervention as some agencies in the government were exempt from complaints of sexual harassment like the armed forces. Habitual harassers mostly escape while the women have been transferred and ridiculed for their psychic behaviour. Empirical research discloses high levels of under-reporting rather than the reverse as the law is still ill-defined and legal remedies slow in cases actually filed. While sexual harassment at the workplace is widely recognized in government employment and the corporate sector, it still does not get the proper juridical response.

Most legal interventions are unsettled on these cases and often lack a coherent rationale. As prospects of legal liability in both the government and private sector are not high, the public disclosure in recent cases, through social media networks, has emerged as a major arena to redress grievances of women.[23] Yet the embarrassment and evidentiary hurdles of procedures and financial expenses remain.

During these controversies, several important themes emerge: first, that sexual harassment refers to a phenomenon where the accused always reiterates the power and authority that comes with one's gender as well as superiority. Second, that the core wrong of sexual harassment consists in injury to individuals as members of a group. Third, that it implies the oppressive enforcement of conventional norms of gender sexual orientation and sexual expression. Finally, the idea of conduct of a sexual nature figures more as a problem to be regulated and less as a liberty to be protected. Relevance of sex role stereotypes and male perceptions of women in earlier cases and the judgments occur consistently. Thus in the Indian context, a permanent feature of many of the harassment cases related to government employees is that harassment is often of a relatively powerless subordinate by a more powerful supervisor who gives unwanted sexual attention. The guidelines and judgments identified sexual harassment as a question of power exerted by the perpetrator on the victim.[24]

Since *Vishaka*, many universities and educational institutions have tried to implement the guidelines and norms prescribed by the Supreme Court. Consequently detailed guidelines were developed both in Jawaharlal Nehru University (JNU) and Delhi University. Presently, a strong redress mechanism exists in JNU known as the Gender Sensitization Committee against Sexual Harassment (GSCASH). It has recorded more than 45 cases in the past three years with complaints leading to expulsions and suspensions. In Delhi University, the Executive Council, in the case of sexual harassment against a professor of the Hindi Department took the decision to place him under compulsory retirement with all benefits in 2011.[25] Another associate professor in the Department of Mathematics, South Campus, was dismissed for sexual harassment. Although in this case, the complaints committee was formed much later as the department did not respond positively to the student till she lodged an FIR against the teacher at the police station.[26] Since then several central and state universities across the country, including a few private universities have shown interest but final regulations and its implementations are still in the preliminary stages.[27]

Within the civil services, one of the most publicized high profile legal cases that hogged the media limelight for many years was that of Rupan Deol Bajaj. Bajaj was an officer of the Indian Administrative Service belonging to the Punjab cadre and then working as the Special Secretary, Finance. In 1988, she lodged a complaint, much before the *Vishaka* guidelines came into force, against the Inspector General of Police, Chandigarh, alleging commission of offences by Mr K.P. S. Gill, the Director General of Police, Punjab, 1988.[28] She complained that in a dinner party, he insulted her in the presence of his guests.[29] After a protracted battle, the High Court of Punjab and Haryana on 20 August 1998 upheld Gill's conviction under Section 354 and section 509 for his actions. He was sentenced to pay a fine and imprisoned rigorously for three months, both of which were later modified.[30]

An elected official D. Ramchandran, the-then minister of social welfare in the state of Pondicherry was accused by his secretary. Radha Bai, an assistant director in the local administration department, of abusing girls in the welfare institutions (see *Radha Bai* v. *Union Territory of Pondicherry*, A.I.R. 1995 S.C. 1476 (India)). He attempted to subsequently molest her and then dismissed her. Judge Paripoornan was of the view that the appellant's removal of service from 1981 was wrong and her actual service rendered as a civil servant had to be taken into account. Although, no punishment was meted out to the minister, the judgment was in her favour as she was entitled to pension and retirement benefits. For the loss of her reputation, she was to be paid a fine of Rs three lakhs.

Mostly it has been difficult to charge either a state official or an elected official for harassment. The government usually declines to share information on complaints of sexual harassment against IAS officers saying it was exempted from disclosure. In the matter of *Girish R. Deshpande* v. *Central Information Commission and others*, the apex court held that information including copies of memos, show cause notices, and orders of censure issued to a government employee qualifies to be personal information and the information being sought is exempt from disclosure,[31] even though harassment charges have been made.[32]

In India's external intelligence arm, the Research and Analysis Wing (RAW), Nisha Priya Bhatia, complained of sexual harassment but her allegations could not be substantiated by the inquiry committee in 2008. She alleged that she was compulsorily retired from service in 2009 in the backdrop of her complaint on sexual exploitation of women employees in RAW. She claimed that as per the rules, the pensions were due to her but even after expiry of two years, the respondents had not finalized the application.[33] Similar to the *Radha Bai* case, no action was taken against the accused and Bhatia's allegations were not addressed, the judgment was sympathetic that she be entitled for the benefit claimed by her as a government employee.

The Indian army, air force, and navy have more than 7,000 female officers who have been inducted since the 1990s. They have been shouldering responsibilities in the non-combat arms.[34] A number of cases of sexual harassment within the defence forces came up which have been resolved by strict organizational enquiry procedures. Women officers feel that they are in a minority and therefore more vulnerable to the undercurrents of sexual harassment in a rigid hierarchical structure of the defence forces. There is also a view that despite the presence of a 'sensitive' law enforcement mechanism within the organization, women tend to avoid reporting out of shame and fear of spoiling one's reputation and track record. This exhibits the authoritative and patriarchal structure of the armed forces despite women being in powerful and responsible positions. In a peculiar case, a young woman officer who had levelled allegations of physical and mental harassment against her superior officers faced a trial by general court martial for her alleged acts of professional impropriety. In most of these cases, women are sacked for indiscipline when charging the seniors for making sexual remarks as in the case of Squadron Leader Anjali Gupta of the IAF in 2005.[35]

These instances go on to prove that no professional sector is devoid of sexual harassment and its grave consequences and victimization as the woman who complains suffers. This also reflects the lack and failure of the complaints mechanism set up by the government, lack of grievances redressal within the hierarchical system of the topmost paramilitary forces of the country, and the inherent weakness of the existing redress mechanisms. Punishments are rare but in case of Major General A.K. Lal posted in Leh, a general court martial held him guilty of molesting a woman officer and dismissed him from army service. Colonel Anurodh Mishra in Jammu and Kashmir, would forfeit six years of his service when considering further promotions as he had molested a fellow officer in 2008.

Two major sexual harassment complaints sent shock waves in the capital—one by a journalist in *Tehelka*. The electronic and print media is a workplace where till now there have been very few court cases, and even fewer judgements favouring complainants in such cases till the *Tehelka* case involving Tarun Tejpal. Before the Tejpal case, however, in a ruling that is probably the first of its kind, a journalist got an order against a media organization for firing her when she had complained of sexual harassment.[36] Eleven years after journalist Rina Mukherjee was fired following her allegations of sexual harassment against a senior, the West Bengal Industrial Tribunal passed an order against *The Statesman*, offering hope of redress for other victims. While this order did not address the harassment angle itself, it was a clear ruling on the way the company acted.[37] Interestingly, the order came at a time when parliament had passed the Sexual Harassment of Women at Workplace (Prevention, Prohibition and Redressal) Act.[38]

The most recent case of a young woman journalist who accused editor-in-chief of *Tehelka*, Tarun Tejpal, of sexual assault shows how reporting of sexual harassment, within the organization could be pushed aside or manipulated. Tejpal admitted to the crime in an email sent to the managing editor and termed the incident 'tragic' and 'a lapse of judgment'. Just like the well-known *The Statesman*, *Tehelka* did not have a sexual harassment complaints committee so the survivor's complaint was not addressed by a committee. During this event however, Tejpal's text messages, to the survivor of the ordeal sent immediately after the incident and a week later were evidence of the encounter. It also included the CCTV footage of the elevators of the hotel where the incidents took place.[39]

In the private sector, the first case after *Vishaka* in which the Supreme Court applied the law was what is called the *Apparel* case. The court upheld the dismissal of a superior officer of the Delhi based Apparel Export Promotion Council who was found guilty of sexual harassment. It was argued that the fundamental right guaranteed under Article 21 of the constitution had been violated in the case and an 'attempt to molest' was equally an infringement of a woman's right to dignity at the workplace as a 'successful attempt of molestation'.[40]

Since *Vishaka*, many cases have emerged in the private sector and in multinational companies. The question of remedies in the Indian context is unclear as the potential for litigation and the compensatory and punitive damages awarded to complainants are rare and minimal. Moreover, tainted CEOs seemed to survive unlike complainants who either leave the organization or face ignominy. Even the press seem to be biased as they usually come out in support of them. I would argue that traditional understanding of harassment in which the harassed woman lacks the capacity to refuse an unwanted sexual relationship at the workplace may or may not be flourishing here in corporate jobs as a newer form of harassment is predominant: as women enter high-paying non-traditional jobs in the corporate sector, men use sexualized conduct to often communicate to women their 'outside' status in the workplace and harm is accomplished through denigration, mocking, or sexualized attention.

In one of the earliest publicized cases, the Mumbai police arrested a partner and head of KPMG India, in a case of sexual harassment at the workplace, filed by a former director. The complainant alleged that he had, along with others, passed lewd comments and asked for sexual favours.[41] The complainant has since then left the firm but the accused is presently heading another company. In yet another case, a California law firm represented an employee of iGate with respect to her claims of sexual harassment against Phaneesh Murthy, CEO, iGate. Mr Murthy was removed from his position of CEO and president for his failure to report his relationship with a subordinate employee. However iGate, a company based in the US, said it found no merit in the complaint of sexual harassment. Murthy said the case was an attempt at extortion: 'Without question, it is a case of extortion. Ever since the first case became public, everybody feels that they have an absolutely easy way to collect money on whatever pretext'.[42] As of now the class actions suit filed against iGate and Phaneesh Murthy in the US, has been dismissed and neither the company nor its disgraced former CEO claim to make any payments.

The chief marketing officer of Idea Cellular, associated with the popular 'What An Idea, Sirji' campaign quit after a subordinate accused him of sexual harassment via inappropriate and personal emails and texts.[43] The company's internal committee could not establish if the claims were genuine because the complainant produced the offending messages in the form of computer print-outs rather than on a phone, and the charged executive preferred quitting to appearing before the investigating committee. In another case, the head of Penguin publishers in Canada, was asked to leave the company after a female employee filed a suit in the local court.[44] Bollywood was under scanner by courts for its shocking discrimination of women who were prohibited from becoming members of the Cine Costume and Makeup Artists Association in a PIL by Charu Khurana in 2015.

In cases involving diplomats as of a UNICEF head in India, the question of immunity obstructs the judicial process. The enquiry by the women and child development ministry in 2007 found there was reasonable cause to believe that the complainant was sexually harassed by Cecilio Adorna, the India representative of UNICEF. women and child development minister, Renuka Chowdhury, ordered an enquiry after the victim approached her, and wrote to external affairs minister, Pranab Mukherjee, seeking withdrawal of diplomatic immunity to the UN official though nothing happened. Instead the complainant suffered retaliation and had her contract terminated.

***

The inadequacies in juridical analyses of harassment is not unique to cases involving gender. Sexual harassment at the workplace takes many forms, from sexually explicit remarks to harassment in cyberspace, over email to sexual assault. There are clearly a number of contextual challenges to advancing women's rights through the judicial system in India. I argued that the judiciary has been hesitant or ineffective in protecting the rights of women on harassment issues as seen in the court's interpretations of these laws. The difficulties that emerge stem in part from the paradigms developed within the law to address the problem of harassment. In Western political theory, Catherine Mackinnon in her path-breaking work viewed sexual harassment of women at work as sex discrimination in employment and defined it as 'unwanted imposition of sexual requirements in the context of a relationship of unequal power' where the major dynamic is expressed in enforcement of two inequalities: sexual and material (Mackinnnon 1979: 3).

MacKinnon's original theory defined two types of sexual harassment, the first about the workplace supervision that conditions the jobs, pay, promotion, and other material benefits, and subjects the employee to sexual forms of abuse. The second is about a hostile environment in which the employee is subject to unwelcome sexual conduct by the employee's supervisors, co-workers, clients, or customers with the purpose of or effect of an offensive working environment. In this analysis, sexual harassment is viewed as a consequence of the expression of gendered inequalities of work. Sex segregation at work is seen as a cause that consigns women to poorly paid subservient female jobs that invited their sexual objectification. However, instead of relying on female sexual subordination, she supplied an alternative account, that it was wrong because it treated women differently from men; it singled them out on the basis of their sex to which men were not subjected.

MacKinnon's equality theory offers us a starting point as it claims that the core wrong of sexual harassment consists in group injury or the subordination of women by men which is achieved through sexual conduct. For her, practices which express and reinforce the social inequality of women to men are clear cases of sex-based discrimination in the inequality approach. The remedy achieved is through anti-discrimination laws which protect workers against discriminatory abuse.

Most courts in India have adopted a standard paradigm of sexual harassment that sees the harasser is the male, the victim, the female. The harassment expresses the sexual desire and consists in unwelcome sexual conduct and targets the complainant. Hence sexual harassment as sex discrimination relies on the presumption that the harassers are heterosexual and so subject female workers to sexual attention that they are not imposing on male workers. Moreover, by seeing sex discrimination as a form of desire, the act of differentiation that makes sexual harassment discrimination, would appear to be normal, a natural part of our social life and the harm of sexual harassment is somehow incidental to the practice of sex discrimination.

Over the years a lot of thinking has gone into sexual harassment that falls outside the scope of the standard paradigm. It is now understood that gender harassment is about engaging in verbal and physical misconduct, not necessarily sexual, but that expresses hostility towards women; co-workers of any rank engage in verbal and physical harassment of gender nonconformists—of masculine women and effeminate men; or sexual orientation or identity harassment. None of these express sexual desire but instead impose sexist standards on others. Power is not always contained in formal institutions but can circulate in many spheres so that we can identify two kinds: (a) horizontal harassment that involves exclusion by those at the same level; and (b) vertical harassment that involves coercion from above. Thus it is not only between superior and junior but also about co-workers that create relationships to sustain hierarchy in place. Given that work is one of the most important distributional goods in our society and is central to most people's sense of themselves, men will try to monopolize good jobs to safeguard their economic superiority and reinforce women's subordinate status in organizations.

Ratna Kapur argues that sexual harassment law produces some of the same problems that occurred elsewhere; there is a tendency to focus on sexual conduct, suppressing sexuality in the workplace and deflecting attention from the more common non-sexual forms of discrimination and abuse in the workplace. But there are some concerns emerging in the Indian context: since the core ingredient of the definition is that the sexual conduct is unwelcome, the burden is conditioned by the complainant's sexual past and mode of dress. In this way waitresses, bar room dancers, and performers become vulnerable to such claims as the definition provides scope for reinforcing assumptions about women's sexuality (Kapur 2005).

One of the groups that are targeted amongst women are those amongst scheduled castes or Dalits, who constitute 16 per cent of the total Indian population. They continue to suffer work-based discrimination, and are extremely vulnerable. Dalit women face more burdens due to caste and gender discrimination. They are subject to systematic oppression and structural violence from their families. Atrocities and violence are used as a means to reinforce the systematic caste and gender discrimination as well as to punish them when they challenge caste and gender norms. Economic and social boycotts are a common tool used by the dominant castes that influences the overall access of Dalits to economic and social rights.

In responding to the murder of two children in Budaun, Uttar Pradesh, many scholars point out the need for understanding of caste and structural violence. The heightened violence and the unspeakable torture that renders people totally vulnerable and powerless are constitutive of caste society where caste atrocity has become the norm.[45] For these reasons, the deliberation of the Justice Verma committee that followed the murder of a young woman in Delhi in December 2012 saw many Dalit groups raising the question of the inequality of protest—was there a similar response after the Khairlanji massacre? Kannabiran rightly points out that 'while all murders result in loss of life and human suffering, targeted murder against members belonging to a social groups that is vulnerable is more serious because it reflects a pattern that systematically reinforces power' (Kannabiran 2014: 14).

Even while the argument so far is to assert a specific right for women against sexual harassment, the elision of difference is defective as violence faced by women is shaped by the dimension of their identities such as caste and class. The attempt to present so far, experiences of women as similar then overlooks the way experiences of Dalit women, for example, is the product of intersecting patterns of patriarchy and upper-caste domination but these do not get represented within the discourse of anti-caste movements or that of women's rights.

Taking forward some of the arguments presented by Kimberle Williams Crenshaw, in a different context, I argue that structural intersectionality or the location of Dalit women makes their actual experience of rape, violence, and harassment qualitatively different from that of upper-class and upper-caste women (Crenshaw 1991: 1241–99). I argued earlier that the support for repairing harms committed against disempowered groups, like women, is stronger when the reform does not challenge the basic structures of society; so law offers   benevolent assistance to deserving complainants only. Attacks on Dalit women are accompanied by arson, looting, massacres, and ethnic cleansing. In this context, the experiences of women who do not share the same class background will be of limited utility for those whose lives are completely shaped by socio-economic factors. Caste and gender are the sites for the particular distribution of social resources that will end up with observable differences in the way Dalit women experience violence relative to other groups. Brutal measures to thwart any attempts by Dalits to secure their rights have a deep impact on the community and produce the desired results to silence voices of dissent that challenge existing societal norms. Violence against Dalit women is a systematically utilized tool to deny the entire community opportunities, choices, and freedom at multiple levels.

Laws are passed on behalf of women on domestic violence, rape, and sexual harassment. These effects are likely to be less for assault survivors like Bhanwari. A significant amount of the resources have to go into meeting needs that are specific to Dalit women, which includes housing, transport, clothing, and even medical assistance. Faced by triple effects of subordination, along with limited opportunities, Dalit women may not be able to meet the requirements, of the law.

The second concept is that of political intersectionality that can be used to highlight that Dalit women are situated within two subordinated groups—between Dalit men and upper-caste women whose opposing political agendas are a dimension of their current disempowerment. By not acknowledging the additional burden of patriarchy and of caste, anti-caste and feminist movements are limited discourses for Dalit women. Thus the assumption of anti-essentialist critiques of feminism that categories like women are not natural merely representations or are actually socially constructed are defective. The argument following from this claim is that since all categories are socially constructed, there is no such thing as women and it makes little sense to reproduce these categories. To say that a category is socially constructed is not to argue that it has no significance as most subordinated people are trying to cope with the way power is dispersed in their lives.[46] Much of the present theories on sexual harassment need to be concerned not simply with the forces that push women within hierarchical structures in workplaces and labour markets; sexual harassment and abuse cannot be separated from the system of caste hierarchies and subordination essential to maintaining present structures of power.

Notes

1. *Vishaka and Ors* v. *State of Rajasthan and Ors*, 13 August 1997 (henceforth *Vishaka*).
2. See Planning Commission (2008: 188).
3. This is to overlook acts that protect women's economic rights: The Employees State Insurance Act 1948, The Plantation Labour Act 1951, The Contract Labour Act 1976, The Equal Remuneration Act, 1976.
4. See World Economic Forum (2013) for claims that the corporate world is not doing enough to achieve gender equality.
5. The Indian economy passed through a crucial downturn in 2008 when the economic growth rate plunged to 5.5 per cent. As the economy has opened up to global players, the external depression has a greater impact than earlier events. See Pearson and Sweetman (2011).
6. For example senior judges, senior police officers, directorships of companies, and editors of newspapers.
7. Around 118 million workers or 97 per cent of the female workforce are involved in the unorganized sector. Most women are working in the agricultural sector and allied fields (crop and live-stock production, horticulture, agro/social forestry) and are classified as agricultural labourers and cultivators.
8. Planning Commission (2008: 189). More than 3 million women or over 12 per cent of all women workers in urban India are domestic workers.
9. For the view that women in India are more prone to victimization in cyber space due to less legal protection, see Saha and Srivastava (2014: 57–67).
10. Pratibha Srikanth Murthy was a 28-year-old BPO employee, of HP Globalsoft in Bangalore, who was raped and killed after leaving home for her night-shift on 13 December 2005. Her murder redefined the idea of safety for working women in the urban areas. Some of the police debated about cancelling night shifts for women employees. See 'Techie rape leaves IT industry shell-shocked', *Times of India*, 24 October 2013. Judge B.V. Guddal awarded a sentence of life imprisonment till death to the accused five years after the crime was committed. Similar cases that raised questions of safety and involved civil society interventions, though outside the scope of this paper, include the *Jessica Lal* case, where the victim was shot dead in 1998 in a public bar and the *Priyadarshini Mattoo* case.
11. The Delhi gang rape case involved the rape and fatal assault of a 23-year-old female physiotherapy intern on 16 December 2012.

12. See Mudhok 2005.
13. See *Municipal Corporation of Delhi* v. *Female Workers (Muster roll) and another* 8 March 2000; *Pramila Rawat* v. *District Judge Lucknow* 10 May 2000; *Air India etc. etc* v. *Nergesh Meerza, Ors,* 28 August, 1981.
14. See Mangubhai (2014: 2–3).
15. For two stages during this moment, see Everett (1979).
16. Renuka Ray, CAD Friday 18 July 1947. See for more Articles in the constitution related to women's rights in 14, 15, 16, 39 (a) and (d), 42, 46, 47, 51 (A)e, 243 (D)3 and (D)4, 243 (T)3 and (T)4.
17. Some of the examples of Acts passed that affect women specifically are: The Family Courts Act, 1954, The Special Marriage Act, 1954, The Hindu Marriage Act, 1955, The Maternity Benefit Act, 1961, Dowry Prohibition Act, 1961, The Medical Termination of Pregnancy Act, 1971, The Prohibition of Child Marriage Act, 2006, Indecent Representation of Women, 1986, Commission of Sati (Prevention) Act, 1987.
18. For a debate on shame and honour vs protectionism, see Kapur and Cossman (1996: 61).
19. See, for example, earlier reports like SEWA (1987) and GoI (1988).
20. See Saheli (1998); Kapoor (1999); Sanhita (2001).
21. The Supreme Court in its judgment in *Medha Kotwal Lele & Ors.* v. *Union of India & Ors* stated that the Complaints Committee as envisaged in the *Vishaka* judgment will be deemed to be an inquiry authority. The report of the Complaints Committee shall be deemed to be an inquiry report under those rules. See *Medha Kotwal Lele & Ors.* v. *UOI & Ors.,* Writ Petition (Crl.) Nos. 173–177/1999, Order dated 26 April 2004. Available at http://www.iiap.res.in/files/VisakaVsRajasthan_1997.pdf.
22. The writer was chairperson of the GSCASH, JNU in 2004–05 and some of the summaries on this law are from that period.
23. The media's role was evident especially in the *Jessica Lal* murder case of 29 April 1999; Also in *Neelam Katara* v. *State & Ors., Crl.Rev.P.* 369/2008.
24. In a rare case, politician and a promoter of an airline, Gopal Kanda is facing rape and abetment to suicide charges after one of the airline's 23-year employee's Geetika Sharma committed suicide. Although in judicial custody Kanda has been now released on bail. 'Geetika Case: HC lets Kanda remain on bail', *Times of India,* 27 May 2014.
25. 'Compulsory retirement for Professor accused of sexual harassment', TNN, 1 July 2011.
26. 'DU reader faces axe for seeking sexual favours', TNN, 31 July 2008.

27. Examples, O.P. Jindal University, Thapar University, and the School of Law and Legal Studies, Guru Gobind Singh Indraprastha University.

28. Under Sections 341, 342, 352, 354, and 509 of the Indian Penal Code (IPC).

29. *Mrs Rupan Deol Bajaj and Anr* v. *Kanwar Pal Singh Gill and Anr* 12 October 1995.

30. After final appeals before the Supreme Court in July 2005 the conviction was upheld and the jail sentence was reduced to probation.

31. 'Centre declines information on sexual harassment cases against bureaucrats', 8 October 2013, Press Trust of India.

32. For a recent case, see D.S. Kunwar, 'Uttarakhand additional secretary held on sexual assault charge', *Times of India*, 4 December 2013.

33. *Ms Nisha Priya Bhatia* v. *Union of India*, 11 May, 2012.

34. Suman Sharma, 'Sexual Harassment not new in Army', *Sunday Guardian*, 12 January 2013; Anand Bodh, 'Woman Army officer accuses seniors of sexual harassment', *Times of India*, 16 July 2008. *D.S. Grewal* v. *Vimmi Joshi and Anr*, (2009) 2 S.C.C. 210 (India).

35. Air Vice Marshal Anil Chopra went on to become an Air Marshal before retiring while Anjali Gupta committed suicide in Bhopal in 2011. In 2008, Poonam Kaur of the army's 5682 ASC battalion posted in Kalka was dismissed for disobedience. In a separate case, Lt Sushmita Chakravarty committed suicide in Kalka, in June 2006 as her duties included arranging late night parties. (see Sharma, *Guardian* 2013).

36. The Statesman Ltd and their workman Rina Mukherjee (Case No. VIII-01/2004).

37. The Statesman Ltd, and their workman Rina Mukherjee (case no. VIII-01/2004) in which the Tribunal ordered that the company should reinstate Ms Mukherjee, and pay her full wages with retrospective effect from the time she was fired in October 2002.

38. The verdict may also help the case of a news anchor/producer in Sun TV, who accused the chief editor of harassment. The latter was arrested, and is out on bail now. On the other hand, Sun TV suspended her from work and has constituted an enquiry against her.

39. The incident took place in *Tehelka's* Think Festival in Goa from 8 to 10 November 2013.

40. *Apparel Export Promotion Council* v. *A.K. Chopra*, 20 January, 1999. S.C. 625 (India).

41. 'Sr KPMG official held for sexual harassment', *Indian Express*, October 9, 2007. Presently Vikram Utamsingh is heading A and M India and is a managing director with Alvarez and Marsal Transactions Group.

42. Goutam Sen, 'Fatal Attractions', *Business Today*, 23 June 2013; also see 4 June 2013.
43. Kunal Pradhan, 'Top idea executive charged with sex harassment quits', 12 August 2010. *Mumbai Mirror*.
44. 'David Davidar Has Not Sexually Harassed Anyone', *Outlook*, 21 June 2010. Lisa Rundle, former Rights and Contracts director, Penguin Canada claimed $423,000 in damages from Penguin for wrongful dismissal and $100,000 from the company. The case was later settled out of court.
45. See Kannabiran 2014: 14.
46. A Prajnya Report, *Gender Violence in India*, (2010) that focuses on violence in public spaces.

References

Baxi, P. 2001. 'Sexual Harassment', *Seminar*, 505, September: 54–59.

Crenshaw, K. 1991. 'Mapping the Margins: Intersectionality, identity politics and the violence against women of colour', *Stanford Law Review*, 43 (6): 1241–99.

Committee on the Status of Women in India (CSWI). 2012. *Towards Equality: Report of the CSWI*. New Delhi: Centre for Women's Development Studies.

Everett, J.M. 1979. *Women and Social Change in India*. Delhi: Heritage.

Government of India (GoI). 1988. *Shramshakti: Report of the National Commission on Self Employed Women and Women in the Informal Sector*. New Delhi: GoI.

Ghadially, R. 2007. *Urban Women in Contemporary India: A Reader*. New Delhi: Sage.

Hooks, B. 2000. *Feminist Theory: From Margins to Centre*. UK: Pluto Press.

Kannabiran, K. 2014. 'Annihilation by Caste', *Economic and Political Weekly*, XLIX (26–27): 13–17.

Kannabiran, K. and R. Singh. 2008. *Challenging the Rule(s) of Law: Colonialism, Criminology and Human Rights in India*. New Delhi: Sage.

Kapadia, K. 2002. *The Violence of Development: The Politics of Identity, Gender and Social Inequalities in India*. New Delhi: Kali.

Kapoor, A. 1999 (ed.). 'Sakshi: Sexual Harassment at the Workplace: A Guide to the Sexual harassment law in India' in *Women Workers' Rights: A Reference Guide*. New Delhi: ILO.

Kapur, R. 2005. *Law and the New Erotic Justice: Politics of Postcolonialism*. New Delhi: Permanent Black.

Kapur, R. and B. Cossman. 1996. *Subversive Sites, Feminist Engagements with Law in India*. New Delhi: Sage.

Karat, B. 2013. 'Insightful and Pathbreaking', *The Hindu*, 28 January.

Mackinnnon, C.A. 1979. *Sexual Harassment of Working Women*. New Haven and London.

Mangubhai, J.P. 2014. *Human Rights as Practice*. New Delhi: Oxford University Press.

Mudhok, S. 2005. *Report on the Status of Women Workers in the Construction Industry*. Government of India: National Commission for Women.

Pearson, R. and C. Sweetman, (eds). 2011. *Gender and the Economic Crisis. Practical Action*: Oxfam.

Rao, N., I. Rurup, and R. Sudarshan, (eds). 1996. *Sites of Change: The Structural Context for Empowering Women in India*. New Delhi: Tulika.

Saha, T. and A. Srivastava. 2014. 'Women at Risk in the Cyber Space', *International Journal of Cyber Criminology*, 8 (1): 57–67.

Saheli. 1998. 'Another Occupational Hazard: Sexual Harassment and the Working Woman'. New Delhi: Saheli.

Sanhita. 2001. 'Politics of Silence'. Kolkata: Sanhita.

Self-Employed Women's Association (SEWA). 1987. *National Workshop on Home-Based Piece-rate workers*. Ahmedabad: SEWA.

Sharma, K. 1998. 'Power vs. Representation: Feminist Dilemmas, Ambivalent State and the Debate on Reservations for Women in India', p. 26., Occasional papers. Delhi: Centre for Women's Studies.

World Economic Forum. 2013. *Global Gender Gap Report*. Geneva: World Economic Forum.

8

Democracy, Deprivation, and Dispossession
Multiple Narratives of Democracy in North India

Badri Narayan

More than two decades after the end of the cold war, democracy remains a paradox and the contradictions of democracy as 'people's power' are becoming clearer. All over the world, various forms of democracies in several countries like Italy, Kenya, Bangladesh, El Salvador, Malawi, New Zealand, Peru, and South Korea are suffering through multiple forms of democratic deficit. In many cases, election as a central method to take democracy forward, fails in many ways. The existing power-holders and dominant sections often dictate governments that emerge out of democratic elections. They create hurdles in ensuring equality and participation as key values of democracy. The US and many Western countries, who take pride in their successful deepening of democracy, also seem to fail on the scale of responsiveness. Although after the collapse of their only global competitor, the Soviet Union, democracy is viewed by many in the West as the only option for ensuring equality and participation for citizens, but some scholars rightly feel the need to develop a system of democratic audit and critical evaluation of the major part of the world who are moving forward seamlessly in the 'transition to democracy' (Beetham et al. 2002).

India is the world's largest democracy. The one achievement which is usually highlighted as an important outcome of democracy in the country is the growing sense of empowerment and breaking the shackles of marginalization by the weaker sections of the society. However, we often miss the fact that empowerment and marginalization sometimes go together, sometimes side by side, at times supplementing each other or countering each other, with the cases varying for the communities that are competing for development in democracy. So marginalization appears in our everyday life in both ways—real and constructed. In its constructed form, it evolves and develops in the context of state-led democracy, which appears as a resource distributing and opportunity providing agency. This can be understood from the narratives of marginalization of different communities, which show how the state-led democracy works as the central locus of identity construction of social groups in our society. It is interesting to observe that these narratives of marginalization mostly emerge as critical and complaint-based against democracy, since these are based on the aspiration and desire for a better life of the marginalized communities.

In the Indian context, the state is perceived as the primary instrument of delivering democracy. In popular parlance, the state and democracy are perceived as synonymous to each other. During our field work in several villages of UP we found that both, the state and democracy are understood by the rural people in their everyday life as '*sarkar*'. The idea of sarkar in India is different from the European meaning of government that is perceived as a rational governing agency. It means the government and powerful people (*huzoor*, modern masters or political leaders—*neta*, powerful people, who may or may not directly be part of the government but attain power in the corridors of the state), who all run the government directly and indirectly or the *sarkar banane ke liye chunav* (election politics for entering in government).[1] This sarkar in its combined meaning of the state and democracy invokes lot of undirected and uncontrollable social aspiration despite the 'global dominance of ideas of liberalization'

(Kaviraj 2005: 2). Sudipta Kaviraj rightly observed that 'there is no end in sight of the Indian society's strange enchantment with the modern state' (Kaviraj 2005: 2). This very enchantment may be the one of the causes of the enormous rise of dissatisfaction against the state and state-led democracy.

This is a very peculiar situation for democracy in Indian society, especially in villages in north India. It sometimes appears that no one seems to be satisfied with democracy. All the people have complaints against the state-led democracy, the major complaint being that the government was not doing anything for them. Both the relatively rich and the poor had similar narratives in the context of state-led policies and development aimed to strengthen and deepen democracy. There may be two reasons for this. Firstly, they felt that the person asking questions might be a government official and so they deliberately enhanced the intensity of their problems in the hope that they will get some benefits. Secondly, the state-led democracy, in its present form, has given rise to a great deal of expectations among the people, which they express in the form of deprivations.

However, when we dug deeper in the psyche of the people through long-term interviews, we found that some presence of state-led development and democracy is found in each person's life even though it is never sufficient. The state-led democracy in India reinvented various methods to fulfill the urges and desires of communities and deepen democracy at the grassroots. Forming categories as a technique of managing democracy appeared as one of the modes of delivering protective discrimination to provide support and the benefit of democracy to the weaker sections of the population. To deepen democracy and attack the caste system, the Indian constitution, along with other measures like the abolition of the caste system, formed a system of reservation based on these categories in three sectors—electoral representation, government employment, and educational institutions (Kaviraj 2005: 13). This reinvention of categories later evolved as a powerful tool of electoral mobilization of marginal communities in India like the SCs, STs, and OBCs, during democratic elections. The demands for shifting categories by upper, middle, and lower castes are the outcome of their growing sense of marginalization in the allotted state location and the hope to come out from it by changing state created categories.[2] In governance, these categories are considered as homogeneous entities but in reality they contain multiple forms of heterogeneities and various layers of social locations for these castes.[3]

It is interesting to observe that sometimes during electoral mobilizations, political parties and the media believe that these categories work well as they help to mobilize a larger percentage of voters in favor of certain political parties. It is only when the distribution of democratic resources takes place that stories of marginalization and narratives of dispossession become visible. Hope for a better future binds them all together. All groups, big and small, come together for a common cause. A case in point is the Mandal Commission agitation, when even smaller groups of OBCs and SCs rallied together for common gains such as government jobs, housing, and other development policies aimed to strengthen the weaker sections and provide equitable social justice within the target group. This was the dream that was shown to these marginalized communities by the ruling political party. The desire of the dominant and vocal sections of these categories to take more share of the resources resulted in an inequitable distribution of resources based on caste. This situation created competition among the different marginalized castes at various levels with the smaller and less powerful being left out of the share of the resources. These communities now want to shift to other categories as they believe that they will get more benefits in this way. The trend among them is to try to shift to lower state-created categories as they feel that these categories are being given more benefits by the government. The ruling political party and other parties use these desires that emerge from the deprivation of these communities for strengthening their base among the respective communities.

Even political parties support the demand of communities to move to lower categories as can be seen by the fact that the Samajawadi Party (SP) government in UP is in the process of sending its recommendations to the centre for including 17 OBCs like Kahar, Kashyap, Kewat, Machuwa, Mallah, Nishad, Kumhar, Prajapati, Dheevar, Bind, Bhar, Rajbhar, Biyar, Batham, Gond, and Tairaha in the SC category. The SP had included these castes in the SC category by managing to intrude in the centre's rights to change quotas and categories. The SP sources accused previous chief minister and Bahujan Samaj Party (BSP) chief, Mayawati, of depriving these castes of their rights to protect her political interests, and in October 2005 a government order (GO) was passed providing equal facilities as SC to these 17 most backward OBCs. This move of Yadav was stayed by the Allahabad High Court following a writ filed by the BSP. After Mayawati became the chief minister she withdrew the recommendations of the previous SP government and quashed it on 6 June 2007.[4] She demanded that the centre should increase the SC reservation quota by another eight per cent before these 17 castes were included. All these recommendations have a vested political interest as these 17 castes that constitute 15 per cent of the total population of UP were capable of changing the forthcoming Lok Sabha election results in favour of the SP. Mayawati feared her defeat and thus withdrew the proposal sent by the SP government earlier.[5]

Indifferent to the vested interests of the political parties, a strong tussle emerged among many middle and most backward castes to be included in the government and state created low categories because of the benefits of reservations and quotas that the low categories enjoy that translate into assured government jobs. While some OBCs wish to acquire SCs status, a section of SCs like Musahar, Nat, Kanjar, Bansphor, etc. are demanding to be included in the ST category as they feel that the STs are given more benefits by the government. This problem is being faced by 62 of the 66 castes among Dalits in UP as only a few big Dalit castes like Chamar, Pasi, Kori, etc. have succeeded in taking advantage of the reservation policies and political empowerment of the Dalits. All the other 62 Dalit castes are very small in number and have low literacy level. Very few youths among them have passed intermediate exams. Many of these castes are engaged in traditional vocations and they have neither diversified nor modernized their caste-based professions. The benefits of government schemes do not reach them because they are not educated and also lack political leadership. Thus, they are unable to make their presence felt in the discourses and debates, within the SCs, and are largely invisible. State government officials, like district magistrates, subdivisional magistrates, block development officers, who are responsible for protecting and developing these castes are not even aware about them.

The leaders of some of these castes held meetings in Barahi Navada, near Varanasi, on 26 November 2012, in Fatehpur on 12 February 2013, and a protest meeting at Ganga Prasad Memorial

Hall, Lucknow, on 7 March 2013, where caste leaders of nine SC groups from Bhadohi, Jaunpur, Varanasi, Allahabad, Kaushambi, Fatehpur, Unnao, Barabanki, Lucknow, and Lalitpur handed over a memorandum to the state government to press their demands of being included in the ST category. These leaders felt that the change in category would help them get jobs in Aaganwadi, accrue facilities of various health schemes, and get the benefits of reservation.

This essay documents the multiple experience of democracy in North Indian society through the narratives of the Musahars, a small Dalit group in eastern UP. These narratives of multiple marginalizations are crucial to understand the articulation of democratic experience by the weaker sections of society. In this essay we trace the sense of relative deprivation of small Dalit groups that emerge out of their narratives of democratic experiences. We explore how state-led categories which had been developed by the state to bring equality in the society, lead to the misdistribution of the resources and produced marginalization in several cases in Indian society. These articulations of marginalization emerge through their everyday life in which they realize the state-led democracy by its presence in the form of various aspects of social justice.

Musahars: Democratic Experience and Desires

The Musahar is a community that is believed to be an offshoot of the Bhuiya tribe of Chhota Nagpur. To the community the word 'musahar' derives meaning that signifies flesh-seeker or hunter (*masu* meaning flesh, *hera* meaning seeker). Some interpret it to signify rat-taker or rat-eater (*musa* meaning rat) (Joshi and Kumar 2002: 20). Musahars belong to the Scheduled Castes and according to the 1981 census, their total population in UP is 126,018. The Musahar (SC) of UP also called Vanmanus, Banjara or Gonrare are mainly distributed in the districts of central and eastern UP. Musahars are the most efficient soil cutters (Joshi and Kumar 2002: 13). According to Asharfi Sadai, 'The Musahar and earth are like a two in one' (Joshi and Kumar 2002: xvi). Their language is Awadhi.

The Musahars of Mirzapur are of an altogether different stock. In the local language, they are called '*vanamanus*', which means forest dwellers. They collect honey and make *pattals* (plates made of leaves). They are a tribal group, once hunters and gatherers, collecting fruits and flowers from forests (Joshi and Kumar 2002: 139). They are mainly landless community that works as palanquin-bearers, agricultural labourers, or labourers in brick kilns, while some are involved in piggery. Modern developmental programmes have made only little impact on them. While earlier, till 1995, the focus of the Indira Awas Yojana was directed on the Musahars only but now this facility has been extended to all SC castes and so the Mushars don't get proper housing facilities as they do not have the voice to claim their rights (Joshi and Kumar 2002: 96). Recent surveys indicate that the spread of education among the Musahars is extremely limited—just three per cent (Joshi and Kumar 2002: 1). According to the 1981 census, only 6.95 per cent of them are literate. In India, the average literacy rate of the Musahars was 52 per cent. Out of this aggregate, 64.13 per cent were men and 39.29 per cent were women (Joshi and Kumar 2002: 90).

The homes of the Musahars are usually small thatched huts consisting of 10×10×6 space (Joshi and Kumar 2002: 7). Goats, cows, oxen, buffaloes are among the major livestock of these people (Joshi and Kumar 2002: 49). Musahar are Hindu by name. Other Hindus neither dine with them, nor accept them into their social fold (Joshi and Kumar 2002: 70). They worship deities like Dudh Beer, Tulsi Beer, Deena Bhadari, Shabari (Joshi and Kumar 2002: 144). They don't have pictures of these gods in their homes. Instead, they make objects of clay and worship these as symbols of their deities. They offer *kasar* or plantain to gods (Joshi and Kumar 2002: 148).

The Musahars like singing, dancing, acting, etc (Joshi and Kumar 2002: 79). They have their own identity. Some people consider them to be a dissipated lot just for the reason that they drink liquor and take pork (Joshi and Kumar 2002: 136). After almost 60 years of post-colonial Indian democracy and governance, the Musahars, in spite of being a part of state-generated development narratives, articulate their own experience of democracy that is quite different from the narratives of other dominant castes. Here we narrate Musahars' narratives of Indian democracy as documented from three villages of eastern Uttar Pradesh, near Varanasi. Their tone, tenor, and diction of telling democratic experiences are quite different from urban educated people. The core of their accounts revolve around how state-led democracy reached them, how they experience it, feel it, and benefit from it. Our focus is to understand their relationship with democracy around the tangible presence of developmental initiatives of the state in the form of housing, loans, education, employment and livelihood initiated under state-made category-based schemes of development and social justice that affect their everyday life.

Experiencing Democracy: Myths and Realities

Our field research among the Musahars, in three villages, reveals the process of their low political visibility among Dalit groups because of their small population, lack of capacity to aspire and acquire for a better share in democracy, and their inability to produce their community leaders; they feel as though they are still standing outside the circle of democratic benefits even among SCs. One may observe their confusion in some cases towards state-generated modernity that reflects through a state-led frame of education, livelihood, and lifestyle. We know that in the Indian context, the state plays an important role in spreading modernity in the everyday life of the people especially in the rural areas (Kaviraj 2005: 1).

The first village that we studied was Dallipur. It is 12 kms from Varanasi, on the way to Jaunpur. The village profiles a mixed caste population with Kurmi (800/900 households), Musahar (250 households), Chamar (400 households), Gupta (100 households), Patel (200 households) and Brahmin (10 households). The village has a primary school, two wells, and four hand pumps. Inside the Musahar hamlet there is a pond, Kajahariya Pokhar. The pradhan of this village is of the Chamar caste (a dominant Dalit caste). The Musahars live in their own hamlet called 'Mushharpatti'.

The second village that we visited was Anai. The village had a voting population of around 3,000. The land of this village is good for farming and nearly 320 households are involved in this sector. A canal flows through this village and alongside there are also 50 tube-wells with an electricity connection. All households have an electricity connection. There is a primary school in the village where children of all castes, including Musahars, study. This village is a part of Mangalpur. The pradhan of this village belongs to the Patel caste. The village has a mixed caste composition with 28 Brahmin households, 60 Musahar households, 200 Chamar households, 60 Khatik households, 25 Muslim households and 200 Patel households. This village is totally illiterate but children of the present generation have started going to school.

The third village was Jungalpur Kathiranv. The population of this village is nearly 22,000 with a voter strength of nearly 15,000. This is a big village with a mixed caste composition. There are 1,500 Chauhan households, 300 Musahar households, 100 Gupta households, 1,000 Patel households, 100 Muslim households, and 20 Yadav households. The pradhan of the village, Arun Kumar Gupta, belongs to the Vaishya caste, which comes under the OBC category. The village has 52 ponds and eight schools. The village has schools, health centres, and is connected to the main road. It has electricity, water supply, and adequate irrigation facilities. All these infrastructural facilities make it appear as an ideal village. My team members and I were involved in constantly documenting the experiences of democracy of the Musahar community in all three villages through long term qualitative interviews.[6]

During our fieldwork, we observed that the presence of state-led democracy in the everyday life of people works simultaneously in different communities in two ways. Firstly, it makes them economically dependent on the state, and secondly, it makes them feel more deprived than other communities. Alongside, among the SC and ST communities, which have been provided special protective discrimination under the notion of social justice through various welfare measures, the communities which have the capacity to acquire and capacity to aspire (Appadurai 2004: 59), have attained a minimum level of development by appropriating a larger share of the welfare measures. In such a situation, many Dalit communities receive only a small share of the benefits through the trickledown effect. However, even among these communities no common pattern is visible. Only the communities, which have assertive organic leaders, are able to claim some share of the benefits. The form in which the claim is made is, however, like that of a subject (*praja*) placing his request (*fariyad*) before the king (*raja*). In fact, the communities often use the word 'fariyad' when describing their demands from the bureaucrats, who are the representatives of the state-led democracy. In such a situation, it often appears that even today the democracy has taken the form of kings and subjects, where the subjects place their requests (fariyad) for a share in resources and welfare measures before the king. The Dalit communities that are able to increase their capacity to make 'fariyad' are able to get a larger share of the democratic resources.[7]

Claiming to be Poorest in Democracy

Musahar respondents began their narratives to prove that they are the most marginal of all SC communities by saying, '*mushar se jyada garib kaun hai*' (who is poorer than the Musahars?).[8] However, it is interesting to know that there are several communities, who are as poor, if not poorer. For example, the Kanjars, who live in the Kanjar basti. They tell very emphatically that they did not get anything from the sarkar (government). Some nominal state benefit reached them through the trickle-down effect. When they accepted that they were getting some benefits from the state they described themselves as being in a comparatively disadvantageous position in comparison with other OBCs and Dalit castes that are more visible in democratic politics and are dominant communities benefitting from the government's social justice schemes.[9]

The experience of democracy, which emerges from their narratives, seems to be true even at the ground level were we to analyze the structure of political parties working in this region. It is shocking to know that there is no Member of Legislative Assembly (MLA) or Member of Parliament (MP), as a representative of any political party, even after 60 plus years of Indian independence. They have around 65 pradhans, who won in the recent local body elections, in this part of UP. So if democracy means political participation they still hold one of the most disadvantageous positions even among Dalit castes. While showing their dissatisfaction about their political participation, Surmati, a 55 year-old woman of Musaharpatti, of Dallipur village, says, '*Humro jati me abe tak kauno lal batti na mila ba bhaia*' (Our caste has never got any red beacon car). Here *lal batti* (red beacon light) is a sign of the ministerial berth that is given to the ministers and chairmen of state bodies by the government.[10]

If democracy means equal distribution of resources by the democratic state, they assert that they have no access to any of the welfare schemes launched by the government for the uplift of the downtrodden sections. The benefits of reservation make no sense for them. In Dallipur village, most of the Musahars are illiterate, except a lone 20-year youth Rajkumar, who has passed the intermediate examination. Some of their children go to school but most of them don't pass high school. Many children drop out of school to become child labourers and supplement the family income. For earning their livelihood, they work as labourers in agricultural fields, brick kilns, etc. About 15 to 20 youths of this caste have migrated to Gujarat in search of work. In any case, the school near their hamlet provides education to the children only till class 5.[11]

The people of this community still live in small, thatched huts. Their patti is like a village slum. This is a harsh reminder of the tangible and intangible artifacts of the Indian democracy that have survived in the last 60 years in these villages. In the name of development, there are some pucca (brick and concrete) houses. These pucca houses were allotted in the 1980s under the Indira Awas Yojana. These dwellings are instead used for rearing pigs, while the villagers themselves live in mud huts. The reason for this is that they were told that these houses were too weak and fragile to stay in. These could collapse any time. These houses had large windows through which ghosts and spirits could enter. Their mud houses either have no windows or have very small ones. These superstitions made them stay away from these dwellings. Ramrati, a woman of the Musahar community of Dallipur told us, 'When Indira Gandhi was alive we were given small houses. The houses have now broken down. We have never lived in those houses because ghosts and spirits can enter into them.'[12]

Dominant and Powerful Dalit Groups Usurp their Benefits

All the Musahars in the three villages complain that no one bothers about them, while the welfare schemes including NREGA are grabbed by other powerful castes. According to Surmati a 55-year old woman, of Dallipur, the entire benefit of NREGA is taken away by the Thakurs, Brahmins, and Kurmis.

Our men only drink and remain at home and there is no unity among them. This is the reason why, inspite of being an SC seat, when Raj

Kumar, the only educated youth of this caste, contested the election of Pradhan, the Musahars were divided in two groups and he lost. Instead, Sunnar Chamar, of the Chamar caste, won the polls.'[13]

The Musahars of this village had several complaints against Sunnar Chamar. According to them, 'Before the elections he used to almost live in this hamlet but after winning the election he doesn't bother about us.' Ramkali, a 65-year old woman says, 'We do not get any benefit of the government's welfare schemes. No one listens to us.' When we asked her why they do not meet political leaders and government officials Ramkali opined, 'The upper castes listen to the people of their own castes. No one heeds to lower castes like us.'[14]

Though poor none of the Musahars of these villages have BPL (below poverty line) or Antyodaya cards meant for the poorest of the poor but instead they all have APL (above poverty line) cards. By no criteria can these poor Musahars be counted among those above poverty line. They say the village pradhan had assured them that they will be given the appropriate card later as their dream is to get the '*lalka karad*' (red Antyodaya card) and '*ujarka karad*' (white BPL card), while they have '*piyarka karad*' (yellow APL card).[15] The Musahars, of Dallipur village, dwell around a pond called Kajrahia Pokhar. Despite of their constant demand for the lease (patta) of this pond, which is the main source of their sustenance and livelihood, they did not get it. But ironically the state and local dominant communities consider their use of the pond as illegal because they don't have the right to use it. The narrative of Ramsurat Baba (65 years), of Dallipur village, about Kajarahia Pokhar (pond) reveals the story of their marginalization by the post colonial democratic state, through which the story of this marginalized community emerged.

> We have been living here for five generations. Cantonment Sahib brought our ancestors here and settled them in order to perform free labour on the landlord's land. Till now no land has been leased to the Musahars. The pond belonged to our ancestors but it has been forcibly taken away from us by the Kurmis. We have appealed to the higher officials for getting back our pond but there is no hearing.[16]

Raj Kumar informed us that in order to get back their pond the Musahars staged a demonstration in front of the district magistrate's office but no action was taken. A little wasteland, along the side of the pond, is used by the Musahars. When the water of the pond rises and fishes are spawned, there are regular skirmishes between the Kurmis and the Musahars.[17]

Narratives of Comparative Disadvantage

The narratives above deal with the feelings of the Musahars regarding their constant ongoing comparative dispossession from their livelihood sources and the poor quality of life in the modern democratic state. Battling against hunger, they have forgotten their traditional cultural resources. When asked if they remembered their traditional folk songs, Phoolmati (55 years), of Dallipur village, said, 'Those who sit under fans and coolers can remember their songs. Our need is to fill our stomachs. We have no time to remember or sing any song.'[18] Sometimes their discourses reflect that their past was better. Due to unequal distribution of democratic resources and malfunctioning of state-led schemes they felt insecure. According to the women of the community, 'Everyone is busy earning and eating. Who is concerned about the poor? All the leaders and officers come here, listen to our problems, give us false assurances and then leave.'[19]

In India, there are provisions for bank loans on cheaper interest rates for disadvantageous and poor communities. In addition there are many micro credit groups with the help of NABARD (National Bank of Agricultural and Rural Development) working in this area.[20] However, even government loans meant for them are beyond their reach. Due to their illiteracy and ignorance they fear taking loans. Lallan (47 years), of Dallipur village, says,

> God knows on which paper they will make us put our thumb impression. In 1980, I took a loan of Rs 5,000, out of which Rs 800 was taken away by the agent. With the remaining money, I bought a pig but it died. I made no profit. All Thakurs and Brahmins take loans on our names. Their loans are written off.[21]

Although they have social interaction with the other Dalit castes, when it comes to getting benefits, they are made to stand at the end of the queue. They are totally deprived. The BSP movement started in this region around the mid-1980s to correct the vices and bias of the upper castes and dominant middle caste-led state democracy. Even during the BSP regime, under the leadership of Mayawati, the Dalit woman chief minister of UP, when there was hope to develop a new Indian democracy, they found no space. In the last 10 years, they never existed in the polity or concerns of our democracy. They did not even get the benefits of the ambitious projects for Dalit villages, like Ambedkar Gram Yojna, during Mayawati's reign. Though the village fulfilled all the criteria for an Ambedkar village, they never got it. Instead, the neighbouring village, which has a Chamar majority, wangled the said status.

When we asked the Musahars of Anai village whether they had taken any loan from the bank they replied in the negative. The reason was that the pradhan had told them that if they took a loan it would need five generations to repay it, as the interest rates were high. Lalai, a resident Anai, added that even if they took a loan, the block office staff and the middlemen took away a large percentage of the money. If a loan of Rs 10,000 was taken, nearly Rs 3,000 was lost as commissions. Although they received only Rs 7,000 they had to pay interest on Rs 10,000. Thus no Musahars applied for bank loans.[22] All from this musaharpatti accepted their poverty as their destiny. Unlike the people of Dallipur village, they are silent about their rights. They somehow manage to exist in the village by performing various menial work. They have neither any agricultural land nor the traditional occupation of making leaf plates.

The residents here feel that they have got nothing substantial from Indian democracy. This caste, despite being a scheduled caste, has not been able to develop the capacity to enjoy the caste status that they rightfully deserve. They have no visibility or voice that could draw attention of the state or democracy towards them. This caste has neither heroes nor the educated lot that is a must for visibility. They cannot come together for democratic politics. Their struggle for two square meals a day is huge. They have no place in democracy. The development projects are far away from them.

While narrating the experience of their everyday life in the village, Lalai, of Anai village, tells us that the Musahars lead very miserable and poverty-stricken lives. He said that his ancestors lived and died here. Earlier, they used to earn their living by making leaf plates from Mahua trees. The plates were supplied to various castes during weddings and other occasions. However, now plastic plates are available. There is almost no demand for leaf plates. He added that the Musahars used to live in the jungles and were dependent on forest products but now with large-scale deforestation, their livelihood has been taken away. Today, they earn their livelihoods by working as labourers in the nearby fields. This is the story of their dispossession in a democratic state.[23]

Lalai told us that the Patels have a stronghold. They control the ponds. Sukhrani, a Musahar resident of this village stated, 'Earlier, we lived in the west of the village but when the population of Brahmins and Thakurs increased, we were pushed to the south of the village.' No Musahar here received any benefits from the government's welfare schemes. He added, 'We do not get any government money or benefits. Whenever some scheme is launched the upper castes grab all the money.'[24]

The women of the village say that they sometimes get some medicines and sometimes a little ration from the fair price shop but they are neither aware of the benefits to which they are entitled. In spite of various government welfare schemes for the uplift of the downtrodden sections they suffer from poverty, hunger, and misery, as they are outside the ambit of these schemes. Although they are all below the poverty line they have not been given BPL cards. After a lot of running round, they were allotted the white APL cards. They only get a little wheat and rice with this card but do not get sugar, kerosene oil, palm oil, etc. When the SP came to power, the Musahars were promised houses but although more than a year has passed they have still not been given houses. When they go to the government officials with their requests (fariyad), they are turned away.[25]

The reason why their requests are not heard by the administration is that they don't have any leaders among them who can submit their fariyad to the sarkar (administration) in an effective way. No one in the village is literate. There is no one to fight for them and place their demands before the political leaders or the government. They have not yet developed their community leaders who can understand the state language and its *niyam-kanun* (rules-regulations) and are able to translate the state language in the community language. They have not yet fitted into the state-led pedagogic democracy.

Fariyadi Matters

The story of Musahars in Jangalpur village is a little different. Here, there is a youth, Srinath, who has emerged as a community leader. He is illiterate but articulate and he has proved to be an effective fariyadi in a couple of cases, which brought a few state benefits. Like in Dallipur village, the Musahars of Jangalpur, also did not have any right over the pond in the village since the Muslims had a 15-year lease on it. They ran from pillar to post to get the lease on the pond but to no avail. However, recently, after a long fight, Srinath, succeeded. He told us,

> I had sent repeated requests and applications to the DM but there was no effect. One day I went straight to the DM's office and told him, 'Huzoor, if you are the king of the government (sarkar), we are the king of the jungle. Huzoor, please give us one chance and see the result. Our wives and daughters do not have place to even throw the ashes of the stoves'.

The district magistrate was impressed by Srinath's attitude and ordered tea for him. He gave him Rs 100 and promised to try to give him the lease on the pond. On the other hand, Hyder Ali, of the Muslim community of the village, who had the 15-year lease on the pond and used to rule over it, was also trying to get the lease extended. However, the DM supported Srinath and the Musahars were given a lease on the pond for 10 years.[26]

Since independence, several five-year plans have been carried out and a large number of welfare schemes have been passed but this is the first time that the Musahars, of Jangalpur, managed to get a lease of the pond. Before this, in 1982, the Musahars were allotted 11 houses under the Indira Awas Yojana. During Mayawati's reign, 18 quarters were constructed and 28 households were given land on lease to construct houses. However, they could not construct their huts on them since the land allotted to them by the pradhan was surrounded by Muslims. They did not allow the Musahars to settle there since the Musahars rear pigs, which the Muslims perceive as not only dirty and unclean, but unholy as well. The Musahars were unable to fight for land in some other part of the village since by that time Mayawati had been removed from power.

Another fariyad of Srinath about distribution of scholarships for their children was also heard by local officials. He informed the researchers,

> Since the Musahars are categorized as SC, when scholarships were distributed to OBC children in the school, the Musahar children were denied the scholarships. My son had told his mother that this time when the scholarships are given please buy me a pair of shoes. However, we were told that the scholarships were meant only for OBC children and the SC would be given scholarships later. After waiting for two months, the scholarships did not come. We felt bad since we had promised to buy shoes for our son. I was angry. I headed for Banaras to meet the DM with my fariyad. I said, 'Sahib, I have brought a fariyad. We are Musahars, poor and illiterate. We are dying of hunger. My son goes to school. It is very cold but he goes bare-footed. The scholarships were distributed to OBC children again yesterday after being distributed to them two months ago. The SC children were not given scholarships. If we had been given, we would have bought shoes for our children. It is very cold.'[27]

The DM said, 'Go, you will get the scholarship within two days.'

However, after two days we did not get the promised scholarship. After two months, when I went to the DM's office for the lease of the pond the DM recognized me. He asked me if I got the scholarship. I replied in the negative. He was angry. He called for his car. After he reached, all of us again placed our fariyad. Several other officers also came. We were given the scholarships.'[28]

Similar to the two other villages, the Musahars of Jangalpur have also not obtained the benefits of any government-loan schemes for the welfare of the poor and downtrodden sections. On asking the pradhan, about the facility of obtaining a loan, he replied that once someone took a loan from the government the person's sons and grandsons will also not be able to repay it. It was because of this fear that most people did not avail of the loans. However, some people did take loans. One of the experiences of taking a government loan was narrated by Lalai of village Dallipur. He said,

> I applied for a loan for Rs 5,000 but got only Rs 4,000. The middle-men and agents pocketed the rest. I bought three pigs. Two died. I

suffered a big loss as the interest increased and the bank officials kept asking me to deposit the interest. I am unable to pay the interest, leave alone the principal. The bank officials and village Panchayats in collusion do not give us the entire amount we had applied for but we have to pay interest on the full amount. It is because of this fear that very few people take loans.'[29]

While maintaining pride in their identity as 'king of the jungle' they claim their dispossession in the modern state but alongside they also continue to disapprove in some sense of the modern state-defined life style. According to them, the reason why the Musahars do not want to stay in the Indira Awas Yojana houses allotted to them is that they see 'ghosts' in those houses and prefer to live in the jungle where they are happier.

***

This study shows that the Musahars, who belong to the SCs and are one of the most marginalized Dalit castes, have several complaints from the state-led Indian democracy. While narrating these complaints and their experiences of democracy they continuously try to prove themselves as 'most poor,' and expression(s) like 'not getting anything from sarkar' appears again and again in their narratives. They feel that other castes, which are dominant and powerful, either upper or middle or even other Dalit castes usurp their democratic rights and benefits. They don't have educated and assertive leaders who can present their fariyad to the local administration. They also don't have their own MPs or MLAs, who can represent them in the government. There is no lalbatti given by the sarkar for any leaders of their community. They hesitate in taking loans from government loan schemes for the SCs and poor. They refuse to live in houses allotted to them under state-given housing schemes because of the traditional notion of community habitat. These are the discourses that emerged from the narratives of our respondents of the musaharpattis, of all three villages, under our study, namely Dallipur, Anai, and Jungalpur.

Thus, in their experience, democracy raises desire but also gives rise to dissatisfactions, which are reflected in their complaints to the state. The state-sponsored schemes empower various communities but also make them more and more dependent on the state gradually. As diagnosed by Sudipta Kaviraj the 'state in the Indian context, as distinct from the European, has been the primary source of modernity. Even in the age of liberal economy the enchantment of state is still undiminished' (Kaviraj 2005: 2). Democracy in contemporary form in India has turned into state-led democracy or 'sarkari cheez'. The political agencies expected to be involved in deepening democracy turned their politics into 'gift politics' like distributing blankets, cheap rice, free tablets and *wajifa* (scholarship) for students, pension schemes, and so on. For these, political parties are not linked with the dissemination of the values of democracy but distributing gifts to allure their subjects (praja) to mobilize them for the coming elections. In this process, all the marginalized castes expect gifts from political parties, which is the only meaning for democracy for them.

It is a notable fact that the caste and communities among middle and Dalit castes, which are numerically dominant, get more attention of the state and political parties due to electoral considerations, as they comprise a larger vote bank. Those who have incorporated well in the state democratic logic of development and modernity through modern state framed education, or have developed their caste leaders, who can represent their demand to the state, get a larger share of the welfare projects of democracy. The castes that have not fully prepared themselves to be accommodated in democracy and in the modernity and development frame, suffer from a democratic deficit.

Despite low numbers, these castes should develop education and collective leadership within themselves that might strengthen the 'politics of presence' among them and give them a voice. However, the renowned post-modern thinker Derrida states, 'Voice alone does not guarantee any presence'. Several other elements must be added to it. This would ensure that others don't drown their voices and present them in a wrong light. It is necessary that within the community, other than the aspiration for development, they should develop such elements that make them 'political'. An eminent political scientist, Rajni Kothari, also suggests the value of political consciousness among caste. He suggests politicization of caste played an important role in the facilitation of democracy and the growth of social awareness (Dirks 2003: 286).

These castes have failed to develop their identity and honour (read caste-based glory). They have still not reached the ground to stand on to strongly express their political and developmental aspirations. They have not been able to use identity and aspirations into their 'politics' and thus use these as resources of growth. They are miles away from the door of democracy. It is must be that these castes should be able to express their political achievement within the democratic framework.

Notes

1. The meaning of terms and concepts like 'state' and 'democracy' is likely to vary between intellectuals and common people, and also between literates and illiterates, underprivileged population of various kinds. (Kaviraj 2005: 2).
2. A similar observation was made by Dirks who says that during the Mandal crisis, caste leaked simultaneously out of the traditional worlds of the subaltern and the village and into the middle-class enclaves of new India. Through the design of the new constitution, the Nehruvian state undertook an immense project of social reform, using the state as the primary instrument to tear down the thousand years' indignities of the caste system (Kaviraj 2005: 13).
3. The state linked various categories in Indian constitution to distribute social welfare to the downtrodden communities. These categories are the Scheduled castes (SCs), Scheduled Tribes (STs) and the Other Backward Classes (OBCs). Presently in Uttar Pradesh the SCs are 64 in number, the STs are 15 in number and the number of Backward classes are 234. The SCs and the OBCs are scattered in various districts of UP. The STs can be found in eastern UP. http://scholarship.up.nic.in/index. asp. Accessed 26 April 2014.
4. 'SP takes on Maya, proposes Dalit status for 17 OBCs', *Milleniumpost*, 2 April 2013, Lucknow, Team MP.
5. 'SP takes on Maya, proposes Dalit status for 17 OBCs', *Milleniumpost*, 2 April 2013, Lucknow, Team MP.
6. Most of the respondents like Ramsurat Baba, Phulmati, Srinath look towards the state for their own benefit and are dependent on the state. The methodology employed to elicit oral histories was the *baat se baat* methodology, which involved extracting information from semi-structured conversation. The purpose was to identify persons of different ages with interesting narratives and an encyclopedic memory

of the past of the village, local history, culture, traditional knowledge, and so on. We chose three sets of individuals from each *patti*, including both men and women, to collect their subjective oral narratives about the village past, in order to see the variation in memory between the various castes, generations, and genders. The three age groups were people above 70 years of age, those in their fifties or thereabouts, and those in the age group of approximately 20 years.

7. Interview with Srinath, village Jungalpur, district Varanasi, by Brijendra Gautam, on 25 April 2013.

8. Interview with Srinath, village Jungalpur, district Varanasi, by Brijendra Gautam, on 25 April 2013.

9. Interview with Srinath, village Jungalpur, district Varanasi, by Brijendra Gautam, on 25 April 2013.

10. Interview with Surmati, aged 55 years, of Musaharpatti of Dallipur village, district Varanasi, on 25 April 2013, by Archana Singh.

11. Interview with Surmati, aged 55 years, of Musaharpatti of Dallipur village, district Varanasi, on 25 April 2013, by Archana Singh.

12. Interview with Ramrati, aged 45 years, of village Dallipur, district Varanasi, dated 25 April 2013, by Archana Singh.

13. Interview with Surmati, aged 55 years, of Musaharpatti of Dallipur village, district Varanasi on 25 April 2013, by Archana Singh.

14. Interview with Ramkali, aged 55 years, of village Dallipur, district Varanasi, dated 25 April 2013, by Brijendra Gautam.

15. Interview with Ramkali, aged 55 years, of village Dallipur, district Varanasi, dated 25 April 2013, by Brijendra Gautam.

16. Interview with Ramsurat Baba, village Dallipur, district Varanasi, dated 25 April 2013, by Archana Singh.

17. Interview with Rajkumar, village Dallipur, district Varanasi, dated 25 April 2013, by Archana Singh.

18. Interview with Phoolmati, village Dallipur, district Varanasi, dated 25 April 2013, by Archana Singh.

19. Interview with the women of village Dallipur, district Varanasi, dated 25 April 2013, by the field staff of Dalit Resource Centre.

20. Interview with the women of village Dallipur, district Varanasi, dated 25 April 2013, by the field staff of Dalit Resource Centre.

21. Interview with Lallan, village Dallipur, district Varanasi, dated 25 April 2013, by Brijendra Gautam.

22. Interview with Lalai, Anai village, district Varanasi, dated 25 April 2013, by Archana Singh.

23. Interview with Lalai, Anai village, district Varanasi, dated 25 April 2013, by Archana Singh.

24. Interview with Sukhrani, village Anai, district Varanasi, dated 25 April 2013, by Brijendra Gautam.
25. Field diary, Dalit Resource Centre dated 25 April 2013.
26. Interview with Srinath, village Jangalpur, district Varanasi, dated 25 April 2013, by Brijendra Gautam.
27. Interview with Srinath, village Jangalpur, district Varanasi, dated 25 April 2013, by Brijendra Gautam.
28. Interview with Srinath, village Jangalpur, district Varanasi, dated 25 April 2013, by Brijendra Gautam.
29. Interview with Lalai, village Dallipur, district Varanasi, dated 25 April 2013, by Archana Singh.

References

Appadurai, A. 2004. 'The Capacity to Aspire: Culture and the Terms of Recognition', in V. Rao and M. Walton, (eds), *Culture and Public Action.* pp. 59–84. New Delhi: Permanent Black.

Beetham, D., S. Bracking, I. Kearton, and S. Weir. 2002. *International IDEA Handbook on Democracy Assessment.* The Hague: Kluwer Law International.

Dirks, N.B. 2003. *Castes of Mind: Colonialism and the Making Of Modern India.* New Delhi: Permanent Black.

Joshi, H. and S. Kumar, (ed.). 2002. *Asserting voices: changing culture, identity, and livelihood of the Musahars in the Gangetic plains.* Delhi: Deshkal Publications.

Kaviraj, S. 2005. *On the Enchantment of the State: Indian Thought on the Role of the State in the Narrative of Modernity.* London: School of Oriental and African Studies.

9

Dalit Capital

Discrimination, Unfavourable Inclusion, and Intersectionality

Aseem Prakash

The chapter attempts to analyse the outcome of the political and economic desire on the part of Dalits to enter the market as owners of capital and trade in various goods and services. The chapter is based on 90 detailed semi-structured interviews with Dalit entrepreneurs conducted in 13 districts located in six states of India.[1] In this endeavour, the first section of the chapter summarizes the results of the experience of Dalit owners of capital while they trade in various good and services. The second section explains that the discrimination and unfavourable exclusion in the markets is caused at the intersection of state, markets, and civil society. Accordingly, it proposes and explains the concept of intersectionality as well its conceptual/ analytical strength to understand discrimination and unfavourable inclusion in the realm of markets. The third section situates the concept of intersectionality in the existing theories of state, markets, and civil society and shows the inability of the dominant theories

Caste related	26 (29)
Earlier restricted and considered taboo	12 (13)
General	36 (40)
Liberalized market	11 (12)
Specialized	5 (6)
Total	90 (100)

to capture these intersecting spaces where discrimination and unfavourable inclusion is caused and sustained. The concluding section explains the limits of intersectionality, that is, it elaborates on the spaces which are beyond the intersection where discrimination may not be practised.

Dalit Entrepreneurs and Unfavourable Inclusion

The business history of Dalit entrepreneurs was reconstructed to understand how market exchange involving them is affected by history, social institutions, collective behaviour, or anything else that lies outside the realm of a narrow market exchange. The accompanying table shows the number of businesses in the sample by general economic type. We have classified businesses into five types. The first covers economic ventures inspired by caste location. These include trade in sanitary ware, bulk washing of clothes, washing clothes for the garment industry, sanitary labour and housekeeping contractors, leather work, hair-cutting saloons, etc. Nearly one-fifth of our respondents entered the market for goods and services associated with their specific sub-castes. The second type relates to trade in goods and services earlier disallowed to Dalits by the Hindu social order. Only 13 per cent of business persons entered the market for such goods and services, which include educational coaching, trade in food and food products, priesthood, etc. Nearly two-fifths of business people are found in the third category, which we have termed general economic ventures. These include smaller economic ventures like trade in wood and fuel-wood, handloom material, grocery shops, etc., as well as big businesses like mining, construction and real estate, production and sale of ceramic ware, and so on. Our fourth category covers the many newer avenues for business which have been created by the opening up of markets and the ongoing integration of the Indian economy with the global economy. These include, among others, trade in communications, electronics and computers, and real estate. Only 12 per cent of the total interviewees were involved in this particular category. Finally, our fifth category covers economic avenues, participation in which is contingent on higher education, specialized training and professional degrees. These include economic activities related to medicine and hospital services. We find that such high skilled and technically qualified business persons constitute a little less than 6 per cent of the total Dalit business persons interviewed.

Discrimination is generally understood as differential treatment of individuals in similar situations. With the rapid transformation of socio-political structures, the sociological norms of purity and pollution defining the relationship between different castes have changed substantially. Yet, although the norms have acquired new forms, the content remains the same—the retention of unequal and hierarchical power relationships between the upper castes and Dalits. In the context of market relationships, the social relationship between the Dalits and the upper castes continues to be shaped by social prejudice against Dalits, which is strategically invoked and executed to meet the demands of market competition. The business histories of Dalit business persons indicate that the actual nature of discrimination faced varies in different sectors of the market and often assumes different forms.

As noted earlier, nearly one-fifth of Dalit business persons in our survey were trading in goods and services, activities which were inspired by their caste location. They earlier worked in a different capacity, offering their labour services to the upper-caste owners. Their entry into the market as owners of capital was treated with contempt by the former employees. One common entry barrier created by the former employers and other market peers involved erecting roadblocks in hiring labour to carry out economic activity. The labourers too, as a group, seem to have gone along with the designs of upper-caste business persons, possibly because their own chances of finding work are mostly controlled by the former.

Second, most Dalit business persons face immense difficulty in securing initial orders for their business. This is generally true for both the sanitary and leather business where the market is controlled by the upper castes. In the case of leather goods, most Dalit entrepreneurs seem to have lost out to big capital and are mostly producing goods on a piece-rate arrangement. Dalits trading as wholesalers and retailers in the food and beverage business are compelled to supply goods at lower prices. If they refuse, the upper caste retailers invoke their caste identity and reject their produce. As retailers, they get credit for a shorter period while procuring food items from the wholesalers. Similarly, Dalits often face negative publicity by their business competitors with regard to their 'impure' caste status when trying to attract customers to their own establishments. In a few cases, the Dalit owner even had to shift the food establishment to a Dalit locality because of an inability to attract clients from a predominantly upper-caste area.

In the category of 'general business' and the new sectors which have come up due to the opening up of the markets, Dalits' efforts were hampered by a lack of access to the state's resources. The biggest handicap was their lack of access to social networks that are controlled by the upper castes who regulate the informal credit market. Short-term informal credit critically influences the success/failure of any business. Dalit business persons are denied access to these informal networks. Even when they succeeded in accessing informal credit, the rate of interest was much higher than the prevailing market rate. The lack of informal credit or being forced to arrange informal credit at high interest rates disempowered them from meeting the deadlines of lucrative contracts which could have helped to scale up their business endeavours to a higher level. Last but not least, Dalits are unable to rent or buy a strategically important physical space for their business due to opposition from upper caste business competitors.

The final category of business, which we have termed as 'specialized', involves those Dalits whose earlier generations had managed to improve their economic status as a result of affirmative policy action by the state. They thus had both the required skills and initial capital to enter into the business as well as to sustain themselves. However, all the respondents noted the subtle experience of caste prejudice, claiming that they were not given the same importance that their upper caste peers commanded. In other words, high class status does not necessarily translate into high social status because of their lower caste.

Any kind of economic activity is critically influenced by the policies of the state. The role of the modern state is crucial because it establishes and legitimizes property rights and governance structures (including labour laws and taxation), regulates credit availability, and also creates and maintains infrastructure (electricity, water, roads, etc.). Dalit entrepreneurs invariably experienced an adverse reaction by the state officials whenever they tried to access the state's resources. In their view, state resources can only be accessed through social networks. They understand social networks as a critical social resource which could enable them to cultivate a relationship with state officials in order to get favourable treatment for enhancing their business ventures.

For instance, many of the Dalit entrepreneurs were denied credit because they were not considered capable of running modern business. They were told by officials that they should not waste the state's precious resources because their business was 'destined' to fail, and they should instead stick to their traditional professions. Dalit entrepreneurs elaborated at length on how kith and kin networks of upper castes, formed through family contacts and marriage relationships, enabled them to access the resources of the state more easily than they ever could. The state resources that facilitate upper-caste business endeavours range from getting government contracts, to ensuring payment of lower sales tax/cess, to flouting municipal laws with ease and without any fear of penalty.

One way to access the state's resources/officials is through paying bribes. In their view, rent-seeking by state officials is rampant and affects every business person, irrespective of caste location. However, what most troubles Dalit business persons is that upper-caste business persons, because of their social network, have to pay lower bribes than they do. This both reduces the transaction costs of the upper castes and also helps them generate a higher surplus. Moreover, Dalit business persons feel that the upper castes have the ability to repeatedly access state resources, which seems to be a remote possibility for them.

A telling example of the role of social networks in accessing state resources is drawn from Madhya Pradesh. The state government had explicitly notified that a specified percentage of total government procurement had to be sourced from Dalit enterprises. Despite being given this exclusive space to do business and earn profit, Dalit entrepreneurs found it difficult to get their payments released. Therefore, many of them had to informally involve upper-caste persons as business partners, whose role was to ensure timely release of payments. In other words, the use of social networks to access the state resources enables upper castes to earn money without investing capital in the business, while a lack of the same, substantially increases the transaction costs for Dalits.

In several instances, we were told that deliberate inaction by state officials under the influence of upper-caste business competitors increased the transaction cost for Dalits. For instance, licences were not granted to a Dalit brick kiln owner and leather goods trader in Pune and Agra respectively, due to the influence of an upper-caste business competitor. Many Dalit entrepreneurs also informed us that Dalits are often forced to withdraw from the market because of the threat of real or potential violence by the dominant caste business competitors. State inaction, in such instances, is more palpable because the law and order machinery routinely refuses to register a first information report.

As is evident from the above discussion, Dalit owners of capital experience what Sen describes as 'unfavourable inclusion' in market processes, though the degree of adversity varies with the location and sector of the markets. In other words, access to market spaces for Dalits as owners of capital is neither entirely blocked (markets having absolutely rigid entry barriers for Dalits), nor are avenues provided for complete integration as equal players (markets being completely accommodative to entry of Dalit entrepreneurs). Further, the tendency of market processes towards absolute rigidity or complete accommodation is not decided only by market processes, but equally by the balance of institutional forces in the wider socioeconomic and political realms. In other words, if Dalit business persons experience unfavourable inclusion in markets processes, duly influenced by the State's (in) action, the roots of the causes lie in the realm of civil society.

It is in the realm of civil society that the ideological architecture of caste relationships are invoked and sustained. It is in the realm of civil society that the resources of social networks are drawn to help business endeavours of upper castes. Again, it is in the realm of civil society that the actual and threatened violence against Dalits is carried out. It is in this context that caste must be seen as a specific form of Indian civil society because on the one hand, caste influences the state (social networks) and on the other, it plays an important role in influencing market outcomes through controlling credit, organizing labour and regulating supply and procurement. Therefore, it is important that we understand civil society not only as a site of democratization; but following the traditional theorists of civil society—Locke, Adam Smith, Hegel, Marx, and Gramsci—civil society should also be seen as a site of accumulation. It is in this context that caste must be seen as a specific form of Indian civil society because on the one hand, caste influences the state (social networks) and on the other, it plays an important role in influencing market outcomes through controlling credit, organizing labour and regulating supply and procurement.

In the course of our empirical investigation to reconstruct the business history of 90 Dalit entrepreneurs, we have tried to analytically explore whether, and to what degree, market outcomes are affected by their ascriptive group identity. Overall, while Dalits are able to enter the markets as owners of capital, they experience, at the same time, numerous forms of discrimination leading to unfavourable inclusion in market processes. We argue that multiple forms of discrimination practised against Dalits are developed and sustained at the intersection of the state, market, and civil society. Accordingly, the main argument of this chapter is that discrimination against Dalits and their unfavourable inclusion in the markets is carved out and sustained at the intersection of state, market, and civil society. In other words, discrimination and unfavourable inclusion in the market cannot be seen as being effected through a single institution. It is practised and sustained through a combination of more than one institution operating simultaneously.

How do we make analytical sense of these multiple institutions (re)producing and sustaining discrimination and unfavourable inclusion of Dalits in the market? We claim that the conceptual approach of 'intersectionality' can facilitate us to understand this complex phenomenon.

Intersectionality

The concept of intersectionality is employed to highlight the importance of taking into account the lived experience of Dalit entrepreneurs at neglected multiple points of intersection. In other words, we
need an approach to reflect multiple subordinate locations as opposed
to one single (non)institutionalized cause of subordination. The
conceptual approach of 'intersectionality' has been borrowed from
feminist studies. The theory of intersectionality in feminist study
endeavours to examine how various social, cultural, and biological
categories like race, gender, class, ethnicity, and religion interact and
create multiple and often simultaneous conditions of discrimination
and social inequality.[2] In crux, the scholars writing on intersectionality argue that these forms of social stratification need to be studied in
relation to each other, conceptualizing them, for example as a 'matrix
of domination' (Collins 2000) or 'complex inequality' (Crenshaw
1991: 1241–99) or intersectional (McCall 2005: 1771–1800) or
'integrative' (Glenn 1999: 3–43) or as a 'race-class gender' approach
(Pascale 2007).

Borrowing this idea from feminist literature, the chapter puts
forth the following claim: The discrimination and unfavourable
inclusion of Dalit entrepreneurs is at the intersection of the state,
markets, and civil society. Intersectionality challenges the existing dominant conceptualization of somewhat rigid analytical
boundaries between these institutions—state, market, and civil
society. It argues in favour of blurred boundaries and the consequent overlapping space which is instrumental in (re)reproducing
discrimination/unfavourable inclusion.

Here, it would be appropriate to delineate our interpretation of
intersectionality in the context of our study on Dalit entrepreneurs,
albeit we borrow extensively from feminist literature. The emphasis in feminist literature is on the multiple axes of subordination as
experienced by women because of the simultaneous operation of
more than one informal institution. Thus the distinct 'experience'
of women that shapes access to status, poverty, and power becomes
central to the analysis. We build on these important insights. Like
feminist theory, we are using the experience of Dalit entrepreneurs as
a means to understand the reasons and sustenance of discrimination

and unfavourable inclusion. However, unlike feminist theory, which analyses (informal) social institutions (ethnicity, religion, race, etc.), we focus on formal institutions that are informalized due to articulation of the worldview of informal institutions (for instance, the ideology of caste) within the formal institutions (state and market).

Accordingly, our analysis of intersectionality is shaped by two central tenets.

First, the values inspired by the ideology of caste present in the realm of civil society get reflected in institutions present in the domain of the state and markets. The mirroring of the values emanating from the ideology of caste in the actions and practices of formal institutions results in blurring the boundaries between state, market, and civil society. Formal rules of the state and markets become somewhat subservient to informal norms dominant in the realm of civil society. Analytically, this blurring of the boundaries produces a space, which is at the intersection of state, market, and civil society where discrimination and unfavourable inclusion of Dalit entrepreneurs acquires its roots, is nurtured and sustained.

Second, the intersectional spaces, though originating in the realm of the state, markets, and society, on intersecting and interacting, transcend their original character and assume unique characteristics with their own sets of norms, rules and behavioural patterns, different and contradictory to the assumed rationalities of state planning and markets.

The Centrality of Intersectionality: Why?

Intersectionality serves a few theoretical and practical objectives. We propose three specific arguments to support our claim that the approach of intersectionality makes us conceptually richer in comprehending discrimination against Dalits and their unfavourable inclusion in the markets.

The Interconnectedness Argument

As already pointed out, it helps us to analytically contest the binaries of state/markets, state/civil society, or market/civil society and show that these institutions are interconnected and operate simultaneously. More importantly, it points to the interconnectedness of various institutions where all the institutions in different realms interact with and shape each other, in an endeavour to retain the unequal power relationship between Dalits and other upper castes. This understanding is particularly important to empower an analytical understanding of the role of state, market and civil society, often acting simultaneously towards marginalization of Dalits.

Social Exclusion versus Discrimination Argument

The focus on intersectional spaces causing and sustaining discrimination allows us to differentiate between exclusion and consequent marginalization due to class location, and discrimination and consequent socio-economic maldistribution due to caste location. The frameworks explaining varieties of exclusion—unequal access to social primary goods (Rawls 1971) or inequality of distribution of impersonal resources (for example, financial resources) and the absence of a mechanism for compensating people with far less personal resources (Dworkin 1981: 283–345) or inaccessibility to basic capabilities (Sen 2009)—are not adequately equipped to explain the socio-economic maldistribution and cultural misrecognition of Dalits sustained by the ideology of caste. This in turn results in methodological failure to analytically capture the spaces where discrimination acquires its roots and is also sustained.

We claim that the approach of intersectionality is useful in addressing this theoretical shortcoming. The approach of intersectionality attests that the power of either of the social groups (upper castes or Dalits) is not constituted at a given moment but is determined and constrained by the history of relationships between social groups. The historically constituted social relationship between social groups helps the formation of social networks which in turn helps to informalize the formal institutions and thereby enable the caste identity to eke out an interesting space between state, markets, and civil society. Thus, this approach is able to analytically capture the socio-political and economic arrangements simultaneously operating and discriminating against Dalits through an array of formal and informal institutions. As in the case of feminist study, it helps us to analyse and prioritize studying 'the powerful, their institutions, their policies, and practices instead of focussing only on those whom the powerful govern' (Harding and Norberg 2005: 2009–15). By studying the intersecting spaces thrown up by the interaction between the state, markets, and civil society, we are able to locate the conceptual practices of power and how they shape everyday social relations.

The Agency and Social Power Argument

The framework of social power derived through caste identity draws its sustenance necessarily through group identity. Social power as experienced at the intersecting spaces can be described as having two interrelated dimensions. First, it has to be seen in the relationship between structure and agency. The dominant upper caste would like to see this relationship between structure (caste system) and agency (ability of the upper caste to prevail against Dalits thereby marginalizing their protest and struggles) of Dalits in the manner of Lukes' conceptualized power, that is, unquestioned reproduction of the world view of upper castes where Dalits continuously serve their social and material interests (Lukes 1974). However, in practice, the power mediating between upper castes and Dalits is far more complex. Dalits, while recognizing their domination and subordination, continuously question, protest, and assert their political agency and in the process, interrogate and question the structure–agency dualism. The upper caste-inspired caste structure is a product of human agency but at the same time also produces conditions for opposition. Thus, power is never held by the upper caste in the form of total power. Instead, Dalits continuously strive towards altering the balance of power, albeit their attempts are not always successful.[3] The result is continuous assertion, (re)negotiation and subversion of the upper caste-held and inspired power, with an avowed aim on the part of Dalits to overcome their subordination.

If our claim that Dalits are conscious of the fact that they are oppressed, dominated, and discriminated by upper castes is true, then how do we explain their unfavourable inclusion where they are allowed entry in the market but not on equal terms?

The intersecting space is a social field where the practice of discrimination is accepted by the discriminated not because the latter accepts her subordinate position consciously and willingly. Instead, it is due to what Rafanell and Gorringe describe as 'clearly motivated by identifiable calculative practices'. 'Power can continue to be exercised not because it overrides calculative agency but precisely because of it' (Rafanell and Gorringe 2010: 610). In other words, Dalit entrepreneurs have either come out of their caste-ordained professions or resisted the tremendous pressure of their former employers to perform manual labour for their benefit, and chosen to enter the markets as owners of capital. In this situation, they do realize that their capacity to oppose and completely resist the illegitimate demands of their business peers is limited. Hence, their choice is to engage with them through an intelligent assessment of constraints in the specific context. Accordingly, they try and organize their personal goals and ambitions strategically in a changed context, where they have to continuously overcome the threat of upper-caste-inspired social sanction of complete exclusion.

From the vantage point of the upper castes, social power is also not permanent. It is continuously reinvented and new ways and means are discovered in their attempts to retain the status quo. This is where the role of social networks explained earlier becomes crucial. The social network in this manifestation is the collective power of upper castes to blur the boundaries between the state, market, and civil society. The intersecting space is in fact an innovation motivated by the collective social power of the upper castes (so as to extract undue and unlawful benefits from the local state), which is created and sustained through a variety of social relationships. The continuous social assertion of Dalits has not only resulted in re-negotiation of power within different social groups amongst upper castes (for instance, an unspoken social contract to articulate their collective voices against Dalits instead of articulating the socio-economic differences within) but have also led to their re-engagements with Dalits where inroads in the markets of the latter cannot be restricted anymore, and therefore informal institutions have to be erected to ensure that they are unfavourably included.

These very social facts require that an analysis of power should appreciate that the upper castes will not voluntarily abdicate their social power over Dalits. Hence, there is a need of formal rectificatory institutions, which can compensate for historical wrongs. The rectificatory institutions, even if eked out, are still controlled by upper castes who may not be ideologically friendly to this idea and hence the execution of the compensatory policies will be marred by repeated failures. Therefore, it is natural and necessary that Dalits recognize these intersectional spaces so as to continuously struggle and claim what is legitimately due to them.

Situating Intersectionality in the Existing Theory of the State, Markets, and Civil Society

How does the approach of intersectionality relate with existing theories of the state, markets, and civil society? The approach of intersectionality has two claims which differ from the existing theories. The same is discussed below.

Claim I: Absence of Theoretical Stress on Social Identity

The claim of intersectionality is that it gives due emphasis to caste identity in shaping outcomes in the markets as well as influencing the state's action crucial to market outcomes. Almost all the existing dominant theories of the state, markets, and civil society are oblivious to this claim.

As far as theory of the state is concerned, we first juxtapose the claim of intersectionality vis-à-vis a society centred theory of state. Under the theoretical framework of Marxism, the most relevant aspect of the theories of state is the issue of the state's autonomy. The state's autonomy is important because the institutions of state are looked upon for creating enabling conditions for equitable participation in the markets as well as ensuring that the regulatory arms of the state are neutral in approach. The thesis of relative autonomy[4] seems to mean three things. First, whether the state is seen in an instrumentalist or deterministic fashion, state power is seen to be deployed in the long term interests of the dominant classes. Second, the state is not seen to be serving the universal interest. The Marxist would believe that the 'capitalist state intervene(s) against capital as well as the working class—especially when individual capitalists or fractions of capital threaten the interests of capital in general' (Jessop 1977: 363). Note, state intervention is only for social groups defined through the (lack of) control of the means of production and not for any social groups defined though ascriptive identities. Thus, Marxism articulates one version of a society-centred approach to study the state which fails to take into account the role of ascriptive identities in shaping the ideology and practice of the state and its associated institutions.

The other version of a society-centred approach to study the state is the pluralist–structural functional approach (Easton 1957: 383–400), Almond (1965: 183–214), (Almond and Powell Jr 1966). There are a lot of differences between the writers elaborating this approach, often quite nuanced in nature. However, the broad points of this approach are as follows. The approach refuses to use the concept of the state and instead uses the term government. The state is seen as too formalistic and legal where the government is seen as reflecting the arena where economic interest groups and social movements contest/ally with each other to shape public policy. The primary difference between the Marxist and pluralist-structural functional approaches is that the former points out to the domination of the state/ government by one section of the society whereas the latter argues that state polices are the result of many interest groups and not one (the ruling class). The state's autonomy is invariably infringed in the pluralist tradition whereas for Marxists, the state is relatively autonomous, on certain occasions, to pursue the specific agenda of capital, that is, protecting the long-term interests of the capitalist class. Second, Marxist theories of state in general and state autonomy in particular are blind to the possibility that any social groups (defined through ascriptive identities) can infringe the autonomy of the state. The pluralist–structural functional approach is opposed to the idea that any particular social group can ever dominate the state. This means that power distribution in the society in favour of one or few social groups is never a permanent aspect of a social structure. Power, in their view, is tied to one or more issues which may lead to coalition building between different social groups and that too, for a momentary or semi-permanent duration (Polsby 1960: 474–84).

These formulations coming from the scholars of Marxist and pluralist persuasions do not sit comfortably with the business histories of Dalit entrepreneurs. At the micro level, the state is seen to be easily accessed through caste and family networks. In the view of the Dalit entrepreneurs, the state is neither an instrument of class rule nor structurally embedded in class relations, providing cohesiveness and stability to class-based domination. Structurally as well as functionally, the state's actions reflect bias towards (dominant) upper castes and more often than not articulate their socio-economic interests. The pluralist–structural functional approach is also at odds with the Dalit view because it fails to recognize that values, beliefs, and ideas shaping the social structure are derived from the ideology of caste. The domination of social groups through the ideology of caste is not a temporary but a sustained and long-lasting social pattern. The power of upper castes over Dalits is not seen as a product of the current combination of socio-political and economic circumstances but is more permanent in nature, deriving its legitimacy from religion and religious scriptures.

In contrast to society-centred approaches, statist theories argue that the state is a force itself and does not aid the interest of a class or social group.[5] They point out that the state officials and managers are able to exercise autonomy in their own right and accordingly pursue their own distinctive interest (Evans, Rueschemeyer, and Skocpol 1985). In the context of state autonomy, the statists argue against the theoretical primacy of class or capital. Instead they point to the 'unified sense of ideological purpose (throwing up the) possibility and desirability of state intervention to ensure political order and promote economic development' (Skocpol 1985: 10). Arguing further, Peter Evans puts forth the concept of embedded autonomy[6]—close ties of bureaucrats to business in which the former retains the ability to formulate and act on preferences autonomously—is the key to the developmental state's effectiveness (Evans 1995: 12). Thus, statists stress on the ideological commitments and a sense of purpose of the state functionaries to not only carve out an autonomous action plan but also to execute it in the universal interest of the nation.

However, Dalit entrepreneurs will even refuse to agree with the statist approach. They point to the embeddedness of state officials in the social structure. The embeddedness derives its strength, shape, and sustenance from the ideology of caste, and kith, kin, and family-inspired networks, enabling the upper castes to access the resources of the state rather than a macro ideological objective catering to universal interests.[7]

In the context of theories of markets, the role of identity has been analysed by numerous authors who can be perhaps safely be clubbed under the disciplinary boundaries of economic sociology, albeit they differ in their ideological positions. Most of economic theory is premised on the assumption that social identities of agents do not influence market outcomes, albeit there are 'powerful exceptions' that show how 'social identities of economic agents can be central to the determination of their economic outcomes' (Deshpande 2011: 38).

Scholars who have followed the neo-classical approach resolutely proclaim that identities restrict competition in the markets, which in turn means inefficient markets, and therefore, they conclude that the role of identities in any economic transaction will eventually wane with the development of competitive markets. The work of Akrelof (2005: 39-55), Lal (1988), and Scoville (1996). highlights that discrimination in the markets on the basis of caste is sustained by collective pressure and anticipated penalty feared by the individual belonging to the upper caste, but it is this individual who is the actual flag-bearer of caste-based discrimination. These penalties can be both imaginary as well as real. The business histories of Dalit entrepreneurs inform us that these anticipated penalties are often used as an excuse by upper-caste entrepreneurs to force an unequal exchange relationship with Dalit entrepreneurs. Use of caste identity from the standpoint of upper caste entrepreneurs, in fact, meets the institutional requirement of mitigating competition from the new player(s), instead of restricting it. The latter has to accept the terms and conditions set by the former because of his fear of complete banishment from the market. The emphasis on the individual as the source of discrimination is at odds with the experience of Dalit entrepreneurs in the markets. Instead, they claim that the focus has to be on informal institutions and how they influence the formal institutions—both in the realm of markets and the state—which sustain discrimination.

New Institutions Economics (NIE) addresses this gap and points out the role of institutions in influencing market outcomes. But NIE retains the role of competition in shaping the markets. It does recognize the role of informal institutions—religion, customs, tradition, norms, conventions, etc.,[8]—and considers informal institutions as given (Williamson 2000: 596). However, North (1981) and Stiglitz (1999) and other authors suggest that informal institutions raise transaction costs and therefore restrict competition and hence are bound to wane off in the long run. NIE is also sensitive to the important role of the state in establishing the institutional framework for reducing transaction costs and promoting competition in the markets. For instance, Stiglitz argues that markets can only function effectively with the parallel development of the modern capitalist state and associated legal institutions.

Therefore, the dominant theories of markets bank on market competition for the demise of the role of identities in influencing market outcomes (as in the case of the neo-classical school) and of informal institutions (as in new institutional economics). Both the schools converge on the point that identities/ informal institutions are detrimental to growth and market competition. However, the narratives of Dalit entrepreneurs recorded by us seem to suggest a probability contrary to this one of a modern capitalist state functioning on impersonal and secular Weberian principles. The strengths of NIE (recognizing the presence of informal institutions) are in fact also its weakness because it pins its hopes on competition (similar to neo-classical school) in the markets as the imperative for economic growth which in turn will lead to the demise of informal institutions, especially the ones which are inspired by social identities (for instance, caste identity).

How do the Dominant Theories of Civil Society differ from the Approach of Intersectionality?

The dominant theories of civil society are not in agreement that civil society is also constituted through social identities like caste. While traditional theorists as diverse as, Locke, Hegel, Adam Smith, Marx and Gramsci recognize that civil society is indeed a site of accumulation, they do not think that social identity can be a factor in creating and sustaining inequality or facilitating accumulation in the markets. Theorists like Gramsci also believe that civil society is also a site where consent of the dominant ideas is manufactured through socio-cultural and political institutions. Likewise, Indian literature on civil society tends to see civil society as either fighting for the deepening of democratic institutions (a theoretical formulation of Marxists scholars) or as normative ideals of liberal ideology which are not situated in the concrete social context. In the latter version, civil society is seen as working along with the state for promoting universal law and social equality. Others in the same theoretical tradition argue that civil society is represented by secular and open mediating institutions like (for instance universities, banks, newspapers etc.). Further, civil society when discussed as political society explores how subalterns are able to strategically negotiate with the ruling class to claim their entitlements from the state. The documentation of the business histories of Dalits highlights a different understanding of civil society. Civil society inspired by the ideology of caste creates conditions for accumulation in the market for upper castes but as a result also acquires coercive and exclusionary characteristics. Accordingly, civil society articulates the ideology of caste and thereby creates institutionalised norms for regulating the interaction of upper castes with Dalits. This interaction so shaped is always unequal and biased in favour of upper castes. It also helps develop informal institutionalised norms for regulating market outcomes as well as interaction with the institutions of the state.

Claim II: Particularity versus Totality

Intersectionality as an approach does not claim to describe or theorise the totality of state, market and civil society. It is merely a lens to understand discrimination and unfavourable inclusion in the markets of Dalits. While doing so, it uses the experience of Dalits and interprets and analyses the state, market and civil society as experienced by them. On the other hand, the dominant theories of state, market and civil society claim to theorise the totality of these institutions. However, we do claim that if the existing macro theories on state, markets and civil society are not able to make sense of the lived realities and experience of Dalits, then the claim of totality will not hold ground since Dalits represent a substantial numerical proportion of the population.

Coda: Limits of Intersectionality and the Value of Normativity

We have tried to show that unfavourable inclusion of Dalits in the market is at the intersection of state, market, and civil society. It also implies that there are arenas beyond the intersection which may not necessarily be discriminatory. Even in the intersecting space, the intensity of discrimination differs. As already noted, we have classified the business endeavours of our Dalit entrepreneurs in five sectors. They are: economic endeavours which have emerged from their earlier caste professions; professions which were earlier restricted for them and for which there were severe sanctions if they chose to pursue them; general economic activities; professions which have emerged due to liberalized markets; and businesses which have arisen due to their command on highly specialized skills. As per our interpretation of the narratives of Dalit entrepreneurs, one can safely conclude that the intensity of discrimination is highest in economic endeavours which have emerged from their earlier caste professions and professional activities that were earlier socially restricted for them to pursue, followed by general economic ventures. Discrimination also exists in the last two sectors—new opportunities emerging due to economic liberalization and economic activities pursued through acquiring specialised skills—but at a relatively lower intensity. Variation in the nature and intensity of discrimination—the ability of upper-caste business competitors to invoke 'caste stereotypes' in order to unfold the simultaneous process of attracting clients and discouraging them from doing business with Dalits[9]—is perceived as not being similar in all sectors of the economy. Dalit entrepreneurs would like to move from the situation of intense discrimination to one of less discrimination, leading to equality with upper caste business peers in the markets. This is precisely the reason why they believe in the normative idea of democracy as well as the normativity in the praxis of the state. Why is normativity cherished by Dalits?

Democracy as a value is appreciated and cherished by Dalits because it promises the value of moral equality. Moral equality for Dalits is a very complex social concept because it entails not only empowered inclusion of each and everybody in the processes that may result in collective decisions and actions, but also a framework of civic society which is able to situate the current socio-economic condition of its constituents in a historical context.

Thus, a democratic state is one, which is able to protect and promote social relations such that social groups take pride in their distinctive identity. It is in this sense, that Dalits fear the danger of the homogenizing tendency of the modern state, where 'particular' and 'minority' social identities are subsumed under the universal, which in their experience implies the identity represented by the dominant upper caste Hindus. If the state promotes and guards particular identities, it would imply that the state is able to intervene effectively in the domain of civil society through the rule of law and restrict exclusionary tendencies. It is through these measures that the state can check unbridled accumulation, often through illegal means, in the sphere of the markets. This nature of normativity would imply a state with administrative and judicial capacity for fair, non-partisan, and non-arbitrary enforcement of its own legal, political, and social code of conduct.

Further, for Dalits, only a democratic state can appreciate their articulation of protest against the oppressive social order. In other words, this would not only entail protection of their rights, respect for their claim for affirmative action (re-distribution) but more importantly recognition of and respect to their agency. This in turn would necessitate that their demands are not violently suppressed. Repression of their demands or rights will invariably benefit the upper castes. Lastly, these normative principles of heterogeneity, administrative and judicial capacity to uphold the rule of law in a non-partisan manner, and appreciation of democratic protest for legitimate demands, including affirmative action to rectify historical wrongs, is seen as the only institutional means to separate and draw a dividing line between the state, markets, and civil society.

Notes

1. These districts are Ahmedabad (Gujarat); Bhopal, Hoshangabad, Raisen, Vidisha (Madhya Pradesh); Aurangabad, Mumbai, Pune (Maharashtra); Jaipur (Rajasthan); Agra, Kanpur, Lucknow (Uttar Pradesh); Hoogly/24 Parganas (West Bengal).

2. See Anderson and Collins (2006), Weber (2004: 121–39), Ore (1994), Crenshaw (1991: 1241–99), Browne and Mishra (2003: 487–513), McGibbon and McPherson (2011: 59–86).

3. For a similar discussion on power in general see A. Giddens (1984: 5–25).

4. In the Indian context, this view is empirically examined and put forth by Bardhan (1984). He argues that the three dominant classes in India—the capitalists, the rich farmers, and the bureaucracy—who compete with each other and as a result, none of them are powerful enough. This in turn makes the state relatively autonomous. Kaviraj (1989), while using the Gramscian concept of passive revolution pointed to the dynamics of class domination where the dominant classes shared power with each other. This helped the state to acquire relative autonomy while heralding the passive revolution. In the post-liberalization era, Kohli (2006) while analysing the explicit pro-business turn, characterizes India as a two-track democracy where the poor are only required at the time of election and rest of the time the elite manage polity in favour of big business.

5. One of the well-known studies on the Indian state shows traces of both the trends—society-centric as well as statist. Rudolph and Rudolph understood the Indian state through the study of organized interest groups. They point out that the Indian state is a reflection of the tussle between demand polity (societal groups dominate over the state) and command polity (state's hegemony prevails over the society) (Rudolph and Rudolph 1987).

6. Embedded autonomy depends on 'an apparently contradictory combination of Weberian bureaucratic insulation with intense immersion in the surrounding social structure'. Both the apparently contradictory elements are required because 'the state that was only autonomous would lack both sources of intelligence and the ability to rely on decentralized private implementation. A state that is only embedded is ripe for capture and dismembering. Only when embeddedness and autonomy are joined together can a state be called developmental'. See Evans (1995: 12).

7. Precisely for this reason Jessop (2006: 119), argues that the statist theory 'involves a fundamental theoretical fallacy. It posits clear and unambiguous boundaries between the state apparatus and society, state managers and social forces, and state power and societal power, the state can be studied in isolation from the society.... (It) excludes…logics such as corporatism or policy networks; divisions among state managers due to their ties between state organs and other social spheres; and many forms of overlap between state and society'.

8. D. North defines institutions as 'humanely devised constraints that structure political, economic and social interaction. They consist of both informal constraints (sanctions, taboos, customs, traditions and codes of conduct), and formal rules (constitutions, laws, property rights)'. See North (1991: 97).

9. It is much easier for upper caste business competitors to dissuade clients from Dalit entrepreneurs by invoking the language associated with the sociological beliefs of purity and pollution in sectors like retail and wholesale food, sanitary ware, education, small general shops/ workshops. The attacks were invariably open and direct. However in sectors like information technology, medical health (nursing homes), etc., the language and practice of discrimination was more indirect and subtle.

References

Akerlof, G.A. 2005. 'The Economics of Caste and of the Rat Race and Other Wonderful Tales', in George A. Akerlof (ed.) *Explorations in Pragmatic Economics*, pp. 39–55. Oxford: Oxford University Press.

Almond, G. 1965. 'A Developmental Approach to Political Systems', *World Politics*, 17 (2): 183–214.

Almond, G. and G.B. Powell Jr. 1966. *Comparative Politics: A Developmental Approach*. Boston: Little Brown.

Anderson, L.M. and P.H. Collins. 2006. *Race, Class and Gender: An Anthology*. Belmont: Wadsworth Publishing.

Bardhan, P. 1984, *The Political Economy of Development in India*. New Delhi: Oxford University Press.

Browne, I. and Mishra, J. 2003. 'The Intersection of Gender and Race in Labour Market', *Annual Review of Sociology*, 29 (August): 487–513.

Collins, P.H. 2000. *Black Feminist Thought: Knowledge, Consciousness, and the Politics of Empowerment*. Boston: Unwin Hyman.

Crenshaw, K. 1991. 'Mapping the Margins: Intersectionality, Identity Politics and Violence against Women of Colour', *Stanford Law Review*, 43(6): 1241–99.

Deshpande, A. 2011. *The Grammar of Caste: Economic Distribution in Contemporary India*. New Delhi: Oxford University Press.

Dworkin, R. 1981. 'What is Equality? Part 2: Equality of Resources', *Philosophy and Public Affairs*, 10 (4): 283–345.

Easton, D. 1957. 'An Approach to the Analysis of Political Systems', *World Politics*, 9 (3): 383–400.

Evans, P.B. 1995. *Embedded Autonomy: States and Industrial Transformation*. New Jersey: Princeton University Press.

Evans, P.B., D. Rueschemeyer, and T. Skocpol (eds). 1985. *Bringing the State Back In.* Cambridge: Cambridge University Press.

Giddens, A. 1984. *The Constitution of Society: Outline of the Theory of Structuration.* Cambridge: Polity Press.

Glenn, E. 1999. 'The Social Construction and Institutionalization of Gender and Race: An Integrative Framework', in M.M. Ferree, J. Lorber and B.B. Hess, (eds), *Revisioning Gender.* pp. 3–43. New York: Sage Publications.

Harding, S. and K. Norberg. 2005. 'New Feminist Approaches to Social Science Methodologies: An Introduction', *Signs*, 30 (4): 2009–15.

Jessop, B. 1977. 'Recent Theories of the Capitalist State', *Cambridge Journal of Economics.* 1 (4): 353–73.

———. 2006. 'The State and State Building', in R.A.W. Rhodes, S.A. Binder, and B.A. Rochman, (eds), *The Oxford Handbook of Political Institutions*, pp. 111–30. New York: Oxford University Press.

Kaviraj, S. 1989. 'A Critique of the Passive Revolution', *Economic and Political Weekly*, XXIII (45-7): 2429–44.

Kohli, A. 2006.'Politics of Economic Growth in India, 1980–2005 Part II: The 1990s and Beyond', *Economic and Political Weekly*, XLI (14): 1361–70.

Lal, D. 1988. *Hindu Equilibrium, Volume 1: Cultural Stability and Economic Stagnation: India, c.1500 BC–AD 1980*, New York: Clarendon Press.

Lukes, S. 1974. *Power a Radical View.* London: Macmillan.

McCall, L. 2005. 'The Complexity of Intersectionality', *Signs*, 30(3): 1771–1800.

McGibbon, E. and C. McPherson. 2011. 'Applying Intersectionality & Complexity Theory to Address the Social Determinants of Women's Health', *Women's Health and Urban Life*, 10(1): 59–86.

North, D. 1981. *Structure and Change in Economic History*, New York, W. W. Norton.

———. 1991. 'Institutions', *The Journal of Economic Perspectives*, 5(1): 97.

Ore, T.E. (ed.). 1994. *The Social Construction of Difference and Inequality: Race, Class, Gender and Sexuality.* New York: McGraw Hill.

Pascale, C. 2007. *Making Sense of Race, Class and Gender: Commonsense, Power and Privilege in the United States.* New York: Routledge.

Polsby, W.N. 1960. 'How to Study Community Power: The Pluralist Alternative', *The Journal of Politics*, 22(3): 474–84.

Rafanell, I. and H. Gorringe. 2010. 'Consenting to Domination? Theorising Power, Agency and Embodiment with Reference to Caste', *The Sociological Review*, 58(4): 604–22.

Rawls, J. 1971. *Theory of Justice*. Cambridge: Harvard University Press.

Rudolph, L. and S. Rudolph. 1987. *In Pursuit of Lakshmi: The Political Economy of Indian State*. Chicago: University of Chicago Press.

Skocpol Theda. 1985. 'Bringing the State Back In: Strategies of Analysis in Current Research' in Peter B. Evans, Dietrich Rueschemeyer, and Theda Skocpol (eds), *Bringing the State Back In*, (Cambridge: Cambridge University Press.

Scoville, J.G. 1996. 'Labour Market Underpinnings of a Caste Economy: Foiling the Coase Theorem', *American Journal of Economics and Sociology*, 55 (4): 385–94.

Sen, A. 2009. *The Idea of Justice*. Cambridge: Harvard University Press.

Stiglitz, J. 1999. 'Formal and Informal Institutions' in Partha Das Gupta and Ismail Serageldin (eds.) *Social Capital: A Multifaceted Perspective*, Washington, World Bank, pp. 59–68.

Weber, L. 2004. 'A Conceptual Framework for Understanding Race, Class, Gender and Sexuality', in S. Nagy, H. Bibber, and M. Yaisiere, (eds), *Feminist Perspective on Social Research*. pp. 121–39. New York: Oxford University Press.

Williamson, O.E. 2000. 'The New Institutional Economics: Taking Stock, Looking Ahead', *Journal of Economic Literature*, 38(3): 596.

PART IV

LEGISLATION AND NEWER FORMS
OF DISCRIMINATION

10

Colonial Construction of a 'Criminal' Tribe*

Meena Radhakrishna

In 1911, the itinerant trading community of the Yerukulas in the Madras Presidency was declared a criminal tribe. This was under a piece of legislation called the Criminal Tribes Act, applied to the whole of British India. Under one of its provisions, special settlements could be established where the criminal tribe communities could be confined in order to watch and reform them. Missionary organizations, of which the Salvation Army was the main one, were put in charge of these settlements and were given more or less complete autonomy as far as administration of these settlements was concerned.

In the first three sections of this paper, an attempt is made to identify some of the strands which wove into the ideological perception, or construction of a criminal in the early twentieth century, as distinct from actual legislation to deal with criminality on the ground. Attitudes to itinerant communities are discussed in some detail with this aspect in mind, as also the Yerukulas' particular relationship with sedentary communities. In the middle part, in the fourth section, I discuss the main features of a criminal tribe settlement called Stuartpuram where this community lived for decades, and still lives. This part discusses the processes by which the Yerukulas were first sedentarized under the Criminal Tribes Act, and then made to work on land owned by the Salvation Army, and finally, turned into regular wage workers in a tobacco factory. The last part, describes the way social and cultural aspects of the Yerukulas' community life were transformed in the Stuartpuram settlement under the supervision of the Salvation Army. This seems to have been an inevitable result of the logic of work on land, or in a factory. The final section discusses the 'historic memory' of the Yerukulas, and their perception of their ancestors as dangerous criminals. This is done through an analysis of a poem that is a part of their oral culture even today, and which is at complete variance with the 'official' version speaking of a useful, honourable past of the earlier generations.

Perception of Nomads

Nomadic communities the world over have always been considered to be more criminal than not, and their 'restlessness' or constant move-ment is considered a troublesome feature by members of sedentary societies. The relationship between itinerant and sedentary commu-nities has become more problematic in modern times. The more the itinerant communities get marginalized to the main sphere of society because of transformative processes, the more they become suspect from the point of view of the sedentary society they interact with. In real terms, their increasing marginality simply compounds the already existing prejudices against them. In Europe, gypsies became gradually marginalized to the established system with the processes of industrialization.[1]

In India, the situation was only slightly different: here the British administration's economic policies, aimed at raising revenue, had made the itinerant communities redundant and anachronistic. The itinerant community of the Yerukulas of the Madras presidency is the focus of this chapter, and it is important to first briefly discuss the trajectory they followed in the late nineteenth century, as far as their gradual marginalization to the sedentary society is concerned.

Members of this community were chiefly traders in grain and salt, operating between the coastal areas of the presidency and the interior districts.[2] They were, at one time, almost the only means of distributing salt in far-flung areas where wheel traffic could not reach. In the 1850s, road and railway networks were established throughout the presidency, and this community's trade—carried out largely on pack bullocks or donkeys—became largely if not wholly redundant.

Further, the famine of 1877 was devastating as far as their salt trade was concerned. A large number of their cattle died, which used to be crucial for carrying their merchandise. And as they were traders in cattle as well, they suffered huge losses during the decade of the famine. Their grain trade, too, suffered drastically during this period, because of the way famines were managed by the British administration, favouring the bigger grain merchants;[3] small traders like the Yerukulas found this item totally inaccessible at a time when their cattle, which carried it, were dying in large numbers as well.

Forest laws of the 1880s prevented them from collecting forest produce, an important item of barter in their trade, and also did not allow them now to collect bamboos and leaves, which they used for making mats, baskets, and brooms, etc. Common pasture land and grazing areas were cordoned off, and not available any more to their cattle.[4]

They were also crucially affected by the new salt policy of the government in the 1880s, which allowed large trading companies to enter the salt trade. A large number of retail outlets were established by the government all over the presidency on railway routes, where salt was now sold through the agents of large company traders.[5]

As a result of the above factors, Yerukulas suffered a massive economic setback as far as the period between the 1850s and 1860s is concerned.

As they become marginalized to the main system, prejudices and myths which already exist about nomads are renewed, or come to the surface more explicitly. David Mayall has pointed out some of these in his discussion on gypsy travellers in nineteenth-century England. Some of these apply to itinerant communities in general, and are discussed in the following paragraphs.

Most importantly, the nomads' lack of property, and supposed lack of due regard for others' property, is seen to be a threat to the established order.[6] Their independence from rigid norms and constraints of sedentary societies is found to be equally objectionable. In fact, itinerancy is seen as a possible escape route for the so-called outcasts and refuse of sedentary societies—if one is an itinerant; it is probably because he or she was not acceptable to the sedentary society.

There have been other charges against gypsies, or migrants or nomadic people: they are escaping from the law, or simply fleeing from hard work of any kind. In agriculture-based societies, the men resent their escaping the hard work of ploughing and tilling, and the women that, or the harder labour of housekeeping and child rearing. In short, itinerancy is not seen as a chosen way of life, but as an aberration of some sort. In fact, their very marginality to the established system is suspected to stem from a deliberate rejection of that system, and this offends the established members of sedentary societies. Accusations of vagrancy, lust for wandering, lack of stability and general purpose in life, restlessness and aimlessness plague all itinerant communities.

In addition, their superior knowledge of the world, acquired during extensive travels, is possibly seen to endow them with greater mental resources and a potential for greater manipulation of others. It is worth emphasizing here that many of the above prejudices are not held so much by the local people, but by the local authorities. In the Indian case, these would mean the British administration, the police establishment, the high caste sections, and the village landlords.

More grievances were added to the standard list of charges against itinerants by the Indian authorities: their lack of predictability of movements implied a potential lack of control; their shifting abodes meant shifting loyalties to different patrons, and so they were seen to be perennially disloyal; the impossibility of taxing them, or raising any kind of revenue out of them, unlike their sedentary counterparts was probably a major irritant to the administration.[7] In addition, for the keepers of social morality, their lack of visible social institutions implied complete disorder in their community life. Their lack of written codes of conduct, and absence of loudly articulated norms of morality implied absolute licentiousness.

At another level, there were more problems. This community had amongst its members acrobats, singers, dancers, tightrope walkers, and fortune tellers. More and more, like their counterparts all over the world, street entertainment provided by them was seen to be a threat to public order. Since they always collected a large interested

crowd around themselves—and were quite a large crowd by themselves—their presence made the local authorities nervous. The British
administration was increasingly inclined to favour forms of recreation
which could be supervised by themselves, and would not precipitate
what they called 'disorderly and riotous behaviour' on part of the
spectators. It is worth mentioning here that in England, all laws
relating to the gypsies were to protect the settled communities from
itinerant ones and never the other way around (Mayall 1988: 180).
Large-scale harassment of these communities by members of settled
communities was a common feature in Europe, and there is evidence
of this happening in the Madras Presidency as well.

It is worth pointing out at this juncture the ambivalences and
contradictions in the attitude of sedentary communities to itinerant
ones. These are symptomatic of the latter's simultaneous usefulness
and marginality to the established systems they have to interact
with. It was, for instance, felt that these communities must be
settled somewhere, but 'not near us, not here'. This is reminiscent
of a similar ambivalence: 'they should visit our village, but should
not stay too long'. Further, they were expected to become a part
of the mainstream, but were expected also to be segregated from
the main society while this was being done, so as not to corrupt
it. They were, in fact, romanticized in imagination, especially in
English fiction and poetry in the case of the gypsies (Mayall 1988:
87). This was for their independent spirit, their dark attractive
looks (or bright clothes and jewellery as in the case of the Indian
'Banjaras'), their supposed healthy outdoor life. In general, there
was a lot of romance and adventure associated with their travels.
However, when confronted in reality, there was fear and dread and
they were shunned if not despised. In fact, a number of English
ladies in their leisure time in India drew Banjara men and women
in a romanticized light while their law-making men folk made them
out to be ferocious criminals. (Banjaras were also declared criminal
tribes by the British administration).[8]

So the important point is that the very nature of the relationship between these two different systems, and the gaps in knowledge of each others' real ways of living will lead to myth-making on
both sides. Unfortunately, we know little about the myths that the
itinerant people have about sedentary societies. At any rate, as far as

sedentary societies are concerned, there is an overarching discomfort, a suspicion regarding itinerants which degenerates into seeing them as established criminals.

Yerukulas and the British

In the earlier section, some of the general prejudices about itinerant communities were discussed. This section looks into some specific additional charges against the Yerukulas, which existed in the minds of the British administrators, and which contributed substantially to their being labelled a criminal tribe. Interestingly, scattered in the official records themselves, there is information collected by the administration for other purposes, which contradicts these very charges. However, since the Yerukulas were an itinerant community, the administrators found it difficult to shake off some of the prejudices they carried with them regarding European gypsies, and seem to have simply superimposed some of these on the Indian counterparts. Moreover, the bulk of their own prejudices were shared by the high caste, landlord sections, on whom the administration relied for first-hand knowledge of Indian society.

The most important of the accusations was that the Yerukulas as itinerants had an 'insatiable lust for wandering aimlessly'. It is important here to point out that their wandering could not have been aimless—they always had fixed trade routes, depending on the demand for their wares; on the cycle of annual festivals and fairs; on availability of raw material for making mats or baskets; and on the season in which the forest produce would be available, or stocks of grain, which they used for barter. Their movements also depended on the salt manufacturing cycle, an important item of their trade, or simply on availability of casual work which they did from time to time. Their routes and schedules of stopping and moving were fixed and cyclic.[9]

The second of the significant charges was that they were idle, lazy, and not keen on hard work. Booth Tucker, the head of the Salvation Army in India wrote of them: 'When we asked them to till the land, or work in a factory, they were shocked. Work? They said, we never work, we just sing and dance' (Booth-Tucker 1916). Now, if they did not work, neither they nor their trade, nor their crafts would have survived for so long. What was being discussed was not whether or not they worked, but the nature of their work. Their work was independent, not time-bound and most important, was not wage work. The third prejudice which had a long life was that of their lack of any social norms, especially regarding their women. Charges of looseness of character, and even prostitution were frequent, stemming from their polygamous practices. Buying and selling of females was another charge, with origins in bride price which they paid at the time of marriages. The myth of their licentiousness had its roots in their unfamiliar social organization (unfamiliar to the high-caste sections), which included freedom in choosing of spouses, easy divorce, widow remarriage, and a marked absence of marriage of girls before puberty. Interestingly, however, this particular view about their immoral women prevailed with the British administrators as well, possibly because of the polygamy component. Ironically, one of the high caste commentators in 1948 held the Yerukulas up as the vision of Indian reformers. He stated that their social norms were what the civilized Hindu society was aiming at through legislation; they should, in fact, 'have been left alone' (as far as attempts to civilize them were concerned) (Aiyyappan 1948: 47).

The final and major charge that plagued the Yerukulas was that of their ostensible criminality. This had two aspects: one was that they had always been criminals—all gypsies supposedly are—and secondly, that they had become dangerous criminals once they lost their earlier means of livelihood (Radhakrishna 1989a: 271–5). As far as proof of the first aspect was concerned, their own alleged folklore was used. It was claimed that 'when they asked their god Subramanya what profession they should follow, he handed them a housebreaking implement!'(GoM 1926: 63). This was supposed to be convincing evidence of their committing thefts and robberies as a profession. In actual fact, crimes attributed to them by the police were seldom proven—this generated another minor myth of their slipperiness and nimble-fingeredness (GoM 1926: 63).

In the annual crime figures of the Madras Presidency, their proportion in the criminal population was always lower than their proportion in the total population. (In fact, sometimes a high-caste category would account for a much higher proportion of total crime in relation to their proportion in the total population in the region) (GoM 1926: 63).

And lastly, the districts through which they regularly passed, or where they stopped for relatively longer periods, did not have a higher proportion of crime than other districts with which they had little contact.[10] Incidentally, when there were genuine crimes committed in areas where they stopped, it was admitted by the police themselves that it was the handiwork of local elements, who got more active whenever an itinerant community was around—these elements were merely using an existing view of itinerants to their advantage, knowing that the crime would be blamed on the itinerants.

However, the second part of this accusation—their becoming criminals because they lost their means of livelihood—is more important. This is because part of this assertion was true: they had lost their chief means of livelihood over a period of time. As mentioned earlier, they used to be salt and grain traders, taking salt from the coastal areas of the presidency into inland areas where wheel traffic could not reach, and bartering it for grain or forest produce. The loss of means of livelihood was correctly attributed to a network of roads and railways which had made their trading activities redundant.[11]

However, it is important to point out that salt was a very important source of revenue for the British administration in the nineteenth century, and the Yerukulas were at one time the only means of distributing it in remote areas, where only 'pack bullocks' could reach (Radhakrishna 1989a). This is the reason why the British administration officially recognized this important aspect of their existence, namely, their salt trading activities. Similarly, they helped in averting famines in far-flung areas, and that is why their grain trade was acknowledged.

The point, however, is that they were never only salt and grain traders. In fact, they did a number of other things apart from these two major activities. They were cattle breeders and traders; dealers in all kinds of forest and agricultural produce; they were casual workers; made baskets, mats, brooms, and brushes, and as mentioned earlier, were also acrobats, dancers, singers, and fortune tellers. They certainly got marginalized drastically as a result of British policies, but they probably did not become criminals, certainly not as a community. They had too many other resources they could still fall back upon. In the Tamil-speaking region, where they were called *koravars*, they continued to be called '*inji*', '*kal*' or '*dabbai koravars*', depending on the work they still did.[12]

The point that is being made is that prejudices against itinerants formed a major strand that fed into the Criminal Tribes Act.

'Hereditary' Criminal

The concept of crime and its causes had been changing all through the late nineteenth century, perhaps even earlier in Europe (Emsley 1987, Jones 1982, Yang 1985). There was a strong school of thought, put forward by criminologists and scientists at one point, which held that crime was inherited over generations in a family through a set of genes (Stepan 1982).

In the Indian context, the concept of a 'hereditary criminal class' remained important and attractive for a long time. This was probably for the reason that this view allowed deflection of enquiries into the causes of crime, and allowed for stringent, arbitrary measures of control. The important point to emphasize here is that the investing of some sections with hereditary criminality was different in the case of India and England. In India it was based not on the notion of genetically transmitted crime, but on crime as a profession practised by a 'hereditary criminal caste'. Like a carpenter would pass on his trade to the next generation, hereditary criminal caste members would pass on this profession to their offspring.[13] In England, a hereditary criminal implied one who had inherited criminality through the genes of a parent or an ancestor.

In India, then, the concept of hereditary crime never really got linked to biological determinism. This happened not because of a genuine advance in the field of genetics, but because the Indian caste system seemed to adequately explain to the British administrator the phenomenon of daunting criminality of at least a section of Indians.

By the end of the nineteenth century, however, it was not the hereditary criminal that the British Indian administrators were looking for any more. Now they were looking for a criminal with more 'scientific' reasons for being one. Clearly, there was a genuine need in these circles to find an explanation for the criminality of such large numbers of people in society. By calling the trait hereditary, the problem was rendered not amenable to resolution or intervention. A genuine social cause had to be identified and dealt with efficiently.

It was in the context of this search that in the first decade of this century, policies followed by the British Indian administration 50 years ago were blamed for destroying the traditional means of livelihood of a number of communities (Radhakrishna 1989a: 271–5). Commission of crime was now directly related to the lack of means of livelihood, and non-availability of work. (Even in England, lack of 'ostensible means of livelihood' made a person qualify as a potential criminal by now.) This further implied that if honest (wage) work could be found for such communities, they could be weaned away from crime.[14]

And this is how the concept of criminality got linked to a secular cause like loss of livelihood by certain communities due to a set of colonial policies, discussed in the last section.

It is worth pointing out here that there was the additional input into notions of criminality by the then developing discipline of Indian anthropology as well. This discipline addressed itself to the study of particular sections of the Indian population, mostly indigenous 'tribal' communities and itinerant groups, and contributed in a very substantial way to the conceptual outline of a criminal in the popular mind. By focusing on bizarre or exotic ritual aspects of the social lives of such communities, and at the same time also on their differential anthropometric measurements, the discipline managed to draw the fine line between a civilized and barbaric individual. In the popular ethnographic literature of the period, a sketch was drawn of a criminal who possessed not just bizarre social customs, but a strange body and psyche as well, 'which had criminality written all over'.[15]

It is important to mention that the Salvation Army also considerably helped public perception of the criminality of groups with which they worked. In fact, over a period of time they were able to define with some authority, for administrations all over the world, what constituted criminality, and in different social contexts, even pointed out who these criminals were—paupers in England, tribals or gypsies in India, aborigines in Australia, New Zealand or North America and so on. The Salvation Army had been working with released prisoners in India a few years before the Criminal Tribes Act was instituted, and this organization was taken very seriously by the government—its officials had evolved categories of criminals like incorrigible, habitual, hereditary, ordinary, worst character, would be good, won't be good, *badmash*, *nekmash* and so on in what they called 'crimdom', and differential treatment was suggested for varying degrees of Indian criminality in a potential 'curedom'. The treatment had to be punitive, deterrent, preventative (sic) or curative (Booth-Tucker 1916: 4).

In any case, the general point to emphasize here is that the category of a criminal tribe was not a sudden development—different stands of social and political opinions and considerations had been shaping the general category of an Indian 'criminal' for several decades. The complexity of these converging currents has not been explored here. A criminal could, for instance, be anyone who resisted the British, or even resisted a local oppressive landlord or high caste member. In addition, the plethora of new legislations that the British introduced created new 'criminals' all the time. These were either people ignorant of the new laws, or those wilfully defiant of the ones which encroached on their traditional rights—for instance, forest laws. To give an example of the broadness and flexibility of the term 'criminal', and the open-ended uses to which the Criminal Tribes Act could be put, it was suggested that the Act could be used profitably 'for combating secret societies, political preachers who might create unrest and so on', in other words to combat the newly emerging nationalist movement.[16]

Settlements under the Salvation Army

Yerukulas were declared a criminal community under the Criminal Tribes Act, 1911. Before going into the substantive part of this section, which discusses a criminal tribe settlement called Stuartpuram, it is important to briefly point out a few salient features of the Criminal Tribes Act, and the way it operated in general.

Firstly, before a community was declared a criminal tribe, 'respectable members' of a village were consulted, who were invariably either headmen, or high caste sections, or landlords; often these categories overlapped. The notified criminal tribe members had to take the permission of the headman before they could enter or leave a village. There is evidence that these headmen-cum-landlords used the Act to extract free labour from the criminal tribe members before they allowed an itinerant community to pass through the village.[17]

Secondly, one of the provisions required the notified criminal tribe members to report to the nearest police station to register their attendance twice a night. These powers were used by the subordinate police for extortions and harassment so widely that it caused some administrative concern (Baird [nd]: 281).

Thirdly, criminal tribe members were forced to work in mills, factories, mines, quarries, and plantations by the police administration as a part of relieving their own vigilance duties, and handing over to the employer's extraordinary powers of control under the Criminal Tribes Act. Under this, even ordinary workers could be declared criminal tribes in case their work performance was not satisfactory, and in fact, in crucial ways this Act also effectively replaced the Workmen's Breach of Contract Act, especially on the plantations. As far as this particular use of the Criminal Tribes Act was concerned, any low caste, vulnerable section of the people, could be declared a criminal tribe and forced to work in an enterprise; any person including a manager of an enterprise could be made responsible for their control, and any site, including an enterprise could be declared a criminal tribe settlement (Radhakrishna 1989b).

And lastly, a section of those declared criminal could be interned into special settlements set up under one of the provisions of the Criminal Tribes Act. The Stuartpuram settlement in Guntur district was one such settlement, and it is here that about 6,000 Yerukulas lived for several decades from 1913 onwards. The settlement was named after Harold Stuart, the moving force behind settlements in general, and a senior government official at that time, in charge of the police. The spirit behind these settlements, thus, can be imagined to be punitive, rather than reformative, contrary to the claims by the administration till much later.

In the 1910s, when the criminal tribe settlements were established in the Madras Presidency, itinerant communities were singled out for settling by policy. The official directive was that 'worst characters, especially wandering gangs' must be settled.[18] The Salvation Army was entrusted with itinerant communities, and sedentary criminals were to be the responsibility of the police.[19] The Stuartpuram settlement, then, became the literal 'site' where the British administration and the Salvation Army together decided to have what they called an 'experiment in criminocurology'. Since the Salvation Army was responsible for a number of settlements and was, in fact, the main organization working with the supposed criminal communities in India, it is appropriate to mention a few details about this organization, and why it would be attractive to the British administration.

The Salvation Army identified itself aggressively with the imperial aims of England of the time. Born in the 1870s, the heyday of British imperialism, it not only called itself the Salvation Army, it cashed in on the popular image of romanticized imperialism by adopting marches, flags, brass bands, and uniforms for its employees. Their head was called 'General' Booth, they had officers who signed 'articles of war', and their newspaper was called *The War Cry*. They had open air 'bombardments', not meetings. They would not say that they were going to start work in a new region, but 'occupy a new territory', and 'declare war' (on ungodliness or whatever) (Parsons 1988: 22). In short, the Salvation Army was a shadow imperial body—self-consciously so—and absolutely identified itself with the aims and projects of England of the time.

General Booth had envisaged for the English poor, what he called city colonies and farm colonies.[20] For the Indian criminal, however, he decided on 'settlements'. Of course, in this case, this imperial term took on a new meaning—the itinerant communities were to be settled down as opposed to being allowed to wander aimlessly.

The Stuartpuram settlement was meant to be a settlement for well-behaved, reformed, and non-criminal members drawn from another criminal settlement, Sitanagaram, also located in Guntur.[21] However, when the Salvation Army was given land in Guntur to set up this settlement, there were a number of protests, posed in different ways. The landlord sections were particularly infuriated, and charged that CT members escaped at night from the settlement and committed crimes. Thus, this settlement was also declared to be a criminal settlement, and a substantial increase in the police force was sanctioned in the area, to intensify patrolling.[22]

The Stuartpuram settlement was initially planned as an agricultural settlement: 500 acres of sandy land and 1,000 acres of swamp land were handed over to the Salvation Army by the government, free of assessment. However, for a number of reasons, the plans failed. Essentially, the land was of very poor quality and the implements of agriculture primitive. Moreover, the Yerukulas were not keen on tilling the land, and made unenthusiastic agriculturists.

Following is an excerpt from a settlement manager's poetic account of his experiences with making unwilling settlers work on land:

> The Salvation Army found it very tedious
> to convert them into good cultivators industrious
> To work on land they were forced and could not be induced
> Though driven like a flock of sheep, the first crop failed...
> No crowbars, no proper spade and no physical strength
> so work turned out did not reach the desired length.[23]
> Again
> In the beginning, I had recourse to a stick,
> I was glad, as it brought the desired result quick
> (Achariar 1926).

Most important, there was fierce opposition by the landlords in the area, who objected to the very concept of low-caste communities being given land, in addition to their fear that paddy land, when suitably irrigated, was very valuable.[24] It was revealed that 'the monied folk of Bapatla [had] counted...on buying the swamp land at cheap rates and rack renting the actual cultivator whenever a crop could be raised.[25] This plan was unwittingly foiled by the administration by parceling out large tracts of land to the Salvation Army. The protest by the landlords was also in a large measure due to their anxiety about losing the services of Yerukulas as agricultural workers on their own land.[26]

All this opposition took place in the era when landlords were important political allies of the British administration, and on balance, the administration decided not to alienate the landlord/headmen sections any further. Irrigation facilities—plans to make available water from the Krishna river to the settlement—were withheld, and alternative means of supporting the settlement had to be now seriously considered.

It was at this juncture, that the Indian Leaf Tobacco Company (ILTD), (a later branch of the Indian Tobacco Company [ITC]) began to be discussed within the administration and the Salvation

Army circles, as possible alternative employers. The ILTD had existed in Guntur district since 1908 in order to procure local tobacco, as the leaf wing of the British American Tobacco Company and Peninsular Company. By 1925, the factory was said to have employed half of the total adult population of the settlement.[27] Essentially, according to government policy, once the infrastructure for the settlement had been provided by the government, the settlements were to be self-supporting. Once income from land was found to be not enough, gradually the settlement became dependent on the factory for the employment of the settlers.[28] The Salvation Army had no other means of finding employment for their charges.

The company's initial contact with the Stuartpuram settlers seems to have been through the mats made by the Yerukula women. The mats and baskets were, in fact, an essential part of the manufacturing process at the factory, and the Salvation Army was the medium through which the sales took place to the ILTD. Slowly, women came to be employed in the factory as regular wage workers, while the men continued to work fruitlessly on land. The financial situation of the settlement was quite stable for a few years after the women settlers from Stuartpuram began work in the ILTD factory. The ILTD management, the Salvation Army, and the administration seemed optimistic about the future progress of the settlement.

In the late 1920s, a process set itself in motion, which changed the balance of forces further in favour of the ILTD and the Salvation Army. This was in the form of the availability of more men workers from the settlement for factory work, and more powers of control for the Salvation Army on settlement land.

In 1928, 'natural flow'—fresh water under the sandy soil was discovered and found to be effective to raise paddy. Water beneath the surface of the sandy soil of the settlement's agricultural land was not brackish as had been believed all along. This revived the interest of the settlers in cultivation.[29] In the same year, the settlers petitioned the government about being given permanent 'pattas' as had been promised.[30] The Salvation Army was firmly opposed to the plan of transferring land to the settlers, and wrote to the officials to this effect.[31] What had happened was that the land had risen enormously in price, 'the place prospered so much that it had its own railway station and villages sprang up like a wild west town after a gold strike' (Watson 1964: 145).

The petition by the settlers had been pending for five years before it was turned down on a number of administrative grounds (re-survey of land will have to be done, more village officers will have to be recruited and so on). The most important official argument, however, was that the concept of permanent pattas was inconsistent with the running of the place as a reformatory settlement.[32] (Settlers were supposed to leave the settlement after their reformation had been achieved, to make place for new criminals.)

Essentially, there had been ominous signs shown by the settlers. There was an indication that the settlers had been found to be not totally without resistance to the policies of the Salvation Army, and had in fact organized themselves into a cooperative society.[33] Members of this society were now preparing to invest their own funds in digging an irrigation channel to improve the land, so that the fruit of the land would then legitimately be theirs, and not appropriated by the Salvation Army.[34]

The response of the Salvation Army was to discharge a large number of settlers from the provisions of the Criminal Tribes Act, and thus from the settlement itself, and transfer them to a new area called the New Colony near the ILTD factory premises. The official requirement of a means of livelihood, before a settler could be discharged from the settlement, was met by finding them employment in this factory.

This plan was fully supported and, in fact, financed by the government. Building a new colony involved digging wells, building huts, and providing other infrastructure, and this was done in great hurry just before the start of the tobacco processing season in 1935, so that the discharged settlers could be immediately employed in the factory. Taking advantage of the situation at this juncture, the ILTD management decided to expand its operations at Chirala.

The problem of men, hitherto tenants of the Salvation Army, had to be sorted out: these men had to be found work in a factory where work processes had been designed to employ mainly women. But there had been a strike by the 3,000 seasonal workers in 1932,[35] and the ILTD had since then been looking out for a more pliable workforce.

In 1933, the manager of the ILTD, Chirala, wrote to the chief inspector of factories, requesting him to exempt the workers in the factory from the provisions of the Factories Act, as the factory needed to work for 12 hours a day, and 66 hours a week.[36] The case made out was on the basis of the nature of the processes themselves. The fact which convinced the administration, however, in favour of the exemption of ILTD from crucial sections of the Factories Act was that 'machine room operatives were drawn mostly from Stuartpuram settlement...maintained by public funds.[37] The manager of the settlement, a Salvation Army official, had written to the ILTD management, urging that the provisions of the Act should be relaxed to enable the men settlers to work as long hours as possible. The 'concession', according to him, if granted, would benefit the administration of the settlement and indirectly make the task of control of criminal tribe settlers easier and cheaper for the government.[38]

This plea to the ILTD Company, in fact, was not inconsistent with the fact that the Salvation Army wanted to discharge as many settlers from the Stuartpuram land as possible and work had to be found for them in order to make out a case with the government for discharging them. These settlers were soon after, in 1935, discharged and transferred to the new colony near the factory on the grounds that 'to walk 3½ miles in the morning for work is not conducive to efficiency'.[39]

The exemption applied for was to section 21 (rest periods in factories), section 22 (weekly holidays), section 27 (limiting of working hours per week), and section 28 (limiting of working hours per day). The exemption which was granted was to sections 27 and 28. It applied to all machine operatives in all tobacco handling and re-drying factories.[40] In this way, the Yerukulas were used as an instrument in a major modification of the law, which was to now cover not just machine room workers from this community in the ILTD factory, but all machine room workers in all tobacco factories in the presidency.

By the beginning of 1935, every available man and woman from Stuartpuram was in the employment of ILTD. ILTD, as a result of the new exemptions, was now working double shifts, from 5 a.m. to 1 a.m. the next morning, except on Sundays.[41] The factory manager was reported to have given the government very good accounts of the Yerukula workers. On the whole, these workers were found to be thoroughly satisfactory by the ILTD.[42] They found regular work in the factory for ten months in a year—a pattern which was to continue for many years.

Rewriting a Culture

Stuartpuram became a large settlement in terms of numbers as whole communities—not individuals—were put in at a time. After all, the Criminal Tribes Act was meant to work with the concept of whole communities. In fact, even the Salvation Army said they were embarrassed by what they called 'this rain of riches'. (They explained this phrase to an intrigued government official: 'To others, these criminals may hardly appear in the light of riches, but to us each bears the image and super subscription of the Divine Mint'.)

This large settlement needed extensive police presence outside to prevent escapes, and inside, the Salvation Army took an attendance up to five times a day, including nights (Radhakrishna 1992). There was strict punctuality and discipline for both children and adults and a system of fines and even corporal punishment to deter disorderly behaviour. There were, incidentally, virtually no outsiders allowed into the settlement for scrutiny, and enquiry committees could enter it only in the 1940s, when the nationalists took up this issue seriously.

The Stuartpuram settlement, as described earlier, was meant to be an agricultural settlement. Though the official rationale was that it should be so because 'agriculture was the natural profession of all Indians', what comes through clearly in the records is the deep anxiety the British administration had for reclamation of waste land, forest land, and swamp land. In fact, land reclamation was synonymous with reclamation of criminal souls. Once cultivable, the land could start paying revenue.

A large tract of waste land was given to the Salvation Army for cultivation by the Yerukulas. This needed some reorganizing of the community's social and cultural priorities. Drastic transformation in the lives of the Yerukulas followed. Most important, of course, was the fact that the itinerant mode of existence was suddenly replaced by a forced settled life. The Salvation Army divided the community into families, which were now the new operational social and economic unit—each family was given a small piece of land, which it was responsible for cultivating, or else punishment followed.[43] The family was further broken up by removing the children to another part of the settlement. The Salvation Army felt that the 'rising generation' should be kept away from their wicked parents, and brought up in a more wholesome atmosphere. Separate schools and dormitories were established for these children, and they were allowed to meet their parents only on Sundays during church activities. The two components of criminals' reformation were moral education, and work. The Salvation Army concentrated on the children for moral education, and on the adult men for work.

Here it is important to emphasize that the Salvation Army did not normally prepare women for wage work in any of its settlements—ideally, they were to be trained in feminine virtues and were expected to sew, embroider, and cook for their families.

In the case of the Stuartpuram settlement, a new division of labour within the family was devised and appropriate gender roles defined. In fact, mat making, which was a traditional activity of both men and women of the Yerukula community, was now handed over exclusively to women, to be combined with other indoor activities.[44] Men now ploughed and tilled the waste land, albeit unsuccessfully.

There were myriad ways in which true women were fashioned out of what the Salvation Army called 'thievish raw material'. For instance, they were taught to pay attention to their appearances. The Salvation Army even held periodic parades of the 'most neatly dressed women' (and gave the winners a prize of one rupee each).[45] The women would also not be allowed to go outside the settlement on a pass if they looked like 'so many vagrants'. The 'before' and 'after' photographs of women in the Salvation Army records show the 'after' version with a completely changed Hinduized appearance, complete with neatly tied saris, oiled hair with flowers, and vermillion marks on their foreheads.

Anyway, after more than a decade of such remoulding, something happened: these newly domesticated women were required to work outside their homes for a wage as the land was found unable to support the families. As already mentioned earlier, the government expected the Salvation Army to make the settlements under their care completely self-supporting once the initial infrastructure had been paid for. Now that there was a severe financial crisis, these women were persuaded or forced in hundreds to go and work in the newly established tobacco factory several miles away.

The Salvation Army had so far been systematically inculcating in them an indoor culture of housekeeping and child-rearing. Now they were expected to walk a distance of seven miles every day, spend a total of 12 hours outside their homes, earning a wage. In fact, the Salvation Army even asked the government to provide crèches for the infants and toddlers in the settlement, so that young mothers could go as well. For the next 10–12 years, the women alone earned as much as 80 per cent of the entire settlement income.[46]

Ironically, while women were the principal earners in their families, the Salvation Army consolidated the new moral code for them. Unable any more to scrutinize their activities, unable also to adhere to the notion of them as dependent wives, the Salvation Army began to take on a more active role in their personal, marital affairs. This was done in order partly to keep their own control and partly to make sure that economic independence did not confound gender identities, as it had gender roles.

Women used to have the freedom to choose their spouses—the Salvation Army now granted permissions for marrying. The Salvation Army officials had always been votaries of proper match-making in settlements, now they became urgently active on the issue. They wrote to the government wanting 'a voice in the choice of spouses'[47] and got it. They were finding to their alarm that bride price, something they had been trying to suppress as it meant mere selling of females, now rose steeply (sometimes as much as Rs 500).[48] The Salvation Army substituted it with dowry, which they gave themselves. It always consisted of saris and vessels for the bride—true symbols of lost domesticity. (Incidentally, in other settlements in the north, the Salvation Army used to insist that the man be able to support his wife before letting them marry—they had to give up that condition here, which they did quite cheerfully.) They also forbade completely what they called 'desertions' by women of their husbands. So ironically, the women lost their autonomy in marital affairs at a time when they were the principal contributors to the family income. It is important to mention here that the ILTD company where the women worked supported the Salvation Army on the severe discipline in the settlement, and their active role in the women's family affairs. In fact, at a later point in time, the ILTD management became quite active itself on the second issue. The discipline—strict punctuality, orderly behaviour, and a system of harsh punishments—resonated well with factory life. On the whole, the ILTD management found that these workers were 'less troublesome' than others, and much more pliable.[49] The Salvation Army's insistence on an irrevocable form of marriage worked in the company's favour as well because they could continue to pay a family wage, which was much lower than the sum paid to an individual man and woman.

As a result of the special exemption from the Factories Act that the government granted to the ILTD, whole families from the settlement had come to be employed in the factory from the 1930s. The men were now working up to 20 hours a day in different shifts.

The ILTD, then, had a new interest in keeping families together at the settlement. I came across at least three petitions by Yerukula men in the company records, where the management was requested to intervene and help them in getting their wives to stay with them. The ILTD obliged in all three cases by threatening the women with loss of their jobs in case they divorced their husbands. Interestingly, I did not see any similar petitions by women.

Historic Memory

So far, the earlier sections have, in effect, dealt with the colonial construction of the Yerukulas' criminality, and the later ones with some of the ways in which their real daily lives were lived out decades ago. It is within this dual context that I am going to try and locate this community's current perception of its own past history.

About 10 years ago, I met the descendents of the Yerukulas in question, still living in the Stuartpuram settlement and working with the very same tobacco factory, the ILTD. When I met them, they were about to be retrenched in thousands, because the factory was going to have a mechanized plant to do the work that these workers had been doing manually. Stuartpuram, of course, was officially not called a criminal tribes settlement any more, and the community, Yerukulas, were not criminal tribes any more—after independence, the Criminal Tribes Act, under which they had been notified by the colonial administration, had been repealed. The Salvation Army, now a much depleted organization both as far as its authority and number of personnel were concerned, was still operating there with a hospital, a school, and other welfare activities.

I spent a long time with the community, both men and women talking about their work in the tobacco factory, the various strikes they had conducted to protest against the mechanization and so on. The workers were articulate, and talked a great deal about their experience with ILTD and were quite emphatic about the unfavourable partisan role of the Salvation Army in their struggle with the company. They also freely expressed their views on the factory management's mechanization plans, which would now make them redundant.

During my stay at the settlement, I noticed that in their leisure time the children and the adults would sing. Sometimes after the day's work, they would gather together and tell each other long tales with much enthusiasm. Slowly, I learnt that the stories they told so often were different sagas of how their forefathers were dangerous criminals; how the Salvation Army had worked tirelessly and selflessly for them for decades; how the tobacco factory had weaned their forefathers away from an earlier life of crime, by giving them employment and so on. Their songs, I found, were those taught by the Salvation Army in praise of Christ.

I wondered how this had happened. When they were so clear about their present destiny, and relationship vis-a-vis the Salvation Army and the ILTD, why were their narratives and songs in such a different tone as far as their past was concerned? I knew by then from official records that this community had been an itinerant one for generations before they were interned in this settlement—in fact, the village community around the settlement remembered their salt and grain trade, and other activities.

However, there were no traces of this relatively recent past etched on their memories in any form. There were no songs or folklore, which in any way reflected links with their earlier itinerant life, or their earlier work. Their stout denial of an itinerant past intrigued me as much as their assertions of an earlier dangerous criminality—and I could not understand this phenomenon till quite recently, when I stumbled upon some official publications of the Salvation Army.

Since I am discussing a community here which was unlettered, and has not left behind any written records, its own folklore (as also folklore about it) becomes an extremely important source of data to understand a whole range of issues. It also becomes very crucial to pose some of the following questions: whether the components of this folklore originated from inside the community, by and large, or from outside; if the latter, then was it an involuntary, 'natural' or gradual transformation/assimilation of versions of their past, or were some of these consciously or 'artificially' introduced; whether the folklore of the community, in however small a way, is a positive reading of its own past, or does the new version/s undermine its confidence or resources to fight its disabilities of the present; have stories or tales about a community, which pass off as its history with outsiders, become a part of the community's own historic memory? And equally, whether subsequent generations of that community keep these narratives alive by making such versions a part of their own oral tradition.

Reproduced here is a poem, which appeared in the Salvation Army newspaper, *The War Cry*. It was called – 'The Crim as we find him in the Telugu country'. It appeared in 1916; a few years after the Stuartpuram settlement had been established. It stands by itself, has no explanation or prose narrative to go with it, and is written by a Major Anandham, a non-Indian Salvation Army officer. (The Salvation Army officials always took local names, but never from the 'criminal' communities with which they worked.) Parts of this poem are reproduced here:

Come listen to me for a moment or more,
For I am a 'crim', yes, I am a 'crim';
There are records against me, yes, more than a score,
I belong to the criminal kind.
I live most by plundering other men's goods,
For I am a 'crim', yes I am a 'crim';
My home is in the jungle way off in the woods,
Oh, I am of the criminal kind.
I watch out for travellers 'long lonely bye roads,
Oh, I am a 'crim', yes I am a 'crim';
And many a 'hold up' I've done on the road,
That's the life of the criminal kind...

Away to the jungle and off to the fair,
I'm only a 'crim'; I'm only a 'crim',
There is booty and plenty awaiting me there,
I belong to the criminal kind.

The reader would have noticed that there is first person address used here—the 'I' dominating the narrative. The Salvation Army muse here is putting forward the supposed point of view of the Yerukulas, but from the point of view of an individual.

Coming to the second edition of the poem which is written about a decade later, it is found to be much edited, changed, and added to. It appears in a book of over 300 pages, written for an international audience by Booth-Tucker, now the head of the Salvation Army. The book in which it appears is called *Mukti Fauj or Forty Years with the Salvation Army in India* (Booth-Tucker ca. 1930: 229). It is a part of a chapter called 'Criminocurology', and has a long prose narrative before and after. The content of this narrative is almost entirely the unfolding of a success story that Booth-Tucker has to tell.

The interesting point about the location of this poem is that it is surrounded with prose which has important details. Here there is a discussion on the tremendous resistance that the Yerukulas offered to their sedentarization, to conversion to Christianity, or work on land or in factories. The poem, however, is quite beatific and ecstatic in tone, as if the Salvation Army just came and conquered. Perhaps the problems could now be talked about, once it is a success story, a story with a happy ending. But still, lack of any resistances in the poem is interesting as this poem, in all essential particulars, represented the myth which the Yerukulas accepted; the resistance which actually took place on the ground was never a part of the myth. Reproduced here are parts of the poem which are newly added to the earlier version, most likely not by the original author but some more senior bard in the Salvation Army.

I've oft been to prison and tasted their fare,
For I am a Crim, yes, I am a Crim!
Learned more of my business profession while there,
Seeing mine is a criminal mind.
And when I get out into freedom again,
I, who am a Crim, I, who am a Crim!

I fool the police, with their cleverest men,
Oh, I'm of the criminal kind!
The longer I follow, the more I delight,
In this life of a Crim, this life of a Crim!
To rob and to plunder, by day and by night,
This life of a criminal kind.

Here the criminal is shown to be a worse one than in the original version—he fools the police with his cleverness, he even learns new tricks of the trade in prison, and in fact, is also sadistic about his pursuit of crime—'the longer I follow, the more I delight'.

This is an important development—the criminal is now shown to be much more dangerous in retrospect, though he has, in fact, been steadily reforming for the last decade in the settlement. At one level it is understandable—the Salvation Army has to show its international audience how unpromising the initial raw material was, to heighten the fact of their success with them. Alternatively, maybe the settlers seemed more criminal as they were actively resisting the Salvation Army when this poem was being rewritten. But in real terms, the new version was an improvement on the earlier one.

In the second edition of the poem, there is an actual break in the narrative when the Salvation Army enters the picture, both symbolically and literally. This break, separating the earlier and later lives of the criminals, is achieved on paper by the device of having the old and the new sections separated by asterisks and it is the newly added section which heralds the new man. It is interesting that this break, symbolic and literal, was absent in the earlier poem written a decade ago and in some ways shows that even the Salvation Army was aware of the rupture that took place in the interim period, as far as the Yerukulas' past and present was concerned.

Thus goes the new section:
The Salvation Army now comes to our aid;
With work for the Crim – yes, work for the Crim!
And for us a pathway to Heaven has made,
For Tribes of the criminal kind...
They give us an offer of work we accept
'Tis work for the Crim – yes, work for the Crim;

> And soon at our task we become quite adept,
> We tribes of the criminal kind...
> At last we wake up to the fact, and the thought,
> "I'm no longer a Crim! I'm no longer a Crim!!
> I'm living by industry, honestly wrought,
> And have changed from the criminal mind!"

The reader will note here that the 'I' of the earlier poem has changed to 'we': there has been great progress made in the intervening years. In fact, the 'we' now includes not only the whole community of say, the Telugu country, but "we, tribes of the criminal kind". (There were at least 3–4 million criminal tribe members in India.) The poem, in fact, is no longer called The Crim as we find him in the Telegu country, but simply, The Crim.

Moreover, the 'we' of the poem now includes not just those who have been reformed but includes the Salvation Army as well:

> So all hands to work, through the storm, or the calm
> We will rescue the Crim, we will rescue the Crim
> And rid this fair land from a menace and harm,
> The tribes of the criminal kind.

There is not only distancing of the reformed ones from the unre-formed ones, there is now total identification the reformed members feel with the projects and plans of the Salvation Army for all Indian criminal tribe members. The newly reformed man is grateful that the Salvation Army has given him an opportunity to work honestly, and give up a life of crime. This is quite interesting, as when I had spoken to the Yerukulas in the 1980s, I found that the content of the two poems is exactly that they also believed: We were dangerous criminals, the Salvation Army came along, gave us work, and we were reformed.

Did they really mean what they said? Were their own stories believed by them? Where were their earlier tales? Why is their present memory devoid of their past? There are several possibilities.

Firstly, the Yerukulas of 1980s do not have any stakes in their past, so they are not going to intervene in versions of that past; their energies are better deployed in fighting for their present, which they were doing. (As mentioned in an earlier section, they were actively engaged in fighting their retrenchment from the ILTD factory in thousands.) Perhaps their emphasis on past criminality is to bring to others' notice their present non-criminality—a sign that they are still not free of the stigma of criminality by communities around them. It is also possible that talking about their past dangerous criminality, their ability once to 'hold up' those in power and terrorize them, gives them a sense of power today: 'We were also powerful once'—a sign of their powerlessness in the present. Another possibility is that this is mythmaking of their own. Belief in their earlier criminality rationalizes their current situation of vulnerability and poverty: 'Because we were criminals in the past, we deserve our present miserable fate'. There is also a touch of both defiance and relief in their loud assertions of past criminality: 'No one can harm us at least today'. And finally, maybe by resigning themselves to this version of their history they will be left in peace by the Salvation Army, or the ILTD, or whoever might challenge an alternative memory of their history.

These were some possible explanations as far as their assertions of past criminality are concerned. About their inability or refusal to remember their itinerant past, it is probably an expression of their discontent with that way of life. As discussed earlier in the essay, they were becoming increasingly marginalized, and begun to be dispensable to the local communities. Even before the Criminal Tribes Act was formally instituted, at least two or three decades before that, they had become vulnerable to police harassment and extortions. Perhaps they finally found peace once they were sedentarized, though it was not in a criminal tribe settlement, they would have liked to become sedentary.

These are mere speculations. The explanation for this collective denial of a collective history, and blanking out of collective memory of their folklore reflecting an earlier life, is probably a combination of all these but around one major fact: there was a severe rupture in the continuity of their lives once they came to the settlement. Folklore and songs and tales can only survive in a lived community life, and one with some continuity, however flimsy, with an earlier life. Under the Salvation Army, in a criminal tribe settlement, the community life was totally broken up and their forced transformation into disciplined wage workers took a toll of their cultural resources.

To repeat here some of what was discussed in an earlier section, firstly and most importantly, from being considered useful if not honourable people, they were officially declared predators on the larger society. Then, their itinerant mode of existence was replaced by settled life. The community as a unit was broken into families, which were now the operational social and economic units. The men's trading activities were replaced by forced work on land and later in the tobacco factory, and the women first forcibly confined to the home, and then forced to become factory workers. Their earlier social practices were considered barbaric and substituted with ones more acceptable to Victorian and brahminical notions of respectability; the women lost their relative egalitarian position in the community, and became increasingly subordinated to men.

Moreover, their children were taken away from them—who could they tell tales to, or sing songs to? It was a fractured community life, with broken bonds and ties. The settlement discipline allowed no meetings larger than six people at a time, except under the Salvation Army's eyes. In any case, there could not be the leisure for telling of tales or singing of songs—both the men and the women worked up to 16 hours a day.

In other words, there were several convulsions of engineered and sudden change in the continuity of their lives, and breaches with the immediate past. What remained of a community was more a confederacy, created by the punitive discipline and the application of the Criminal Tribes Act.

The social and cultural resources, gathered over generations, were probably irreparably destroyed with the violence of change that each of the breaches implied. The system of relationships and other social balances that communities evolve to sustain themselves seem to have been wiped out in this particular case because of a lack of continuity between the present and the past. Ironically, it was not until both men and women began work in the tobacco factory that some semblance of a collective or community identity began to emerge again, because of a shared environment, however restrictive. By then, however, it appears that their past history had already been rewritten in their memories.

There is a clue to the gradual way in which a rupture from their past took place. Their real lived experience, once they were beginning to be labelled criminals, was at complete variance with their earlier existence as legitimate traders. There was the Salvation Army inside the settlement, and if they managed to escape, the police outside. In fact, the police were a major constituent of their new psyche, as the possibility of a life outside the settlement, if they managed to escape, was clouded with their ubiquitous presence.

> They hunted me, haunted me, hounded me ever,
> I was a 'crim', they said I was a 'crim';
> And my honest intentions were scorned all the more,
> I was branded the criminal kind.
> So I gave up my struggle and thought it my lot,
> For I was a 'crim', yes, I was a crim,
> With the rest of my fellows, the Sircar I fought,
> Being marked as the criminal tribe.

The rupture is also expressed in a telling manner in the following two instances that F. Booth-Tucker told his international audience in an amused manner, fully aware that absconding from the settlement spelt terror for the settlers:

> One of our women officers was conducting a meeting amongst a number of tribesmen. She had been speaking to them...about the necessity of resisting the temptations of Satan. 'Who is your greatest enemy?' she asked, 'The Police', 'But, I mean, your spiritual enemy, the enemy of your souls.' They persisted, however, in repeating the answer. The officer was forced to change the subject and had to give them a chorus to sing instead (Booth-Tucker ca.1930: 13).

Recounting another instance, he recalled that a Salvation Army officer asked his Yerukula pupils, 'I have a friend that's ever near—never fear. What does that mean?' 'Don't be afraid of the police, god will look after you', came the prompt reply (Booth-Tucker ca.1930: 13).

But the most poignant is the way, before the rupture became complete, their prayers changed, which used to be for the peace of their dead and the health of their children: 'Spirits of our fathers, help us. Save us from the government and shut the mouths of the police' (Booth-Tucker ca.1930: 12). So this was the mental soil on which so powerful a myth, so convincing a version of another history could be sown. The important point to emphasize here is that the Salvation Army had consciously spun it, improved upon it, and intended to plant it years before it was actually made their own by members of the Yerukula community. As indicated earlier, there was resistance on the ground to the components of this version while it was being spun.[52] Now being passed on to new generations, this new history faces no such resistance.

Ironically, the official records of the British administration, the ILTD factory, and the Salvation Army contradict much of what the Yerukulas believe today. These sources not only grant the Yerukulas an 'honourable' past, they speak of the resistance that the community offered to forces which challenged the legitimacy of its existence at various stages. Equally ironically, it is the official sources which acknowledge the lack of any real basis for branding the community a criminal one.

The oral traditions of the community, which are supposed to 'recover' an 'authentic' past, reconstruct over and over again the criminal that the larger society had once invented, by passing on a constructed version of their history to their children and grandchildren. This version, as the chapter attempts to show, did not originate out of the way their actual lives were lived, but was purposefully introduced into the oral culture of the community about seven decades ago.

It will be appropriate to end with what the 'Crims' in the 1920s were meant to be thinking of themselves and their situation from the point of view of the Salvation Army:

> Now (work) is our watchword, from day unto day,
> There is hope for the Crim; there is hope for the Crim,
> *We wipe from our minds our sad record away,*
> We tribes of the criminal kind. (*emphasis added*).

Notes

* The author and publishers gratefully acknowledge *Economic and Political Weekly* for the permission to reproduce this essay, originally published as an article, 'Colonial Construction of a "Criminal" Tribe: Yerukulas of Madras Presidency', *Economic and Political Weekly*, 8–15 July, 2000, pp. 2553–63.

Earlier versions of this chapter were presented at the Nehru Memorial Museum and Library, School of Oriental and African Studies, Oxford, and Cambridge. I am grateful to the participants of these seminars for very useful discussions and comments. Issues raised in this chapter have been discussed with a large number of other scholars and friends, some of whom have decisively moulded their final shape. I thank all of them. All the Government Orders (GOs) were consulted at the Tamil Nadu Archives and Andhra Pradesh Archives. The Salvation Army documents were consulted at the organization's archives at the International Heritage Centre, London.

1. For an excellent account of gypsies in England, see Mayall (1988).
2. For an account of their trading activities, see Radhakrishna (1989a).
3. See, Government of Madras (1867), Government of India (1878: 49), Bhattacharya (1965: 1–22); Ambirajan (1971: 20–28).
4. Government of Madras, 'Administration Report of the Forest Department (Southern and Northern Circles), Madras Presidency for 1889–90, p. 27. Revenue for grazing went up from Rs 40,138 in 1883–84 to Rs 1,43,845 in 1889–90 (GoM, Report of the Forest Committee, Madras, 1912, Vol. II, pp. 7, 32).
5. A detailed analysis of the Report of the Salt Commission, 1876, Madras, makes this fact clear.
6. This para and the one that follows draw largely from Mayall (1988).
7. I am grateful to D. Washbrook for bringing to my notice the point about taxing.
8. Banjaras were a community much more in evidence all over India, unlike the Yerukulas who operated only in the limited Telegu regions of the Madras Presidency. In fact, Banjaras were called the 'exporters' of grain and salt to distant provinces and regions by the Madras administration, and Yerukulas termed 'local' traders. Essentially, Banjaras were a numerically larger community, operating on a much larger scale, traversing a much larger geographic area. For the same reason they escaped the Criminal Tribes Act for a longer period compared to the Yerukulas, being relatively less vulnerable.
9. Judl 239, 24 September 1918.
10. Judl GO 1071, Back nos. 51–53, dt August 1870. IGP to Chief Secretary to Government, Fort St. George, Madras, 19 May 1870, No. 3016.
11. For a detailed discussion on the process by which the Yerukulas lost their varied means of livelihood, because of a set colonial economic policies, see Radhakrishna (1989a).
12. PWL GO 225L, 26 February 1929.

13. Quoted in Nigam (1990).
14. This essentially meant that the CT members, as a government policy, were to be parcelled out to the owners of mills, factories, mines, and quarries as workers, as also to plantation owners (Radhakrishna 1989b).
15. For a detailed discussion on some of the currents which went into the making of the discipline of anthropology, see Radhakrishna (1997).
16. Home (Judl) 2764, dt 23 November 1916.
17. For a general discussion on this issue, see Radhakrishna (1989b).
18. For an account of criminal tribes settlements, see Radhakrishna (1992).
19. *The War Cry*, London, June, 1913. *The War Cry* was the official organ of the Salvation Army.
20. General Booth had spelt out his plans to salvage the English poor in his detailed work, 'In Darkest England and the Way Out' (Salvation Army, London, 1890). The criminal settlements in India were inspired by those ideas [Radhakrishna 1989b: Appendix].
21. The Salvation Army called Sitanagaram a sieve through which the criminals had to pass and be tested, and 'only those who responded to the treatment could find their Cannan in Stuartpuram' (Judl GO 3219 (Mis), 21 December 1915).
22. Note on the Stuartpuram settlement, Note, 1925.
23. Though the account is of another section of the Yerukula community in another Salvation Army, managed settlement, the same could be said of Yerukulas in Stuartpuram as well.
24. According to the Salvation Army sources, it was Rs. 1000 per acre (Booth-Tucker ca. 1930: 232).
25. Demi official letter from Guntur Collector to Stuart, Member of Council, 20 March 1915 in Judl GO 2509, 14 October 1915.
26. Notes to Judl GO 2509, October, 14, 1915, comments by Inspector General of Police.
27. Government of Madras, 'Administration Report of the Labour Department', Madras, 1925–26.
28. PWL GO 2394L, August 23, 1929; PWL GO 2338L, August 19, 1930; PWL GO 1313L, 17 June 1932.
29. The acreage under paddy almost doubled in 1928. Government of Madras, 'Administration Report of the Labour Departmant, Madras, 1928–29.
30. PWL GO 1147L, 26 May 1933.
31. Salvation Army records at the Stuartpuram settlement, Bapatla. Letter from Manager to Deputy Tehsildar, Chirala dated August 26, 1930. The policy so far had been that the tenancy of the family was taken

away if its members were found to be resorting to crime. This could not be done if the family owned the land.

32. PWL GO 1147, 26 May 1933.

33. This society, called the Stuartpuram Yerukula and Staff Tenants' Cooperative Society came into existence in 1926 and was free of patronage, unlike other such societies, of the labour department or Christian organizations.

34. Government of Madras, Administration Report of the Labour Department, Madras, 1934–35.

35. Government of Madras, Administration Report of the Labour Department, Madras, 1932–33.

36. Devt. GO 1315, 27 October 1933. Commissioner of Labour to Secretary to the Govt. of Madras, Devt. Department, October 1, 1933, enclosing letter from the ILTD Manager to Chief Inspector of factories, 22 July 1933.

37. Devt. GO 1315, 27 October 1933. Commissioner of Labour to Secretary to the Govt. of Madras, Devt. Department, October 1, 1933, enclosing letter from the ILTD Manager to Chief Inspector of factories, 22 July 1933.

38. Devt. GO 1315, 27 October 1933.

39. PWL GO 2671L, 6 December 1934.

40. Devt. GO 1315, 27 October 1933.

41. PWL GO 2726L, 17 December 1935.

42. Govt. of Madras, Administration Report of the Labour Department, Madras, 1934–35.

43. Judl GO 2308, 22 September 1916; Note, 1925.

44. The notion that this was primarily a women's job seems to have not been confined to the Salvation Army. It is interesting to note that the Yerukulas under a Roman Catholic priest underwent a similar division of labour. Home (Judl) GO 1534, 14 June 1916.

45. Booth Tucker, Mukti Fauj, ca. 1930, p. 234.

46. PWL GO 1313L, 17 June 1932.

47. Home (Judl) GO 1759, 5 August 1918: Booth-Tucker to Member of Council, 12 July 1918.

48. Home (Judl) GO 1759, 5 August 1918: Booth-Tucker to Member of Council, 12 July 1918. As the Salvation Army official put it, girls who had been straightened out and cured of drinking habits were sold to the highest bidder.

49. PWL GO 1654L, 6 July 1928.

50. February, 1916.

51. Booth-Tucker, *Mukti Fauj*, ca. 1930, p. 229.

52. Even according to the Salvation Army, 'We encountered many difficulties. The tribe was nomadic and resented internment, nor did they like the work in quarries…In fact they objected to everything. Even the six hundred donkeys which they brought with them entered into the spirit of their non-cooperating masters. (*Mukti Fauj* 1930: 228). Another account speaks of their, 'resentful mood', 'argument and scuffles', 'protestations and threats of violence' towards the Salvation Army officials (Baird n.d.: 131). The records at the ILTD factory, Guntur, and the official documents record the assertions and resistance of the Yerukulas as workers in the factory, especially after they got organized as ILTD Workers' Union.

References

Achariar, M.C.T. 1926. *History of Aziznagar Settlement*. Vrinddhachalam: Dass Press.

Aiyyappan, A. 1948. *A Report on the Socioeconomic Conditions of the Aboriginal Tribes of the Province of Madras*. Madras: Government Press.

Ambirajan, S. 1971. 'Political Economy and Indian Famines', *South Asian Studies*, 1 (August): 20–8.

Baird, W.B. n.d.(unpublished). *The Call of the Jackals*. London: Salvation Army Archives.

Bhattacharya, S. 1965. 'Laissez Faire in India', *Indian Economic and Social History Review*, 2 (1): 1–22.

Booth-Tucker, F. 1916. '*Criminocurology: The Indian Crim[sic] and What to do with Him: Being a Review of the Work of the Salvation Army among the Prisoners, Habituals and Criminal Tribes of India*, Simla (India): Liddel's Printing Works.

———. 1930. *Mukti Fauj or 40 years with the Salvation Army in India and Ceylon*. London: Marshall Brothers.

Emsley, C. 1987. *Crime and Society in England, 1750–1900*. New York and London: Longman.

Government of India (GoI). 1878. *Report of the Indian Famine Commission, Parts I, II, and III*, Vol. I, p. 49. Government of India.

Government of Madras (GoM). 1867. *A Memorandum on the Madras Famine of 1866*, Madras: Government of Madras.

———. 1926. 'Note Showing the Progress Made in the Settlement of Criminal Tribes in the Madras Presidency up to January, 1925', Madras: Government of Madras.

Jones, D. 1982. *Crime, Protest, Community and Police in Nineteenth Century Britain*. London: Routledge and Kegan Paul.

Mayall, D. 1988. *Gypsy Travellers in the Nineteenth Century.* Cambridge: Cambridge University Press.

Nigam. S. 1990. 'Disciplining and Policing the Criminals by Birth, Part 1: The Making of Colonial Stereotype—The Criminal Tribes and Castes of North India', *Indian Economic and Social History Review*, 27(2): 131–64.

Parsons, G. 1988. *Religion in Victorian Britain, Vol. 1 (Traditions).* Manchester and New York: Manchester University Press.

Radhakrishna, M. 1989a. 'From Tribal Community to Working Class Consciousness: Case of Yerukula Women', Review of Women's Studies, *Economic and Political Weekly*, XXIV(17): 2–5.

———. 1989b. 'The Criminal Tribes Act in Madras Presidency: Implications for Itinerant Communities', *The Indian Economic and Social History Review*, 26(3): 271–5.

———. 1992. 'Surveillance and Settlements under the Criminal Tribes Act in Madras', *The Indian Economic and Social History Review*, 29(2): 171–98.

———. 1997. 'Colonialism, Evolution and Anthropology: A Critique of the History of Ideas 1850–1930', Research in Progress Papers, *History and Society*, New Delhi: Nehru Memorial Museum and Library.

Stepan, N. 1982. *The Idea of Race in Science: Great Britain, 1800–1960.* London: Macmillan.

Watson, B. 1964. *A Hundred Year's War.* London: Hodder and Stoughton.

Yang, A.A. (ed.) 1985. *Crime and Criminality in British India.* Arizona: University of Arizona Press.

11

Deconstructing Emerging Disability Legislation in India

Renu Addlakha

Background

India was one of the first countries to sign the historic United Nations Convention on the Rights of Persons with Disabilities (UNCRPD). This commitment has given rise to a flurry of activity, particularly in the legal sphere. Initially, there was an attempt to amend laws on disability in the country, such as the Persons with Disabilities (Equal Opportunities, Protection of Rights and Full Participation) Act, 1995 (PWD Act) to make them compliant with the UNCRPD. However, it was soon realized by disability rights groups that the discursive location of national disability legislation and the Convention were so disjunctive that no amount of revision or amendment could make them compatible. The ministry of social justice and empowerment of the Government of India proposed 108 amendments to the PWD Act including 50 new provisions: but it was soon realized that only a totally new disability law could operationlize the ideals and recommendations of the UNCRPD. Subsequently, the Mental Health

Care Bill (MHCB), 2013, and the Draft Rights of Persons with Disabilities Bill (DRPDB), 2013, were proposed by the government. While the former was passed by the Upper House (Rajya Sabha) on 19 August 2013 leading to the repeal of the existing Mental Health Act of 1987, the DRPDB could not be introduced in parliament because of severe criticism by groups of disability advocates who accused the government of tinkering with the submitted draft leading to a disjuncture between the UNCRPD and proposed legislation. In the light of these developments, the DRPDB has been referred to a Standing Committee of Parliament awaiting further action. The purpose of this chapter is to see to what extent the principal provisions of these bills fulfil the goals of equality and non-discrimination in a society not only deeply riven by multiple inequalities but also thoroughly permeated by ideologies of sexism and ableism.[1]

Persons with disabilities are the most neglected and disempowered section of the population. Due to their marginalized status, they are denied the fundamental civil, political, social, and economic rights that are the prerogative of all citizens in a democracy. Two events, which triggered public outrage and a nation-wide debate, clearly highlight the extent of the utter dehumanization of persons with disabilities in our society. One was the forced sterilization of women in a home for the mentally disabled in Pune district in 1994. The primary reason given for the hysterectomies was maintenance of menstrual hygiene. The other was the burning to death of 28 inmates in a private mental asylum in Tamil Nadu in 2001. The inmates of the Erwadi Dargah were chained to their beds and could not escape the flames that engulfed their thatched huts. Their cries for help were ignored by the asylum owners, who mistook them for the usual outbursts of the mentally ill. The Supreme Court took *suo motu* cognizance of this horrific incident and called for a nation-wide review of treatment facilities for the mentally ill, both in the public and private sectors.

More recently, two judgements that have generated much discussion in the area of reproductive rights and disability are the *Niketa Mehta* and the *Nari Niketan* cases. In the former, that came before the Mumbai High Court, a young middle-class urban couple, Haresh and Niketa Mehta, along with their doctor, approached the court for permission to terminate the woman's pregnancy in the 25th week due to the discovery that the foetus might be born with a serious congenital heart defect. According to the Indian Medical Termination of Pregnancy Act 1971, the upper limit for abortion of a foetus is 20 weeks. The court constituted a medical team and after much deliberation and media hype, the plea of the petitioner was rejected. Within one week of the judgment, the woman had a miscarriage (Addlakha *et al.* 2010: 176–81). In the latter case, the Chandigarh Administration petitioned the Punjab and Haryana High Court to terminate the pregnancy of a 19–20 years old unmarried, mildly/moderately intellectually disabled orphaned, pregnant woman residing in a state-run institution for the mentally challenged in Chandigarh. The court in its orders dated 9 June and 17 July 2009 permitted termination of the pregnancy. Subsequently, the young woman petitioned the Supreme Court, through her advocate, to be allowed to continue with her pregnancy against the order of the state. Due to the urgency of the situation on health grounds, the Supreme Court passed an order immediately in favour of the petitioner to continue with the pregnancy (Addlakha 2010: 34–6).

According to conservative estimates derived from the 2011 Indian Census, 2.1 per cent of our population suffers from some form of disability which in absolute numbers is approximately 26.8 million persons. Using a wider definition of disability, which includes conditions like diabetes and cardiovascular disease, the World Health Organization (WHO) estimates that 6 to 10 per cent of the population suffers from identifiable physical or mental disability. That comes to over 90 million persons in India.[2] Such phenomena as war, ethnic conflict, HIV/AIDS, industrial injuries, and road accidents are increasing the number of disabled persons. Ironically, enhanced life expectancy has increased manifold the incidence of old age-related, chronic disease-induced disabilities worldwide as well.

But what is a disability and what does it mean to be disabled in the first place? Disabilities may be congenital or from birth. For instance, most intellectual disabilities are congenital. Malnutrition and micronutrient deficiencies may result in disabling conditions in children in the form of stunted physical and mental growth. When disabilities are acquired later in life due to accidents, injuries, or advancing age, they may be characterized by an episodic upsurge of symptoms and/ or progressive degeneration. Many neuro-psychiatric illnesses like schizophrenia, multiple sclerosis, and Alzheimers disease fall in this category. A disability may be static such as the loss of a limb due to an amputation. Then there are also hidden and visible disabilities. Diabetes and epilepsy are hidden disabilities while leprosy and blindness are visible conditions. A disability generally has two components that is, the medical limitation and social prejudice, which often gets translated into discriminatory behaviour towards the disabled person. In legal documents and policy statements disability, is defined in terms of what qualifies for public assistance.

Historically, there has been a deep-rooted cultural antipathy to persons with disabilities. Throughout the ages the disabled have been looked down upon with disdain, almost as if they were sub-human. They have been portrayed as medical anomalies, helpless victims, and a lifelong burden for family and society. Even in religion and mythology, negative characters were attributed some form of deformity, be it Manthara, the 'hunchback' in the Ramayana or Shakuni, the 'lame' uncle of the Mahabharata. Indeed, the law of karma decreed that being disabled was the just retribution for past misdeeds. Such constructions of the disabled by the non-disabled has the dual effect of not only justifying the complete marginalization and disempowerment of a whole population group but also leads to the internalization of such negative stereotypes by the disabled themselves. This acceptance translates into passivity, dependency, isolation, low self-esteem, and a complete loss of initiative. Pity, segregation, discrimination, and stigmatization became normalized in the management of persons with disabilities. Needless to say, the plight of women with disabilities is even worse, since they have to confront the double oppression of gender and disability. And in a country like India it may be a triple burden if one takes account of the omnipresence of poverty.

After the Second World War, countries in Western Europe, Japan, and the United States were faced with the challenging task of rehabilitating a huge number of disabled soldiers. This historical necessity placed disability at the centre of social welfare policies in both Europe and the United States, leading to a marginal mitigation of the negative social perceptions. But the most significant outcome of this process was the organization of disabled persons themselves into a vibrant social movement along the lines of the women's movement. Through self-advocacy by disabled persons, the concept of disability was redefined not as personal tragedy necessitating therapy but as collective oppression necessitating political action (Oliver 1996). In this perspective, the focus shifts from the inability of persons with disabilities to adapt to the so-called 'normal' environment to the failure of the social and structural environment to adapt to the needs and aspirations of the disabled. As advocates for equal rights for disabled persons, these disability organizations lobbied with national governments for a barrier-free environment, inclusive education, affirmative action in employment, in addition to the whole range of civil, political, social, and economic rights to which all citizens are entitled in a democracy.

The Universal Declaration of Human Rights[3] of the United Nations in 1948 introduced a rights-based approach to disability. Every person has certain natural or inalienable human rights by virtue of being a person. These rights cannot be violated under any circumstance. They constitute what in essence it means to be human. Article 25 of this UN Declaration explicitly states that each person has the right to security in the event of unemployment, sickness, disability, widowhood, old age, or other lack of livelihood in the circumstances beyond his control. It is assumed that persons with disabilities are entitled to all the rights upheld by the Human Rights Charter as also other rights instruments such as the International Covenant on Civil and Political Rights and the International Covenant on Economic, Social and Cultural Rights, even though disability per se as a ground of exclusion and discrimination is never explicitly mentioned. It may be noted that the above human rights instruments came into operation during a period of time when the concept of disability had just begun to take shape in international law.

The international climate was made more disabled-friendly by subsequent UN declarations specifically for the welfare of persons with disabilities.[4] The year 1981 was declared as the International Year of Disabled Persons. A World Plan of Action concerning Disabled Persons was adopted by the General Assembly in 1982 for the implementation of which 1983–1992 was proclaimed the United Nations Decade of Disabled Persons. In 1993, the General Assembly adopted the Standard Rules on the Equalization of Opportunities for Persons with Disabilities.[5] The culmination of the United Nation's work on disability has been the enactment of the UNCRPD in 2006.

The impact of the international human rights movement and anti-poverty initiatives have transplanted the issue of disability from that of social welfare to one of social development. Development essentially means inclusion. If the needs and aspirations of a whole population group are not taken account of, then social development in the true sense of the word has not taken place. Disability is both a cause and consequence of poverty. They reinforce each other, leading to increased vulnerability and exclusion. Poverty exacerbates the opportunities of persons and disability further marginalizes them, making it impossible for them to have access to basic conditions of life like health, education, transportation, and employment. For women with disabilities there is the added burden of gender bias and discrimination, which further exacerbates their life conditions.

Instead of giving rights to disabled citizens and empowering them, a culture of charity and welfare has been systematically promoted in India since the colonial period. Medical rehabilitation, including distribution of assistive aids and appliances, special schools, vocational training in low-end occupations, and sheltered employment, have been the pillars of state policy for the disabled. Furthermore, electoral politics of caste and gender have pushed the disabled to the margins of the political landscape, making them a weak political constituency. They have in fact been systematically disenfranchised by the political system. Things began to change marginally after 1981 (International Year of Disabled Persons) when the issue of disability was opened up at the national level. The changing international climate focusing on human rights and empowerment of marginal groups impelled the government to make some policy changes such as token reservations in educational institutions and employment. But real progress in the form of concrete legislation to deliver the promise of equality of opportunity and social justice only came in 1995 with the passage of the Persons with Disabilities (Equal Opportunities and Full Participation) Act. Other legislation soon followed. One of the positive outcomes of economic liberalization and globalization has been the introduction of a view of disability as a human rights and development issue rather than simply a matter of charity and welfare.

Disability Legislation in India

The fundamental right to life enshrined in the Indian constitution provides the guarantee of life with liberty and dignity to all persons resident in India. The right of persons with disabilities to respect, dignity, and freedom is part of this generic right to life. There is a broad constitutional provision in the Preamble of the Indian constitution on the part of the state to guarantee equality of opportunity and a life of dignity to all its citizens, including persons with disabilities. Although there are no explicit references to the disabled as such in the constitution, they may, however, be derived from provisions dealing with welfare of other identified vulnerable groups. Article 14 guarantees equality before the law; Article 15(3) enjoins the state to make provisions for the welfare of women and children. Article 39A of the Directive Principles of State Policy directs the state to ensure that no citizen is denied justice on the basis of economic and other disabilities. Similarly, Article 41 enjoins the state (within the limits of economic policy and development) to make effective provisions for securing the right to work, to education, and to public assistance in cases of unemployment, old age, sickness and disablement and in other cases of undeserved want. Then, Article 46 of the Directive Principles of Sate Policy enjoins the state to promote with special care the social and economic interests of the 'weaker sections'.

As Justice Bhagwati has pointed out, through innovative changes to the process for instituting proceedings, ascertaining facts, and granting discretionary remedies, the Indian courts have stepped beyond their traditional domain to render justice to women, children, bonded laborers, and other oppressed sections of society. Notably, the Supreme Court has affirmed that both the Fundamental Rights enumerated in Part III of the constitution and the Directive Principles enumerated in Part IV, must be interpreted harmoniously. This is illustrated in several judgments relating to guaranteeing rights to persons with disabilities. For instance, in the landmark judgment *Indra Sawhney* v. *Union of India*,[6] a seven-judge constitutional bench of the Supreme Court of India held that the spirit of Articles 14 [right to equality], 15(1) [right against discrimination], and 16 [right against discrimination in public employment] allowed for affirmative actions for persons with disabilities. In a more recent judgment *Union of India* v. *National Federation of the Blind*[7] in which the petitioner claimed that Sec 33 of the PWD Act regarding reservation in employment for the visually disabled was not being implemented, the Supreme Court ruled that the cap of 50 per cent on reservation did not apply in the case of 3 per cent reservation for disabled persons in public employment. The court rejected the centre's argument that 3 per cent reservation to disabled would see quotas exceed the 50 per cent cap as it said 49 per cent reservation to SCs (15 per cent), STs (7 per cent), and OBCs (27 per cent) in government jobs was vertical in character, while the benefits to the disabled were horizontal in nature.

If a chronological analysis of state policies towards the disabled is undertaken, the period can be divided broadly into two phases. The first phase would extend from independence to 1995 when the parliament enacted a comprehensive legislation on disability. In this period some administrative measures to alleviate the plight of disabled persons were undertaken which gained momentum after 1981, the International Year of Disabled Persons. But the major fillip came with the passage of 'The Persons with Disabilities (Equal Opportunities, Protection of Rights and Full Participation) Act, 1995'. This piece of legislation heralded a new phase in the disability rights movement in India.

There are primarily four legislation enactments that directly concern physical and mental disability, namely,

1. The Mental Health Act of 1987
2. The Rehabilitation Council of India Act, 1992
3. The Persons with Disabilities (Equal Opportunities, Protection of Rights and Full Participation) Act, 1995
4. The National Trust for the Welfare of Persons with Autism, Cerebral Palsy, Mental Retardation and Multiple Disabilities Act, 1999.

The Mental Health Act of 1987

It needs to be remembered that unlike the physically disabled, historically, there have been many legal disqualifications for both the mentally retarded and mentally ill based on a presumption of mental incapacity and incompetence. For instance, under the Indian Contract Act, a person of unsound mind is ineligible to enter into a contract, and under the Indian Succession Act she does not have testamentary capacity to dispose of property. A person of unsound mind cannot engage in litigation nor can she be charged in a court of law. Under the Hindu Marriage Act, insanity will automatically render a marriage null and void. Unlike the physically disabled, employment in government service, voting, and election to public office are other deprivations which affect the mentally disabled.

Prior to the passage of this Act, lunacy was the generic term used for all types of mental afflictions and the Indian Lunacy Act (ILA) of 1912 governed the treatment of the mentally disturbed through the regulation of mental hospitals. This Act was based on notions of mental illness, which are no longer tenable. The Indian Psychiatric Society had drafted and actively canvassed for the adoption of a more liberal mental health legislation soon after its inception in 1948. The old Lunacy Act, however, continued to be in operation till April 1993 when it was replaced by the Mental Health Act of 1987. The Indian Lunacy Act enabled a magistrate, with or without medical opinion, to declare a person to be insane, order her incarceration, and appoint caretakers to look after the lunatic's property. The Act placed far more emphasis on the property than the well-being of the afflicted person. While 'lunatic' was summarily described as 'an idiot or a person of unsound mind', there were 46 sections dealing with the administration of her property. Furthermore, the ILA made no distinction between the mentally ill and the mentally retarded, nor did it make any mention of the patient's rights or informed consent for treatment. Its explicit purpose was simply to safeguard society against the danger posed by the lunatic rather than to provide therapy and guarantee basic human rights to the mentally disturbed.

In contrast to the ILA, the Mental Health Act (1987) has a whole section dealing with the protection of Human Rights of Mentally Ill Persons.[8] It also differentiates between the mentally ill and the mentally retarded and eschews the use of such terms as 'lunatic', 'insane', 'idiot', and 'unsound mind'. A mentally ill person is simply defined as one who is in need of treatment by reason of any mental disorder other than mental retardation. The Act calls for regular visits by visitors to duly licensed psychiatric hospitals at least once a month, and also contains provisions for setting up of a Mental Health Authority.

The main beneficiaries of the Act, the persons with disabilities, are attributed no capacity in the legal sense to take decisions except for in one section where they can voluntarily admit themselves into an institution. Once admitted, voluntarily or otherwise, they cease to have any control over their lives. They may be discharged only upon recommendation by a team of doctors and their condition is thereby medicalized to a great extent. The court too, plays an excessive role in the determination of the fate of the patients. The Act focuses greatly on the institutions and their governance. Little attention is paid to regulating the conditions of the inmates.

It is interesting that the gender element emerges in section 42 of the ILA and Section 50 of the Mental Health Act 1987 wherein they women are 'protected' from attending a committee hearing in public. The concerned panel may make alternative arrangements to interview the women at their convenience in accordance with the Civil Procedure Code.

The Rehabilitation Council of India Act, 1992

One of the major lacunae in the programmes for the disabled has been the lack of trained manpower. The Rehabilitation Council of India was constituted in 1986 under the Societies Registration Act as an apex body to standardize and monitor training in the disability sector in the country. In 1992 it was converted into a statutory body under the Rehabilitation Council of India Act. The Act came into effect on 23 June 1993. Prior to this, existing programmes in the fields of rehabilitation and special education were ad-hoc and uncoordinated in nature with no standardized syllabi. There was a need not only to standardize manpower training and service delivery, but also to regulate organizations and institutions working in the disability sector. One way of maintaining both standards of professional practice and quality of services is through the creation of a Central Register of certified rehabilitation professionals and organizations. In establishing uniform standards in the field of rehabilitation, the RCI covers a range of professionals such as psychologists, speech therapists, social workers, physiotherapists, occupational therapists, and other specialists working in the field of disability. There is also a need to facilitate systematic research in this area. The RCI Act addresses all these concerns.

The Persons with Disabilities (Equal Opportunities, Protection of Rights and Full Participation) Act, 1995

As a signatory to the Proclamation on the Full Participation and Equality of People with Disabilities in the Asian and Pacific Region, which was adopted at a meeting in Beijing in 1992 to launch the Asian and Pacific Decade of Disabled Persons (1993–2002), the Persons with Disabilities (Equal Opportunities, Protection of Rights and Full Participation) Act, 1995 (henceforth PWD Act) was passed. This is a landmark legislation, which has catapulted disability as a central human rights issue. Today it is the lynchpin of all state policies on disability in the country. It is the main tool of redressal for individual violation of human rights. It frames the partnership between the government agencies and the NGOs working in the disability sector. It is increasingly being used to encourage the private and corporate sectors to enhance employment opportunities for persons with disabilities. Several shortcomings notwithstanding, one can safely aver that it is the most comprehensive measure for empowerment of the disabled in the country. The main objectives of the PWD Act are to lay down modalities for comprehensive development of programmes and services and equalization of opportunities for persons with disabilities by making special provisions for their integration into the social mainstream. The other objectives are:

1. To spell out the responsibilities of the state towards prevention of disabilities, protection of rights, provision of medical care, education, training, employment, and rehabilitation of persons with disabilities.
2. To create a barrier-free environment.
3. To remove any discrimination against persons with disabilities in sharing of development benefits vis-à-vis non-disabled persons.
4. To counteract any abuse or exploitation of persons with disabilities.

The Act sought to achieve these goals through an administrative structure comprising central and state co-ordination and executive committees, and central and state commissioners of disabilities. Prevention and early detection of disabilities, provision of aids and appliances, free primary education, accessibility in transport and the built environment, reservation in education and employment in the government sector, and social security are some of its most important provisions.

The National Trust for the Welfare of Persons with Autism Cerebral Palsy, Mental Retardation and Multiple Disabilities Act, 1999

This is a special legislation applicable to those suffering from autism, cerebral palsy, mental retardation, or multiple disabilities through the constitution of a national level trust to look into their welfare. Its aim is to work for affirmative action for categories of persons whose disability may render them incapable of self-care in daily life and independent living. The purpose of this legislation is to empower a specific group of disabled persons to live in the community. Essentially protectionist and promotive in nature, the aim of the trust is to safeguard the interests and protect rights of a highly vulnerable section of the disabled population.

The national trust supports programmes which promote independence and guardianship where necessary; and addresses the life concerns of those persons who do not have family support or protect interests of such persons after the death of their parents and caregivers. The trust also supports organizations rendering support in the event of crises in the family of such persons.

The trust comprises a board of public servants, parents associations, NGO representatives, and persons with disabilities. It received from the government a onetime contribution of Rs 100 crores for the corpus fund. It receives contributions in the form of donations, bequests, benefactions, and transfers from private individuals and organizations for the welfare of disabled persons. In rendering assistance preference would be given to women with disabilities, persons with severe disability, and the disabled elderly.

Interestingly, this Act has a stronger gender component than the other existing legislations on disability. The ministry for women and child development has a representative on the board. Section 11(3) of the National Trust Act gives preference for setting up hostels and homes for women along with hostels for persons with a severe disability and senior citizens with disabilities.

Proposed Legislative Regime for Persons with Disabilities in India

As Addlakha and Mandal (Addlakha and Mandal 2009: 62–8) have pointed out in their analysis of disability jurisprudence in India, prior to formal legislative enactments the concept of disability largely fell within the ambit of mental health/disability, which was a recurrent issue across a range of legislative domains such as marriage/divorce, adoption/guardianship, property and criminology. A person of 'unsound mind' could not adopt, marry, contract, vote or run for elected office.[9] Underlying mental disability/health legislation was the undisputed construction of the mentally ill/mentally disabled person as essentially incapable of looking after herself and acting in her best interest. Consequently, a whole array of legal categories were generated to describe, justify, and solidify the legal (and by extension social) incapacity of the person labelled mentally ill or deficient. Unsoundness of mind, mental infirmity or insanity, dangerousness, legal incompetence, diminished culpability, lack of autonomy and self-determination, legal representation, surrogate decision-making, and guardianship became the bulwark of mental health law. Ironically, what precisely constitutes unsoundness of mind or insanity in the legal context was never defined with the judges relying on the testimony of expert witnesses (psychiatrists) in determining its existence and impact. Courts did not distinguish between imputed disability and the resulting incapacity. There was, however, no ambiguity regarding the non-person status of the mentally disabled persons: those placed under guardianship, for instance, lost all their personal/property rights, and confinement was deemed as the most suitable solution; there could be postponement of civil and criminal trials allowed on grounds of insanity.

The situation of persons with physical disabilities in the legal sphere was even more amorphous. Highlighting the generalized notion of mental infirmity, Amita Dhanda cites the following to highlight the ambiguity:

> The expansive ambit of 'mental infirmity' was also demonstrated in Ramlal v. Mt. Laxmi,[10] wherein the High Court held that a plaintiff whose physique was so affected by paralysis that he could not speak except for making a few sounds, and could not stand on his feet for more than a couple of minutes, was allowed to file through next friend even though his mind was not affected and he was able to understand the questions put to him and signify answers by means of gestures. It was perhaps the multiple nature of the physical disability suffered by the plaintiff which led to him being considered 'mentally infirm' because, in S Muthasankara Nadar,[11] a physically disabled person who was unable to walk was not permitted to take recourse to this order. In Nanak Chand v. Banarasi Das,[12] it was held that while the order was applicable to totally deaf and dumb persons, the incapacity of persons who were partially deaf and dumb would require enquiry (2000: 281).

The paradigm shift instituted by the UNCRPD lies in rejecting the presumption of incapacity that occurs upon the existence of a disability and the consequent disqualifying regime.[13] Like any other human rights instruments, it is by nature universal and non-derogable. Its core principles are autonomy and self-determination, equality, and non-discrimination. It proposes an inclusive and universal paradigm of legal capacity compatible with a regime of rights rather than systems of welfare. These rights are to be actualized through reasonable accommodation,[14] informed consent, and freedom of choice.

In the light of the need to establish synchrony between international law and national laws, there has been a total overhauling of disability legislation. While amendments have been suggested for the Rehabilitation Council Act 1992 and the National Trust Act 1995, the Mental Health Act of 1987 and the Persons with Disabilities Act 1995 have been drafted afresh. In the remainder of this chapter an attempt will be made to analyse some of the core changes incorporated in the Mental Health Care Bill 2013 and the Draft Rights of Persons with Disabilities Bill 2013 with a particular focus on how gender concerns have been incorporated in the proposed legislations.

Specific Definitions of Key New Terms

The new legislation is marked by the incorporation of some new terms with specific definitions; For instance, Section 2(j) of the DRPDB clarifies that 'high support needs' means an intensive support—'physical, psychological and otherwise, which may be required by a person with benchmark disability for daily activities for participating in all areas of life including education, employment; family and community life, treatment and therapy'.

Then, both the DRPDB and the Mental Health Care Bill (MHCB) provide a specific definition of caregiver as 'any person including parents and other family members, who with or without payment provides care, support or assistance to a person with disability (DRPDB Section 2(f) and 'paid or unpaid, relative or other, but one who resides with the person with mental illness and is responsible for him/her) (MHCB 2013 Section 2(d)). Since the majority of caregivers (paid or unpaid) are female, this clause is an indirect recognition of the importance of gender in the disability sector.

New Categories

The DRPDB takes on board the broad definition of disability put forward by the UNCRPD; Section 2(q), which defines a person with disability as 'a person with long term physical, mental, intellectual or sensory impairment which hinder his full and effective participation in society equally with others'. The earlier approach of listing a limited number of conditions, such as blindness, low vision, hearing impairment, etc., that count as disabilities under the law is replaced by a broader understanding of the concept contained in international discourses. However, such a broad definition notwithstanding, the schedule recognizes 19 categories of disabilities with the additional proviso 'Any other category as may be notified by the central government' in Clause 20.

Some radical changes in core concepts are also found in the MHCB. While mental retardation has been dropped from the

MCHB (Section 2r), substance abuse (alcohol and drug addiction) have been incorporated as valid mental illness categories.

Disability and Legal Capacity

Chapter II (5) of the MHCA breaks the historically embedded equation between mental illness and legal incompetence, since mental illness does not mean unsoundness of mind until decreed as such by a competent court highlighting the distinction between medical and legal notions of insanity. Stripping the concept of mental illness of its legal trappings, the MHCA states that mental illness shall be determined only in accordance with such nationally or internationally accepted medical standards. Furthermore, Chapter II (4)(states that proof of a person's current or past admission to a mental health establishment or treatment for mental illness shall not by itself be a ground for divorce. This is a path-breaking formulation, since the insanity plea has been used very often to deprive persons suffering from disability (particularly mental illness) of the exercise of their fundamental rights and freedoms. It has been disproportionately used against women in divorce cases (Dhanda 2000).

Although legal capacity has primarily been discussed in the context of mental illness and psychosocial disability prior to the enactment of the UNCRPD, the concept is now germane to any disability legislation. The DRPDB provides specific elaborations on the theme of legal capacity in Sections 12(1), which dwells on the matter in the context of ownership and inheritance of property, financial control, and access to financial credit. Section 12(2) allows for a caregiver being disengaged when there is a conflict of interest in an economic transaction between the former and his//her ward. A person with disability may alter or annul any support arrangement, Section 12(3). Then, the privacy, autonomy, and dignity of the person with disability shall be respected by the person providing support, Section 12(4).

Right to Autonomous Decision-making

One of the fundamental principles of the UNCRPD is that persons with disabilities are autonomous with an inviolable right for decision-making regarding their life. While in the DRPDB attempts have been made to increase autonomous decision-making powers of the person with disability, it stops short by retaining provisions of plenary and limited guardianship instead of shifting to a regime of supported guardianship endorsed by the UNCRPD. Section 13(i) of the DRPDB defines plenary guardianship as

> ...a guardianship whereby subsequent to a finding of incapacity, a guardian substitutes for the person with disability as the person before the law and takes all legally binding decisions for him and the decisions of the person with disability have no biding force in law during the subsistence of the guardianship and the guardian is under no legal obligation to consult with the person with disability or determine his or her will or preference whilst taking decisions for him...

Section 13(iii) defines limited guardianship as '...a system of joint decision which operates on mutual understanding and trust between the guardian and the person with disability'.

However, it is in the proposed mental health legislation that the real radical shift is visible. In the MCHB there is a whole chapter on mental illness and capacity to make mental health care and treatment decisions (chapter II). Another important change is not presuming that a past history of hospitalization is evidence of the existence of mental illness in the present. Section 3(4) clearly states that prior hospitalization in a mental health facility though relevant shall not be determinative of the person's present or future mental illness. This is a very important change from the Mental Health Act of 1987, which regarded past psychiatric treatment as prima facie evidence of the existence of mental illness.

But perhaps the most revolutionary ideas in the MHCB are the concept of advanced directive as presented in Chapter III. Advance directive simply means prior consent in writing on the manner in which a person may or not may not be treated when mentally ill. It can involve refusal of all treatment. It can involve the selection of a nominated representative to make decisions for the person in a situation when s/he is rendered incapable of doing so herself. An advance directive is composed when a person is considered to have the capacity for autonomous decision-making, but it is invoked during the period a person does not have the capacity to make mental health treatment decisions. Like a will, it shall be made on plain paper signed by the person in the presence of two witnesses, and deposited with the district mental health board. It shall be attested by a medical practitioner certifying that the person has the capacity to make mental health care and treatment decisions at the time. Like any written testament, it can be revoked, amended, and cancelled by the concerned person.

The revolutionary assumption of the advance directive is that all persons with mental illness have legal capacity, but may require varying levels of support from nominated representatives to make decisions. According legal capacity to a person with a diagnosis of mental illness overturns existing legal regimes that automatically rob the individual of autonomy upon declaration of mental illness. However, an advance directive is not valid in the case of emergency treatment, highlighting how the medical regime continues to override all other conditions.

Humanizing the Institutional Regime

Section 4(i) of the DRBDB guarantees the right of a person with disability to live in the community and requires the government to provide '… access a range of in-house, residential and other community support services, including personal assistance necessary to support living with due regard to age and gender' (Section 4(2). While the emphasis in the new legal regime is on community-based treatment (ambulatory care, half way homes, short stay homes, group homes, etc) over mental hospital-based treatment to enhance social inclusion, an attempt has also been made to remove the more dehumanizing aspects of mental hospitals. In addition to protection from physical, mental, verbal, and sexual abuse (including chaining, head tonsuring), the right to protection from cruel, inhuman, and degrading treatment aims to guarantee privacy and ensure personal hygiene (especially menstrual hygiene for women). To undercut the segregation paradigm, the MHCB proposes rights to personal contacts and communication during hospital stay, which means right to send and receive calls, mails, emails, and visitors. Furthermore, the law mandates decent remuneration for work undertaken during hospitalization.

But perhaps the most important change in this connection from a gender perspective is that not having a family or being homeless are not automatically considered valid reasons for extending incarceration when the patient is otherwise medically fit for discharge. Mental hospitals in India have an overwhelmingly large number of long-stay female patients, many of whom are not discharged simply because no relatives come forward to claim them.

Concluding Remarks: Engendering Proposed Disability Legislation

One of the most important new dimensions of the DRPDB and the MHCB is an attempt to integrate a gender perspective in various articles. The idea of intersectional vulnerabilities is put forward with specific mention of the need to protect in particular women and children with disabilities. There is greater synergy with the UNCRPD in explicitly addressing issues of reproductive rights, livelihood concerns, violence, and abuse, and penalties for offences against women with disabilities (like sexual offences, forced termination of pregnancy, forced sterilization), in different articles. The proposed disability law also calls for greater representation of women in the various committees like National and State Commissions for Persons with Disabilities.

There appears to be comparatively greater gender-sensitivity in the composition of the DRPDB, which could perhaps be attributed to the greater association between disability and women's rights discourses within civil society and to some extent in the academy. This is in contrast to the almost total domination of mental health issues by psychiatrists in the MHCB. The first explicit reference to gender comes in chapter V on 'social security, health, rehabilitation and recreation' in the DRPDB. Section 23(2) states that the appropriate government will develop schemes and programmes while giving due consideration to the diversity of disability, gender, age, and socio-economic status. Section 23(3d) guarantees support to women with disabilities for livelihood and for upbringing of children. Clause i of the same section talks about caregiver allowance to persons with disabilities with high support needs; although gender is not mentioned in this provision but the reality is that the overwhelming majority of caregivers all over the world are women. Section 24(2k) in the same chapter explicitly mentions the need to cater to the sexual and reproductive and health care needs of women with disabilities. Again, in Chapter V of the DRPDB on special provisions for persons with benchmark disabilities, specific reference is made to women in the allotment of agricultural land, housing, and in all other poverty-alleviation development programmes (Sections 36a and b).There is also a provision for representation of women with disabilities from civil society in the central and state advisory boards on disability (Chapter XI). Lastly, specific provisions for protection of women with disabilities appear in Chapter XVI dealing with penalties committed against persons with disabilities. The gender-specific crimes cited are violations of the modesty of a woman with disabilities (Section 105b), sexual exploitation (Section 105d), termination of pregnancy without her express consent (Section 105f). However the latter is waived if the woman suffers from a severe disability backed by the opinion of a registered medical practitioner and the consent of the guardian.

While occasionally mentioning women, the MHCA does not recognize gender-based discrimination and gender-specific difficulties. In Section 7, 'discrimination on any basis' would probably refer to gender-based discrimination, but it is not explicitly mentioned. Section 9(iii)(g) states that adequate provisions to cater to women's needs while menstruating form an integral part of the minimal health standards that all mental health facilities must adhere to appears more of a footnote. There are no specific provisions for creating awareness of the extra disadvantages faced by women with psychosocial disabilities. Also, the committees and panels constituted by the government under this Act do not provide for adequate gender representation.

Thus it can be seen that several lacunae notwithstanding, preliminary attempts have been made to synchronize the proposed domestic disability legislation with the international standards put forward by the UNCRPD. It remains to be seen how these proposals fare in parliament and what eventually emerges in the form of the law of the land.

Notes

1. Ableism, is discrimination in favour of the able-bodied, while disablism may be defined as discrimination on grounds of disability.
2. Estimates of the total number of persons with disabilities in a country vary depending upon the definition of disability used, degree of impairment, and survey methodology, including use of scientific instruments for identification and measurement of the disabling conditions.

3. Human rights may simply be defined as those natural and fundamental rights essential for a decent life as a human being. They are possessed by every person simply by virtue of being human, irrespective of nationality, race, sex, religion, class, or disability.

4. In 1971, the General Assembly adopted the Declaration on the Rights of Mentally Retarded Persons, which stipulates that the mentally retarded are not only entitled to basic human rights like everyone else, but they also have special rights corresponding to their special needs in medical, education, and social fields. In 1975 the Declaration on the Rights of Disabled Persons was adopted, which proclaimed equal civil and political rights of disabled persons.

5. These rules were aimed at facilitating development of national disability programmes of member states so that disabled persons can exercise all the rights and freedoms as their non-disabled counterparts. These standards provide a scheme to address all the needs of persons with disabilities in accordance with the principles of human equality, dignity, and respect. They deal with provision of medical services, education, employment, and social security; in fact, all issues that contribute to raising the quality of life of this group.

6. IR 1993 SC 477: 1992 Supp (3) SCC 217.

7. Civil Appeal No. 9096 of 2013 arising out of SLP (Civil) No. 7541 of 2009.

8. The Act categorically states that (i) patients may not be subjected to any indignity (physical or mental) or cruelty during treatment; (ii) patients may not be used for research purposes unless this is of direct benefit to their diagnosis and treatment; (iii) the responsibility for allowing research lies with the relatives of an incompetent patient. Voluntarily patients may not be used for research, even if it is to their benefit, without their consent; and (iv) patients must be granted basic rights in conformity with human dignity (Section 81). This section becomes all the more relevant in the light of the fact that a person loses her civil rights to vote, contract, and hold property upon being medically certified as being of unsound mind.

9. Despite enactment of a range of disability legislation, most of these disqualifications still hold because different laws have not been amended in the light of a rights-based regime.

10. AIR 1949 Ajmer 48.

11. 1972 STC 242.

12. AIR 1930 425.

13. The UNCRPD removes the dichotomy between physical and mental disabilities. Article 1 states that the aim of the Convention '...is to pro-

mote, protect and ensure the full and equal enjoyment of all human rights and fundamental freedoms by all persons with disabilities…'; Article 3 (a) unequivocally endorses right to autonomy and freedom of choice of all persons with disabilities; Article 12 on equal recognition before the law unambiguously states: 1) parties reaffirm that persons with disabilities have the right to recognition everywhere as persons before the law, 2) parties shall recognize that persons with disabilities enjoy legal capacity on an equal basis with others in all aspects of life, 3) parties shall take appropriate measures to provide access to persons with disabilities to the support they may require in exercising their legal capacity. Article 12 further reiterates the freedom of choice (with or without support) of persons with disabilities in matters relating to property ownership, banking, mortgage, and other financial matters. Article 9 on access states that the right to assistance, material and human, is a fundamental right of every person with disability and in no way interferes with her legal competence and capacity. It recognizes that in some cases and at some times assistance may be required to exercise capacity but such assistance may be provided without annulling the competence of a person giving rise to the concept of supported rather than substituted decision-making.

14. 'Reasonable Accommodation' refers to the principle of providing for appropriate modification and adjustments wherever needed to ensure that the disabled enjoy all the rights and freedoms on an equal basis with the non-disabled, provided that such modification or adjustment does not impose a disproportionate or undue burden on the concerned person or agency.

References

Addlakha, R. 2010. 'A Legal Precedent: Reproductive Rights of Mentally Retarded Persons in India', *Indian Journal of Medical Ethics*, 7 (1): 34–6.

Addlakha, R.I. Gevers, M. Callon, and J. Cheu. 2010. 'Disability-selective Abortions in India: Individual Choice, Disabling Environments and the Socio-Moral Order', in *Difference on Display: Diversity in Art, Science and Society*, pp. 176–81. NAI Ultgevers Publishers.

Addlakha, R. and Mandal, S. 2009. 'Disability Law in India: Paradigm Shift or Evolving Discourse?', *Economic and Political Weekly*, XLIV (41 and 42): 62–8.

Dhanda, A. 2000. *Legal Order/Mental Disorder*. New Delhi: Sage.

Oliver, M. 1996. *Understanding Disability: From Theory to Practice*, New York: St. Martin Press.

12

Discrimination and Sexual Minorities in India

Revisiting the *Naz* Judgment

Poonam Kakoti Borah

The decade of the 1990s brought about a huge transformation in the political landscape of India. Opening up of the economy, rise of communal politics, and resurgence of identity politics left an indelible mark on the nature of Indian politics. Civil society activism based on issues such as protection of civil liberty, violation of women's rights, development induced displacements and discrimination against Dalits demanded attention from the Indian state. While these were the developments at home, several other momentous world events were happening like the disintegration of the USSR, rise of multicultural claims, and emergence of ethnic conflicts with which it coincided. New social movements around issues like ecology and sexuality also gathered momentum, at around this time. Issues which were hitherto considered as secondary became the rallying points for mobilization.

Sexuality, traditionally understood as a non-issue in the realm of politics, enters the discourse on citizenship first through the feminist intervention and then through the gay liberation movements of the

1960s. Second-wave feminism showed how sexuality, which was considered as private and personal, was in fact a public and political issue. The Stonewall riots of 1969 was the founding moment of the gay liberationist movement.[1] Thereafter gay and lesbian cultural spaces and political organizations in the West such as the National Gay Liberation (USA), Gay Liberation Front (UK), Lambda (USA) and ACT UP (USA) speaking on behalf of the 'peripheral sexualities' were born. The gay liberation movement challenged the medicalized and negative understandings of homosexuality. As the understanding of homosexuality has moved from an essentialist biological position to a social constructivist position, emphasizing positive self-definitions, more and more people have come out of the closet.

Sexuality was hardly a matter of concern in Indian public forums in the 1960s and 1970s, the hey-days of the gay liberation movements in the West. It is only in the 1990s, with the arrival of HIV/AIDS, that sexuality becomes a politically salient category to be reckoned with. Till then, homosexuality remained an invisible sexual practice and homosexual identity absent (Kole 2007). The proliferation of political mobilization around sexuality issues happens in the backdrop of the discriminatory anti-sodomy statute, Section 377 of the IPC.[2] While the Indian constitution guarantees equal protection of law, and equality before law, the very presence of Section 377 creates, on the basis of sexual orientation, two ranks of citizens: the normal-heterosexual and the deviant-homosexual. Keeping in mind the consequences that law has on public understanding of morality, the judgment of the Delhi High Court in the *Naz Foundation* case is a high point of the Lesbian Gay Bisexual Transgender (henceforth LGBT) movement in India. The two-judge panel of the High Court of Delhi held Section 377 of the IPC violative of Articles 21, 14, and 15 of the constitution of India. The judgment, in effect, removed direct discrimination against homosexuals but indirect discrimination as well as structural discrimination persists.

This chapter is an attempt to look at discrimination towards sexual minorities in India, from the perspective of existing laws. While trying to understand the nature of discrimination faced by sexual minorities in India, this chapter looks at the idea of direct and indirect discrimination, perpetuated by institutions and limitations of a legalistic approach. While critically engaging with the law in order to ensure non-discrimination, this chapter also argues that a re-looking into ideas of privacy and tolerance become imperative in order to fight discriminations that emanates from our binary thinking. Furthermore, it juxtaposes two cases of discrimination to show how indirect discrimination is much more widespread and has been used by institutions to discriminate against those who do not conform to ideas of 'normal' sexual orientation.

This chapter is divided into five broad segments. Section One deals with the concept of discrimination and provides an account of how discrimination has been understood as direct and indirect, structural and institutional. Section Two discusses the broad framework in which discrimination has been addressed in the Indian constitution and sets the background in which discrimination against sexual minorities is discussed. This part of the paper also elaborates on both direct and indirect institutional mechanisms that lead to discrimination against sexual minorities. Section Three of this paper deals with two specific cases of discrimination separated in time by the momentous *Naz* judgment: the arrest and detention of activists in Lucknow (2001) and the case of Professor S.R. Siras (2010). It is significant that in both these cases public morality structured the arguments against the victims of discrimination. Section Four of the paper discusses two legal judgments: the *Naz Foundation* judgment of 2009 and the *Koushal* judgment of 2013. These two judgments have shown two contradictory positions that courts can take towards cases of discrimination. Finally, towards the conclusion, this chapter argues that the struggle against discrimination needs to engage equally with laws that directly or indirectly disadvantage sexual minorities as well as those structures of our thought, which privileges heterosexuality and entrenches its normality.

Conceptualizing Discrimination

Discrimination as a concept has occupied a simultaneous position with equality in our political imagination. Discriminations emanating from cleavages in society, such as those of race, gender, class, caste, amongst several others have triggered widespread demands of equality. Inequalities emanating from such differences are considered as the resultants of discrimination. In fact, the entire 'rights revolution' of the present times is an extension of the protests against inequalities and discrimination. Human rights documents from the UN proscribing discrimination regards that discrimination 'includes any distinction, exclusion, restriction or preference... which has the purpose or effect of nullifying or impairing equality before the law or the equal protection of the law, or the recognition, enjoyment or exercise, on an equal basis, of all human rights and fundamental freedoms'.[3] However, the widespread use of the term belies its definitional ambiguity.

Discrimination has been used in scholarly works to indicate a value-laden concept wherein members of a socially salient group are targeted, directly or indirectly, individually or institutionally, in order to marginalize and exclude them. While conceptualizing discrimination, Kasper Lippert-Rasmussen states the general character of discrimination as:

> X discriminates against (in favour of) Y in dimension W if: (i) X treats Y differently from Z (or from how X would treat Z, were X to treat Z in some way) in dimension W; (ii) the differential treatment is (or is believed by X to be) disadvantageous (advantageous) to Y; and (iii) the differential treatment is suitably explained by Y's and Z's being (or believed by X to be) (members of) different, socially salient groups (Lippert-Rasmussen 2006: 168).

Where, the variable 'X' can refer to both individuals and groups of individuals, as well as governments, private companies, and social structures; and 'Y' and 'Z' refer to (groups of) persons and human beings as well. For Lippert-Rasmussen, an instance of discrimination is bad to that extent that it makes the discriminatees worse off in matters such as social status, legal recognition, income, education, or freedom from subordination and oppression. In his account, discrimination is directly related to harm and therefore, discrimination against Blacks, women, and the elderly remain morally indefensible (Lippert-Rasmussen 2006: 168).

While race, caste, and gender have been brought to the fore in the foregoing century as important markers which structure discrimination, sexual orientation also has been recognized as another axis of such treatment. A cursory examination of patterns of discrimination reveals that in all such cases, two groups of people are not only treated differentially but this difference leads to disadvantage for one group. So, race-based discrimination not only differentiates Blacks and Whites, but also places Blacks at a relatively disadvantageous position in comparison to Whites. Similarly, gender-based discrimination differentiates as well as disadvantages women in comparison to men. Discrimination emanates from the relative powerlessness of a particular group and is entrenched by institutional structures, which again are a product of the same power differentials.

Discrimination has been variously categorized as direct and indirect, individual and structural, de facto and de jure, intentional and non-intentional discrimination.[4]

Direct discrimination has been understood as intentional discrimination that explicitly aims to disadvantage the members of certain socially salient groups. Direct discrimination may be practised by an individual or an individual firm as well as by the state. While an individual may practise direct discrimination by refusing access to members of a socially salient group into his premises, the state practises direct discrimination when it permits policies of racial segregation in schools, denies certain jobs opportunities to women, and legalizes the practice of untouchability.

Indirect discrimination is marked by the lack of explicitness. Discrimination emanates mainly from institutions rather than individuals. Indirect discrimination refers to the uneven consequences that flow from policies, which in the first instance appear to be free from any intentional discrimination. An appropriate example of indirect discrimination, on the basis of sex, would be the way in which women are disadvantaged in the labour market because of the distinction made between skilled and unskilled work. While women are not restricted entry into the labour force today, unequal income is generated due to the patriarchal biases which are inherent to such a structure.

Another important distinction that is drawn is between structural discrimination and institutional discrimination. According to Pincus, structural discriminations are difficult to de-mystify because the intent to cause discrimination is not as visible as it in institutional discrimination. Structural discrimination emanates from cultural values of a society and from principles of social organization and therefore, its eradication would require changes in pedagogy while institutional discriminations can be fought through arguments that expose the immorality and illegality of a particular act (Pincus 1996). Institutional discrimination is manifested in the form of state laws and therefore, easier to resist.

Non-Discrimination in the Indian Constitution and Sexual Minorities

In opposition to this harm-based account of discrimination, another approach to understanding discrimination is that of viewing it as destructive of human dignity. Kalpana Kannabiran asserts that practices of segregation, seclusion, negative stereotyping, exclusion, chronic mistreatment, and collective violence undermine the dignity of individuals. Placing discrimination practised against certain groups in India, Kannabiran argues that liberty should be inter-twined into the discourse of non-discrimination. In a way, her conceptualization has shifted the grounds of our understandings of equality and non-discrimination by placing liberty into the framework (Kannabiran 2011). Equality as non-discrimination was woven into the framework of the constitution through Articles 14, 15, and 16. In *E.P. Royappa* v. *State of Tamil Nadu* (1973), it was held that the basic principle which informs both Articles 14 and 16 is equality and inhibition against discrimination.[5] The Supreme Court observed that:

> From a positivistic point of view, equality is antithetic to arbitrariness. In fact, equality and arbitrariness are sworn enemies; one belongs to the rule of law in a republic while the other, to the whim and caprice of an absolute monarch. Where an act is arbitrary it is implicit in it that it is unequal both according to political logic and constitutional law and is, therefore, violative of Art. 14, and if it affects any matter relating to public employment, it is also violative of Art. 16. Articles 14 and 16 strike at arbitrariness in State action and ensure fairness and equality of treatment.[6]

The Indian constitution is a unique document not only because it establishes equality as non-discrimination but also because its approach to equality is underpinned with an acknowledgement of difference. Under the constitution, therefore, provisions allowing protective discrimination towards backward classes are present under Articles 15 (4) and 16 (4).[7] Under the ambit of the Indian constitution matters related to removal of discrimination are not just dealt through negative but also through positive interventionist measures.

Demands for recognition of difference and diversity are not new in Indian politics. Difference based politics in India witnessed another major change with the emergence of a sexuality based politics. Though sexual orientation was never considered as a ground for the creation of a socially salient group, with the arrival of HIV/AIDS, sexuality becomes a politically salient category to be reckoned with. In a curious twist of binaries homosexuals were cast against the heterosexuals not just as the deviants but also as the diseased. The movement which emerged thereafter in India had to fight a battle on two fronts: to eliminate the barriers in access to health rights and to fight for positive self-recognition of the community (Kole 2007).

Notwithstanding the sensitivity of the Indian state to the claims of religious, ethnic, and linguistic minorities, the inherent heterosexual ideology of the Indian state prevented it from recognizing sexual diversity as a reality. Discrimination, both direct and institutional is visible through Section 377 of the Indian Penal Code (1860) which is reflective of the 'heterosexual matrix' in India. The grant of political equality notwithstanding, the curtailment of civil and social rights of the sexual minorities defeats the state's claims of non-discrimination of sexual minorities qua citizens.

While direct institutional discrimination in the case of sexual minorities is visible through Section 377, indirect institutional discrimination is visible through certain other criminal and non-criminal laws that do not directly aim to discriminate them but disproportionately disadvantages them. Section 292 of the IPC, which makes obscenity a criminal offence, though intended for application towards all, has mostly disadvantaged publications intended for circulation among sexual minorities. Protest plays staged by sexual minorities also face the same fear of criminal prosecution due to the Dramatic Performances Act, 1876. One significant instance of indirect discrimination towards sexual minorities occurred in 1997 when a consignment of 'Trikone', a magazine for sexual minorities in Asia published in America, was confiscated under Section 11 of the Customs Act, 1962, which banned the import of any goods to India which 'affects the standards of decency or morality'.[8] Moreover, under the Juvenile Justice Act, 1986 neglected juveniles can be taken away from their parents by the state and put in a child care home. The definition of a neglected juvenile, however, has serious implications on gay and lesbian couples because parents are considered as unfit if they lead an immoral or depraved life.[9] In all these instances, a recurrent theme of 'deviancy' as opposed to public morality is visible and, therefore, discriminates against their life choices, not only by differentiating sexual minorities from others, but also by disadvantaging them at the same time.

As far as labour laws are concerned, dismissal of service on grounds of moral turpitude can hang as a Damocles' sword on the sexual minorities. Moral turpitude, understood as, 'conduct that is considered contrary to community standards of justice, honesty, or good morals', effectively stands as a barrier to the 'coming out' of sexual minorities.[10] Effectively, then heterosexual individuals need not shroud their personal life in mystery due to fear of dismissal (except in few cases of adultery) while for sexual minorities, such disclosures may mean dismissal from their jobs. Additionally, provisions of the Employees Provident Fund Scheme, 1952; the Payment of Gratuity Act, 1972; Workmen's Compensation Act, 1923, and The Employees State Insurance Act, 1948 all define the nominee or dependent (as the case may be) in a narrow sense to include relations by blood and marriage (Desai 2002). In other words, these provisions assume heterosexual relations as the norm and thereby render all non-heterosexual relationships invalid for benefits that accrue from a marriage.

Thus, the criminality of the regular life of sexual minorities is not just entrenched by Section 377 of IPC but by a range of other laws which demarcates and discriminates between heterosexuals and non-heterosexuals. That this criminalization of ordinary life is based on public morality and not on constitutional morality is significant. Section 377 of the IPC is an example of direct institutional discrimination against sexual minorities in India. It reduces questions of love or intimacy, desire or longing to 'carnal intercourse against the order of nature' and sets up a regime where the lives and loves of LGBT persons are read within the framework of 'unnatural sexual acts' (Narrain 2011: 254) nevertheless, it has fostered the emergence of a queer community in India by promoting a shared sense of marginality and injury. 'The opposition to this state of marginality gave birth to a queer political consciousness forged in the crucible of struggles around the law. This emergence of a queer political consciousness is signposted by activist publications like the 'Less than Gay report'(1991), 'Campaign for Lesbian Rights'(CALERI report) (1997), 'Humjinsi' (1999), and the PUCL-Karnataka Reports on human rights violations against sexuality minorities and the transgender community in 2001 and 2003 respectively. These documents, as they articulated a greater vision for queer rights, were significant milestones for change and created a foundation for a demand for rights' (Narrain and Gupta 2011: xxii). In recent years, the lesbian, bisexual, gay, transgender, and *hijra* peoples and communities in India have effectively and consistently raised their concerns in larger social, legal, and political contexts. Increasing, the discourse of non-discrimination has focused attention on the ways in which indirect institutional discrimination acts as a catalyst in entrenching criminality associated with the lives of sexual minorities.

The Pervasiveness of Indirect Institutional Discrimination: A Study of Two Cases

While discussing discrimination with reference to sexual minorities in India, two significant events separated in time deems attention. The first occurred in July 2001 in Lucknow, while the second occurred in February 2010 in Aligarh. While in the first event police targeted individuals working for NGOs working in the field of HIV/AIDS intervention, in the second event a university suspended one of its faculty members for an act of sodomy performed within the confines of his 'private' home. The unfolding of discriminatory treatment in both these cases is different. However, what runs as a unifying theme is the differential and disadvantageous treatment meted out because of their association with an 'outlawed' sexual practice.

The emergence of HIV/AIDS on the global stage in the 1980s triggered a series of preventive measures, leading amongst which was that it fostered the growth of several health-related NGOs with international funding. These NGOs worked to create awareness regarding unsafe sex, which was one of the major causes of AIDS. The target groups for these NGOs were the high-risk groups such as sex workers and homosexuals. However, these NGOs faced a peculiar problem when working with homosexuals in India: though the practice was prevalent, the label of the 'homosexual' was rejected and therefore, interventions became difficult because targeted individuals refused that they were homosexuals. This led the concerned NGOs to innovate a new term—MSM or men who have sex with men—as a way forward to generating awareness on safe-sex practices amongst the high-risk groups. Two organizations which were involved in the fight against HIV/AIDS in Lucknow were the Naz Foundation International (henceforth NFI) and the Bharosa Trust. While NFI is based in London and registered in the UK, Bharosa is a local Indian NGO that receives technical support from NFI. Both these organizations collaborate with the National AIDS Control Organization (NACO) and because these were operating from Lucknow, were working with the Uttar Pradesh State AIDS Control Society (UPSACS), and therefore, the ambit of their activities fell within the limits of the governmental policies.

Media attention on these two organizations fell on 8 July 2001 when the police raided the premises of these two organizations and arrested four persons from NFI and Bharosa under Section 377 of the IPC, accompanied by S120B (Conspiracy), S107 (Abetment), S292 (Obscenity), Section 60 of the Copyrights Act and Sections 3 and 4 of the Indecent Representation of Women (Prohibition) Act. The act of the police ran contrary to the state's policy of AIDS prevention, as these organizations were involved in generating awareness on safe-sex practices. However, the raids were justified by the police stating 'moralistic' claims that these organizations ran a gay club and were promoting homosexuality, which was antithetical to Indian culture. Despite the fact that these organizations denied these allegations, and produced reports and documents, which established the nature of work they were engaged in, the police refused to acknowledge the legality of their work. The arrested members were in jail for almost 47 days and were abused, beaten, and threatened during this period. Only when the bail was granted, the lawyers who fought the case for the organizations found that Section 377 was removed from the charge-sheet. This leads to the question, then as to why were these individuals who were carrying on their duties keep in jail for a prolonged period. The answer seems to be hidden in the statement of the chief judicial magistrate who reasoned while denying bail in the first appeal, that 'a group of persons indulging in these activities... (is) polluting the entire society by encouraging the young persons and abating them to committing the offence of sodomy'.[11] It is noteworthy that the organizations faced the wrath of law not because their activities were illegal but because of the 'unnaturalness' associated with the act of sodomy and stigma attached with HIV/AIDS. Public morality again acts as the arbiter of justice and decides the ways to discipline the 'deviant'. The Lucknow case justifies Lippert-Rasmussen's principle of discrimination as bad, to the extent that it causes harm is justified.

Another instance where the harm of the principle of discrimination can be tested is the case of Dr Siras of Aligarh. On February 9, 2010, Dr S.R. Siras of Aligarh Muslim University was handed his suspension notice from his University under Section 40 (3) (c) of Aligarh Muslim University Act of 1981 which gave the vice-chancellor of the said university powers to suspend a teacher against whom a complaint of misconduct is alleged. A day before the aforementioned sequence of events took place, Dr Siras was filmed, discretely by some miscreants, in the privacy of his residential quarters when he was engaged in an intimate act with a consenting male adult. The persons who were involved in filming claimed to be from the press and threatened Dr Siras with the release of these tapes in the media. In the meanwhile, administrative officials from the university also gathered at Dr Siras' residence and offered to calm down the entire issue. However, the next day a suspension notice was served and after a fortnight, the university served Dr Siras with a charge-sheet with the charge that he 'has committed act of misconduct in as much as he indulged himself into immoral sexual activity and in contravention of basic moral ethics while residing in Quarter No. 21-C, Medical College, AMU, Aligarh thereby undermined pious image of the teacher community and as a whole tarnishing the image of the University'.[12] Dr Siras was also issued a memo demanding that he vacate the university residence. His plight, however, did not end there as the media highlight caused difficulty in locating an accommodation. While the university was adamant on non-revocation of the order, the Allahabad High Court in its order, dated April 2010, stayed his suspension notice as well as the order that mandated his vacating the university residence. That the High Court of Allahabad asserted the right to privacy as a fundamental right is reminiscent of the Naz Foundation argument. But, the court categorically asserted that applicability of the *Naz Foundation* v. *Union of India* does not arise in the said case. The jubilation resultant to the decision of the High Court which marked an end to the unlawful suspension of Dr Siras, however, was marred with his death under 'mysterious circumstances' on 7 April 2010. The tragic unfolding of events in Dr Siras' life and death is a pointer towards the discrimination which structures the lives of sexual minorities. Discrimination, relating both to employment as well as housing, is seen in the case of Dr Siras. The pervasiveness of discrimination emanating from sexual orientation is evident from the fact that Dr Siras' academic stature and class location did not act as safeguards against discrimination and consequent violation of his dignity. Despite the fact that the *Naz Foundation* case had legalized homosexuality within the confines of the 'private', the case of Dr Siras points out how changes in law and society have not been in tandem. Moreover, one should also not lose sight of the fact that the Allahabad High Court's decision not to apply the *Naz* judgment is a sad rejoinder to the initial exhilaration shown by LGBT groups in June 2009. That institutions entrench public morality and turn a blind eye to constitutional morality is one of the lessons that can be drawn from the entire episode. Also, it is significant to note that in this case the harm principle of Lippert-Rasmussen is carried to its extreme where discrimination leads not only to a disadvantageous position but to the very annihilation of Dr Siras' life itself. In the light of these cases, therefore, it becomes important to re-examine the celebration surrounding the *Naz Foundation* case. In order to entrench a society free from discrimination based on sexual orientation, foundational questions regarding the naturalization and normalization of heterosexuality and the family have to be asked:

At present, the issues raised by the LGBT movement are multiple: creating public visibility for the identities and issues, building community and safe spaces for people to be able to reach out to each other, providing support networks, fighting for legal recognition and

rights, providing safe health care services, articulating and questioning the politics that makes all sexuality other than hetero-normative
suspect, building alliances nationally and well as internationally with
other movements, connecting the politics of gender and sexuality
with other politics, and working with multiple strategies towards a society where all genders and sexualities would be respected and treated
equally (Narrain 2007: 261).

Looking for the social in the assumed 'natural' could take forward
the movement against discrimination. And while looking at discrimination based on sexual orientation, one also cannot lose sight
of the intersectionalities that cut across an individual's identity. The
effort, then has underpinned by the understanding that 'the premise of change with respect to sexuality is as much about change in
societal mores as it is about legal change' (Narrain 2007: 261) and
therefore, shifting the terms of discourse from the demand for legal
protection only to an associated process of questioning the limits of
law becomes essential.

Reversal of the *Naz* Judgment: Direct Institutional
Discrimination in the Aftermath of the *Koushal* Judgment

Across the world, currently around 80 countries criminalize same-sex
relationships. While countries such as Nigeria and Uganda have passed
legislations banning homosexual relations in as late as in January
and February 2014, constitutions of countries such as South Africa,
Ecuador, Portugal, and Bolivia explicitly prohibit any discrimination
on the basis of sexual orientation. A proposal for de-criminalization
of homosexuality was first put forward in the Wolfenden Report of
1957 in the United Kingdom. Thereafter, national as well as international courts have been instrumental in revoking discriminatory
provisions against LGBTs.[13] Despite such developments, Section
377 of the IPC has not yet been revoked, implying that homosexual
behaviour is a punishable offence. The endurance of Section 377
in the Indian law book is a legacy of the colonial period which has
withstood any change over the century.

In 2001, the Lawyers Collective HIV/AIDS Unit, on behalf of
Naz Foundation, filed a constitutional challenge to Section 377

in the Delhi High Court on the grounds of equality, privacy, and freedom of expression. The judgment which was delivered on 2 July 2009 was a historic 105-page document that overturned a 149-year-old discourse. The operative conclusion of *Naz Foundation (India) Trust* v. *Government of NCT, Delhi and Others* held Section 377 of the IPC is violative of Articles 21, 14, and 15 of the Constitution of India 'insofar as it criminalizes consensual sexual acts between adults *in private*' (emphasis added). In technical terms, the judges 'read down' Section 377. The decision founded on the constitutional principles of dignity, privacy, and equality was significant because it recognized that Section 377 persecutes and marginalizes a significant group of the population because of their sexual non-conformity, 'They are subject to extensive prejudice because of what they are or what they are perceived to be, not because of what they do.'[14] Throughout the legal reasoning of the judgment, the judges exhibited an ability to empathize with the pain of the sexual minorities. The Naz Foundation bench displayed great courage and craftsmanship in fashioning a historic decision heard loud and clear, not only in India, but across the world.[15] It signified an important change in the ethos of the country, not by any political upheaval but by a judicial pronouncement. As Rukmini Sen has commented, 'Occasionally the judiciary, as an important arm of the state and as an articulator of counter-majoritarian viewpoints, gives expression to what it considers to be the soul of the Constitution' (Sen 2009). Interpreting the constitution to respond to the changes in time could be a challenging task and Naz Foundation did fundamentally alter the relationship between a large disenfranchised, silent, dispersed, and discriminated minority and the hegemonic majority.

Though heralded as one of the most radical judicial pronouncements in the recent past, the judgment should be accepted with care because of the emphasis it places on the privacy argument. Arvind Narrain points out that the legal challenge asking for de-criminalization of sex in private has only limited consequences for the wider queer community as Section 377 would be operative with respect to the public space. He points out how Section 377 happens to affect mainly those persons who do not own any private space and hence are forced to engage in sexual encounters in parks or other outdoor spaces. The judgment, therefore, has limited significance for those sexual minorities who are located at the bottom of a class hierarchy (Narrain 2004).

For Martha Nussbaum, an argument based on privacy has narrow consequences as privacy is class-linked. She remarks that 'if certain forms of behavior are protected on the grounds that they take place in the "private zone" of the home, then people who don't have such a convenient zone of privacy will be disadvantaged. Thus call girls, who operate out of their home or in expensive hotels may achieve protections that are denied to streetwalkers' (Nussbaum 2002: 257). Legal pronouncements based on privacy arguments for Section 377, therefore, not only display a class bias but also run the same danger of creating similar hierarchies between good homosexuals and bad homosexuals.

Vikram Raghavan, commenting on the contradiction that is created by the operative conclusion of the judgment has commented that 'under this interpretation, Section 377 may still be freely applied to prosecute "non-private" conduct between adults in a public place' (Raghavan 2009). Relying on privacy is problematic in the Indian case because much of the cases involving police intimidation and harassment involve conduct in public places. Moreover in the Indian context, where the 'private' is constantly intruded by family and neighbours, many gays are forced to bond in public spaces.[16]

While this chapter agrees that the argument of privacy has a class bias, it seeks to extend the argument further and argues that the High Court by retaining the public/ private binary has circumscribed the rights of the sexual minorities. The *Naz* judgment had freed lesbians and gay men from the threat of being labelled as criminals—endowing them with a sense of dignity—as long as the condition that they remain in the private sphere is met. However, the decriminalization of homosexuality by the Delhi High Court has addressed only one dimension of their exclusion from 'full and equal membership' of the political community. Persisting discriminations such as those pertaining to employment, marriage, and social security benefits demonstrate that the fight against discrimination is far from completion. In the words of Diane Richardson, 'lesbian and gay men are entitled to certain rights of existence, but these are extremely circumscribed, being constructed largely on the condition that they remain in the private sphere and do not seek public recognition or membership in the political community. In this sense, lesbians and gay men, though granted certain rights of citizenship, are not a legitimate social constituency' (Richardson 1998: 89).

By reading down Section 377, the High Court instead of celebrating sexual difference had ushered in a politics of tolerance and assimilation. The judgment echoed the sentiment that 'all public (as opposed to private) discrimination against homosexuals be ended and that every right and responsibility that heterosexuals enjoy as public citizens be extended to those who grow up and find themselves emotionally different'.[17] It, therefore, followed a simple equality which sits comfortably with our understandings of direct discrimination.

Notwithstanding the lacunae of the *Naz* judgment, it has been widely acclaimed for 'it asserts that queer people are indeed a part of the Indian nation and also states that the judiciary remains an institution committed to the protection of those who might be despised by a majoritarian logic. It has initiated a fundamental debate on notions of choice, personal autonomy and our fundamental right to live' (Narrain and Gupta 2011: xxxiii). The jubilations that followed the *Naz* judgment did not, however, last for long. On 11 December 2013 in a Civil Appeal filed by Suresh Kumar Koushal and another, the Supreme Court of India held that 'Section 377 IPC does not suffer from the vice of unconstitutionality and the declaration made by the Division Bench of the High Court is legally unsustainable'.[18] The *Koushal* judgment generated widespread reactions across the country as it swept away all the progress that had been made from 2009 to 2013. Concerns regarding the well-being of the lesbians and gays who had 'come out of the closet', after the *Naz* judgment were raised. Moreover, the *Koushal* judgment made a reversal of the entire *Naz* judgment by denying sexual minorities not

> merely the right to perform same sex acts but also their status as minorities, describing them as 'minuscule', ruling as 'not proven' the terror and torture they undergo at the hands of police, and holding laconically that theirs was not a complaint against denial of identity rights but an unsustainable plea for immunity for the performance of acts contrary to 'nature' (Baxi 2014: 12).

The judgment left the ball in the court of the parliament, arguing that it is the appropriate authority to 'consider the desirability and propriety of deleting Section 377 IPC from the statute book or amend the same as per the suggestion made by the Attorney General'.[19] That, this judgment was delivered by Justice Singhvi (and Justice Mukhopadhyay), who has been liberal in using the powers of judicial review is also a noteworthy feature. In fact, the court in a strange way, states that, 'on several occasions, merely because courts in foreign countries have taken a different view than that taken by our courts or in adjudicating on any particular matter we were asked to re-consider those decisions or to consider them for the first time and to adopt them as the law of this country'.[20] The *Koushal* judgment, therefore, stands as a unique example of regressive judgments by the Supreme Court of India which denies the existence of discrimination against sexual minorities in India and attributes judgments emphasizing non-discrimination (of sexual minorities) as being pronounced under foreign duress.

In view of the impending general elections of 2014, major political parties at that moment had shown particular interest in removing Section 377 IPC but in the aftermath of the election results, the voices that have come forward have given suspicious signals, causing much anxiety among the community.[21]

Effectively, therefore, the *Koushal* judgment had taken the case of sexual minorities to the pre-*Naz* period denying all the advances that had been made and celebrated. While *Naz* suffered from the drawback that it advocated a simple equality model which denied the possibility of radicalizing the politics based on sexuality; *Koushal* overturned whatever progress *Naz* had led to. It allows direct institutional discrimination to continue, segregating persons on the basis of sexual orientation, and criminalizing a section on the basis of their sexual desire.[22]

***

Within a liberal paradigm there is a widespread belief that particular identities (such as being gay or lesbian) can be tolerated as long as the borders of the public/private binary is secured. The basic assumption of tolerance is that differences should be tolerated as long as they do not constitute any harm to public order. Tolerance does not bring about any transformation, it simply accommodates the difference of the 'other'. Couched in this language, homosexuality is seen as a biological deviation and therefore homosexuals can be tolerated, as they are not responsible for their sexual orientation. However, this tolerance has to be limited to the private realm. Amnesty International, reporting for countries where tolerance is adopted as the official policy has reported that, in cases of transgression to the public realm, targeted attacks on lesbians and gay men have led to killings.[23] The High Court fails to explore this dimension of tolerance and therefore, it was feared that the *Naz* judgment would keep structural discrimination intact, despite its successful attempt at fighting direct discrimination.

The High Court had ignored that the sexual minorities are claiming not just equality but also respect—which is possible only by acknowledging gay identity in the public. The idea of gay men and lesbians 'coming out' is underpinned by the idea that asserting one's sexual identity is desirable, as certain fears and inhibitions are successfully left behind. Asserting that sexual minorities have begun to come out, Jonathan N. Katz states that:

> We have been the silent minority, the silenced minority—invisible women, invisible men. Early on, the alleged enormity of our 'sin' justified the denial of our existence, even our physical destruction. Our 'crime' was not merely against society...but 'against nature'... Long did we remain literally and metaphorically unspeakable... that time is over...gay people are moving out—and moving on—to organized action against an oppressive society.[24]

Lesbians and gays, who were expected to confine the expression of their sexuality to the private realm so as not to contaminate the public realm, have begun to contest such restrictions through Gay Pride marches and creation of alternative public spaces. The ability to be 'out' and publicly acknowledge sexual difference is therefore crucial to the ability to claim rights.[25] 'Coming out' as a strategy signifies the repudiation of the public-private dichotomy. However, in the Indian context the Delhi High Court by hinging on the privacy argument accepts that it is possible to conceive of sexual orientation as a strictly private matter. The model that the court adopts is the simple equality model where the sexual minorities push merely for an agenda of legal reform. Notwithstanding the importance of legal reform, this model means 'little more than homo conformity with hetero society...it is parity on heterosexual terms—equal rights within a framework determined and dominated by straights'.[26] This approach aspires for assimilation, instead of social transformation. The decision of the court has created another level of exclusion—that between the good homosexual and the bad homosexual. This creates a distinction between 'some people who are allowed to live their lives freely in both public and private; others are allowed freedom only if they keep significant aspects of their lives private and privatized'.[27] In a nutshell, it can be said that the *Naz* judgment, attempting to erase one form of discrimination, creates a different form of discrimination. However, in a curious twist of the legal tale, direct discrimination has arisen from the ashes through the *Koushal* judgment, claiming resilience and threating to disrupt the project of non-discrimination against sexual minorities. Though law cannot be the horizon of equality, the case of sexual minorities makes it explicit that the legal battle is far from over and the struggle to dismantle binary categories of hetero-sexuality/homosexuality has to go on simultaneously with attempts for non-discrimination.

Notes

1. For more on the Stonewall riots and the development of the gay rights movement in the West, please refer to Wolf (2009).
2. Section 377 of the Indian Penal Code reads as:
   'Of Unnatural Offences: Whoever voluntarily has carnal intercourse against the order of nature with any man, woman or animal shall be punished with imprisonment for life or imprisonment of either description for a term which may extend to ten years and shall also be liable to fine.
   Explanation: penetration is sufficient to constitute carnal intercourse necessary of the offence prescribed in the section.'
3. Article 1 of the International Convention on the Elimination of All Forms of Racial Discrimination. Available at http://www.ohchr.org/EN/ProfessionalInterest/Pages/CERD.aspx. Accessed 09 November 2013.
4. For more see, Link and Phelan (2006: 528–9); Hunter (1992); Pincus (1996); Doyle (2007: 537–53); and Gruhl (1932: 23–40).

5. While Article 14 declares that 'The State shall not deny to any person equality before the law or equal protection of the laws within the territory of India', according to Article 16 (1) 'There shall be equality of opportunity for all citizens in matters relating to employment or appointment to any office under the State (2) No citizen shall, on grounds only of religion, race, caste, sex, descent, place of birth, residence or any of them, be ineligible for, or discriminated against in respect or, any employment or office under the State.'

6. Cited from http://indiankanoon.org/doc/1416283/. Accessed 10 November 2013.

7. For a detailed discussion refer to Galanter (1961).

8. Chapter IV, Prohibitions on Importation and Exportation of Goods of the Customs Act, 1962. Available at http://www.cbec.gov.in/customs/cs-act/custom-act-1962.pdf. Accessed 09 November 2013.

9. Chapter II (14) Competent Authorities and Institutions for Juveniles of the Juvenile Justice Act, 1986. Available at http://www.vakilno1.com/bareacts/juvenilejusticeact/juvenilejusticeact.html. Accessed 09 November 2013.

10. West's Encyclopedia of American Law, edition 2. Available at http://legaldictionary.thefreedictionary.com/moral+turpitude. Accessed 09 November 2013.

11. Quoted from J. Csete (2002: 19).

12. Cited from http://www.fridae.asia/newsfeatures/printable.php?articleid=9724. Accessed 15 November 13.

13. Prominent examples include: *Romer* v. *Evans* case of 1996 (USA), *Dudgeon* v. *United Kingdom* case of 1981.

14. *Naz Foundation* v. *Government of New Capital Territory of Delhi and Others*, Delhi Law Times Vol. 160 (2009) Para 94.

15. Raghavan (2009).

16. In fact, the significance of gay cruising spots such as parks, bars, and bathhouses have been constantly asserted upon by gay activists, while for lesbians safe spaces which have some element of being public include house parties and membership-based organizations.

17. A. Sullivan quoted in Lister (2002: 201).

18. *S.K. Koushal* v. *Naz Foundation and others*, 2013, p. 97. Available at http://judis.nic.in/supremecourt/imgs1.aspx?filename=41070. Accessed 15 December 2013.

19. *S.K. Koushal* v. *Naz Foundation and others*, 2013, p. 98. Available at http://judis.nic.in/supremecourt/imgs1.aspx?filename=41070. Accessed 15 December 2013.

20. *S.K. Koushal* v. *Naz Foundation and others*, 2013, p. 97. Available at http://judis.nic.in/supremecourt/imgs1.aspx?filename=41070. Accessed 15 December 2013.

21. For more please see: http://archive.indianexpress.com/news/homo-sexuality-sonia-rahul-gandhi-dismayed-over-supreme-court-verdict-quashing-gay-rights/1206936/. Accessed 13 December 2013 ; http://timesofindia.indiatimes.com/india/Political-parties-back-LGBT-rights/articleshow/27231226.cms. Accessed 13 December 2013; http://indianexpress.com/article/cities/mumbai/mixed-response-to-cong-promise-to-decriminalise-homosexuality/. Accessed 27 March 2014. But statements made by stalwarts like Rajnath Singh and Harsh Vardhan who are a part of the ruling NDA government has caused much insecurity among the members of the community, please see: ihttp://www.telegraphindia.com/1131214/jsp/nation/story_17679913.jsp#. U7S2QZSSy_Q. Accessed 13 December 2013; http://timesofindia. indiatimes.com/india/Health-minister-Dr-Harsh-Vardhan-questions-stress-on-condoms-in-AIDS-fight/articleshow/37173742.cms. Accessed 25 June 2014; http://www.gaylaxymag.com/latest-news/bjp-mp-from-bikaner-to-table-anti-homosexuality-bill-in-lok-sabha/. Accessed 14 December 2013; At the same time, BJP Lok Sabha MP from Gujarat Balakrishna Shukla is a supporter of LGBT rights, please see: http://scroll.in/article/659523/In-Modi's-Gujarat,-a-BJP-MP-champions-gay-rights. Accessed 26 March 2014.

22. In the light of the *Koushal* judgment in December 2013, the Naz Foundation (India) Trust has filed a Curative Petition in the Supreme Court, as the last resort, on 31 March 2014. It has sought for an oral hearing of the petition as well as an interim stay on the *Koushal* decision. Please see, http://www.lawyerscollective.org/updates/naz-foundation-files-curative-petition-challenging-supreme-court-judg-ment-section-377.html. Accessed 01 May 2014.

23. Amnesty International cited in Richardson (2000: 82).

24. Katz cited in Bamforth (1997: 1).

25. J. Pakulski cited in Richardson (2001: 158).

26. Tatchell quoted in Bamforth (1997: 251).

27. Jakobson and Pellegrini quoted in Lee (2011: 159).

References

Bamforth, N. 1997. *Sexuality, Morals and Justice: A Theory of Lesbian and Gay Rights Law*. London and Washington: Cassell.

Baxi, U. 2014. 'Naz 2: A Critique', *Economic and Political Weekly*, XLIX 12(6): 12.

Csete. J. 2002. 'Epidemic of Abuse: Police Harassment of HIV/AIDS Outreach Workers in India', *Human Rights Watch*, 15(5). Available at www.hrw.org/reports/2002/india2/india0602.pdf. Accessed 20 September 2011.

Desai, M. 2002. 'Civil Laws Affecting Gay Men and Lesbian' in B. Fernandez (ed.) *Humjinsi: A Resource Book on Lesbian, Gay and Bisexual Rights in India*, pp. 93–99. Mumbai: Combat Law Publications.

Doyle, O. 2007. 'Direct Discrimination, Indirect Discrimination and Autonomy', *Oxford Journal of Legal Studies*, 27(3): 537–53.

Galanter, M. 1961. 'Equality and "Protective Discrimination" In India', *Rutgers Law Review*, XVI: 42–7.

Gruhl, E. 1932. 'Discrimination', *Annals of the American Academy of Political and Social Science*, Vol. 159, Part 1: Power and the Public. pp. 23–40.

Hunter, R. 1992. *Indirect Discrimination in the Workplace*. Sydney: The Federation Press.

Kannabiran, K. 2011. *Tools of Justice: Nondiscrimination and the Indian Constitution*. New Delhi: Routledge.

Kole, S.K. 2007. 'Globalizing Queer? AIDS, Homophobia and the Politics of Sexual Identity in India', Globalization and Health, Available at: 3:8. http://www.globalizationandhealth.com/content/3/1/8. Accessed 18 August 2009.

Lee, J.C.H. 2011. *Policing Sexuality: Sex, Society and the State*. London and New York: Zed Books.

Link, B.G., and J.C. Phelan. 2006. 'Stigma and Its Public Health Implications', *Lancet*, 367: 528–9.

Lippert-Rasmussen, K. 2006. 'The Badness of Discrimination', *Ethical Theory and Moral Practice*, 9(2): 168.

Lister, R. 2002. 'Sexual Citizenship', in E.F. Isin and B.S. Turner (eds), *Handbook of Citizenship Studies*, p. 201. London: Sage.

Narrain, A. 2004. 'The Articulation of Rights around Sexuality and Health: Subaltern Queer Cultures in India in the Era of Hindutva', *Health and Human Rights*, 7(2): 3–24

———. 2007. 'No Shortcuts to Queer Utopia: Sodomy, Law and Social Change', in B. Bose and S. Bhattacharyya (eds), *The Phobic and the Erotic: The Politics of Sexualities in Contemporary India*, pp. 255–62. Calcutta and Oxford: Seagull Books.

———. 2011. 'A New Language of Morality', in A. Narrain and A. Gupta (eds), *Law Like Love: Queer Perspectives on Law*, pp. 253–77. New Delhi: Yoda Press.

Narrain, A. and A. Gupta (ed). 2011. 'Introduction', in A. Narrain and A. Gupta (eds), *Law Like Love: Queer Perspectives on Law*, pp. xi–lvi. New Delhi: Yoda Press.

Nussbaum, M. 2002. 'Sex Equality, Liberty and Privacy', in Z. Hasan, E. Shridharan, and R. Sudarshan (eds), *India's Living Constitution*, pp. 242–83. New Delhi: Permanent Black.

Pincus, F.L. 1996. 'Discrimination Comes in Many Forms: Individual, Institutional, and Structural', *American Behavioral Scientist*, 40(2): 186–94.

Raghavan, V. 2009. 'Navigating the Noteworthy and Nebulous in Naz Foundation'. Available at http://lawandotherthings.blogspot. com/2009/07/navigatingnoteworthyandnebulous-in_08.html. Accessed 07 July 2009.

Richardson, D. 1998. 'Sexuality and Citizenship', *Sociology*, 32(1): 83–100.

———. 2000. *Rethinking Sexuality*. London: Sage.

———. 2001. 'Extending Citizenship: Cultural Citizenship and Sexuality', in Stevenson, N. (ed.), *Culture and Citizenship*, p. 158. London GBR: Sage Publications Inc.

Sen, R. 2009. 'Breaking Silences, Celebrating New Spaces: Mapping Elite Responses to the 'Inclusive' Judgment'. Available at http://lawando-therthings.blogspot.com/2009/07.html. Accessed 07 July 2009.

Wolf, S. 2009. *Sexuality and Socialism: History, Politics, and Theory of LGBT Liberation*. Chicago, IL, USA: Haymarket Books.

13

Discrimination and Exclusion

A Case of Dalit Muslims in India

Md. Aftab Alam

This study explores the issues related to the silence imposed historically, socio-economically and politically on the Dalit Muslims. It brings to the fore their voices and visions, issues and struggles, shares their achievements and critically highlights weaknesses and limitations. There is an attempt to address the issues of discrimination and exclusion of Dalit Muslims, their identity, their ambiguous relationship with other Dalits, and the assertion of their rights and dignity.

Muslims are the largest religious minority in India. According to the 2001 census, they constitute 13.4 per cent of India's total population. However, due to lack of sufficient research, we do not know much about the socio-political dynamics of this religious minority group which is a diversified community. There has been an attempt to represent Muslims as a single, monolithic, homogenous group not only in political terms, but also in social science discourses. Issues surrounding infringement of religious freedom and questions about state bias towards Muslims has been subject to scholarly scrutiny. These kinds of representations have been facing a serious challenge in recent times due to the emergence of the perspective of understanding Muslim society from below/its margins. Various studies point out the discrimination faced by certain sections within Muslims due to their caste background.

The Indian constitution refers to SCs, STs, and backward groups but we do not find any mention of 'Dalit Muslims' as a category. They are also absent from academic discourses and the debates of mainstream politics. The census report usually enumerates the different castes included as SCs. But in these reports, we do not find even a reference to the category of 'Dalit Muslims'. We need to discuss their problems, sufferings, and in a way expand Habermas' notion of 'public sphere'. The deeply disturbing fact, however, is that the public sphere of our society does not even deem it necessary to hold discussions on this group. The media have never included this group within the ambit of their discussion. That is why, it is important to underline at the outset that the issue of Dalit Muslims in India is a highly deficient area of study within the domain of social sciences. Indian democracy, despite its various pitfalls, has over the years unleashed forces of democratization among various social groups, including marginalized ones (Kohli 2001).

> However, the paradox of Indian democracy is that the social and political position of the Indian Muslims has been left untouched by the working of Indian democracy. Moreover, it has not unleashed forces of democratization within the community. Thus, the initiation of wider social and educational reform within the community is yet to start. Through this kind of research we can successfully create a congenial condition for serious discussion on multi-faceted problems faced by Dalit Muslims.

The chapter examines the prevalence of caste among Indian Muslims and its historical background. It deals with the social inequality among the Muslim community as a widely accepted phenomenon. It tries to critically analyse the well-accepted categorization of Muslim society into three broader units, that is, *Ashraf, Ajlaf,* and *Arzal*. Many Muslim scholars find that tenets of caste that exist in the community are a result of Hindu social influences. But these kinds of arguments have oversimplified the problem of caste among Muslims and hold the 'low born' Hindu converted to Islam responsible for maligning pure Islam.

It then moves on to explore the Dalit Muslim question and the issues of discriminations, social exclusion/inclusion, and recognition. It also focuses on how caste becomes a source of discrimination and exclusion from the mainstream. And finally, it highlights the issues of backwardness and then moves on to critically engage with the question 'Why did the state not recognize Dalit Muslims?'.

The theoretical part on Dalit Muslims acknowledges the existence of caste inequality among Dalit Muslims. It raises the question, 'Why has Dalit Muslims as a category not been recognized yet by the Indian state?' Drawing on the work of Muslim *Ajlaf* (mean and lowly) intellectuals and activists, my own insights and field work, I suggest the existence of a category Dalit Muslims in India. This work contends that most sociological research on caste among Muslims is impressionistic, lacking proper empirical research; castes (*zat/biradari*) among them have territorial specificities with their respective associations or *biradari* panchayats and marriage restrictions; there is an occupational hierarchy corresponding to caste; caste among Muslims is as rigid as among the Hindus; the caste system and system of biradari and zat cannot be separated from each other. It suggests that there is a need for rich and in-depth ethnographic research on Dalit Muslim castes or *Arzal* category, including the attitude of non-*Arzals* towards *Arzals*. The fact that their non-representation and absence from every sphere is linked to exclusion, which brings us to the debates surrounding inclusion/exclusion, discrimination, and finally/specifically recognition of this deprived masses.

The chapter also attempts to provide an ethnographic profile of Dalit Muslim castes/communities, an oscillating community, between the Hindu and Islamic religions. The problems faced by them because of this, in socio-economic and religious fields are also discussed. It studies the forms of discrimination, stigma, social distance and structure of domination faced by Dalit Muslims in Bihar. There is no work on untouchability among Muslims, but it exists, although the forms and nature of untouchability have changed in recent times. These marginalized communities, have not been studied so far due to lack of data, lack of social categorization, and background status or variety of other reasons.

It also deals with the question of Dalit Muslims, the Presidential Order of 1950, and judicial perspectives. As we know that Dalit

Muslims have faced discrimination within the Muslim community, this chapter argues that they have also been discriminated by the Indian state. Moreover, excluding the Muslims of scheduled caste background from the purview of the policy of protective discrimination leads to political marginalization. Therefore, recognition of this hitherto marginalized community can be helpful to reduce their backwardness. The chapter argues that a secular state that does not concern itself with religious differences and has no preference for one religion over another, cannot go into the details of religious prejudices of one section against the another. It needs to treat equally various sections which are similarly located in the society or have suffered the same kind of discrimination, exclusion, and marginalization. Therefore, in this context, Dalit Muslims need to be treated by the Indian state identically. The rest of this chapter summarizes the specific constitutional grounds on which special treatment for SCs is based, the major constitutional issues involved, and provides a summary of some of the major cases that have come up on these issues.

Discrimination and Exclusion of Dalit Muslims

Constituent assembly members linked democracy with the politics of non-discrimination. Therefore, they tried to ensure that in independent India no one is discriminated against on grounds of caste, colour, religion, and gender; that is, no one would be excluded arbitrarily from public life and all would be equal before the law. Generally, the differences that arise from specific caste practices were regarded as the main source of discrimination. The practice of untouchability got special attention among various caste practices. The forced segregation and exclusion (of various kinds) of the lower castes from all aspects of societal life was identified as the major source of inequality, discrimination, disadvantage, and finally, exclusion.

Despite being a successful democracy, India continues to remain a deeply hierarchical and unequal society in both social and economic terms. There are groups, which have historically been victims of exclusion, and continue to face deliberate discrimination due to the operation of retrograde social processes like the caste system. There are also other groups which have become victims of exclusion in postcolonial India primarily due to their minority status in a divergent social plurality. In the light of these premises, Zoya Hasan examines the concept of 'politics of inclusion' from the perspective of policies and political processes (Hasan 2009: 227–39). She takes this position with the purpose of offering constructive intervention in the debate on social exclusion and argues for a democratic pluralistic refashioning of political communities in India. The Indian constitution included only Hindus and Tribes under the SCs and STs. In 1956, Sikhs were included as well after they agitated and much later in 1990, Buddhists too were included.

While discussing the social structure of Indian Muslims, prominent scholars like Imtiaz Ahmad and Zoya Hasan brought forth the theoretical debate 'can there be a category called Dalit Muslims' (Ahmad 2007; Hasan 2009). Analysing the socio-economic situation of Dalit Muslims vis-à-vis other socio-religious groups (SRG), Hasan identifies the Dalit Muslims and argued for their inclusion in the scheduled caste list. She pointed out that 'from the evidence marshalled in the NCM report (2008), there is a strong case for including Dalits in the Muslim and Christian communities in the SC category because, as the report says, they are Dalits first and Christians and Muslims only later' (Hasan 2009).

Theoretically, Dalit Muslims as a discriminated, marginalized, and excluded category has been established. They share and face all the attributes of Hindu Dalits and the state needs to recognise their deprivation and socially degraded condition.

There is, therefore, a need to extend the discussion to those Muslim castes which share the attributes of the scheduled castes but are denied recognition and entitlement as SCs. Several issues require discussion for an understanding of the situation of those Muslim castes which share the attributes of the SCs, but are denied recognition and entitlement as SCs (Ahmad 2007). These issues will be discussed before going on to reflect on their situation in contemporary India.

Professor Niraja Gopal Jayal points out that the framework of caste domination is retained in Indian Islam (Jayal 2006: 30–4). The foregoing facts clearly show that, despite egalitarian teaching of Islam, social divergence is the characteristic feature of the Muslim society. The Muslims of India though forming a religious community sharing basic Islamic precepts, do not form a 'community' in the anthropological/sociological respect. The Indian Muslims are differentiated among themselves into various groups and subgroups on the basis of ethnic, social, and cultural distinctiveness among them. The groups and subgroups in Muslim society are arranged in stratified order and social inequality is rampant among them.

Therefore, to substantiate the earlier statements, this section attempts to provide an ethnographic profile of Dalit Muslim castes/communities, an oscillating community, between the Hindu and Islamic religions. It examines the problem of inequality and discrimination faced by the Dalit Muslims. The problems faced by them because of this, in socio-economic and religious fields, are also discussed here in brief. It studies the various forms of discrimination, stigma, social distance, and structures of domination faced by them in Bihar in order to understand their awareness of their own identity as Dalit Muslims and their relationship with the changing social structure. This section also studies their customs, rituals, beliefs, and other cultural practices. There is no work on untouchability among Muslims, but it exists, although the forms and nature of untouchability have changed.

These marginalized communities, have not been studied due to lack of data, lack of social categorization, background status, or a variety of other reasons. While social and economic conditions of Dalits have been extensively studied, intensive ethnographic studies of specific Dalit communities have been rarely undertaken. This tradition did exist in the past, which we find in the writings of British ethnographers, and has been continued to some extent by the anthropological survey of India. But most of the contemporary literature has not addressed the problems faced by Dalit Muslim communities.

There are lots of such cases of caste-based discrimination among Muslims which could be read in newspapers from time to time. My research attempts to reveal/highlight caste-based discrimination against Dalit Muslims in India.

Given the significance of the subject, there is a need for rich and focused ethnographic research on such castes in order to understand the attitudes of the non-Arzal castes and groups towards the members of the Arzal category and to gauge the extent and intensity of discrimination suffered by the latter today. It is possible that with the introduction of sanitary toilets and other technological changes the

Arzal castes no longer engage in the demeaning and defiling occupation of scavenging but social distance from them continues to be maintained. It is also possible that the forms of discrimination and stigmatization practised against the Arzal castes have changed, but they may have taken other forms. Only focused social research can indicate the contemporary situation of the Arzal castes in contemporary Muslim society (Ahmad 2007: 258–65). Several of these aspects have been addressed in this research study and the data from the field reveals that Dalit Muslims are at the bottom of the social hierarchy and suffer discrimination in day-to-day life.

Untouchability is alive in the countryside though fear of law and rising Dalit Muslim assertion seem to have curbed its crude manifestations. It can be observed during marriage ceremonies or entry into a mosque. Dalit Muslims' participation in social activities has improved; some people are invited for wedding feasts. But the improvement stops there. Around half of the respondents said they wait for others to finish eating before they can eat, while many said that they are expected to wash their plates after eating. The primitive manifestations of untouchability still exist, but in a different form.

As many as one-third of respondents said they were not served food and water in non-Dalit Muslim homes while many claimed being served in separate vessels. Some of the Khan and Ansari families, I spoke to, concurred with this.

Dalit Muslim children are still growing with the stigma of being from an inferior caste. While seating arrangements are common in schools, Dalit Muslim kids in many cases are asked to take the back benches. Also, many are served mid-day meals separately from other children. Upper-caste Muslims too agreed that there were no Dalit Muslim teachers in their village schools. Vestiges of medieval society became apparent when upper castes and OBCs, if only a handful, revealed they served Dalit Muslims in towels or their upper garments; while some poured water directly into the cupped Dalit Muslim hands for drinking instead of giving a tumbler. A few cases showed that barbers used separate instruments for cutting the hair of Dalit Muslims. Dalit Muslims are still forced into services seen as 'menial' like sweeper, scavenger, grave digging, carrying out animal sacrifice, etc. There can be no doubt whatsoever that Dalit Muslims are socially known and treated as distinct groups within their own

religious communities and are invariably regarded as "socially inferior" communities by their co-religionists' (GoI 2008).

Universally practised forms of discrimination and exclusion
include social and cultural segregation, expressed in various forms of
refusal to have any social interaction; endogamy, expressed through
the universal prohibitions on Dalit–non-Dalit marriages and through
severe social sanctions on both Dalits and non-Dalits, who break this
taboo. Social segregation also extends to the sphere of worship and
religious rituals, with separate mosques and priests not being uncom-
mon among Dalit Muslims.

In short, in most social contexts, Dalit Muslims are Dalits first
and Muslims only second. Forms of discrimination of Dalit Muslims
include various modes of subordination in mosques, as well as
insistence on separate burial grounds. Occupational segregation and
economic exploitation are also very common and usually related
practices, though somewhat less widespread than segregation or
marriage bans. Untouchability is sometimes practised, but is not
widespread, and its forms vary greatly.

The members of Dalit Muslims/Arzals are excluded both physically
and socially. From a physical point of view, they tended to inhabit
excluded localities and did not mix with the members of the other
two categories. When it came to social intercourse, their relationship
was characterized by strict maintenance of social distance and deference so that the members of the Arzal castes had minimal and limited
interaction with the members of the other castes.

Considering the severely stigmatized and extremely excluded so-
called Arzal castes, Imtiaz Ahmad argues that two questions need to
be disposed of (Ahmad 2006). One is whether these castes should
be recognized and entitled to benefits currently given to the SCs?
One argument often advanced is that Muslims do not have castes
and therefore the benefit of reservation to SCs cannot be extended
to them. This is a fallacious argument to say the least. Public policies
are not based on ideologies, which is an extremely contested arena
with no ground for believing that the state's understanding of the
Islamic ideology is necessarily correct. Public policies are based on
objective realities and seek to address social problems as they exist
at the ground level. If extremely excluded and severely stigmatized
castes exist among Muslims, there is no ground that the strategy

of ameliorating such groups should not be applied to them. There exists a strong case for extending the benefits of the SCs to severely stigmatized and extremely excluded Muslim castes, and any attempt to shy away from this obvious action would expose the state to the allegation that it is indirectly seeking to prevent the depletion of the 'Hindu community' by ensuring that the SCs stay within the Hindu fold and if they hanker for those benefits they should change over to Hinduism and one of the other religions of Indian origin whose deprived sections are included in the category SCs. The state's secular credentials will remain in doubt so long as this argument is adhered to.

The second question is whether these Muslim castes should be recognized as SCs only when there is demonstrable evidence that they converted from one of the SCs. This was also the test applied in the determination of Sossai's claim to be granted concessions being extended to the SCs. Among other things, his claim was rejected as he could not demonstrate beyond the shadow of a doubt that he or his ancestors had necessarily descended from one of the SCs (GoI 2008). It is necessary to remember that in most of these cases we are dealing with castes whose caste histories are wholly unrecorded. Moreover, where is the basis for presuming that all such castes in other religious traditions are necessarily descendants of the SCs? It is possible that they may have come into existence autonomously as a result of subsequent colonization under Muslim domination. Muslim elites may have forced some groups, irrespective of whether they earlier belonged to the SCs or not, to perform certain functions for them and their current stigmatization may not be the result of their conversion to Islam but may owe itself to their subsequent domination. Under the circumstances, requiring the severely stigmatized and extremely excluded castes, whether among Muslims or Christians, to pass the test of originating out of the SCs would amount to failing them on a priori grounds. This would militate against the spirit and intentions of the constitution. The scale of justice has to be balanced to ensure that similarly placed social groups are treated equally and evenly without religion (an anathema in a secular state) being brought into play to deny some of them equal treatment under the law. It is intriguing to see the plight of Dalit Muslims in Bihar. They are worse off in terms of any indicator. No study can claim to be totally representative because of social and regional diversity. But I am trying to make it as comprehensive as it can be as an empirical study.

The NCM study and the Sachar committee report endorsed that Dalit Muslims were the worst off as compared to Dalit Christians and their counterparts in other communities like Hindus, Buddhists, and Sikhs. Their condition was worse in urban areas. Dalit Muslims are completely absent in the affluent group for urban India, it highlighted. The report said there was enough evidence to justify the SCs status for the Dalit Muslims. If no community had already been given SC status, and if the decision to accord SC status to some communities were to be taken today through some evidence-based approach, then it is hard to imagine how Dalit Muslims could be excluded. These kinds of studies which focus on the ethnography of discrimination can be considered/used as evidence.

Dalit Muslims: Encountering Various Forms of Caste-based Discrimination

There are various forms of caste-based discrimination which a Dalit Muslim faces in his/her day-to-day life. One can safely argue, and particularly, based on the findings of this research, that there is now considerable evidence of Dalit Muslims being deprived and discriminated in every sense of the terms. Various forms of caste-based discrimination are highlighted below.

Untouchability

Concepts of purity and impurity, clean and unclean castes, do exist among these Muslim groups. Dalit Muslims are seen as unclean and impure by Ashraf Muslims. Some of the respondents confirmed that untouchability in its evident forms has declined; some still consider it as widely prevalent and practised by Ashraf. Nevertheless, different forms of untouchability are still experienced by the Dalit Muslims. Many of the respondents narrated regarding refusal to drink water from the same glass/vessel by Ashraf. Further, higher castes had to be addressed using honorific terms and bodily deference in front of them became an important marker of caste identity. It was very much evident while this research was going on. Many a time, I observed that when an upper-caste Muslim used to cross from a Dalit Muslim locality, they used to offer 'salam' (greetings) with respect but the attitude of the upper caste people revealed how lowly and mean they considered the Dalit Muslims. An upper-caste Muslim does not even deem it fit to sit with the Dalit Muslims.

The caste group maintains separate utensils and does not share the same utensils with lower castes and in some cases do not allow the latter to touch the water source. They are often given left-over food to eat.

Nats and Bakkhos were segregated in separate hamlets and were denied basic amenities available to the rest of the mohallah. Even other Dalit Muslim castes were segregated largely in the outskirts of the village/mohallah. They were discriminated in the mosque as well. In few cases, they were asked to sit in the last row. Some of the Dalit Muslims have built their own mosques, although, a kaccha built mosque. This is what I saw in the Taj Nagar area. Distance and differentiation in social life was maintained between the lower and higher castes through various means. Further, a large majority felt that there was no significant difference in the attitude of the upper caste Hindus towards Dalit Muslims, although, they had good terms with their counterparts among Hindus. Moreover, the majority of Dalit Muslims argued that they suffered discrimination at the hands of co-religionists. It is important to highlight that generally practices of untouchability continue to persist and defines social interaction among different caste groups even though they are not manifest. For instance, amongst the Dhobi caste of Muslim origin based in Patna it is felt that other Muslims do not come to attend their wedding feasts because they serve meat with their hands. Also, low castes celebrate festivals in seclusion of the upper castes and there is little social inter-course between them. There is a constant rue that if there is a death or a wedding amongst the upper-caste Muslims, the Dalit Muslims make it to the occasion even without being called. However, even if the latter send special invitations for such occasions, no one from the upper castes turns up. The exclusion is experienced more as an indifference of the higher castes.

Dalit Muslim colonies are segregated from the upper castes' localities and most of the civic amenities like hospitals and schools are
centred around the upper castes' residences. Furthermore, there is a
spatial discrimination, in a few cases, towards the Dalit Muslims in
allowing them entry into the mosque. Even in graveyards there are at
times, walls/divisions that separate the Dalit Muslim graves from the
upper-caste ones.

Endogamy

It is evident from the findings that conversion did not bring about a
fundamental change in the institution of family and marriage among
Dalit Muslim converts. Rules of marriage, inheritance, and social customs remained unchanged. No inter-caste marriage in these villages/
mohallahs was witnessed and endogamy was observed. It needs to
be pointed out that endogamy, hereditary membership, and distinct
ritual status are features of Muslim communities. The Ashrafs used
endogamy for reinforcing group identity and subsequently, were able
to raise their social standing in the hierarchy of Muslim groups by
employing endogamy. All these Dalit Muslim castes are characterized
by endogamy, and are hierarchically ranked. Social exclusiveness was
practised among these groups.

This study shows that how caste identity remains an important
determinant in shaping marriage practices in Muslim society. By
and large, inter-caste marriages are rare and have a caste backlash
through religiously backed panchayats. There are instances of
such marriages, the opposition meted out to them, their survival
at the face of these oppositions, and the partial acceptance of the
couples by their communities long after their marriages. In one such
instance, a boy from a Dalit Muslim family fell in love with a girl
of a Sheikh family. However the caste barriers between the couple
remained insurmountable and they decided to elope. However, the
village communities found them and the couple had to undergo
separation.[1] Further, though modes and methods of marriages are
not discussed in detail, it appears that *dhobis*, *halalkhors*, *bakkhos*,
pawariyans, *machuaaras*, *naalwaaras* and *nats* all are mainly endoga-
mous caste groups.

Occupational Segregation

Caste-based occupational segregation is evident amongst Dalit Muslim groups. Groups bearing distinct names are associated with traditional occupations. Dalit Muslim groups are organized more or less like Hindu Dalit castes. Occupational hierarchy based upon caste and status is determined by that nature of occupation.

Representation of Dalit Muslims in state and central government services as well as other services like the police, civil, defence, and public enterprises, political parties, as well as secular politics, religious bodies, ministerial berths, government institutions, minority educational institutions, etc., seems to be almost nil and on an average more members are dependent upon lesser number of earning members. Ashraf Muslims monopolize high social rank and become culturally assertive in terms of sharing public spaces like mosques, graveyards, etc. In this context, the following castes of halalkhors, *lalbegi*s, *bhatiyara*s, *gorkhan*, bakkho, *mirshikari*s, *chik, rangrez,* and *darzi*s constitute the most stigmatized castes among the Muslims. Even though most of these caste members are in transition from their older professions but they feel that they are still recognized by others (upper-caste Muslims) in relation to their older professions. Thus they say for e.g. that a halalkhor's progeny is seen as halalkhor always and is denied social position available to others. This study shows that out of hundred Dalit Muslim households with a population of more than 600, only 8 are educated at higher than matriculation level and all are unemployed, only 5 are in government jobs in total — two of them as peons, another two as sweepers, and one as a constable in police. Historically, there has been discrimination in office, government, and administration between high- and low-born Muslims. Mosque and dargah, etc., draw their clergy primarily from the upper castes.

Social and Cultural Segregation

Dalit Muslim castes such as halalkhors, lalbegis, nat, bakkho while not refused permission directly (in most of the cases) in religious places, these distinctions are observable in social gatherings. In some cases, separate mosques were built for different castes. Social life is segregated around caste lines. The division between high-born versus low-born Muslims was important in determining social status. Further, status was marked by social exclusiveness. There was existence of separate quarters, intimate social intercourse was dictated by the status groups. Mostly, separate seating arrangements are observed at social functions. Social groups that are low in the hierarchy need to provide deferential treatment to those above them. Among few Dalit Muslim castes, like Bakkho, Nat etc. there has been a survival of Hindu rituals centring around birth, marriage, and death even after embracing Islam. During this study, it was found that quite often than not, their names are found to be a Hindu name or partially Hindu name. In few cases, in situations of great social distance between groups there are separate mosques, qazis (priests) religious organizations, and burial grounds as well as segregated residential quarters. Social life is defined along caste lines, namely occupation, commensal relations, social intercourse governed by caste. Some restrictions around commensality and inter-dining operate, though these are less elaborate than their Hindu counterparts. Commensal restrictions are based upon notions of social hygiene and cleanliness. Subordination of Dalit Muslims are expressed through forms of dress, terms of address, as well as by physical posture. Dalit Muslim castes represent social, political, economic, as well as ritual status. In a few instances, minor disputes were settled by caste panchayats.

Dalit Muslims experience deep forms of social and cultural segregation within society. These assume several different forms that mark their everyday life. There are cases where the derogatory puns are hurled at Dalit Muslims. For instance terms like Bhatiyara are both an abuse as well as the name of a caste. The group, historically considered as keepers of working classes inns, besides the upper castes' sarais, where their women (were) are seen as to be indulgent into prostitution, is sexually stigmatized. The social positions of various castes like Bakkho, Nat, Manihar, Halalkhor, etc. are demeaning. All the Dalit Muslim castes face constant ridicule and denigration and are excluded from mainstream and high occasions of the communities, including weddings and festivals.

During interviews with lower caste Muslims, I was reminded of this social fact time and again.[2] While it would be fair to criticize the Ashraf Muslims for practicing caste endogamy, lower-caste Muslims too are not free from it. During my stay in a predominantly Muslim area, that is, Phulwari Sharif (large locality) and other areas, I noticed that lowest-caste Muslims (Dalits) were abused by the intermediate caste Muslims freely. The lowest-caste Muslims lived in a separate area of the town, and the locality was known by its caste name, bakkho toli, where bakkho reside, chamrauli, an area where the chamars (an untouchable Hindu caste) live. Lalbegi and halalkhor (Dalit Muslims) also lived there. Ansaris and Iraqis, of somewhat higher rank, who are in substantial numbers, have minimal and functional contacts with these Dalit Muslims; for the most part they have their own separate worlds. Yet the Pasmanda Muslim Mahaz has a sympathetic following here and one wonders if such practices do not defeat the very purpose of its politics. As we know, PMM tries to foster a broad alliance of backward and Dalit Muslim castes (Ansaris constitute a backward caste), but these kinds of gaps between both the communities will weaken their politics. However, it needs to be pointed out that many of the respondents admitted that they are closer to Ansaris (a backward caste) compared to any other Muslim castes (upper castes—Ashrafs).

Further, caste-based discrimination takes its most evident form in practices around worship and burial. Though the mosques are not exclusively for one caste or a set of castes, the upper castes are expected to offer their prayers from the first few rows and Dalit Muslim castes behind their backs. As stated by the respondents, in the times of conflict, the Dalit Muslim castes stand to lose from the mosque space as well. The dead of the Dalit Muslim castes, in most cases are to be buried separately under the supervision of the Dalit/backward Muslim Maulvis. The Halalkhors based in Phoolwari Sharif in Patna say that they can cremate their dead only in the cemetery allocated to their caste members. Otherwise the common grievance is that upper-caste Muslims evade attending feasts, social functions, mosques, funerals, etc. and this is accentuated by the fact that most of the Dalit Muslims are geographically segregated.

This study finds that a majority of the respondents did not have access to safe drinking water, further while Ashraf and Ajlaf castes lived in better houses than Dalit Muslims (Arzals), the majority of the Dalit Muslims lived in mud houses. Their houses are mainly found in the suburbs of villages/mohallahs and areas on the outskirts. Members of the Nat and Bakkho castes got a few houses built under the Indira Awas Yojna under Laloo Prasad Yadav's regime.

Economic Discrimination

It has been found that political power, economic advantages, and social privileges centre around Ashraf castes. Occupational castes that are low in the hierarchy have a very low standard of living. Ashrafs maintain hegemony over resources and institutions of the community. And there is a deliberate exclusion of Dalit Muslim castes from sharing of resources. Dalit Muslims' landholdings are found to be dismal. Due to physical (or residential) segregation and social exclusion on account of the notion of untouchability and impurity, they suffer from a general exclusion.

Most of the Dalit Muslim women work as daily wage labourers marked by insecure livelihoods and employment. These women often engage in selling toys, plastic chairs, and other small items door to door, mostly these are barter-like transactions. They collect garbage, scraps and other rejected/old stuff from these households and sell them in the scrap market.

Economic marginalization of the Dalit Muslim communities is perpetuated and coincides with their social and cultural marginality. Thus, as stated above, occupational representation in government and state services is almost negligible. Most caste groups subsist on occupations and professions that are of a lowly scale and are often viewed disparagingly by society. This is compounded by the fact that on the whole there is increasing deprivation in the absence of opportunities of education, employment on the one hand, and lack of any social, cultural, or economic capital on the other.

Dalit Muslims are also excluded from participation in certain categories of jobs (the sweeper being excluded from jobs inside the household such as cooking) and cannot purchase certain consumer goods (such as vegetables or milk) because their occupation and physical touch is considered 'polluting' or 'unclean'.

Social Change and Forms of Protest and Resistance

Social change: Over a period of time, there has been social change taking place within the Dalit Muslim community. With the introduction of a cash economy, and loss of traditional occupations, the former dependencies associated with the jajmani system have been undermined. There was a greater dependence on the market for work and credit (to some extent). The state intervention with regard to Dalit Muslims will help in the social mobility of these excluded groups. However, withdrawal from village services like grave digging, carrying fire pots at funerals, etc., withdrawal from patron–client relations, and from generalized dependence as village servants has led to further deterioration in some cases.

While there has been a gradual diminishing of traditional caste roles, these have been substituted by minor and lowly professions that come to be the share of Dalit Muslim castes and on the whole there is an increasing deprivation. For example, the Bakkhos used to sing praises at the time of childbirth in families but over time have moved to selling steel utensils in exchange for old clothes from people. Bhatiyaras have started making *tikiya*s of coal for the hookah but with the hookah also going out of vogue they have taken to driving horse carts (*tanga*) and running food stalls at the railway platforms. Most communities articulate that much has not changed except those who were nomadic, like bakkhos and nats have been granted land under Indira Vikas Yojna (single-room accommodation) but the overall social condition has only deteriorated.

Forms of protest over caste-based discrimination: There has been an emergence of the Dalit Muslim movement for the self assertion of Dalit Muslims. There have been agitations through mass mobilizations. There exist both organized and unorganized forms of protest by Dalit Muslims. Forms of protest were addressed to the state including both organized mass action as well as appeals to the state.

In a few cases, there has been formation of Dalit Muslim mosques. Dalit Muslim leaders, like Ali Anwar and Dr Ejaz Ali are also adopting various religious strategies to achieve greater equality, dignity, and respect. These include critiquing Ashrafs, attacking caste discrimination, highlighting the notion of equality enshrined in Islam and inner transformation.

The last two decades has seen an increasing mobilization of Dalit/ backward Muslims especially in some parts such as Bihar, Uttar Pradesh, and Maharashtra. It is significant to note that 'Dalit Muslims have raised their voices for social justice' (Verma 2010: 61). A political and social struggle has been undertaken by Dalit Muslims and their leaders with an attempt to bring the issue of social discriminations faced by them to the fore of society as well as politics. Many Dalit leaders have tried to convince the upper-caste Muslim members that caste exists within Muslims but such leaders are often marginalized and sometimes also threatened. Resistance on a daily basis centres around being more assertive towards articulating their neglect by upper-caste communities. This has often produced intense caste conflict between different groups such as conflicts over burial space, cremation, rights over place of worship, etc.

The prominent political leaders among them are; Ali Anwar, Rajya Sabha M.P. and Dr Ejaz Ali, former Rajya Sabha M.P. These leaders are working with the Dalit Muslim castes on which this study is based. While interacting with the Dalit Muslims in the localities and being in the field, it came to the notice that certain facilities in these areas were provided by Ali Anwar and Ejaz Ali. In certain Dalit Muslim localities, where there was no road, Ali Anwar built the roads with the help of his MPLAD funds. In certain areas, it was noted that a tube well was provided by Dr Ejaz Ali. It is important to emphasize that these political leaders are responsible for making the Dalit Muslim movement heard and mobilizing their masses. They are rooted in their constituency and people in these areas admit the fact that now at least they are able to raise their voices. This study has tried to trace and establish a linkage between these Dalit Muslim castes and two prominent leaders of Bihar (and their organizations) representing Dalit Muslims' concerns. Moreover, all the shortcomings and failings of the movement apart, they have made their point that Dalit Muslims are lagging far behind in every sense of the term and have faced the worst forms of discrimination by their co-religionists in general and the Indian state in particular.

What we see is that the worst forms of discrimination and exclusion which include social and cultural segregation, expressed in various forms of refusal to have any social interaction; endogamy, and through severe social sanctions who break this taboo. Occupational segregation and economic exploitation are also very common and usually related practices, though somewhat less widespread than segregation or marriage bans. Untouchability is practiced, but in different forms and intensity in different areas.

There is now considerable evidence of Dalit Muslims being deprived, discriminated, and excluded in every sense of the terms.

Looking at the findings of this research, one can argue that Dalit Muslims are of the most marginalized, discriminated, and excluded community today and they need further state intervention

In the previous section I have argued that Dalit Muslims face the worst forms of discrimination and exclusion. Of late, there have been political mobilization and democratic assertion of Dalit Muslims under the leadership of Ali Anwar and Dr Ejaz Ali (All India Pasmanda Muslim Mahaz [PMM] and All India Backward Muslim Morcha [AIBMM] respectively). There are a number of organizations struggling for Dalit Muslim reservation and to pressurize the government to include Dalit Muslims in the SC list as they were in it before independence. PMM and AIBMM are working in various states. In Maharashtra, All India Muslim OBC Organization (AIMOBCO), under the leadership of Shabbir Ahmed Ansari, is working amongst Dalit & OBC Muslims. On 25th July 2008, a petition was lodged in the Supreme Court by the AMKS for the inclusion of Dalit Muslims in the SCs Category which has been denied under the Presidential Order of 1950. In an important development for the PIL lodged in the Supreme Court by the AMKS for inclusion of Dalit Muslims in the SCs category, the counsel court ordered the Union of India to file a counter affidavit to the writ petition 13 of 2008 within the granted period of four weeks.

The Sachar Committee report (which is accepted by all sections of the Indian Muslim community) reports the existence of the caste system among Indian Muslims:

> Since the Constitutional (Scheduled Caste) Order, 1950, popularly known as the Presidential Order (1950), restricts the SC status only to Hindu groups having 'unclean' occupations, their non-Hindu equivalents have been bracketed with the middle caste converts and declared OBC. Thus, the OBCs among Muslims constitute two broad categories. The halalkhors, helas, lalbegis or bhangis (scavengers), dhobis (washermen), nais or hajjams (barbers), chiks (butchers), faqirs (beggars) etc., belonging to the '*Arzals*' are the 'untouchable converts' to Islam that have found their way in the OBC list. The momins or julahas (weavers), darzi or idiris (tailors), rayeens or kunjaras (vegetable sellers) are *Ajlafs* or converts from 'clean' occupational castes (GoI 2006: 193–4).

Based on these findings, the Sachar Committee categorized Indian Muslims into three major categories such as: '1—[...] Those without any social disabilities, the Ashraf, 2—those equivalent to Hindu OBCs, the Ajlaf and, 3—those equivalents to Hindu SCs, the Arzal. Those who are referred to as Muslim OBCs combined 2 and 3 (GoI 2006: 193–4).'

Thus the claim that all Muslims are equally deprived is not correct. True, by and large, Muslims are deprived and face discrimination at the hands of communal Hindu forces. But within the Muslim community, Muslim SCs, STs, OBCs are more deprived than Ashraf Muslims. Almost all the Muslim organizations and educational institutions have been founded, headed, and controlled by Ashraf Muslims. The majority of jobs in these institutions are held by them. The Sachar Committee reports also says:

> [...] The incidence of poverty is highest among Muslim-OBC (38%) followed by Muslim General (35%) [...] Overall, the conditions of Muslim-OBCs are worse than those of Muslim-General [...] Within the Muslim community a larger percentage of Muslim OBCs fall in low income category as compared to Muslim-General [...] Within Muslims, Muslim-OBCs are slightly lagging behind the Muslim-General in high income group (GoI 2006: 211–13).

However, the criteria of inclusion and standards of evidence remain the most contentious issues. The second issue concerns the standards of evidence on whatever set of criteria that is adopted. Here again there seem to be two issues involved. One is that of the quality of the evidence, that is, the standards of competence and levels of expertise that it demonstrates. The second issue is that of the extent (or 'quantity') of the evidence and the related consideration of arriving at an overall judgment on a body of material that is bound to present a complex and heterogeneous picture. Further clarity on these issues is perhaps only possible after the fact—that is, after a body of material is presented to the courts and they come to some judgment as to their worth on the above counts. However, government tries to avoid according SC status to Dalit Muslims and Christians. It cites the difficulty that in case the scheduled caste converts to Islam and Christianity are accorded the status of SCs, administrative difficulties at the time of issuance of caste certificates would arise because of the difficulty in determining in many cases, their pre-conversion caste standing (GoI 2008: 69–70). Christianity came to India several centuries ago and conversions have been taking place since then. The difficulties in precisely and objectively deciding the determination of pre-conversion caste origin would open the floodgates for issuing bogus SC certificates which, even in the present circumstances, is a cause for concern. There has been opposition as well to the demand for inclusion of Dalit Muslims and Christians. Zoya Hasan examines the concept of 'politics of inclusion' from the perspective of policies and political processes (Hasan 2009: 227–39). She takes this position with the purpose of offering constructive intervention in the debate on social exclusion and argues for a democratic pluralistic refashioning of political communities in India. The Indian Constitution included only Hindus and Tribes under the Scheduled Castes (SCs) and Scheduled Tribes (STs). In 1956, Sikhs were included as well after they agitated and much later in 1990, Buddhists too were included. The three reasons why other minority groups in India like Christians and Muslims were not considered backward and hence not included in these categories are as follows:

1. Theologically there is no caste system in these religions.
2. It would be incompatible with the concept of Indian 'secularism' if religious criteria were to be used to define backwardness.
3. It would undermine national unity.

Apart from the reasons listed earlier, it is also true that these religions are not considered Indian since they originate from outside the region though there is the apprehension, especially espoused by the right-wing Hindutva forces, that reservation for Dalit Muslims and Christians would lead to religious conversion. One has to understand that Dalit communities of these religions are discriminated against simply because Islam and Christianity are not indic religions. This poses a serious question on the secular credentials of India. Excluding Dalit Muslims and Dalit Christians from the SCs category (Presidential Order of 1950) is illogical and an anomaly in our constitution. This anomaly needs to be rectified at the earliest. The National Commission for Minorities, Sachar Committee Report, and the Ranganath Misra Commission has already recommended the inclusion of Dalit Muslims and Christians into the SC list.

Members of the constituent assembly saw democracy as a powerful instrument of emancipation. To end existing forms of discriminatory practices, particularly those of exclusion and segregation resulting/ embodied in the caste system, the constitution provided for equality before the law. Simultaneously, to overcome the effects of years of segregation and subordination, they envisaged/devised a system of reservations, as part of its policy of positive discrimination.

The Kaka Kalelkar Committee Report, in one of its sections dealt with the issues of 'the backward amongst the non-Hindus' (GoI 1955). The report admitted that Muslims and Christians also practise the caste system. It highlighted the fact that the bulk of the Muslims and Christians in India are converts from the Hindu fold. This conversion was encouraged by the fact that Islam and Christianity were fundamentally opposed to caste. The 'lower castes' in the Hindu fold left their traditional religion of the ruling race because they felt assured that in that way they would be free from the tyranny of caste and caste prejudices. The report noted that except for the four upper castes, namely *Sheikh, Syed, Moghul,* and *Pathan,* all the other Muslim castes were inferior and backward.

Non-recognition of the socio-economic nature of the Muslim backwardness issue was indeed a major roadblock in changing this environment. The 1955 Kaka Kalelkar report on the backward classes had, for the first time, recognized the Muslim OBCs on par with their Hindu counterparts; and said that they were eligible for job reservations, since 'there are a number of communities amongst them that are suffering from social inferiority in their own society and social backwardness'.

These recommendations remained only on paper and it was for the Mandal Commission later to give a due recognition to the problems of these classes. Importantly, the Mandal Commission treated the majority of the Muslim population as OBCs deserving reservation in government jobs and educational institutions. This worked out to be much more than the proportion of Hindu population treated as OBCs.

Later on, when the Supreme Court upheld the Mandal quota, the Muslim OBCs automatically came under the purview of reservation. But still, there were a lot of implementation issues to be sorted out. The working guidelines used by the bureaucracy in most states and their ignorance about the issue—as well as the lack of awareness amongst the Muslim OBCs—were coming in the way of the actual implementation of the Mandal recommendations.

Both the commissions, the Kaka Kalelkar Commission (1955) and the B.P. Mandal Commission (1980) have emphasized the lower status in the caste hierarchy as a determining factor for 'backwardness'. The state High Courts as well as Supreme Court like the two Backward Class Commissions, accepted 'caste' as a basis of classification in a series of their judgments.

***

Social stratification along castes is a reality among Muslims in India. The chapter de-bunks the myth of representing/looking at Muslims as a single, monolithic, and homogenous group. It also highlights the prevalence of caste among Indian Muslims and its historical background. I examined several issues for an understanding of the situation of those Muslim castes which share the attributes of the SCs, experience/suffer the worst forms of discrimination and exclusion, but are denied recognition and entitlement as SCs. I have discussed several of these issues in the preceding sections and reflected on their situation in contemporary India.

This study, while relating the question of Dalit Muslims with the issues of discrimination, exclusion, and recognition, has tried to boldly contest the Presidential Order on several grounds. This Order, going completely against all notions of secularism, democracy, and social justice, declares that such benefits would be limited only to those Dalits who claim to be 'Hindus'. However, two amendments were made in this Order and thereby two minorities, Sikhs (1956) and neo-Buddhists (1990) were re-included in this category. But Muslims and Christians have still been out. So why should Dalit Muslims, too, not be included in the list of SCs? Whether or not social discrimination suffered by Dalit Muslims can be proven in a court of law or not on the basis of established definitions of social disabilities, there is no compelling evidence to justify their exclusion from the SCs category. Yet, the positive recommendation of the Ranganath Mishra Commission to amend the Presidential Order to include Dalit Muslims in the SCs list has been put on hold. As long as the religious criterion remains in place the SCs category will include

Dalits of certain religions and exclude others regardless of their social position. The state's secular credentials will remain in doubt so long as this criterion/argument is adhered to.

This research has tried to provide a more grounded picture of the situation of the castes that constitute Dalit Muslims/Arzals. It demonstrates that in terms of day-to-day social interactions the Dalit Muslims exist on the margins of society. This research explored the areas related to commensality, endogamy, sociality, various forms of discrimination, and stigmatization practised against Dalit Muslims castes. It shows that they are engaged in the lowly occupation of scavenging, confine their marriages within the group, and are excluded into separate residential quarters in the villages as well as the towns in which members of the other categories do not live. It all leads to their severely stigmatized and extremely excluded conditions.

Notes

1. An interview with the respondent, Amiruddin Nat, Urf 'Pathak', 27 February 2010, in Patna, Bihar.
2. The observation is based on fieldwork conducted in February–April and July 2010 in Patna district and adjoining areas in Bihar.

References

Ahmad, I. 2006. 'Recognition and Entitlement: Muslim Castes Eligible for Inclusion in the Category "Scheduled Castes"', Paper presented at the workshop on 'Conferment of SC Status to "Untouchables"/Dalits converted to Christianity/Islam: Issues and Challenges' held at Tata Institute of Social Sciences, Mumbai, on 18–19 August.

———. 2007, 'Can there be a category called Dalit Muslim?', in I. Ahmad and S.B. Upadhyay (eds), *Dalit Assertion in Society, Literature and History*, pp. 258–65. New Delhi: Orient Blackswan in association with Deshkal Society.

Government of India (GoI). 1955. Report of the Backward Classes Commission, headed by Kaka Kalelkar. Delhi: Government of India Publications. 30 March.

———. 2006. *Sachar Committee Report*, Prime Minister's High Level Committee on Social, Economic and Educational Status of the Muslim Community of India. New Delhi: Government of India.

————. 2008. *National Commission for Minorities Report on Dalit Muslims and Christians, Dalits in the Muslim and Christian Communities: A Status Report on Current Social Scientific Knowledge*, prepared by Satish Deshpande. New Delhi: Government of India.

Hasan, Z. 2009. *Politics of Inclusion: Caste, Minorities, and Affirmative Action*. New Delhi: Oxford University Press.

Jayal, N.G. 2006. *Representing India: Ethnic Diversity & the Governance of Public Institutions*. Palgrave, New York.

Kohli A. (ed.). 2001. *The Success of India's Democracy*. New Delhi: Cambridge University Press.

Verma, V. 2010. 'Reinterpreting Buddhism: Ambedkar on the Politics of Social Action', *Economic and Political Weekly*, XIV(49): 61.

Index

Editor and Contributors

Renu Addlakha is a Professor and Deputy Director at the Centre for Women's Development Studies (CWDS). Her books include *Deconstructing Mental Illness: An Ethnography of Psychiatry, Women, and the Family* (New Delhi: Zubaan Books, 2008); *Contemporary Perspectives on Disability in India: Exploring the Linkages between Law, Gender and Experience* (Saarbrucken, Germany: LAP Lambert, 2011); editor of *Disability Studies in India: Global Discourses Local Realities* (New Delhi: Routledge, 2013); and the co-editor of *Disability and Society: A Reader* (New Delhi: Orient Blackswan, 2009).

Md. Aftab Alam is an Assistant Professor in the department of Political Science at Zakir Hussain College, University of Delhi. Apart from research papers, he has written research reports for government institutions such as National Commission for Backward Classes, National Commission for Minorities, Ministry of Social Justice and Empowerment.

Poonam Kakoti Borah is an Assistant Professor in the Department of Women's Studies, Gauhati University. She was formerly teaching undergraduate students at Indraprastha College for Women and St. Stephen's College, University of Delhi.

Tarunabh Khaitan is an Associate Professor at the Faculty of Law and the Hackney Fellow in Law at Wadham College, University of Oxford. He has recently published a monograph titled, *A Theory of Discrimination Law* (UK: Oxford University Press, 2015).

Narender Kumar is an Associate Professor at the Centre for Political Studies, Jawaharlal Nehru University, New Delhi. He is the author of two books, *Dalit Policies, Politics and Parliament* (New Delhi: Shipra Publishers, 2004) and *Scheduled Castes and Panchayat Elections in Haryana* (New Delhi: Indian Social Institute, 2001) besides co-authoring three books and various articles.

Badri Narayan is Professor at the Centre for the Study of Discrimination and Exclusion in Jawaharlal Nehru University. Besides having written a number of articles both in English and Hindi, he has recently authored *Kanshiram: Leader of the Dalits* (New Delhi: Penguin, 2014) and *The Making of the Dalit Public in North India: Uttar Pradesh 1950–Present* (New Delhi: Oxford University Press, 2011).

Aseem Prakash is an Associate Professor and Chairperson, School of Public Policy and Governance, Tata Institute of Social Sciences, Hyderabad. He has published *Dalit Capital: State, Markets and Civil Society in Urban India* (New Delhi: Routledge, 2015).

Meena Radhakrishna is former Professor, Delhi School of Economics and Sociology, University of Delhi. She is the author of *Dishonoured by History: 'Criminal Tribes' and British Colonial Policy* (Hyderabad: Orient Longman, 2001).

Daniel Sabbagh is a Senior Research Fellow at the Centre d'études et de recherché internationales (Sciences Po-CERI/CNRS). He is the author of *L'Égalité par le droit: les paradoxes de la discrimination positive aux États-Unis* (Paris: Économica, 2003). It was partly published in English under the title, *Equality and Transparency: A Strategic Perspective on Affirmative Action in American Law* (New York: Palgrave, 2007). He has co-authored and co-edited several books.

Nidhi Sadana Sabharwal is Associate Professor, Centre for Policy Research in Higher Education, National University of Educational Planning and Administration, New Delhi. She is co-editor with Sukhadeo Thorat of *Bridging the Social Gap: Perspectives on Dalit Empowerment* (New Delhi: Sage, 2014).

Anand Teltumbde is Professor with Vinod Gupta School of Management of Indian Institute of Technology, Kharagpur. He has authored eighteen books. Some of his recent books are, *Persistence* *of Caste* (London: Zed Books, 2010) and *Khairlanji: A Strange and Bitter Crop* (New Delhi: Navayana, 2008).

Sukhadeo Thorat is Chairman, Indian Council of Social Science Research, New Delhi and former Professor of Economics, Centre for the Study of Regional Development, School of Social Sciences, Jawaharlal Nehru University. He has published 20 books, more than 100 articles and has been awarded Padma Shri, Mother Teresa International Award for the Weaker Section and Minorities, and Dr Ambedkar Chetna Award. He is the author of *Dalits in India: Search for a Common Destiny* (New Delhi: Sage, 2009).

Vidhu Verma is Professor and Chairperson, Centre for Political Studies, School of Social Sciences, Jawaharlal Nehru University, New Delhi, India. She is author of three books, *Non-discrimination and Equality in India: Contesting Boundaries of Social Justice* (London: Routledge, 2012); *Malaysia: State and Civil Society in Transition* (USA: Lynne Rienner, 2002); and *Justice, Equality and Community: An Essay in Marxist Political Theory* (New Delhi: Sage, 1999) besides articles in several journals.